GERMAINE DE STAËL

*To Greta,
my ultimately
faithful friend.
— Ted,
2017.*

Madame de Staël in 1797. Sepia drawing by Jean-Baptiste Isabey (1767–1855). Reproduced by permission of the Louvre Museum, Cabinet des dessins.

GERMAINE DE STAËL, DAUGHTER OF THE ENLIGHTENMENT
The Writer and Her Turbulent Era

SERGINE DIXON

an imprint of Prometheus Books
59 John Glenn Drive, Amherst, New York 14228-2119

Published 2007 by Humanity Books, an imprint of Prometheus Books

Germaine de Staël, Daughter of the Enlightenment: The Writer and Her Turbulent Era. Copyright © 2007 by Sergine Dixon. All rights reserved. No part of this publication may be reproduced, stored in a retrieval system, or transmitted in any form or by any means, digital, electronic, mechanical, photocopying, recording, or otherwise, or conveyed via the Internet or a website without prior written permission of the publisher, except in the case of brief quotations embodied in critical articles and reviews.

Inquiries should be addressed to
Humanity Books
59 John Glenn Drive
Amherst, New York 14228–2119
VOICE: 716–691–0133, ext. 210
FAX: 716–691–0137

WWW.PROMETHEUSBOOKS.COM

16 15 14 13 12   8 7 6 5 4

Library of Congress Cataloging-in-Publication Data

Dixon, Sergine.
    Germaine de Stael, daughter of the Enlightenment : the writer and her turbulent era / by Sergine Dixon.
       p. cm.
    Includes bibliographical references and index.
    ISBN 978–1–59102–560–3
    1. Staël, Madame de (Anne-Louise-Germaine), 1766-1817. 2. Women authors, French—19th century—Biography. 3. Authors, French—19th century—Biography. 4. Women authors, French—18th century—Biography. 5. Authors, French—18th century—Biography. I. Title.

PQ2431.Z5D59 2007
843'.7--dc22
[B]

                                                                    2007033210

Printed in the United States of America on acid-free paper

For Christina, who loves to write.

CONTENTS

Introduction — 9

The Nurturing — 17

PART ONE: TUMULT AND TERROR

1. Moments in Time — 31
2. Germaine's World — 43
3. Germaine's Pen — 53
4. The Rape of Unity — 61
5. The Hydra Unleashed — 73
6. Passion Analyzed — 85

PART TWO: TYRANNY

7. Confrontation — 103
8. In the Company of Gods — 115

9. In the Company of Men and Women	125
10. Sailing, Full Sails	137

PART THREE: TALISMANS

11. The Test of Sorrow	151
12. The Test of Success	165
13. The Path to Glory	177

PART FOUR: LIBERATION

14. The Price of Glory	193
15. The Testament	205
Conclusion	219
Epilogue	229
Postscript	237
Afterword	241
Acknowledgments	245
Notes	247
Select Bibliography	281
Index	297

INTRODUCTION

Born Anne-Louise-Germaine Necker in Paris on April 22, 1766, Germaine de Staël possessed one of the most brilliant minds of her time. Feeling and an extremely kind heart permeated her writings as they did life itself. I hope to establish this while placing her literary and political texts, her reminiscences, therefore the 'oeuvre', in the context of French history's extraordinarily agitated periods—the Revolution and the Napoleonic era.

Since Madame de Staël's death in 1817, descendants issued from Madame de Staël's daughter Albertine de Broglie (1797-1838), family names being those of d'Haussonville, d'Andlau, Luppé, de Pange and le Marois, have reigned high in the panoply of early biographers of their ancestor. They published continuously while sharing much of Germaine's correspondence with the reading public, this up to and including the 1960's. Collaborating with Germaine's son Auguste de Staël (1790-1827), her cousin Madame Necker de Saussure (1765-1841) published the author's complete works in 1820 and 1821 with Treuttel and Würtz in Paris. Other editions of the complete works followed—Didot, in Paris, in 1844 and 1861; Lefèvre, in Paris, in 1858; then Slatkine, in Geneva, in 1936, being given an imprint by Longchamp in 1949. In the year 2000 the Champion publishers in Paris inaugurated a series of the complete works.

To a large extent, the venerable group of initiators just mentioned also offered first critiques of the 'oeuvre'. This gave the impetus for a plethora of biographies and critical studies in Europe and America early in the nineteenth century, starting with, for example, the *Mélanges de lit-*

térature et de politique by Germaine's longtime friend Benjamin Constant. Tributes, criticism alternately partial and impartial, and the search for the authentic Germaine de Staël continued on. Publications have transpired also from Germaine's contemporaries in letters, journals, and autobiographies—among others François René de Chateaubriand, Elisabeth Vigée-Lebrun, Lord Byron, Juliette Récamier, Wilhelm Schlegel, Charles de Villers, Simonde de Sismondi, Henri Meister, Jean Bernadotte, Louis de Narbonne, Adolf Ribbing, Pedro de Souza, and Elizabeth Hervey. Carefully edited and often presented with biographical substance, these works have offered variations on the theme of friendship.Concern often capped friendship, for if Germaine was generous, she was also exacting.

Staëlean scholarship has become prodigious. In time, articles have appeared in literary journals on both continents. Many found their way into more than fifty-five European Staëlean Notebooks (Cahiers Staëliens) founded by the Society of Staëlean Studies (Société des études Staëliennes) first issued seventy-five years ago. Currently, the Société holds 235 members. Madame de Staël's descendant Count Othenin d'Haussonville, who has published extensively concerning his ancestor, presides over it. Moreover, the publication of the correspondence of Madame de Staël began in 1962 thanks to Béatrice Jasinski who, until her death in 2001, presented seven volumes of letters supplemented with careful documentation and biographical material. The scholars Georges Solovieff, Norman King, K. Kloocke and Simone Balayé took the challenge of further examining Madame de Staël's now recognizably massive correspondence, discoveries of more letters having continued.

Undoubtedly, ten thousand letters treasured so far are a golden antechamber to the persona of Madame de Staël. A lifetime of thought and sentiment brought happiness, but anxiety and sorrow as well. There is a common denominator in this epistolary legacy: enthusiasm. More important still, at the same time, an exceptionally powerful self-analysis has invited biographical commitment. Publications have also revealed reactions from Germaine's correspondents, to name only a few of the many, again François René de Chateaubriand, for instance Friedrich von Schiller, tzar Alexander I, Arthur Wellesley duke of Wellington and Thomas Jefferson. One person did not respond personally to Germaine's letters: Napoléon Bonaparte.

One approaches such a legacy with trepidation. Published throughout two centuries and hailing from different parts of Europe, interpretations of Madame de Staël's letters have sometimes allowed curiosity, conjecture, judgemental habits and mediocrity's abetted taste for sensationalism to offset pure historical description and explanation, if not admiration. Where the facts of Germaine's life are concerned, unfortunately, the onerous fad for denigration has come into the picture. In contrast, Jasinski's exemplary respect for correct historical context and truth-seeking concerning facts honor her subject's monumental letterwriting. Here, trepidation can subside.

Concerning the 'oeuvre', that is to say the public legacy, the late Simone Balayé's parting advice to her 'searchers' (chercheurs) was simple: read the 'oeuvre', she said, read on! Balayé's biographical and critical labors reveal the degree to which she practiced her counsel. Since the 1960's her growing leadership in the Société's organization and colloquiae, her texts that have echoed each other in chronological and bibliographical assistance, her editorial support of translations of Madame de Staël's novels *Delphine, Corinne ou l'Italie*, of the texts *On Germany* (*De l'Allemagne*) and *Ten years in exile* (*Dix années d'exil*) by Avriel Goldberger from 1987 to 2000, such activity honored her subject. Balayé also published essays on *Delphine* and *Corinne ou l'Italie* between 1984 and 1988. A remarkable analysis had preceded these during one of her numerous colloquium offerings, *On the Subject of Pre-Romanticism*, a paper recently included in her text of 1994—*Madame de Staël: To Write, To Struggle, To Live* (*Ecrire, Lutter, Vivre*). At once critic, analyst and biographer, Balayé here juxtaposed elements of continuity and what she called 'rupture' in Staël's output, the author's political resilience and individualism contrasting with a lifetime's exposure to the demands and particularly the narrowness of the society in which she lived, though soon enough, that society would be shattered. Balayé's claim can be considered her ultimate message to those eager to follow her lead: the beauties of the Enlightenment, she writes, were always with Madame de Staël. It was only with the abuses of the Ancien Régime that Germaine broke. One had to understand that she was a political person, philosophical also in the sense that she envisaged a new intellectual era. Germaine suffered from the genocide of the 1790's and despaired over the despotic consequences of the young Revolution's failure to act on its pure republican principles. But with her, resilience and the passionate hold of the ideals of her young years made her attentions turn away from despair and toward the future.

While Balayé's 1979 text *The Enlightened and Liberty* (*Lumières et*

Liberté) re-examined her claim of individualism, she expressed admiration for a colloquium presentation given ten years earlier by R. Mortier at Coppet, Madame de Staël's home near Geneva. It was called *Madame de Staël et l'héritage des Lumières.* Indeed, the subject invited reflection. It is still an avenue for consideration.

Simone Balayé's energetic performance has inspired many, particularly those who have held to her discipline, stayed close to the 'oeuvre', and abstained from publicity-seeking interpretation. Madelyn Gutwirth's text *Madame de Staël, Novelist—Emergence of the Artist* (1978) came eight years after her having published *Staël, Rousseau and the Woman Question* and before her examination of the novels *Delphine, Corinne or Italy* as well as the *Essay on Fiction.* In 1972, Jean Starobinski also compared Madame the Staël and Jean-Jacques Rousseau; Lucia Omacini presented extensive studies of both *Corinne or Italy* (1980) and *Delphine* (1987); Norman King examined *Delphine* from the perspective of S. de Sismondi's thought (1979); Charlotte Hogsett wrote *The Literary Existence of Germaine de Staël* (1987); among other subjects of study, Frank Paul Bowman focused on the polemics surrounding Staël's *Considerations On the French Revolution* (1988); Karina Smurlo's *Fire and Feminine Discourse in Corinne or Italy* (1999) came barely ten years after G. Gengembre's *A Woman Revolutionized.*

Articles by these writers have appeared in the Cahiers Staëliens along with offerings by Jasinski and Balayé. I hope to be forgiven for not having named all of the latter's colleagues—her esteemed 'searchers' (chercheurs) as she called them. All as well as newcomers to Staëlean scholarship are present in my bibliography though decidedly, avenues are open for further investigation. Meanwhile, translated selected writings have come to light in addition to the full Goldberger texts thanks in part to Vivian Folkenflick's *An Extraordinary Woman* (1987).

Factual biographies of Madame de Staël are mentioned in the bibliography, but there is no doubt that Germaine has been examined, judged and often misjudged regarding the society she created around herself and nurtured with forceful and unbounded affection. Exaggerated attention to this has deflected from consideration of her intelligence, it has also belittled a sensitivity which, if carefully studied, connects with her intelligence. Later manifestations of melancholy show the degree to which this connection became an introversion. A careful reading of Germaine's letters and works will bring out the crystals of intelligence and sensitivity combined. The ebb and flow move from love to disillusionment in her rapport with others, to conflicts and humiliations. While both enthusiasm and idealism persist, she portrays her relationships unabashedly in fiction and even in nonfiction. At the very same time, in her letters she constantly exercises a self-analysis which reveals the anxieties raised in the course of relationships too complex, too unexpected or unpredictable to accept outright. Inwardly and outwardly, privately and publicly, here was a life consciously attached to human relationship or, shall we say, to love. But in thought and feeling, while Germaine lived very much in relation to her time, she treasured her loves and lamented over their loss—which included a personified France—and the creative self moved on unrelentlessly. Because of this, Madame de Staël's compulsive act of writing merits continued investigation.

There is no risk here of a separation of the writer from the person, of the latter falling off, so to speak, from her historical performance. This is so because in and out of writing, as her first moment of entry into society concurs with her entry into the publishing world, she is historically unique. Then, if it is true that the private, letter- writing person and the public, publishing person are inextricably bound together, the challenge is ours to describe and at best explain the development of her experience from impulse to impression, perception, and reflection onto the action of her pen.

A question arises: did experience demolish her enthusiasm? Simple as the question may seem, the answer offers significance from the perspective of literary history: Germaine was not a romantic, that is to say, not quite yet. Her enthusiasm was vigorous; granted, she was nurtured by the writings of Jean-Jacques Rousseau, but by those of Montesquieu and Voltaire also; she developed her recognizably political disposition so that the outcome, for her, came in the form of republican idealism. At this point, therefore, the Staëlean melancholy, for one, her political idealism, for another, must be assessed in their own right if we wish to let her come forth tangibly, the person with pen in hand.

Of necessity, the drama of her time demands description, particularly where the thrust into revolutionary genocide will be concerned, then Napoléon's meteoric ascendancy. The latter will impose itself on Madame de Staël's own rise in political reputation, her success as a writer, and the oppression she will have to endure year after year. Forcible and extraordinary as those events were, she reacted promptly and with keen perceptivity. Granted, a representation of history—if not that particular history due to a large cast of characters many of whom were inextricably bound to each other by ambition, greed and self-interest—such a heavy representation risks overcoming the attention to a single life. I hope to have avoided the risk and carried out the historical task adequately while highlighting Staël's idealism which, contrary to many of her friends and acquaintances, was steady and passionate.

Consider that before the drama unfolded, Madame de Staël was part of the last generation nurtured by the great 'luminaries', as she called them: those who came to Suzanne Necker's salon and highly respected her father Jacques Necker. Barely twenty during the Revolution's first tumult, then maturing within sights, sounds and repercussions of terrorism, and soon after seeing the signs of despotism, she was bound to express dismay, horror, revulsion, and for a period of time disillusion. Up to and including the last piece of writing, she questioned the initial Revolution's failure. As a republican and idealist, her mind and heart were troubled, for to her, the original principle of liberty had been mutilated.

Into and through her forties, Madame de Staël bore emperor Napoléon's order of exile and his police surveillance. Napoléon could not bear her so-called ideology, her ebullience, and her influence on others. For many of those difficult years, her courageous resilience maintained the intellectual outflow buoyed by her emotional personality. Hence the characteristic intimacy of her writing: political but literary, all in one.

What is the ideal society? What is the ideal relationship between men and women? Her questions fill her work during thirty years. She appealed to her readers to develop independence of mind. She went from this to a cosmopolitanism reaching from individuals to other nations. Those who read her, and came to know her, experienced her impact. Some were perplexed, as I mentioned earlier, others fully agreed with her ideas. Many were writers themselves and like her were in the throes of publishing. As in Voltaire's Ferney at the time of Germaine's birth, a steady group of literary and political friends gathered at her home in Coppet or came to her Paris salon. For most of her friends, Germaine's emotional agitation, brilliance of mind, sensitivity and vivacity defined her personality. But over and above everything else they admired and respected her for her authorship. They considered her writings insightful, innovative, and focused. Some found in her works those same components of the personality they had defined for themselves. They defended her before her critics. She too published essays in self-defense. Germaine's relationships also developed through her correspondence and during her travels in France, Switzerland, Italy, Germany, during journeys in England, Russia, then Scandinavia and England again before the final return to France.

By definition, enthusiasm connects with a youthful disposition. Therefore, we must ask ourselves where this characteristic came from, what made her young years project that quality into maturity, and made her want to impart it to others in writing. Sustained by it, Madame de Staël's emotional kind of intellectuality merits attention from the perspective of its nurturing.

THE NURTURING

Young man, take this and read. . . . As I am better disposed to have you exercise your mind rather than to instruct you, whether or not you adopt my ideas does not matter to me so long as they will have your full attention. Others will teach you how to know the forces of nature; what matters to me is that you have decided to test your own forces. Adieu!

Denis Diderot, 1754[1]

Powerful elements dominated Germaine Necker's childhood and adolescence: her mother's tutelage, excitement generated by the newly created Encyclopedia, the intellectual ambiance in her mother's salon, the mutual affection between Germaine and her father, and increasingly overbearing political events. Each element made mental and emotional impacts. The first combined love and intellect in the mother as well. The very young child returned the maternal affection effusively. Fragile tentacles of self-analysis and psychological perceptivity formed quickly. "I simply must write to you," Germaine wrote to Suzanne Necker during a short parental absence. "My heart has tightened, I am sad. . . . You can find all kinds of consolations in yourself, but all I can find in myself is you."[1] She was barely twelve years old.

In most of the letters written soon after, the emotional bond nearly pushed aside tentacles of the mind, but only nearly. Germaine considered her education a personal venture; she was anything but a passive child. "While educating myself," she wrote to her mother, "my aim is to be more pleasing to you."[2] She was already placing herself in time, and in the context of society. But because of the mother's moral hold on her child, that placing was only secondary; the mother came first as the best example in the process of learning. This happened when it came to learning the English language, which Suzanne loved, while with Germaine the facility for language was quickly evident. Soon, she was encouraged to express her thoughts on paper, which her mother did as well. Germaine's first efforts with the pen were carefully supervised. In mid-May 1779, during Germaine's fourteenth year, Madame Necker complimented her on her "own good heart," but, she added, "your style is somewhat out of hand. Don't push yourself beyond your own bounds ... just as you praise and caress me. ... The fault is quite common at your age. When one has lived more one learns that the veritable way to please and to interest others is to paint exactly one's thought without enlargement, then the writer's manner has something original and truthful as against comparisons taken from things that are out of reach."[3]

Of Provençal origin, Suzanne Necker was born near Lausanne in 1738. Her father, a Calvinist pastor, educated her in the classics, philosophy and theology. At age twenty-six, in 1764, she married the wealthy financeer Jacques Necker who like her had come to Paris shortly before this. With a prestige applied to the husband she worshipped, Suzanne determined to conquer Paris and soon opened a salon. 'Salons' were known to have been held as far back as the Renaissance. Well-to-do ladies hostessed gatherings of prestigious writers and artists, scientists, diplomats and other political figures whose ideas did not always meet but whose conversations brightened the reunion days. Wit shone and polite argument often emanated from guests' own publications. Suzanne thus found her niche in Paris society, well aware that her brilliant guests also visited other salons—those of her elder Marie-Thérèse Geoffrin (1699-1777), Madame Claude Helvétius whose husband (1715-1771) published the sensualistic text *On the Mind* (*De l'esprit*), and Madame Paul Henri d'Holbach (1723-1789); the latter's *Système de la nature* expounded materialistic and atheistic views. While Suzanne enjoyed her arena, she kept to her personal rule of wanting to please, though without exaggeration. Her manner was serious and could be persuasive. The writer-philosopher Denis Diderot (1713-1784), one of her earliest visitors, came with his friend the mathematician Jean Le Rond D'Alembert (1717-1783). Their *Encyclopédie* already earned much success at the time of Suzanne's salon opening. Diderot remarked on his hostess's prettiness and flattered himself that she was "in love with me" and, he added, she is witty—"un bel esprit."[4] Diderot perceived Suzanne's sensitivity to questions of moral principle; he teased her, noticed her tears, and apologized. Later, Suzanne questioned him on the subject of the soul. Her confrontation received harsh treatment. "The soul," Diderot replied, "has a secret history . . . it is a dark cavern, inhabited by all sorts of beneficient and maleficent beasts. The wicked man opens the cavern door and lets out only the latter. The man of good will does the opposite."[5] Suzanne discovered Diderot's intense respect for English philosophy, literature and political administration, and his agreement with the British thinker John Locke (1632-1704) on the primary importance of sense experience as well as Locke's democratic ideas. Diderot's sharp criticism of the French government had met censure and one imprisonment. Paris's judiciary parlement was the bane of his writing years. He was silent, though not verbally.

Suzanne Necker accepted the eclecticism of her salon, nevertheless she held on to Calvinistic principles. She acted on these in her charitable works. This did not enter the agendas of the other 'grandes dames' of her day. She did join these, however, in canvassing to have her intellectual friends enter the French Academy, Jean-François marquis de Saint-Lambert (1716-1803), Etienne de Condillac and d'Alembert. Openly applauding her husband's successes in business, Suzanne lived a secondary, somewhat introverted life by quietly venting anxieties in writing. Soon, therefore, this interest attached itself to her child. The rapport between mother and child presented introversion on one hand, extroversion on the other, effusiveness being entirely Germaine's. Reserve, composure, empathy, attention and listening, all of these Suzanne hoped to pass on to Germaine. "One must observe oneself," she wrote, "master oneself, and never allow temper to flare as this can cause irreparable damage." Self-control in comportment . . . gesture and voice are also part of the art of pleasing."[6]

When Germaine entered adolescence, Suzanne's deep love for literature transmitted itself to her. The seventeenth century playwright Jean Racine and Baron Charles Secondat de Montesquieu (1689-1755) came into this transmission. And then, Shakespeare. English authors were within arms' reach: Locke, Milton, Pope, Dryden, Swift, and Richardson whose novels Diderot often praised for their moral quality. Newly translated German novels, dramas and poetry—particularly Wieland and Lessing—entered the Necker library as well as English publications of the 1760's such as Thomas Gray, Lawrence Sterne and Oliver Goldsmith.

Always within sight were the poetry and prose of François Arouet known as Voltaire (1694-1778). His introduction to French readers of English thought and parliamentary life fascinated Suzanne. She developed a cult for the venerable poet. When he came to Paris to be honored, Germaine, then aged twelve, was taken to visit him. Often at the theatre, Germaine learned many of his plays. Next to Racine, Voltaire became her favorite French author. She composed playets in paper cut-outs, and recited poetry in the garden of Saint-Ouen, doctors having recommended fresh air and exercise away from Paris. On first hearing the music of Glück, Germaine requested lessons on the clavichord, which she mastered easily.

Still very young, Germaine also accompanied her parents to England to see a Shakespearean performance by David Garrick. On journeys to Versailles and Fontainebleau, mother and daughter read together. Then one day, Germaine was admitted to the Friday salon. Sitting straight and listening were the orders of the weekly ritual. Guests sometimes came forward. The young girl never forgot their thoughtfulness. Regular visitors besides Diderot and d'Alembert were the naturalist Georges comte de Buffon (1707-1788), whose eloquence Suzanne termed the ultimate quality of genius; the playwright Jean-François Marmontel (1723-1799), who once encouraged Germaine to write a report on Montesquieu's *Spirit of Laws (L'Esprit des lois);* and among others the journalist-critic Jean-Baptiste Suard (1732-1817), whose affection Germaine returned in kind. In time, other guests captivated Germaine, Thomas Jefferson (1743-1826), for example, who during his five-year diplomatic assignment in France came with young Marie Joseph marquis De La Fayette (1757-1834). Later, Germaine communicated with Jefferson as if the day of his visit had only just happened. In a similar manner, she maintained her affection for La Fayette.

Germaine's childhood companion Catherine Huber remembered a salon dinner during which Germaine "listened, her eyes following the conversation as if she wanted to race ahead of the words, eager to express her thoughts." To Huber, the mobility of Germaine's face showed an understanding "of even the most remote political subjects."[7]

The Necker library became a magnetic companion to the Friday salon. There came the newly translated *Werther* by Johann von Goethe (1749-1832). The German writer entered Germaine's panoply of revered authors. Tragic tales that instilled a contemplative mood easily affected her, so did gloomy and warlike legends like the Scottish Macpherson's *Poems of Ossian* with their bristling foretaste of romantic fury and strange lands. Diderot's friend baron Melchior Grimm (1723-1807), often a familiar face in the Necker household, conveyed this new kind of excitement in his popular review *L'Année littéraire (The Literary Year)*.

Germaine described the emotional impact of her studies: "Love for studying," she wrote, "has all the characteristics of passion . . . It offers a goal . . . toward which the progress is a certitude. . . . Studying takes one through a series of new objects, and makes one feel an eventfulness that nourishes thought, occupies and animates it without outside interference. . . . This kind of impulse . . . connects with one's future just as the chain of thought involved has had a connection with curiosity and the effort that has been made."[8] Undoubtedly, Germaine's enjoyment of reading drew from her inner disposition. Powers of concentration and reflection were securely anchored.

Though both mother and daughter were still within affectionate reach of each other, Germaine experienced a distancing from her imperious tutor. Reading old and new publications and salon conversations alternated. The world burst into Germaine's life with glories past and present, with notions concerning the future as well. Volume after volume, up to the last in 1772, the *Encyclopédie—The Dictionary of the Sciences, Arts and Trades*—gave evidences of scientific progress and proposed social and political reforms. The ferment was strong. It fought clerical and royal censure until the end.

The writers whom Diderot invited to contribute to his massive project astounded aristocratic and bourgeois readers alike, articles and essays pouring through the fabric of the hefty tomes that criticized the government and the Roman Catholic church. On the surface, the eagerness for reform quickly became manifest. Below the surface, the attacks on superstitious beliefs, on the question of belief itself, drew philosophical scrutiny. Concurrently, the question of the object of belief, namely divinity, came to the surface. Were there powers determining life's destiny? Were these only ideas? Sharply different personalities addressed these questions. Some, like Etienne de Condillac (1715-1780), echoed John Locke's claim that ideas are not innate and only come through sensory experience aided by reflection. Others, overtly materialistic and aetheistic, questioned royalty's divine right to power, particularly if divinity was not real, and God did not exist. The *Encyclopédie* became the vehicle for a cause: it was time for a change. In the not so distant past the venerable academician Bernard de Fontenelle (1657-1757) wished to see philosophy liberate itself from internal polemics and become accessible to a wide reading public. His wish came true. Philosophy concerned itself not only with the individual but with society as a whole, hence the social adjunct to thoughts of reform.

Montesquieu gave the *Encyclopédie* its initial political stamp. He depicted frivolity, religious intolerance and the French monarchy's claim to absolutism. Voltaire seconded Montesquieu's consideration for the English parliamentary system. In publications of his own such as the *Essay on Mores* (*Essai sur les moeurs et l'esprit des nations*), while calling himself a deist and therefore respecting the existence of a providential principle, Voltaire rather concentrated on human misdeeds and misfortunes. His attacks on prejudice, superstition, ignorance and injustices brought by these were sharp and persistent: the ills had to be crushed. While Montesquieu had wistfully correlated human nature with the nature of things, in *Candide or Optimism* (1759), Voltaire drew human nature with a prickly pen that left his readers breathless. *Candide*'s irony and pathological realism would be remembered by all, old and young.

During the first printings of the *Encyclopédie* a Genevese named Jean-Jacques Rousseau (1712-1778) discoursed on the so-called value of the sciences and the arts. According to him, civilized society's moral carelessness festered greed and corruption; society denatured mankind. Many interpreted Rousseau's claim as a refutation of progress. Rousseau was misunderstood: the nefarious appendages of civilized society were the real culprits. But Rousseau caused dismay among the men of letters of his time. Though congenial during young adult years spent in his native Switzerland and soon after in Paris, later on his presence became abrupt, unconventional, reclusive and generally disconcerting. Those who did understand his claim and his passionate style offered friendship—Diderot and Voltaire for a few years, Grimm, d'Holbach, and for a short time the Scottish philosopher-historian David Hume (1711-1776), who welcomed Rousseau in Britain.

Like many of her generation, Germaine's mother found enchantment in Rousseau's novel *Julie or the New Héloïse* (*Julie ou la nouvelle Héloïse*) (1756). It had caused a sensation even before Suzanne opened her salon. During the 1740's and 1750's, Rousseau composed operas. He angered the elderly and beloved composer Jean-Philippe Rameau (1683-1764) by his unwelcome criticism. Nevertheless, Diderot elicited from Rousseau articles on music for the *Encyclopédie*. Ill health and susceptibility to literary criticism made Rousseau a near recluse. In 1762, the *Emile or Education* and *The Social Contract* were banned. Later works still flowed with his passionate concern for the fate of ordinary man. "I believe strongly in everything that I write," he stated.⁹ Few grasped the connection between his attitude as a writer and the troubled personality it came from. Germaine was bound to ask questions sooner or later.

Suzanne Necker disagreed with Rousseau's notions concerning the education of young girls. She maintained that these merit a vigorous curriculum including latin, history, geography, literature, recitation, music and foreign languages. Suzanne acted accordingly. That which transpired in Germaine's reading and salon experiences negated Rousseau's call for a simple, quiet household and feminine self-abnegation.

In time, Rousseau's concern for the citizen's place in society touched sensitive chords in the class-conscious society of the dying eighteenth century. The open-minded sensed the logic of the *Social Contract* according to which promises were made by a sovereign people to itself. In such a political philosophy, everyone's innate moral sense was uppermost in the scale of human values. Diderot sympathized with this notion: "grandeur . . . has to connect with feeling, not with fantasy or excess of religious devotion motivated by fear . . . otherwise nothing would be sublime in mores . . . and virtue would become minute."[10] Montesquieu had deplored fantasy, having seen, he said, "men who can act on principle . . . for each one depends on a general law."[11] Voltaire expressed a similar view of human nature from the perspective of the historian: "I would like to discover what our society was like in olden times, what arts were cultivated . . . what homelife was like, this being more interesting than the wars and so many examples of human cruelty history insists on telling."[12]

The moral thrust coïncided with scientific progress, both brightening their century. The German philosopher Immanuel Kant (1724-1804) observed the explosive array of publications in England, his own country, the Netherlands and France including the seventeenth volume of the *Encyclopédie* in 1772. He was moved to offer the classic definition of the term Enlightenment (Aufklärung):

> It is man's exodus from his self-incurred tutelage . . . the cause lying not in any weakness of the understanding, but in indecision and lack of courage to use the mind without the guidance of another.
> Dare to know (sapere aude)! Have the courage to use your own understanding; this is the motto of the Enlightenment. [12]

Kant agreed with Rousseau on the subject of religious belief. "The greatest ideas concerning divinity come from reason alone," Rousseau wrote in the *Emile*. "... Look at the spectacle of nature, listen to your inner voice. Did God not say everything to our conscience, to our judgement? Can human nature possibly say more than this?"[14]

The public was silent, but this was not so in correspondence and private salon conversations. Consequently, the last decades of the century presented their political phenomenon: republican idealism. Tentacles stretched in every possible direction, most of all into religious belief and political conviction. Many among the educated young, and certainly those who possessed a precosciously mature outlook on the world and in particular the society that had nurtured and sheltered them, many indeed instantly grasped at these tentacles—Germaine Necker among them. But to some of her elders, the question of human value in relation to religious belief remained a preoccupation. Germaine's father, Jacques Necker, exemplified such a concern.

A protestant bourgeois, Necker's success in business affairs, his entrepreneurial manner, self-confidence, and perceptivity regarding public opinion nevertheless harbored private religious feelings. For him, philosophy may well have defined human nature for what it was, dignified yet open to corruption, but the important question now at issue concerned what ordinary citizens thought as members of the body politic. From his experience with the working world above and below his own status, he wanted to bring the urgency of this question into focus. As he did so in conversation and in writing, religious feelings and faith in human nature never left him. Fortuitous circumstance brought Jacques Necker into the political arena. Born in Geneva in 1732 of German and French ancestry, success in banking brought wealth after having come to Paris in 1750. His marriage to Suzanne Curchod in 1764 was happy. He stood by his wife in her salon, aware of the respect surrounding them, delighting in Germaine's precocity. His reputation grew, his expertise caught the attention of court officials who, though riddled with prejudice and extravagance, knew the need for financial assistance. Necker in turn paid attention to the monarchy. He admired Louis XVI's finance minister for the efforts made to redress the economy. Robert de Turgot (1727-1781) was an ideologue of progress, an encyclopedist who had lectured at the Sorbonne University shortly after Necker's arrival in Paris. Aging, austere and increasingly disillusioned, Turgot wearied of the court's attempts to maintain their frivolities through intrigues. He looked at the nation with dismay: "The nation is a society composed of different orders that are poorly tied to each other and of a people whose members have but few bonds and where, consequently, everyone is preoccupied with his own interest. Nowhere is there a common, visible interest."[15]

Turgot's court appointment ended abruptly in 1777. Necker was called to Versailles. Enchanted, charming and somewhat naïve, this bourgeois protestant of Swiss upbringing found himself catapulted into Versailles' self-contained pleasures and before a court's condescending gaze. He well knew from reading that Louis XVI's ancestors had known only one side of the public: its favors and its praises. During Louis XV's long reign, public opinion supplanted praise. Resentment grew against taxation privileges that favored the nobility, aristocracy and the church at the expense of all other royal subjects. Proliferating pamphlets and newspapers expressed ironic criticism. The dire economy, the uneven pricing of bread, for one, raised daily exclamations of discontent.

Necker gave in to obsequiousness before his monarch. He loaned part of his fortune to the king. He did not forget Turgot's parting comment, but pressures came against his attempts for reform. He first addressed the problems of wheat distribution, of income and expenses among provincial administrators and court officials, and of poor communication between the government and provincial judiciary parliaments. His grasp of these needs attested to his feeling for the nation as nation before its monarch. He published his first financial report. Shocked by this publicity, court and king forced Necker to resign. The year was 1781.

Proud, Necker attempted to react to the blow with moderation, and to detach from feeling. He later described the moment's somber intimations of things to come:

> My government occupation which brought me close to the king allowed me to discover the first signs of a Revolution. Some of these signs were real, others pronounced. That is what I have seen. First of all, the great force of public opinion. It strangely affected me.[16]

Diderot and Buffon praised Necker, but his successor Charles de Calonne (1734-1802) pointed out statistical errors, and the Paris parliament rejected his suggestion that provincial assemblies be created. The court, which had steadily refused his entry into the king's council, had become an enemy for life.

In spite of intimations, Necker's sense of moderation and propensity to meditate on religious concerns prevented him from foretelling the full extent of coming events. It was not so very long since the death of the unhappy Rousseau, whose *Héloïse* Necker had esteemed. He had complimented the author for having pushed "everyday virtues to their highest level without discouraging those who wanted to reach it."[17] Nor could Necker anticipate the reversal of a desperately hesitant king calling him back to the royal desk.

At home, Necker wrote a text on financial administration, published three years later, also a short piece called *The Happiness of Fools*. "Because fools are unaware of their own folly," he wrote, "they enjoy unalloyed happiness in self-contentment, whereas the man of genius, lucid in self-analysis, knows only torment and incertitude."[18] Simplistic and touched by vanity, the momentary respite from anxiety amused Necker. More complex, the text *On Financial Administration* contained an equally telling remark: "The heart of man is a tableau that one must see from the distance from which the wise director of nature has placed him."[19]

Germaine Necker greatly admired her father. With finesse and judgement regarding his character, she sensed her father's inner reaches: caution in judging others, respect for religion. She long remembered his comment on the heart of man. The years 1777 to 1785 represented new fruits of Germaine's nurturing period: her desire to write, and her deep love for her father. Happy to express her thoughts among old and new friends in her mother's salon, frank and kind in her manner, Germaine exuded an intoxication with words, and knowledge of the importance of effort in the search for ideas. She took her talent seriously, writing a short piece called *The Inconvenience of Living in Paris*. Enjoying the fresh air at her parents' country estate, she practiced elocution and recitation out of doors and read Voltaire's classical tragedies, Beaumarchais' *Marriage of Figaro*, Bernardin de Saint-Pierre's *Paul and Virginia* and Lawrence Sterne's *Sentimental Journey*. A recent trip to England had enchanted her, including a visit to the House of Commons.

Often present in his wife's salon, Necker's showed eagerness for reform. Like Montesquieu and Voltaire, he expressed his admiration for the English parliament and used the salon to sound out his idea for a national and representative convocation. All admired his energy, his rapid intelligence and seductive gravity, flashes of vanity notwithstanding. Speaking in the intimacy of Suzanne's salon presented no difficulty. With Suzanne, a project for the opening of a hospice came true, and later a hospital. Suzanne's health was failing. A nervous condition kept her away from the salon. Necker found comfort in the company of Germaine whose vivacity of mind and encyclopedic curiosity he enjoyed. He perceived her sensitivity, but the fact, also, that she abandoned the composure of her childhood. She danced the minuet in the salon, sang, and recited excerpts from Virgil, English poetry and the Old Testament. Germaine grieved for her father's political demise. Sympathy was as much a part of her as ambition. She realized that the public had been affected by Necker's departure from Versailles. Her *Journal* indicates strength of self-analysis, perceptivity, and a first distancing from the nest:

> Father wants me to beware of writing . . . calling this a weakness of self-esteem . . . he worries, seeing me write his portrait.[20]

A journey with her parents to the south of France was organized for the sake of Suzanne's health. Germaine wrote poetry, elliciting from the legend of Sapho and Phaon the troubling concept of lovelessness. Except for rare moments of exaltation, poetry, she knew, was not exactly her calling. Necker purchased a substantial property near Lausanne, next to the village of Coppet. Germaine followed her parents, but missed Paris. She wanted to continue attending French Academy nominations. At one of these she heard her father's brilliant eulogy to Jean-Baptiste Colbert (1619-1683), Louis XIV's valued finance minister. Just as it had for her father, the feeling for history had become part of Germaine. To live for history "like kings," she wrote in her *Journal* in 1785, and "to feel for history when writing about oneself elevates one's perspective . . . but risks losing naturalness."[21] In last moments of adolescence, Germaine was all thought, all feeling. Understanding her father's fall from glory, she conversed with him on his project for a text called *The Importance of Religious Ideas*. She applauded him for having pulled his mind away from political vicissitudes.

She was told that she was of marriageable age. Though admitting to herself that reality, she found the yearning for a "calming of one's soul" a disturbing element at that time in her life. However, she reflected that reality, after all, was the "basis" of her enthusiasm, peculiarly philosophical as the latter seemed to be.[22] Germaine was ready for young adulthood, two forces acting: the intellect, and feeling.

> My mother exclaimed to my father: "Once again I have found in your daughter the sensibility, the physiognomy of her childhood." "I believe," my father replied, "that she has lever lost it."[23]
>
> Germaine de Staël, *Journal*, 1785

Part One
TUMULT AND TERROR

1.
MOMENTS IN TIME

July 14, 1789, the Bastille has been stormed. Bleeding, the governor's ghostly head is paraded on a tall spike before a howling, half-drunk populace. Behind the populace, somewhat apart, elegant young people stand silent, eyes aghast. They are children of the aristocracy and of the new Parisian bourgeoisie, struggling journalists and young writers full of vigor and idealism.

The fate of the unfortunate governor of the Bastille, the marquis de Launay, will not dissipate easily from minds and hearts of these young people, particularly when their minds are open to reflection and their hearts are generous. Germaine Necker de Staël is part of this generation, she is their peer and a writer as well, with a mind and heart akin to theirs. The shock will reverberate. The feeling of terror will be contagious. Fear will remain, and for a long time. To any young and intelligent person who loves France and identifies with it, all the more so if that person was born in Paris though from parents of a nearby country, of Protestant upbringing, and who has an attachment for France because it is the land of her childhood, for Germaine indeed, the experience of terror and fear will have tenacious after-effects.

Roars of the mob foment hysteria. Like a contagious disease, anger spreads, poisoning the city, then other cities. Those who have entered the Bastille and pillaged it for weapons are poised to aim at Versailles. Made aware of the fever that infests not only Paris but the nation at large, the court is frantic in a pathologically deliberate act of indifference. The same royal disease had filled the last decades of Louis XV's reign.

Like her peers, Germaine will ever pose the question, to herself at first, then to all who will come into her world in conversation and in writing: what caused this terrible moment? Other questions will follow and superimpose themselves: what will happen to France? Will it be vulnerable to others? The prior question will return at the end of Germaine's political agitations nearly thirty years later.

What caused this terrible moment? Hunger and poverty, and the long, wearying exasperation that went from silence to lament, threatening cries and finally murderous action. Three quarters of the population of France consisted of the peasantry of whom twenty million were poor. Their lower-class Parisian compatriots were in an equal state of dejection. They preceeded the peasantry in their revolt. Turgot and Necker had been right in their premonitions concerning public opinion. By the early 1780's, from intellectual aristocrats and their bourgeois counterparts down to laborers and the jobless, an amorphous public conscience had evolved, but new visible and audible elements of public life were affecting mores and concurrently, thought. Newspapers, books, open-air spectacles, moralizing canvasses, acts of devotion to nature and scorn for ostentation, speech-making in praise of virtue, societies of friends, such were the elements that created and nourished public conscience. Oratory became common; it reached the hungry and poor.

The vicar of Chartres, Emmanuel Sieyès (1748-1836), a writer who later entered politics, called for individual effort in putting one's conscience into action.[1] While men like Sieyès spoke of effort, the peasantry could only be slow and sluggish in response. Bad crops, antiquated agriculture, bitterness against absentee landlords compounded their misery. Silence changed from submissiveness to action. In olden times, everyone revered the king, all considering themselves his subjects and hoping for his interest and assistance. In the eighteenth century, neither of these were forthcoming. Reverence died.

When the fifteen-year-old Austrian princess Marie-Antoinette, daughter of empress Marie Therese and the Germanic emperor Francis I, arrived in France in 1770 to marry sixteen-year-old Louis XVI (1754-1793), festivities overwhelmed the gaping public. Momentary happiness filled the air. Through the artifice, the multitude barely saw their prince. Except for his coronation in Reims four years later and one furtive journey to a northern naval town, Louis seldom left the gilded microcosm of Versailles. Before and through her child-bearing years, Marie-Antoinette showed a taste for the Paris opera and theatre so that the populace did see her, but Louis seldom accompanied his queen.

The hunt and solitude were Louis's major interests since youth. He was shy and taciturn though not unkind. He read Montesquieu, David Hume's history of England and studied commerce and law. Volumes of the *Encyclopédie* and Rousseau's *Emile* came to his reading table. His impressions are not known, for Louis only recorded details of the hunt. His father, then his mother, died of tuberculosis during Louis's adolescence. He was often told that all of France looked up to him, and that a weak king could well encur public disdain and end like the English Charles I. During the year of Louis's marriage, Diderot sent a message urging him to renounce royal extravagance and abolish the fiscal privileges of nobility and clergy.[2] The apostrophe was not heeded. Louis XV had kept his grandson away from the king's council. Added to his ignorance of administrative affairs, his natural timidity was bound to develop into chronic hesitancy.

High prices of wheat and the fear of a bread shortage afflicted many. How could Louis face the government's economic difficulties? Pleading his youth with his ministers, he did meet with them, and listened. He perceived that they were moving counter to the absolutism that had been engrained in him. In 1774, his minister of state Jean-Frédéric comte de Maurepas (1701-1781) expressed wishes for a temperate monarchy. Louis's finance minister Turgot agreed with Maurepas to prepare a re-activating of the old parlement, the august body of magistrates who deliberated and acted as a court of justice. Louis's irresolution regarding such a diminishing of his power of veto and censure (lettres de cachet) flared under the concerted pressures of his entourage: Marie-Antoinette, for one, whose friends and expenses Louis tolerated; court intrigues that moved like the wind and affected Louis's ministerial choices every which way; Louis's brothers the comte de Provence and the comte d'Artois whose influences wavered according to those intrigues; finally the public, before whom timidity so tortured Louis that the ministry had to help him rehearse his speeches. The parlement of Paris felt public pressure in turn. Some magistrates criticized the government.

So far, Louis exercised firmness in only one thing: his belief in the absolutism of his position. He was unable to implement this belief and therefore rule like his ancestors for whom favors and praise sustained the concept. These disintegrated when Louis's grandfather ended his reign in corruption and indolence. In 1775, riots, sedition and pillage erupted in the provinces. They were quelled. Louis heard echoes of calumnies, if not directly at his reading table. Voices foreign to him were approaching Versailles.

He responded: "In all fairness, I should try to help bring happiness to a people who contribute to mine. From now on I shall better look after them. . . . The task is heavy."[3] The gesture came too late.

The new secretary of state, Chrétien de Malesherbes (1721-1794), a friend of Voltaire, suggested a convocation of the states general. In the old régime, this body of consultlants chosen from clerics, aristocrats and wealthy bourgeois were invited by the monarch to express opinions on pressing matters. They had been convened in the former two centuries during financial crises and royal rivalries. Malesherbes anticipated Necker's wish. The very thought of such a reunion repelled Louis, yet he showed an interest in tax reforms, agreeing also that religious intolerance and forced labor (the 'corvée') were nefarious. Voltaire greeted the news of Louis's interests with alacrity. But the ministry's outcry was fierce. Lack of funds was their first concern. Louis gave in to their criticism, including Marie-Antoinette's. Malesherbes resigned, and Voltaire's other friend Turgot was ousted. So close to the end of life, Voltaire felt the sting of disillusion.

Differences in circumstance, personality and character are history's puzzling preponderances when individuals come to share responsibilities. As we know, Jacques Necker exuded respect, devotion, and eagerness during his first royal assignment. Courteously, Louis acquiesced to the bourgeois banker's presence; he needed funds to cover costs and refill the royal coffers. Necker failed to carry out his projects for reform; intent on power and grandeur, the ministry had been malevolent toward the 'republican' Necker. After his ouster in 1781, court festivities continued as much as ever. So did public libels, and costs brought on by the war with England. Public agitation grew. Necker's tentative tax reforms were undone. Intent on having the court on his side, the new finance minister Calonne engaged in speculation and loans and momentary distributions of bread to the poor. Louis's respite from anxiety was illusory.

Calonne made one serious attempt to redress the deficit: as Turgot and Necker had done before him, he suggested a reunion of notables in Louis's presence. Antiquated, as it had not been held since 1626 under Richelieu, nevertheless on February 22, 1788, one hundred and forty-four royals, nobility, clergy and municipal officers met Louis. His speech was inaudible. Calonne admitted to a deficit, and blamed his predecessors. Fear of the loss of tax privileges caused dissention at court and soon, the dismissal of Calonne. The public clamored for Necker. Louis's choices of finance ministers caused further internal oppositions.

By July 1788, Louis found himself hounded by calls for a new assembly. The parlement attracted larger audiences: young lawyers, admirers of the American Revolution, and the jobless. Instigated by Louis's brother young count d'Artois (1757-1836), the court manoeuvered to suspend the parlement. Louis further resisted divulging royal expenses. In August, under public acclaim, the parlement defied Louis and met in the Palais de Justice. Aided by his new finance minister Etienne Loménie de Brienne (1727-1794), formerly archbishop of Toulouse, Louis bluntly exiled the group to Troyes. The notables were disbanded. Louis was harshly criticized. Royal troops came into the city. Clubs closed. Pressures mounted against Louis, from magistrates on one side, and relatives on the other. The parlement rallied. This time it formally demanded the opening of the States General. Refusing, Louis imposed personal edicts against the very body created for royal reprimands. Replying with calls of 'despotism', the parlement renewed its call. Magistrates were arrested, but it held on. Provincial parlements joined in the revolt.

The period between July 1788 and July 1789 spread chaotic enmity. Louis found himself virtually alone. Vociferous and menacing, multitudes took to the streets of Paris. At Versailles, all reproached Louis out of fear that he would agree to the parlement's demand. In the presence of a mob, Louis met it once again. Magistrates listened to his quiet oration on the virtue of obedience—a belated theme.

If history lives by contrast and coincidence, it does so by continuity also. Moderate, positive voices came from other parts of the nation's society. These belonged to a generation ten to fifteen and even twenty years older than Germaine. The impact of the Enlightenment had been a mature experience for them. Writers, intellectuals enamored with the concept of liberalism, they were ready to politicize their idealism. Many came from the nobility who did not live at court. They were joined by well-read bourgeois active in commerce, industry and law. They formed the Party of Patriots. Jacques Brissot (1754-1793), a journalist living in England, led the popular *Courrier de l'Europe*. Soon, such journals gained a hold on Parisians and readers far afield. The daily ritual was well noticed by the police, courtiers, and the king. Some arrests ensued. Oddly, journalists were sometimes protected by the king's democratically inclined cousin Louis Philippe duc d'Orléans (1747-1793). Eager for reform, wanting the parlement to survive, the patriots presented their platform: end all feudal laws, and for a new beginning, create a constitution. Meetings were held in small groups. They were passionate encounters. Deeply inspired by the American constitution, La Fayette invited Thomas Jefferson to private consultations before the latter's return home after five years of service as diplomatic envoy to France. The future president of the United States (1801) and author of America's Declaration of Independence (1776), Jefferson was well acquainted through extensive correspondence with the recently formulated Constitution of the United States. The American law took effect only a few months after Jefferson's meetings with La Fayette. Fourteen years younger, La Fayette treasured his four years of service to the American cause (1777-1781) as he did the filial esteem for the man now eager to assist in the new French cause. La Fayette's inspiration survived numerous disappointments.

Other liberal aristocrats joined the patriots. In their midst stood the ebullient Honoré Riqueti comte de Mirabeau (1749-1791). He wanted a limited constitutional monarchy after the English model. Persuasive in and out of oratory prowesses, Mirabeau did a memorable deed: he raised funds among the patriots. Thus, optimism and oratory ardor met. But public anger flowed counter to the patriot spirit. It changed the color of journals and pamphlets. Pillage increased. Crops still failed. Rioters intercepted grain transports. A solemn parlement met once again in the Palais de Justice. Louis, his relatives and ministers came, hoping to legislate some loans. French and Swiss guards accompanied them. Reluctantly, Louis promised to convene the States General in 1789. He now had the royal family against him.

On August 25, 1788, Brienne left. Louis recalled Jacques Necker to his desk. The request filled Suzanne Necker with apprehension. Necker expressed scruples, but Germaine applauded. For such a young political being, the circumstance was exalting. But for her father, now named minister and admitted to the royal council, there remained but one avenue: in an emotional message, he put his fate in the hands of his king and queen. Germaine's excitement subsided. "In other circumstances," she wrote, "I would gladly have told this news, but a ship so very close to floundering has been given to him . . . my admiration barely suffices to inspire confidence toward coming events."[5]

Necker obtained Louis's consent to reinstate the parlement and project the States General meeting for January. The patriots urged Louis to give the latter a democratic composition, as writers had wished during the Enlightenment. New clubs opened, political societies emerged, reading and welfare groups, and revitalized salons. Pro-patriot newspapers went to the provinces. The mathematician Marie Jean marquis de Condorcet (1743-1794), senior to most patriots, decided to join them. So did a young priest recently made bishop of Autun, Charles-Maurice de Talleyrand (1754-1838). Patriots became the Club Constitutionnel, which Germaine joined some years later. Sieyès founded a club; his motto reflected an unmistakably philosophical conviction: the sovereignity of the people.

Arguments erupted when it came to voting powers among the three Estates. They stretched on, pillaging continued during another hard winter. Libels against the king and queen and even Necker erupted. Counter to this veritable paper war, Sieyès published a pamphlet entitled *What Is the Third Estate?* He praised industriousness. Regarding the social order, Sieyès excluded the privileged. Rousseau's influence was clear in this attack on society's old hierarchy. Anyone elected as a deputy to the promised meeting, Sieyès added, "necessarily represented the whole nation."[6] Then at last, the moment arrived for a first representative election to the resurrected political body. A lawyer from Arras named Maximilien de Robespierre (1758-1794) entered the third estate. Germaine met him in her parents'salon. His personality puzzled her; an element of distaste stayed in her memory of him. But she could not foresee the degree to which his ideas for a constitution differed from those of his new colleagues, pre-conceptions coming from such a disturbingly complex person. Later, it became evident that he maintained a bipolar view of human nature whereby there existed meanness on one side and a strangely naturalistic belief on the other. Robespierre's oratorical and organizational ascendancies moved steadily and firmly. Elections proceeded into the spring of 1789. The public fixed its intense gaze on the 'Tiers' while the other two estates showed determination to defend their privileges. Though monarchists, they did agree to go against despotism. In April, impatience and anger fed further riots, French guards were attacked and killed.

On May 4, the entry of the delegates into Versailles projected solemn expectation, as Germaine saw from her window seat. But beyond the windows of the royal chapel of Saint Louis, the irrational current flowed, and reverberated. Pillage spread to other French cities. The 'Tiers' took the name Commune, and called itself the Assemblée Nationale. In June, disagreements between the ministry and the court became known. Aided by Sieyès, Necker offered to verify the powers of each of the three orders.

Unfortunately, by the end of June, in disarray over the loss of a son, Louis attempted an inexplicable volte-face: to dissolve the States General. He expelled all from the assembly hall. Deputies re-assembled in the tennis court and pledged allegiance to a constitution. Louis came with his guards. He spoke of equality and liberty, stunning the audience into immobility. He knew that some clergy and nobility were joining the Tiers assembly. Newly termed 'Constituante' and presided by the scientist Jean Bailly (1736-1793), all witnessed a distraught, unpredictable monarch. The court held a 'Scéance Royale' to which it did not invite Necker. It reprimanded the assembly, ordering it to leave. Mirabeau resisted on its behalf. Fearing that Necker might resign, numerous Tiers delegates went to his home and pleaded with him to stay on. He agreed, ". . . but look at this people," he added, "and the blessings they bestow on me. . . . before two weeks perhaps it will follow me with pelting stones."[7] Necker returned to work, hoping to find food supplies for the needy. By the end of June, under much argumentative duress and with an impatient injunction from the king, the Tiers were joined by the clergy and nobility into a single assembly. La Fayette proposed the first consideration: a declaration of the rights of man.

Positive and negative forces combatted each other. Guards defected, confusion spread disorder in military levels. On July 9, Louis refused to have the remaining guards leave his side. He destituted himself of the one man who could have mediated the impasse between himself and his people. Secretly, he sent Necker away. Aware of the assembly's discord, the public turned to murderous rage. On July 14, it vandalized military depots, amassed weapons, and stormed the Bastille.

On the same day, Germaine and her mother rushed to Brussels to meet Necker then on his way to Switzerland. Once the royal secret was divulged, Necker's departure caused general panic.

During those first days of the Revolution, reversals had moved like the tremors before an impending catastrophe. Shock and dismay prevented a foretelling of any kind, and the speed of the events made this even less possible, certainly for the time being. On a young person like Germaine, the first impact came with the news of the Bastille's murderous destruction. She went to look at the fortress's ruins. She learned that prisons had been forced open and that grenadiers were freed to help the populace. How could this have happened only two months after an event that she saw and considered unique in the annals of French history—the great procession into the chapel of Saint Louis? This was her first question.

Her exhultation had been personal. At twenty-three, she did understand the importance of the Versailles convocation. She gave the event the quality of permanence. Moreover, the court's gyrations surrounding an indecisive monarch, its acts of self-interest and internal rivalries were familiar to her. Through conversations at home and her contacts with the *Courrier de l'Europe* and the *Journal de Paris*, she knew even since 1787 that outbursts against the privileged class were steadily increasing. She agreed with Thomas Jefferson that "all the tongues of Paris have been let loose."[8] Germaine too felt the prick of a rapidly changing journalism. "Pamphlets appear each day," she wrote, "libels are so vindictive that freedom of the press seems to exclude all but personal attacks. . . ."[9] But for being young and her world secure until now, Germaine's political anima was still in effervescence.

Since her first reading of Montesquieu's *Spirit of the Laws*, Germaine had espoused the ideal of representative government. Versailles's May event thrilled her because it meant a potential realization of Montesquieu's dream. In ecstasy before the défilé, she felt the possibility of that realization, but only, she reflected, if France held together. "France is about to offer a grand spectacle to Europe," she wrote at that time, ". . . it seems to me that its spectators should give in to emulation, but what are to be feared are the minds of the various provinces, of all subdivisions likely to diminish the force of the common goal and push it away from its center."[10] In spite of the emotional impact, Germaine already possessed the practical sense congenial to politics.

Seated at the window, she noticed the imposing figure of Mirabeau among the deputies attired in their black garments. Later, she remembered that "on seeing for the first time in France representatives of the nation . . . the physiognomies of the deputies expressed more energy than that of the monarch, and this contrast must have caused concern in circumstances where, nothing being established, strength was needed on both sides."[11] She did not know then the degree to which this contrast would intensify. But her excitement maintained itself thanks to her attachment for her father.

Necker had stood before the large body borne out of all kinds of societies within the nation: the sincerely patriotic, those secretly intent on fighting the privileged classes with measures more forceful than polite debate, and those ready to exploit a splendid opportunity to satisfy their ambition. Necker's three-hour homily on equality, before he even spoke of taxes, then on one of his favorite projects—provincial administration—met sporadic applause. Before anything else, the question of privileges had been what the deputies wanted to hear. His persistent reference to dangers to the nation irked them. It may have jarred the positive feeling of participation in the nation's new adventure.

Still, Germaine was enchanted. Her new political persona bonded with the father she admired, this bewigged, lofty servant to the king, standing proudly in embroidered velvet, bravely facing what she could only see as a respectable and respectful assembly. But her euphoria did not last. Between that moment on May 5th and that of July 14th, she understood that the latter's upheaval demolished any possibility of a lasting entente within the States General, let alone in each of its bodies. In time she learned that revolution began not only with bloodshed, but with a drawn-out spectacle of quarrelling infecting the debates on financial reform and representation. Instinctively, she was troubled by the presence of Mirabeau and by his inflammatory speeches. She most probably knew through her father that Mirabeau disliked him and had formed a little-known liaison with the court. Soon, she saw the numerous and incomprehensible hues of passion in this large political environment: ambition, vanity, envy, and vengeance. These were things that she soon depicted with her pen.

There came a respite two days after the fall of the Bastille. This moment bore another kind of solemnity: Louis appeared at the town hall balcony wearing the red, white, and blue revolutionary cockade. Just returned from Brussels for a third recall, Necker stood beside Louis. The marquis de La Fayette had come with a newly formed citizens' militia. Germaine, who had seen rioters walk alongside Louis's coach into Paris, once again gave in to exultation. To her, the crowd's spontaneous acclamation "blocked for ever the silence of a land governed by a court."[12] Louis stood passively. Smiling after the return to Paris which Germaine described as triumphant, Necker praised the public and the assembly for their attempts at forming a constitution. The crowd roared in approval. "Never did a man among those not seated on a throne enjoy to such a degree the affection of the people,"[13] Germaine wrote. This was an unbelievably happy moment. The name 'Necker' seemed lifted to the heavens. Later, she recalled this feeling in such a manner. Before her now, she witnessed her father's enjoyment of his apotheosis. She reflected that nothing could equal "the emotion that one feels before the acclamations of a multitude."[14] She felt the presence of the nation as that of a being full of sound and motion. May 5th, July 14th, and July 16th were never forgotten.

"... so many events, unfortunate, glorious, unbelievable, have agitated me for such a long time. . . . I am asking myself: have a thousand years gone by in one year, one month, two weeks? Perhaps I am living in another world. . . . Who can perceive from afar the small causes of such great effects?"[15]

Germaine de Staël, August 16, 1789

2.
GERMAINE'S WORLD

> How I resist waking up! Fearing like this the day's beginning, is it not part of happiness, as if dreading the moment when all remembrances re-enter the heart, prefering to life a picture of nothingness? . . . No, the feeling of the self subsists, and it is that which characterizes one's moral existence.[1]
>
> Germaine de Staël, *Journal*, July 1785

The three years that precede Necker's first recall to the government (1788) are for Germaine a manifold coming out in society. She has reached her nineteenth birthday and will be entering her twenty-second year. Marriage, anxiety over the illness of her first child, disillusion in love, friendships, political concerns, sympathy for her father in his disappointment and for her mother due to her ill health, and throughout, multi-facetted writing projects. At a glance one realizes that the private Germaine and the public baroness de Staël-Holstein intermingle. They will never separate. The two personae are one. Now as well as during continuing years Germaine will live from impulse and will write from impulse inwardly and outwardly, all in one.

Except for the tender letters to Suzanne Necker at age twelve, first impressions come into the *Journal* written during the summer of 1785. This brief work has already offered us a glimpse of her sense of history, of her original definition of metaphysical thinking, of compliments to Jacques and Suzanne Necker including admiration for her father's text *The Importance of Religious Ideas*, finally Germaine's having witnessed Necker's comment on her own sensibility. The *Journal* reveals other impressions that are significantly more mature, thus posterior to the effervescences of youth. One remarkable instance is the phrase 'the feeling of the self' (le sentiment de soi). Introspection here points to the concept of moral existence. Germaine has felt the need to write, to encompass the meaningful and the trivial into a testimony of herself.

Carefully examining her social environment, Germaine notes the conversational acumen of visitors to her mother's salon. The pen is energetic. It sketches the carefully planned gestures and teasing gossip that are mandatory staples of social intercourse and reputation. These are portraits in miniature, small literary exercises flicked with satire. But she quickly returns to the subject of moral existence, a much preferred food for thought. Reflecting that the elevation of the soul is rare, she finds comfort in thoughts about her father, knowing that he possesses that rare quality. Her attachment to him will long be a source of comfort, natural and real. Wanting to portray him, she imagines putting all kinds of different men into one man, each symbolizing one of Necker's qualities—eloquence, finesse, gaiety, sensibility. Why, she asks, are we unequal in our attributes, why is this so at different times, so that the same person can be passionate and suddenly turn cold?

Much as the *Journal* is brief, it has the characteristic of an unfolding, as if one opened an envelope. By association of ideas, thoughts concerning her father lead to a less welcome presence—the 'other' man whom she has just met. The *Journal* is circumspect, as if the pen hesitated to open the subject. The attention deflects, and ink flies into a tangent, idealizing conjugal love. The writer barely knows her fiancé baron Eric de Staël-Holstein. Imagination aiding, she anticipates happiness in marriage to him. When the pen comes to the point of Monsieur de Staël, we are shown a man who "is honest, incapable of doing anything wrong, but is sterile and without resilience (ressort). He cannot cause unhappiness except by not adding to the happiness of another. . . ."[2]

The mood changes, and is explanatory. Considering all circumstances, marriage to the Swedish aristocrat was the only convenient arrangement possible. Necker's need to safeguard his wealth had long pre-occupied him. For ten years he had negotiated toward a settling of Germaine's future. His regret over the loss of his court position, anxiety over Germaine's eagerness to participate in politics, the many hours spent at her desk, which disturbed him, these were some of those circumstances. Germaine mentions her awareness that the young and brilliant English prime minister William Pitt (1759-1806) had been a candidate in this matter. Though Suzanne favored the idea, the question was one-sided, for Germaine does not mention a reply. She opines that she could not and would not live in England. But she expresses regret in not having the chance to bind her fate to that of a great man. She concludes that after all, she is the daughter of Monsieur Necker and to her, this is her real name.

Scruples and the analysis of Eric de Staël trouble her. Admitting that she has accepted her parents' decision, Germaine knows beforehand that this will not be a marriage of love, or certainly not at the outset because of the issue of character. Her emotional temper is such that she will leave one small door open to love, perhaps later. While it is known that pages have been torn from the text, a cry of regret of another kind ejects from the *Journal*'s last pages: "I would have liked to have been adored by all and to sacrifice everything to one object only."[3] Up until now the *Journal* has allowed exaltation to have a measure of release. However, the emotional intensity of the cry belies confusion in Germaine's heart, perhaps even panic. She has never been away from her parents for long periods at a time. At this point, she is full of love for them, and particularly for Necker. She faces an impending other love with trepidation. It will be another kind of love. She cannot identify her panic.

Beyond the *Journal* and to us in retrospect, elements in Germaine's relationship with Necker have to be taken into account: M. de Staël is completely unlike Necker—agreeable but placid, courteous but reserved, intelligent enough to notice, for one, the court's ineptitude, but unmotivated; Germaine's affection for Necker dominates all feeling at this time;[4] his greatness has overwhelmed her; having worked with him on his text on religion, she has come to appreciate his seriousness and insight. The paternal pseudo-religious inspiration will be permanent. Therefore it was not possible for Germaine to think of resisting Necker's marriage settlement, or even of reproaching him after the fact.

The conditions imposed by Necker via communication with M. de Staël's godfather king Gustave III of Sweden were that Eric would be made ambassador to France, would retain the post several years, and would not take Germaine to Sweden. The diplomatic appointment lent an aura of distinction irresistible to Parisian eyes and opinion. Were this enough to bring calm and contentment at home, only time would tell. Germaine's personal happiness was in the balance. Calm and contentment were foreign to her. The contract was signed by the royal family and the ceremony took place on January 14, 1786, in the Swedish embassy in Paris. Germaine wrote a letter of farewell to her mother.

M. de Staël appeared elegant and pleasant. He was Germaine's senior by seventeen years. He had no wealth of his own, so that Necker created a pension for him. A freemason like many of his generation, he had long been an 'habitué' at Versailles, thus familiar with Marie-Antoinette's festivities and developing intrigues. Definitely not of Germaine's world socially, mentally and evidently with little intellectuality, M. de Staël was temperamental and prone to feelings of humiliation. Altogether an indolent reflection of ancien régime mores, he was astute enough to sense and express to Gustave III the atmosphere of corruption at court and its ignorance of administrative know-how. But he could not meet the new and energetic ideas his wife espoused. She had quickly attuned herself to the events of 1789. Like every serious and politically disposed person of her generation she had started to grasp the immediacy of a new society. M. de Staël did realize that Germaine was bound to hold on to this idea wholeheartedly. He also discovered that he could not bear her possessiveness. At the same time, she was disenchanted. Unhappily marred by the loss of their infant child, theirs became a turbulent intimacy. M. de Staël's homecomings were less and less frequent. He fell into dissipation and incurred debts through extravagance. His heterosexual behavior became known. Germaine reproached him for having abandoned her at a time when her soul "was pure and the heart open to a sensitive rapport.... You will regret having left a young person who had been entrusted to you,"[5] she added.

Germaine experienced a mixed reception at Versailles. "The baroness is not pretty," one of Marie-Antoinette's courtiers remarked, "but she has a good mind, gaiety, amiability; she is well brought up and full of talents."[6] Her eyes "sparkle with genius," an old friend of the family remarked, "her hair the color of ebony falls on her shoulders in soft curls and with features more pronounced than delicate, one felt the presence of something above the destiny of her sex."[7] A friend of Germaine's mother exercised rather blunt perspicacity: "Granted, she has been raised within principles of honesty and virtue, but she is indelicate in manner and so very spoiled in her self-opinion that it is impossible to make her see her lacks. She is imperious and willful.... On every subject she has an uncommon assurance for a person of her age."[8]

Germaine felt increasing dismay concerning her husband. Self-analysis having become natural, she understood the uneven impressions she made on others. Once again, she examined herself, and did so with empathy for her husband. In a letter to him near the end of the summer of 1788, she wished for an end to their mutual torment:

> If the woman one has married because of convenience in position and fortune has brought disappointment, one must weigh in the silence of reason and conscience the direction that should be taken. If a wife's faults do not incur crises, if, most of all, there remain enough qualities to inspire love, the worst avenue one can take is that which you are now taking.[9]

M. de Staël shirked Germaine's persistant demands. Her letters were numerous and often plaintive. Before her remonstrance, barely ten months after the marriage, she had made things clear concerning her position: "I am pure and I love you. What do my faults matter . . . why do they upset you since they have no bearing on my heart and besides, will pass with my youth?"[10]

Reproaches alternated with requests for attention and affection. Short relief came when she accompanied her parents to health spas. In mid-September 1786 she described to Eric her father's teasing comportment: " he regains some of his former gaiety with me. He amuses himself by tearing out of my hands letters I have just received, and making me lose my temper. . . ."[11] But Germaine relished rare moments when her husband manifested "tender attachment, a proof of his good heart."[12] Still, he could not be firm with her, nor could he face her impetuosities and her constant moving about. Signs of jealousy over her display of affection for old family friends alternated with gratefulness for her having paid his debts. [13] During fifteen years, the relationship gradually cooled; it dwindled into nothingness.

The year of her marriage, Germaine opened her first salon at the Swedish embassy, on rue du Bac. She was following her mother's example, but the orientation differed. Suzanne Necker had created her social ambiance primarily in order to enhance Necker's reputation. For Germaine, the salon became her raison d'être. It reflected the blossoming intellectuality that she shared with peers, and the enjoyment of being with established writers, politicians, journalists, diplomats and beloved old friends like Jacques comte de Guibert (1744-1790) whose election to the Académie française Germaine attended. She applauded Guibert's wanting to cut back the privileges long given to nobility in the militia. Regular visitors to her gatherings were Condorcet, the economist Adam Smith (1723-1790), Thomas Jefferson, Thomas Paine, the physician G. Cabanis (1757-1808), the poet A. de Chénier (1762-1794), and La Fayette.

For all concerned, these were memorable reunions and encounters. A positive, genuine camaraderie evolved. Considering differences in occupation and age, the soon to be called 'ideologues' shared the passion for governmental reform, a deep veneration for Voltaire, and Germaine's enthusiasm. The assembly deputy Charles Maurice de Talleyrand unabashedly borrowed money from Germaine. Later, he did not hesitate to snub her. There came vicount Mathieu de Montmorency (1767-1826), Sieyès' close friend and one who, like La Fayette, had served in America and was now eager to play a part in the anticipated new government. Montmorency became the youngest delegate in the States General where he promptly spoke in favor of abolishing the nobility's fiscal privileges. He also became Germaine's lifelong confident and advisor. Whereas the latter was her peer, Talleyrand was her senior by twelve years. At that time Sieyès also became a close friend. Twenty years Germaine's senior, he soon entered the Assemblée Constituante. Sieyès brought someone to Germaine's salon: the thirty-year-old count Narbonne-Lara (1755-1813), godchild of Louis XVI and war minister. Soon to become minister for foreign affairs, the personable and handsome Narbonne confided in Germaine, expressing his admiration for America in its transformation into independence. He too held a republican ideology, this being so in spite of his aristocratic lineage. Narbonne had strong desires for governmental reform, and like Montmorency was willing to renounce his tax privileges. Germaine fell in love with Narbonne.

Hers was not the only politically oriented salon. Before the first bloodshed of 1789 the marquis de Condorcet welcomed in his salon Adam Smith, Jefferson, Paine, La Fayette and a young Swiss writer named Benjamin Constant (1767-1830). Conversations shone in both the Madame de Staël and Condorcet salons. All shared the desire to move along with the newly created Assembly, to define and support the implementation of reforms. First and foremost came the need to clarify as well as possible the idea of a new French constitution. As has been mentioned, at this time their shared idealism harbored the notion of a constitutional monarchy, the assumption being that Louis XVI would concur and thus retain his position on the throne in a secular capacity.

Germaine energetically agreed to this line of thinking. She did remember the danger her father had envisioned. But another kind of danger threatened that concerted assumption. It was more personal, closer to home, and direct: the increasingly virulent press's criticism of particular members of the aristocracy. Germaine's uncontrolled impetuosity became a toy for the press. She was playing with fire.[14]

Talleyrand and Sieyès were men who controlled their feelings. They exercised caution out of wisdom, like Sieyès, out of maneuverability for Talleyrand. Even so, after July 16th and outside the safe salons where a new constitution was being amicably discussed, the populace's resentment unleashed itself. An electrifying medusa rose from it. It was too late for ideas of grandeur among friends in a comfortable ambiance.

Who was baroness de Staël, now aged twenty? Young indeed, she rebelled against sedate comportment. Enthusiasm ruled. She developed a conversational style of her own, intelligent, aggressive, and captivating. Boredom was the great enemy in and out of the salon. She wanted to shine. Necker, Rousseau and Voltaire were her divinities, Necker always, Rousseau in a troubling manner at that time. She had read his works thoroughly and was just then attempting to explain the Rousseau phenomenon with her pen. On the rough copy, intimations of a justification appeared, for he had also troubled others. What was Germaine really like then? So far, she could not seduce physically; she was learning to do so with eloquence.[15] She loved her salon, the vivacity and intellectuality of which equalled her own. She was its queen, a queen who developed into many outward selves yet within, all facets were held by impulse and a uniform, highly intelligent frame of mind. And in the privacy of the desk, Germaine's pen was put to work.

Political tension strengthened new friendships. Trust in the future and in human nature in general held on, this being so with Germaine's friends as well. Condorcet, for one, was writing his *Inquiry Concerning a Historical Tableau of the Progress in Human Spirit*. His peer, Antoine de Lavoisier (1743-1794), published agricultural statistics and projects for land reform. A dedicated chemist and physicist, Lavoisier became a deputy as his friend Condorcet was chosen to lead one of the chameleon assemblies.

Elsewhere in the publishing arena, strangely discordant voices challenged the optimism of Germaine's world. Emanuel Swedenborg (1688-1772), whose visionary writings had chagrined Kant, regained popularity, Gustave III of Sweden being a new adept. Then came the marquis Donatien de Sade (1740-1814), a scandalous figure in life, and scandalous enough in print to bring on life imprisonment. Sade wrote *One Hundred and Twenty Days of Sodoma* while in the Bastille. Pierre Caron de Beaumarchais (1732-1799), courtier, watchmaker and financial entrepreneur, blatantly ridiculed the upper class. The popular and prickly *Marriage of Figaro* (1785) verbalized a hopelessly pessimistic portrait of society. His foreboding of reaction against social discrimination was taken seriously even though the tone was archly comical, also the more so for being satirical. Genres like these were part of the eternal eclecticism of the Paris book world. Moreover, there came gentle voices: Rousseau's friend Henri Bernardin de Saint-Pierre (1737-1814), whose *Indian Hut* Germaine read to her salon; Saint-Pierre's *Paul and Virginia* continued appearing in the press through 1788; N. Restif de la Bretonne (1734-1806) presented *The Nights of Paris* at that time; Rousseau's *Confessions* came posthumously; though the last volume had been completed in 1772, the *Encyclopédie* enjoyed a continuing renown; some of the final volumes featured articles on literature by one of Germaine's favorite family friends the playwright Marmontel; beyond French borders, the young German idealist Johann von Schiller (1759-1805) wrote didactic poetry that reached France in 1788; his drama *Don Carlos* had been staged in 1785.

In the midst of this publishing flurry, the English pamphleteer Paine wrote his radical text *Dissertations on Government*. Paine had been in America in 1774. His *Common Sense* had gained much esteem among American revolutionaries. His *Rights of Man* incurred stern criticism from his homeland, but French patriots revered his writings and considered him one of theirs. However, political radicalism endangered individual reputations. Germaine understood this. For the time being and knowing well that agitations would most probably cause Necker's return to the royal court, she held her political ardor in check except in her salon and in the extensive correspondence. She sent news bulletins to M. de Staël's godfather Gustave III, sometimes in Swedish as she was learning her husband's native tongue. These were veritable exercises in political and precision writing. The ardor was not restrained for long and was bound to find its way in far more than exercises. Also, much as private conversation and reporting on the subject of growing turbulence contributed to political thinking among friends, she attended all along with the activity of writing, which gradually became her modus vivendi.

The *Journal* had been an act of pure introspection. It had a style of its own. At times it flowed loosely, nearly at random, at others it grasped fanciful and abstract concepts altogether most unlike her father's pronouncements where words were marshalled as means to action. Germaine's new desk activities were unlike the fashionable romanesque manner of writers like Isabelle de Charrière (1740-1805), whose *Letters from Lausanne* (1785) were clearly autobiographical, or Claudine marquise de Tencin (1685-1749), mother of d'Alembert and Montesquieu's friend, whose still popular historical novels and tragic love stories flooded the book world with romances that held sway more than two generations.

While Germaine had a serious project in mind, she also provided semi-serious amusement, possibly as a diversion or perhaps as an experiment. Short, sentimental tales expounding virtues, loss and melancholy were popular then. Original and quaint, their heroines were madwomen (folles) lamenting over their unfortunate state and expressing acute sensitivity to society's indifference. In June 1786, Germaine sent her *Madwoman of the Forest of Sénart* to her parents' friend Henri Meister (1744-1826), then assistant to her old friend Melchior Grimm, and for publication in the *Correspondance littéraire, philosophique et critique*. The single scene is brief: a man walking in the forest comes upon a young women who is asleep. Awaking, she is startled, covers her face with a veil, and as the man approaches she speaks incohently, barely revealing in her exaltation a yearning for an imaginary loved one. They part, no action having occurred except the flow of sentiment. The style is simple and direct, like a perfectly expressed emotion. The narrator's presence in this short prose passage is equally succinct: the man walking in the forest is more than a reflection of the author. With a flick of the pen, he, as narrator, is emotion personified. Within this momentary piece, Germaine has combined the ideal and the real. This kind of creativity may have been partially subconscious, and partially autobiographical. Nevertheless, the blending held true to an artistic principle. It became her principle.

> I was someone who experienced everything with emotion. Touched, my heart was open to every sensation imaginable.[16]
> Germaine de Staël, *La folle de la forêt de Sénart*, 1786

3.

GERMAINE'S PEN

> Oh! If pity comes to my unhappy heart,
> Let me suffer my destiny in peace;
> Please, no more words about love or marriage!
> To be forever free, that is my only desire.[1]
>
> Germaine de Staël
> *Sophie ou les sentiments secrets*, 1786

During her twenty-first year, Germaine experimented with characterization. She turned to versification. Her first and fully structured piece in verse is the drama in three acts *Sophie or Sentimental Secrets*. It was most probably composed during the year of her marriage. The action takes place in France where an English garden adorns an elegant castle. Sophie's tutor, count de Sainville, encourages his English guest lord Bedford, who is in love with Sophie, to expect that the young woman will agree to marry him. To her tutor's dismay, Sophie resists the offer. She cannot bring herself to express her sentiment of love for de Sainville, but Bedford, distressed in his love for her, perceives her secret. He pleads his case before Sophie. An anonymous letter implicates the count in an affair. He admits this to Sophie in confidence, though without divulging the name of the loved one. Impressed by her tutor's proud disregard for calumny, Sophie comforts the trusting countess de Sainville. Affectionately, the latter enjoins Sophie to accept Bedford's offer of marriage. Melancholy overwhelms Sophie. She rejects the notion altogether. The count's life is threatened, and Bedford goes to his friend's rescue. The countess sees Sophie's disarray, perceiving in turn the young woman's secret. The countess persistently enjoins Sophie to marry the English guest who is about to leave. Sophie finds refuge in a small temple in the garden, using a key given to her by the count. She finds a bust of herself crowned with flowers. The count enters. They confess their mutual love, but, filled with distress, Sophie leaves for regions unknown. The countess forgives her husband, and calm returns.

Considering the circumtance in time, is Sophie entirely a creature of the imagination? Has the poetic adventure relieved Germaine of the complex, pseudo-filial yearnings expressed in her *Journal*? Where is the line of demarcation between the ideal and the real in Sophie's story? Only conjecture can answer these questions, and conjecture is often unkind, if not false. Sophie is a creation dominated by sentiment. More than this, she is not a real person but sentiment itself. Persons, actions, gestures and words surrounding her are all under the spell of the tyrant love. Abstract and tense compared with the popular romanesque genre of the time, this play gathers heat from the agitations of all who are prey to this sentiment. Inspiration from classical Greek tragedy and seventeenth-century dramatic poetry has surely come into Germaine's pen. However, Germaine has also read S. Richardson's *Clarissa Harlowe* (1753). Much as shame and death destroy Clarissa, Sophie stands intact, and only wistfulness and departure remain at the end. Violent pursuit and action do not happen here. Nor are there antipathies among the four personae. Sophie lives in an internal world of feeling, profoundly tortured by it. This is the only element of violence. Clarissa is all flesh and blood, palpable, vulnerable to the extreme, her virtue forcibly thrust out of existence. Sophie is ethereal. She will walk away, vibrant and victorious, her virtue untouched. She has had to liberate herself. She will not be happy, but within her, the feeling of the self subsists.

Germaine's disillusion in marriage and her first child's illness filled 1786 and 1787 with stress. She did not give in to despondency. Writing provided the needed buoyancy. It did so the rest of her life. At certain times she was disconsolate, for example when Necker received the royal order ('lettre de cachet') to leave Versailles. Germaine comforted him. When his successor Calonne was dismissed in turn, then Brienne, and menacing crowds became a political force of their own, malaise intensified and permeated every level of society. One short hiatus occurred when Louis XVI made his first promise to gather the States General and to give his consent toward the institution of a first States Assembly. Germaine, her father and their friends regained some of their old optimism.

At that time she occupied herself with serious writing. She expressed in the preface to the tragedy *Jane Gray* that she wanted to do something useful. This is her second experience with dramatic verse. Germaine prefered "Gray" to "Grey" in her text's title and use of the name.

The misfortune of the English sixteenth-century princess Jane Grey is "one of the great lessons of past centuries," Germaine wrote in the preface to her play. "Jane's youthfulness encouraged mine," the author continues, "I would so have liked to raise admiration of a similar kind, of the rare mixture of strength and sensibility in the face of death itself."[2] Germaine's new heroine indeed will face death. Glory rather than tragic circumstance is the focus here. While pleased to offer this work to her friends, Germaine reveals her fascination with the historic example of one's having sought happiness through glorious sacrifice, "the only thing to which I can now aspire."[2] The venture is daunting, for she is drawing from one of English history's most dramatic contests for royal power. In 1553, the main character is seventeen and surrounded by war-mongering men. Germaine omits Jane's subsequent nine days of royal supremacy, which Marie Stuart will destroy.

Married to the ambitious duke of Northumberland's son, a husband whom she loves, Jane laments the death of Henry VIII's only son, Edward VI, her father-in-law having been the prince's regent. Northumberland is poised to lead his army against Mary Stuart and even the young Tudor Elizabeth I in order to gain the crown for his son and Jane. But she proclaims disinterest in ambition and a preference for quiet study. However, she acknowledges with melancholy that her destiny is in the hands of others. She is aware of Northumberland's plan, to which her husband lord Guildfort complies. But grandeur is of no interest to Jane. Virtue is her motto. Indignant, Northumberland will lead his army against Marie. Jane and Guildfort pledge their love, and Guildfort leaves to be at his father's side in battle. The tide turns. Jane and her husband must consider finding refuge in France. Jane urges Northumberland to renounce his plans, but he refuses, full of resentment, greed and fury in his defeat. Guildfort is torn between his love for Jane and his duty to his father. Count Pembroke, who loves Jane and now leads Marie's army, offers to save Jane's life and Guildfort's as well, but Jane rejects the offer. A trial is set for the defeated: first, Northumberland, then Guildfort, then Jane, who are summarily led to the tower. Jane meets Pembroke once again, pleading for her husband's life and for an end to pride and vengeance. She offers her own life in exchange. Guildfort is brought before her. Imprisonment has enraged Northumberland, who is executed. Jane and Guildfort are reunited in death.

Two centuries before Germaine wrote this tragedy, Jane Grey was a creature of reality indeed. She was in the world, committed to it by high rank and the overbearing circumstance of royal rivalry. As Germaine explains in her preface, she wanted others to to experience the same admiration she had felt before such force and such sensibility, both of which made Jane face execution "and know the price she had to pay . . . life itself."[3] The political rivalry among three princesses is the problem of the play. Attempts to solve this problem originate in one man's ambition and greed. The action engulfs Jane's father-in-law and subordinate son in combat against Marie, the first and rightful contender to the throne, which Jane acknowledges. The author establishes her subject's sensibility in her first speech: she is twice happy, she tells her friend Clarice, for seeing her again after a long absence; she refuses to exercise judgement against her war-obsessed father-in-law; she explains that in her marriage to Guildfort virtue has welcomed love.

Jane's force of character is most evident when she declares to both her husband and his father the legitimacy of Marie Stuart's pretention to the crown. Knowing one's duty, she adds, is tantamount to having the power to carry it through. Should Northumberland gain military ascendancy over Marie, awarding the crown to his daughter-in-law would be a false grandeur. Regarding invoked religious commands, Jane continues before the stupefied Northumberland, God is the law she will obey, not the orderings of manoeuvering zealots. When the news of Northumberland's defeat reach Jane, knowing that both she and Guildfort will perish, she resolves to think only of her attachment to her husband. Happiness, tolerance, equinanimity, integrity, and faithfulness, all unfold from Jane's speeches as the tragedy moves toward the end. Filled with passion, these qualities are the warmth and colors of the drama. Their sounds and images are sadly true. The color black intercepts, and it is cold. Here, Germaine's attention to the character of Northumberland is significant. Greed and ambition are the motivating forces. As a historian, Germaine can only give one answer to the enigma of such passions: "All human evil lies in the human heart."[4]

Germaine offered *Sophie* and *Jane Gray* to her reading public in 1790. However, having written these two plays, she turned to a prose project on which she had long reflected, and published it in 1788. She was entering her twenty-third year. "There is no official tribute to Jean-

Jacques Rousseau," she wrote at the beginning of her essay *Letters on the Writings and the Character of Jean-Jacques Rousseau* (*Lettres sur les écrits et le caractère de Jean-Jacques Rousseau*). "I felt the need to express my admiration for him," she continued, "moreover, it has been a pleasure to retrace the memory and impression of my enthusiasm."[5] Germaine remarked that while she was twenty-two at the time of writing, Rousseau had been forty during his own first publication. Surely, she added, "his heart and mind must have calmed, so that he could concentrate on his work."[6] Why was there such a need for calm? Passion had dominated Rousseau's youth, Germaine specified. Writing did not come easily to him. "To choose within the rushing elements of his thinking he needed the time and efforts that mediocre men need to acquire thought itself."[7]

With the eagerness of an avowed biographer, Germaine stressed how a very young being consumed with passion indeed could not live and reflect all at once. Only later would such a person as he be able to address abstract ideas with depth.

Germaine traced the path of Rousseau's thinking from the early discourse on the utility of sciences and arts to the later body of work which clearly echoed his first claim: human nature has blotched nature's work. Logically, the problem of good and evil and the quest for happiness became Rousseau's dominating concerns. Germaine interjected that too often and too strongly Rousseau "linked the arts and sciences together, whereas the effects of these two human institutions differ entirely." [8] She explained that Rousseau may have erred in taking science's progress as a cause rather than as an effect. In this sense a clearer balance of plusses and minuses was needed.

Rousseau assumed that good and evil are everywhere, the young biographer pointed out, and later works again may offer a clearer definition of this generalization. At the same time his preoccupation with the origin of inequality among men led him to reveal fully his deep-seated hatred for civilization's institutions. However, Germaine added, while claiming that the state of nature was perfectly respectable, he overlooked the human drive for knowledge. For her, this drive was as much a part of human nature as it was a means to happiness. Still, one could justify Rousseau for having come to such a pronouncement. As she put it, his "reduction"[9] of the human heart was based on experience. To an incredible degree, Rousseau had felt personal unhappiness within society in his later years. Glory as a writer came to mean nothing to him.

How well Rousseau expressed hatred for vice, and love for nature! For Germaine this constituted Rousseau's strength as a writer, and in her opinion this talent placed him alongside Montesquieu. Qualities of warmth and eloquence well compensated for the lack of proposed remedies to man's so-called institutionalized condition. Those qualities came from the writer's soul. Thus, on reading him, Germaine reflected, one could sense where the animation came from: the character of the man. Rousseau's emotional impact was a constant in his writing, he was persuasive, logical, particularly in the discourse on public festivities where patriotism, freedom and morality reign as one, benefiting all. Yet, the inroads of pride among men living in society are nefarious. He opined that men hold on to their personal sense of freedom less tenaciously than women. In times of oppression this difference causes men to "sink below their natural level of tolerance."[10]

Aware that her enthusiasm could be criticized, Germaine resolved to try to comment on Rousseau's *La nouvelle Héloïse* "as if time had aged my heart."[11] While we have before us the dramatization of a moral idea, she continued, and as Héloïse commits herself to a moral fault, what matters from the writer's point of view is the effect of this event more than its story. At best we, the readers, are left with a re-animation of love for virtue. With a talented writer like Rousseau, fictions "as in truth" have the power to depict both the passions and the innocence which "agitate and calm successively."[12]

Germaine's predilection for *Emile* was deep. Here, her emphasis on Rousseau's condemnation of prejudice is significant, for with him it has harmed knowledge itself. It has erased the trace of every knowledge human nature ever possessed. Understanding this has to be the basis for education. Germaine's predilection now allowed her to establish a reconciliation between the literary mentor's binding of the sciences and the arts with one of the great precepts of the Enlightenment, namely the pursuit of knowledge.

The path Germaine took in order to defend Rousseau well demonstrates her intellectual lineage. We remember that she is a child of the Enlightenment, that she was born when her family and its social entourage were reading Montesquieu, and Voltaire's *Essays on Mores*. The materialistic physician Julien de La Mettrie (1709-1751) and his *Natural History of the Soul* were also known at the time. A recapitulation of Germaine's intellectual nurturing must respect the element of diversity, the thrust of the Enlightenment being admirably manifold. Therefore, the presence during the first half of the eighteenth century of materialism, not to mention atheism, has to be remembered. These went against the grain of idealism and deism, they were just there during Rousseau's time, and later during Germaine's as well.

Rousseau's friendship with the materialist-atheist d'Holbach speaks for open-mindedness. Moreover, he attended lectures on chemistry with Diderot during the pleasant years preceding his multiple quarrels. His *Emile* appeared in 1762, therefore at the very center in time of the Enlightenment's kaleidoscopic explosion. As we know, so had Mr. Macpherson's strangely gripping and secretly invented *Ossian*. Such fascinating beings—Héloïse, Emile and the mystical Ossian—had catapulted onto the laps of the aristocratic and bourgeois readers of that time, men and women alike. This was a most pleasant prescription for the cult of feeling. Though still young, Germaine far from escaped this. For the generation reaching maturity at the end of the eighteenth century and for those growing up in the early nineteenth century, *Héloïse* reigned on the bedside table. It did for the artillery officer named Napoléon Bonaparte.

Germaine's defense of *Héloïse* is calm and measured compared with her ecstasy over *Emile*. Here, she cannot resist emotion before Rousseau's vision of a society free of prejudice, for she writes that ". . . if women, rising above their fate, dared become tutors to men, if they knew how to say what men should do, if they had feelings appropriate to this concerning men's actions, what a noble destiny . . . !"[13]

Where Rousseau's political writing is concerned, Germaine quickly reached the crux of the *Contrat social*, namely the imbalance of general well-being and self-interest. For Rousseau, she added, the character of the lawgiver is the all-important question. Pulling attention away from his definition of the general will, she applauded Rousseau's focusing on the importance of a ruler's qualification for his role as such. She was thinking of the coming States General, of Louis's disposition and of her father working once more at the helm of what could become an ideal and magnificent political body.

The *Lettres* end on the subject of Rousseau's character. The young biographer is well aware that a justification of Rousseau the man is lacking. French aristocratic society, not having known that Rousseau suffered a growing and debilitating physical illness, harshly blamed him for his independent, reclusive lifestyle and his over-sensitive reaction to criticism. Héloïse, a creature of the writer's mind, bore her share of condemnation for having failed morally. The elegant, pleasure loving, shallow and hypocritical society of the 1760's had enjoyed this kind of castigating exercise. But now, Germaine was looking at the man whose *Confessions* had just been published. She discerned his personal pride, the eloquence which, if provoked, was impressive, and the over-sensitivity tyrannized by a powerful imagination. According to Germaine, Rousseau's imagination misled reason during relationships with others. Why did he abandon his children, Germaine asked. An unpleasant wife maneuvered him with the misconception that the children's affections would turn away from their father. He, doubting his strength as a father, gave in to her subterfuge. This was Germaine's interpretation of Rousseau's behavior regarding his children and his being under the influence of his wife.

The portrait is that of a troubled, conscience-stricken soul. Since then, society has held to a belief in Rousseau's suicide. Yet with the aid of Germaine's accolade, above the agitation and disillusion, the humane quality of kindness remains, extending beyond the thinker's immediate reach, far into the world of fellow beings.

> Some will reproach me for treating so soon of a subject very much above my own strengths.... But who can dare predict the progress of one's mind?... Besides, is it not during one's youth that one owes the deepest gratitude to Rousseau?[14]
>
> Germaine de Staël, 1788
> *Lettres sur les écrits et le caractère de Jean-Jacques Rousseau*

4.
THE RAPE OF UNITY

> I am indignant against this vile man Mirabeau. Bring me his abominable piece of writing, but do not mention this to my father: one must not trouble his astonishing calm, which few are able to maintain, even if equal to him in genius.[1]
>
> Germaine de Staël, May 27, 1787

As the summer of 1789 came to an end, public admiration for Necker waned. Germaine became concerned for his safety. Attacks against him were coming from both sides of the revolutionary spectrum—the royals, and the populace. In a letter to king Gustav III in mid-August she explained the situation in the following manner:

> I have seen the one closest to me in the world at the helm during the recent storm; I now realize that a court intrigue is supporting the nobility's exaggerated pretentions. It assumes that Versailles holds the entire kingdom in its hands and dares to think that it can destroy the force of the people by overthrowing M. Necker, if not the king as well. Such an intrigue has been led by count d'Artois. He has done it all. It has persuaded the king that his cause and the nobility's are one and the same.[2]

Germaine made this comment barely one month after Necker stood by his king before a jubilant crowd at the Paris town hall. Now in her twenty-fourth year, cognizant of events at Versailles, she exercised mature perceptivity. The nobility's illusion, its daring, and power over Louis XVI became so many other causes of conflict and eventually danger to the nation. In her fear and hatred of Mirabeau and those whom he influenced, in her astuteness as well, therefore through feeling and intelligence, Germaine became a political person. These actions of the court nobility were more than 'other causes'. They were primary causes. From now on they engulfed Louis in the embraces of his courtiers. He was no longer alone. But in another sense, he stood irremediably distant from the people of France.

When Germaine said that d'Artois 'had done it all', she meant that he took a pivotal position at court, thus turning his older brother's attention away from his people. This was surely the greatest test of Louis's strength of will. But little strength remained. His condescending manner had irritated assembly deputies to the point of anger. His daily journal entry read 'nothing', even on July 14; nothing had been killed during the hunt. Aside from character, Louis's inability to make clear decisions had most to do with the influences that bore down on him. The court's obsession with self-interest closed his dialogue with the nation, a dialogue barely started at Necker's side a month earlier.

During regular attendance at assembly sessions, Germaine experienced the other side of the attacks against her father. Oratorial rumbling around him gradually swelled into a cacophonous roar. Mirabeau attacked him directly and through him, the king. Aggressive publications including Mirabeau's own met their counterparts in the general press. Men of questionable character took the revolutionary challenge, one by one. In articles and pamphlets, their outbursts were virulent.

Mirabeau's vehemence reigned until 1791. He interrupted Necker, and rudely described him as a man without talent. What was the origin of the Mirabeau phenomenon? Surely, the explosive temperament was genetic. But he had been poorly treated by his father, like young Jean-Jacques Rousseau. Before his election to the Third Estate Mirabeau led the municipality of Marseilles with an iron hand. Money was his passion. He engaged in pamphleteering, plagiarized, and exploited his oratorical success by obliquely attacking the king. Unabashed, he pitted Sieyès against Necker. His gesture of calling for patriotic contributions was laudable, but less so were his numerous visits to Louis and Marie-Antoinette. Some uttered the word 'treason'. As for Germaine, she could not take her eyes off Mirabeau when he spoke. She quivered, seeing how he disliked her father. Instinctively, she knew that by his presence Mirabeau destroyed all hope of political entente, let alone calm.

Outside the assembly walls, discontent spread. Citizens watched and listened. Discontent was not only personal to every emotionally-prone individual. It transpired from what was happening inside those walls. The so-called 'estates'—nobility, clergy and 'Third' (Tiers)—constantly and doggedly reworked the lists of representatives, requests accumulating, griefs and private interests frustrating attempts at efficiency. Soon, factions threatened to dislocate the assembly. Outside, and to maintain order, La Fayette took charge of a nightime guarding of the estates' hall (salle des états). In late August, he led the 'garde bourgeoise', a citizens' militia purported to defend the Revolution. At that time, with Necker and Germaine both attending the debates, first major changes in the government took place. Against the outcry of his courtiers, Louis submitted to the will of the assembly which now adopted the name 'nationale'; he officially requested nobility and clergy to join the Tiers. In an unusually swift concert, committees declared civil equality, abolished the hated royal orders of arrest (lettres de cachet), ended all privileges, and proclaimed the Declaration of the Rights of Man and of the Citizen which had been proposed originally by La Fayette.

Reactions among the populace who had followed the debates were ecstatic. Counter reactions to the four explosive motions were as swift as the assembly's committee work had been: Louis's brothers and several courtiers left France. First, count d'Artois, who went to Germany, then count de Provence, to Germany also and later England. Numerous members of the nobility then proceeded to emigrate. Some created an intelligence system in Lyon, others who went to Germany started working toward a coalition against France among European powers. In September of 1789, talk of military action against the nation and the arrival in Versailles of a Flanders regiment alarmed the multitude. Those who remained at court welcomed these troops. Suspicion led some to think that a plan was considered to dissolve the States General. Even if this were so, the project was not mentioned to Necker. On October 14, 1789, Louis entered the assembly hall, bowed to the deputies, and spoke on peace and order. This infuriated the Parisian populace. Within twenty-four hours, a multitude of women marched to Versailles. Before the guards could respond, the royal family and the assembly were brought to Paris.

Germaine witnessed the insurrection. Excitement, hope, and premonitions overwhelmed her. She well knew Versailles' internal agitations. Her own excitement led her to indiscretions. Her father had a just confidence in her intelligence, but condoned her verbal turbulence. Germaine's hope that her father would rise above the tumult thanks to his capabilities stayed with her, besides, she loved France too much to remonstrate against it at this point, which many around her did in mournful tones, including her mother. Separating the nation from her mind and heart was out of question. Her feelings toward France became maternal in time, but they never diminished. As for premonitions, however, somberness set in. Her letter to Gustav III of August 16, 1789, had anticipated the 10,000-strong march to Versailles:

> My father found all powers either overwhelmed or reduced to nothing. Here was a government led by force, an old nation become infantile rather than returned to its youth . . . with liberty obtained before the public mind could grasp its meaning, a mind incoherent in ideas, contrasts among characters and circumstances in the assembly make one shudder. My father must help Louis regain his authority. If the troops do not obey the king, this country will be lost. . . . The court's contrariness has fed public arrogance, and abandoned all to violence.[3]

Where the national assembly was concerned, certain personalities did draw attention to themselves. Their differences did make an observant witness like Germaine tremble indeed. This was so notwithstanding the fact of Mirabeau's domination, his agitations and vehemence feeding adulation in and outside the assembly walls. 'Contrasts among characters and circumstances', as Germaine said, could not have been sharper from our point of view. For instance, among the deputies there stood the tall Charles Maurice de Talleyrand-Périgord, whom Germaine had recently met. Raised in the church and intensely political in mind and ambition, Talleyrand soon appointed himself leader of assembly members of the clergy willing to accept the projected constitution. He was elegant, suave, persuasive, and mobile in political loyalty, which was not visible to all including Germaine at first. He caught her esteem—some have said affection—, charm and finesse aiding. Political cunning and agility helped him surmount the vicissitudes of the Revolution during and beyond their devastating effect.

Mild-mannered Philippe, duke of Orléans (1747-1793), also a deputy, called himself Philippe Egalité. Raised in the pseudo-court atmosphere at the Parisian Palais Royal, here was a royal Bourbon cousin of Louis XVI professing an interest in democracy. However, he had monarchical ambitions, even to the degree of considering the status of regent to Louis's son should circumstance allow this. A fanciful man, Philippe's monarchical disposition strengthened at the hands of

Choderlos de Laclos (1741-1803), author of *Les liaisons dangereuses*. Since the novel's publication in 1782, renown allowed Laclos to influence the impressionable d'Orléans. Philippe was ridiculed by the revolutionaries; he became their victim.

The marquis de La Fayette was perhaps most in public view during the three years preceding the Revolution's turn from tumult to terror. He was close enough to Louis to be given the role of military protector, yet distant also to voluntarily create an armed control by and for Parisians during public demonstrations. Though youthful in manner and disposition, La Fayette respected discipline as a point of honor. He felt that Parisians should exercise self-protection, for he understood them well. He remained a monarchist, but on the proviso that Louis would accept a constitution. Proud of his participation in the American Revolution, he wanted to apply that glory in his native country. He joined meetings, clubs and the assembly, speaking and offering action every step of the way. Like Germaine, he was outspoken and anxious to realize his political dream of a constitutional monarchy. Like Talleyrand, he was visible indeed, but there the similarity ended. La Fayette was affectionate, he conscientiously loved his country, and shared this feeling with compatriots for years to come. Germaine was in his affections, as she was in his. The esteem both George Washington and Thomas Jefferson felt for La Fayette attested to the sincerity of his character.

From the dark undercurrent of public opinion there came a man overflowing with zeal, partiality and invective. Swiss by birth, Jean Paul Marat (1743-1793) was first active in science and medicine. Once in Paris, he founded the newspaper *The Friend of the People* (*L'Ami du peuple*). Systematically, he dispersed copies among printers in three sections of the city. His ceaseless anti-monarchism swayed the public. His words incited to violence. While Mirabeau exuded aggression, Marat the journalist and deputy poured hatred and virulence. One day, hatred turned against him.

Such personalities, all four energetic in their role as deputies, gave the assembly the thrust of difference. It stemmed from their upbringings in the church, royalty, the military, and science. These were their first circumstances. Though young, Germaine could discern character differences and sense matters of belief, but she could not foresee where these would lead. Naturally pro-monarchist, the duke d'Orléans later took a fateful step away from loyalty to his cousin Louis. Marat's revolutionary ire took him to the bitter end of bloodshed. Talleyrand's loyalties were to himself, whatever happened and wherever self-interest took him. La Fayette's resilience connected always with endeavor toward the nation, pride in his accomplishments, enough so to surmount temporary political disillusion. His constant of patriotism held firmly.

From 1789 to 1791 the assembly changed its title from 'nationale' to 'constituante' and finally 'legislative'. Internal factions progressed. Clubs emerged outside the assembly, though deputies participated in these argumentative and ardent bodies. Bourgeois merchants and lawyers joined them. The Cordelier Club led by the powerful orator-lawyer Georges Danton (1759-1794) gradually formed a leftist opposition within the assembly. It influenced members of the Tiers. The young writer Benjamin Constant, then studying at the German University of Brunswick, felt the danger of this kind of opposition. "Everything promises," he wrote, "and nothing holds. . . . We are destined for something of which we have absolutely no idea." [3a]

In the old Dominican convent of the Jacobins, Mirabeau, Sieyès, and La Fayette and their democratic friends formed the Jacobin Club. They invited talented young men whose upbringing and education promised a sensible political caucus. But the club evolved and entered the assembly, bringing along negative elements that its founders could not possibly have foreseen. The Revolution had engendered mental moods unpredictable and far from conducive to unity of thought. The Jacobin movement manifested contrariness, it confronted patriotism with skepticism, resentments, and objections motivated by personal ambition. To make matters worse, royalist clubs flirted with the populace, who responded with anger and boycotted their meetings. Out of the assembly's Jacobins a menacing body emerged called the Mountaineers (Montagnards). Solidly camped, it proceeded to destroy political unity altogether.

Through their combined leadership, Sieyès and his friend Condorcet, who at one point presided over the assembly, tried in vain to contain the vituperative Montagnards. Moderate stances that had respected the idea of a constitutional monarchy now vanished. Germaine had sympathized with this attitude, then considering herself a 'constitutional' republican. This felt like a pleasant relation to democracy, but it was short-lived. This was as far as Germaine could go in the political activism maintained in her salon. Precaution now spoke to her. Thus and for some years, the force of circumstance closed the political door before her.

When the assembly dissolved the parlements, ordered the secularization of the church and took away its funds, jubilation ran high. But now, the assembly's own internal power play threatened its initial representative quality with destruction. How then could the assembly listen to Necker's repeated entreaty to follow the English constitutional system as the correct model for a government? His *Observations on the Deficit* met with ridicule and with vicious attacks in *L'Ami du peuple*. Necker's idea that a limited legislative monarchy could sustain executive royal power was now out of question. The legislative body became pervasively national.[4] By auction, it appropriated the clergy's properties. It proclaimed the transformation of provinces into eighty-three departments. It abolished monastic vows and suppressed all feudal rights. It reduced bishoprics. All clergy were made to give the oath of loyalty to the constitution under threat of prosecution. Finally, the legislative assembly eliminated all ranks, titles, honors and it reiterated the end to prerogatives of the nobility.

This was the beginning of the end for royal authority. One wonders what the hapless Louis XVI could possibly have thought, so totally out of tune with his country, when asked to be present at the July 14, 1790 Fest of the Federation at the Paris Champ de Mars. Marie-Antoinette was at his side, the Neckers, the duke d'Orléans also, and La Fayette with fourteen hundred guards, before a magnitude of three hundred thousand citizens. Dressed as an ordinary citizen, Louis gave the oath of civic allegiance. Deputies from all departments of France applauded. Were they applauding him? Essentially no, but only a political abstraction pseudo-materialized by the appearance of districts, their representatives, banners, music, four hundred priests, an arch, an altar where the former priest Talleyrand presided at mass. To the huge cry 'Vive la nation!', 'Vive le Roi . . .' barely echoed in the distance.

In retrospect, Thomas Jefferson expressed regret concerning Louis at this sad juncture in the monarch's life:

> The King was now become a passive machine in the hands of the Assembly. . . . Had he been left to himself, he would have willingly acquiesced in whatever they should devise as best for the nation. A wise constitution would have been formed, hereditary in his line, himself placed at its head; with powers so large as to enable him to do all the good of his station, and so limited, as to restrain him from its abuse. . . .[4a]

For Necker, the summer of 1790 may have been the harshest ever. Still a hard worker and sincere in his preoccupation with grain distribution, he was no longer in tune with the assembly's cacophonies. His old self-confidence and reputation were gone. Crops having failed again, grain became scarce, and riots continued. No longer able to impose his will, aching with nostalgia for the Versailles consultations with his king, and now filled with self-justification, Necker felt that now it was time to leave. "My intentions are pure and honest," he said, ". . . and if, by accepting my place in the ministry I have lost personal peace, at least I am sure that my conscience has not been troubled."[5] Necker left Paris on September 8, 1790. His old friend Georges count Buffon decried the uneventful departure: " Never has a minister left with more incognito. . . . The indifference of the French is astonishing. No satires, no praises, nothing, not a word; a chair falling in the Tuileries makes more noise than the departure of a man adored fifteen months before . . ."[5a] From the Swiss canton of Vaud, Necker continued to send memos to the assembly and to publish articles on governmental administration. Naively, he mailed his *On Power* (*Du Pouvoir*) to the king who had borrowed a large part of his fortune. Though awkward, the gesture had its reason: Necker still defended the principle of monarchy.

Suddenly, on March 2, 1791, Honoré Riqueti count Mirabeau died. In the circumstance of time, this death signaled the doom of the idea of a well-represented constitutional body. A passionate era ended. Voices were now colder, and actions methodical. Whereas Mirabeau had kept open communication with the aristocracy, now that the assembly had completed a large segment of its revolutionary decrees, it became a prosecuting force. Marat, Robespierre and the latter's friend Louis de Saint-Just (1767-1794) snatched the reins of the assembly. From now on, anyone connected with the aristocracy suffered stinging, life-threatening attacks.

Germaine was not exempt from affront. She was caricatured and grossly described. "She is not even French," one newspaper said, "and she will always be among the women from whom one flees."[6] Newspapers proliferated, and compounded more political division.They were libelous and so numerous as to tyrannize everyone's daily routine irrespective of individual opinion, even for just a moment. Public opinion festered as if diseased. The venerable *Gazette littéraire de l'Europe* created in 1764 by Necker's friend Jean-Baptiste Suard (1732-1817) was thrown off its pedestal. Royalist papers like *L'Ami du Roi* were satirized by the *Journal de la cour et de la ville* and others like *La Chronique scandaleuse* and *La Lanterne magique nationale, Les Actes des apôtres*. These were quickly written, printed and distributed, emulating Marat's *L'Ami du Peuple*. The reactionary journals *L'Orateur du Peuple* and *Le Journal politique national* broke the balance of equitable journalism, flooding the Palais Royal stalls with indecent rancour. Opposition came from *L'Ami des patriotes*, also from the *Journal des Débats* created in 1789, but the latter took ten years to earn ascendancy over the public. The royalist *Mercure* held on until August 1792. It is thought that in 1791 Germaine wrote an article for Suard's other journal *Les Indépendants* but if so she withheld her name, and posed the following question: What are the signs of the opinion of the nation's majority? Journalism being mobile and prone to excess, articles written by the deputy-secretary to Danton, Camille Desmoulins (1760-1794), stunned with their irony, by "a clarity of formula intercepted by uncertainty of thought . . . then a violent, ferocious declamation."[6a]

The mood in Germaine's salon changed. All anxiously witnessed the assembly's dislocation into left and right segments—Jacobins versus Girondins. Many of the latter hailed from the Gironde-Bordeaux area. Their moderate stand infuriated the feverish Jacobins. As war minister, Narbonne, Germaine's new love, often met the Girondin deputies Brissot, Talleyrand and La Fayette in Germaine's salon, this being in fact committee reunions.[7] Critics were well aware of these meetings. Strangely enough, Germaine earned more rancour from aristocrats and from those embittered in their lot who resented her father. She was hurt by this. In a letter to king Gustav III in September, 1791, she was nostalgic. When the States General opened, she lamented,

> the lights of intelligence and the excellent intentions of the king offered tremendous hope for a free and happy constitution. But the fanatic intoxication of the nation distanced this possibility. Why do the aristocrats who have been oppressed to the point of leaving reproach those who in a perfectly good will hoped to form a constitution? . . . why at first did they accuse my father of favoring the Third Estate whereas they, the privileged, should have risen to the level of justice itself?[8]

Germaine was pleading her father's case, and her own as well. The premonition that the Revolution would fail because of the behavior of the nobility agitated her. Their exit en masse, their growing conspiracy against France offended her loyalty and her attachment to the idea of a republic where the priority would be justice for all. She never abandoned this concept, and the premonition stayed with her. Still attending assembly meetings, her overview of the assembly's predicament made her dread a dangerous turn for the nation, an impending separation of powers more frightening than what her father had envisaged.

In her private life during 1789, 1790, and 1791, Germaine bore considerable tension. Barely one month before the solemn opening of the States General, she lost her first child, little Edwige-Gustavine. The wound inflicted by this death became an integral part of her; it increased her natural propensity for melancholy. It was as if now, it were a secret duty to be melancholic. Writing did not flow easily. Even her letters reflected nervousness and distress brought on by the combined political and personal traumas of those years. Affection did calm her, however. In the summer of 1790 she composed a warm eulogy for Jacques-Antoine Guibert, long esteemed and whose ideas for general and military reform she admired. She did not publish her compliment. She wrote two verse dramas called *Montmorency* (1790) and *Rosamonde* (1791), but did not publish them. Germaine put aside three short stories written in 1786— the last children of her young writing years: *Mirza, Adelaïde and Théodore*, and *Pauline*, all published in 1795. But now, after the revolutionary outbreak, she reassessed the first of these—*Mirza* —, and penned a short preface to the story. Her interest in fiction was holding fast even though the essay on Jean-Jacques Rousseau had proved highly successful; it had made her reputation as a writer. Therefore, the two genres—fiction and nonfiction, subsisted.

The preface to *Mirza or Letter from a Traveller* was probably written in 1791. She pointed out that the story "only offered feelings of the heart." But her pen swiftly reverted to the recent political outbreak which "has affected individual sentiment, and one does not know what route to offer hope itself... nor what principle can possibly guide public opinion from now on through the errors of party politics, and lead once again to a proper, brilliant goal."[9] Interestingly, due to its wistfulness and because of her concern for public opinion, her present comment substantiates that the newspaper article of 1791 was most probably hers, at least as the title would indicate. The manner in which the short preface to *Mirza* was written reflects Germaine's obsession with what she called the 'grandeur' of the early, ceremonial events at Versailles, their initial impact, and their disheartening consequences. Here, the story of Ximeo, head of an African village, and of his love for Mirza, the young African girl defiant of Europe's cruel slavery trade that has shattered her world, of Ximeo's act of duty to his country at war, his imprisonment, Mirza's offer to take his place, then her sacrifice, the vibrant images in such a young fiction project a perceptively romantic acceptance of suffering in love.

Shortly after Necker left Paris in September 1790, Germaine's parents retired to Coppet near Geneva. The recently acquired Italianate chateau overlooking the lake possessed a handsome park within sight of the Mont Blanc. This became a haven of peace and quiet for Necker. It gave Suzanne Necker respite from the stressful years in Paris and the possibility of improvement in her health. Germaine was not enthused with such peace and quiet. After a short stay in Coppet she opted to return to Paris. Suzanne's distress had extended to her daughter. She disapproved of Germaine's relationship with Narbonne, and she was less and less capable of coping with anxiety. Her resentment against France, constant complaints concerning the revolutionary explosion, aggravated the tenuous rapport between mother and daughter. Restrictions, the illness that made Suzanne gyrate from firmness to weakness troubled Germaine. Love for her mother was strong, but the growing attachment to Narbonne drove her attentions away from the new parental home, and led her back to Paris.

Perhaps the recent attachment relieved Germaine from the emotional oppression consequent to what now appeared to be, at least in her mind, the revolution's ominous failure. This became more acute as the assembly shifted in mood and structure toward violence, the public press assenting. On June 1, 1791, Germaine wrote to Eric from Coppet—her many letters to him being either amicable or ironic depending on her husband's physical ailments and his cold indifference: "As I will not know anyone in this new legislature, I hereby submit my resignation from politics," she wrote. ". . . Belles-lettres will capture my leisure . . . , besides, the society of Auguste is charming."[10] Germaine had given birth in Coppet to her first son Auguste, Narbonne's child, on August 31, 1790. If not an anomaly, 'resignation' from politics was surely motivated by an unhappy mixture of discouragement and fear, both sharply political feelings, the circumstances of a sojourn in Coppet in the parents'ambiance and a child's birth aiding reflection. Therefore, Germaine's decision simply had to be momentary.

Eric expressed dismay. His extravagances were costly. The revolutionary enmity toward aristocracy jeopardized his position. As for Auguste's father, count Louis de Narbonne, ambition, zest at work and proverbially seductive exploits were the most evident characteristics. Perhaps a son of Louis XV, Narbonne had been at the court of Louis XVI since 1785. He was well educated, and raised in the military lifestyle. He possessed a regiment and became Louis's war minister. He was successful in this. He and Necker esteemed each other. He joined La Fayette,

Condorcet and Talleyrand in Germaine's salon, all supporting the Gironde. Narbonne savored Germaine's acumen in conversation, her amiability and frankness. For him and at that particular point in their lives, her susceptibility to form a liaison agreed with his volatile temperament. Her passion for Narbonne had many complements, most remarkably, the serious political sympathy that she easily imparted to her close friends. Notwithstanding his charm and élan, traits that she admired in her father, at this stage of her young maturity her passionateness and the aches of marital disillusion surely initiated the emotional rapport.

Germaine openly exulted in her conquest of Narbonne. In letters subsequent to the arrival of little Auguste, the victorious feeling prevailed. Later letters revealed a tempest. Her possessiveness and his inconstance extinguished the fires of Germaine's first passion within five years. Beneath such short-lived happiness, France's misfortune haunted her. Forever, they filled her mind with the unanswerable question of political disunity.

> The sentiment of admiration should never leave a people. Only from it can all degrees of affection derive between the magistrates and the governed. Where can appreciative and calm judgement be found in our numerous associations? Can one thousand men decide according to their own lights? Is there not an animated impulse that can reach this multitude, one so difficult, and so hard to unite in one opinion?[11]
> Germaine de Staël, *De la Littérature*, 1800

5.

THE HYDRA UNLEASHED

> A whole lifetime of reflection is needed before the spectacle of these last two years, and I need to refer to my baptismal certificate to remind myself that I am only twenty-four years old.
>
> Germaine de Staël, September 16, 1791[1]

Madame de Staël clearly assessed the French political upheaval of the years 1789 to 1791 in her newspaper article *To what Signs One can Recognize the Opinion of the Nation's Majority* (*A quels signes peut-on reconnaître l'opinion de la majorité de la Nation.*) Published on April 16 1792 in *Les Indépendants* and though unsigned, it has been documented as hers.[1a] As if the nation were diseased, in clinical strokes of the pen, Germaine diagnosed contradictions that swayed public opinion : fear inspired by the press, reason countering this with Girondin moderation, hatred for the royal regime versus desire for a new government, insurrection quelling pleadings for calm. Germaine contrasted political moderates with the envious and those given to exaggeration. The Jacobin hatreds prolonged suspense. Ignorance of what liberty is, yet the violent snatching of it added confusion, while the aristocracy cried out. But some were too silent or too hypocritical, egoïsm ruling. Germaine firmly projected her belief in order and her fear of despotism. She felt the nation's pulse through those contrary elements.

Concerning Mirabeau, perhaps the oratorical despot had confused license with liberty. Did he not know that law had to be maintained? She granted that the nation's grief over his death moderated judgements against the stunning political figure.

Ancient abuses were now being cut down, but time was short, and all could see that now there were "but two parties, the royalists and the republicans."[1b] Enmity had to end for the sake of everyone's understanding of liberty. We must speak up, and rise above suspicion. Germaine's republican call is youthful, but she marshalled two forces for the sake of argument: logic and perspective. These never left her pen. Her particular kind of activism anchored itself and remained the contextual part of her writings.

Germaine participated in the Society of Friends of the Constitution. Other political clubs developed, but with different sounds. The Cordeliers was founded by Georges Danton, who led the vociferous band of Montagnards. Concurrently, Louis's call for troops to deter Parisian riots had broken his chance to be part of the government. His last act of resistance met with disdain. The Assembly continued abolishing ranks, titles, and all prerogatives of the nobility. The provinces were fragmented. Intrigues plagued efforts toward reorganization. July 14, 1790, had seen but a momentary tribute to its recalcitrant king.[2]

Germaine felt the populace's malevolent hysteria. "It dances from morning 'till night, it is happy, puts on airs to show this in the presence of its enemies . . . this new regime amuses it, pulling it away from the boredom of its habitual occupations."[2] The wind had changed. In 1792, the court's enmity against the Assembly widened. Clergy and nobility who had not left Paris drew closer to each other in ire. While rioters shouted demands for a new ministry, revolts within the army led many to leave and join foreign troops. Officers who were court aristocrats sought appointments abroad and left for Baden and Coblenz. Feeling threatened by the growing emigration, the Assembly decreed death to the fugitives and confiscated their property while ordering the clergy to swear allegiance "to the nation, its law, the king."[3] Forces of disorder swept every segment of the country's society into an uncontrolled path. With only a few exceptions, no right-mindedness entered this hot and swift path. Jean Marie Roland was such an exception: husband of the political journalist Manon Roland and minister of the interior in the spring of 1792, Roland created a bureau of information on revolutionary ideals, but this was suppressed as Girondin powers weakened.

The assembly fell into a pattern analogous to that of a police state. Louis showed less and less interest in negotiating for a peaceful governmental arrangement. Marie-Antoinette's brother Leopold II of Austria signaled that a coalition might help the French king. Indeed, European powers expressed their alarm, Leopold having met Frederick Wilhelm II of Prussia. Louis negotiated. After the royal family's attempted escape and arrest in Varennes, rancor deepened. The word 'Republic' was heard. During an immense assemblage, Danton harangued passionately, and some killings occurred. La Fayette had to disperse the crowd with his twelve hundred guards. Danton became a suspect; he had accepted bribes from Louis's brother, Philippe of Orléans. Animosities disrupted the work of the Assembly which now gave itself a last name: the Legislative. Continual changes in the ministry weakened it. Attacking moderate Girondins, Danton and Robespierre held power, distrusting each other.

The Assembly became the stage for personal vindictive wars. At large, France experienced rural terror. Emigration further drained away educated efficiency and self-control. Before leaving the war ministry—for he was demoted along with all of Louis's ministers on March 9, 1792—Narbonne had ordered one hundred and fifty thousand men to come to arms. Most of these were unprepared for military action. Then, with barely three military units, and soon only two, France entered into war with Germany and Austria. Other countries soon entered the conflict. It lasted twenty-three years.

Much as Germaine's love for Narbonne was a response to his appeal, her disappointment in marriage spurred the youthful yearning for attention. At first, Narbonne's infatuation was genuine, but it did not last. Her fires burned longer, paralleling events that thundered around them. Emotional and political tensions grew high; that she survived them during the period between 1792 and 1795 can be considered a miracle. One reason for this may have been her passion for Narbonne.

Germaine's letters to Narbonne intimate this survival. She was overwhelmed above political anxieties and even concerns for her family. But the returns were poor. With her, the experience produced a kind of writing replete with every imaginable enticement to the loved one. For today's reader, the letters lose their initial intensity once thrown to the wolves of public analysis, also, the intensity is nearly always single, as in a monologue. Out of respect, the modern reader can reach a good understanding of Germaine by empathizing with her repeated cries of anguish in a substance congenial to her character as a writer.

Germaine needed to write as the devout need to pray, to calm her passion, she said. Narbonne did not seem to have that need. In spite of his troubling silence, it seemed impossible to her that he should have negative feelings. She could not bear his absence. She specified that she was easy to understand for she "ceded to but one impulse, one idea, one sentiment . . . that this intoxication seems to grow . . . events teaching me to detest men (the Jacobin extremists) while love increases for the one who has surpassed my imagination."[4]

Narbonne lost his position at court at the time of the assassination of Gustav III of Sweden. Germaine stayed in Paris near her salon friends. As France declared war against Austria, Narbonne momentarily joined La Fayette in the army of the north, then returned to Paris. That summer, Germaine attended the renewed 'fête de la fédération'. She heard someone shout that the nation was in danger. Along with Condorcet, she well knew that governmental arbitrariness had set in like an infection. Forces abroad were bound to add to the disease. It has been thought that after having seen Louis XVI wear the red revolutionary cap at a Tuileries event on June 20 1792, Germaine and Narbonne offered Louis an escape plan; Marie-Antoinette rejected it.[5]

Distrust of the aristocracy increased, instigating pursuits and arrests. Narbonne, Germaine and their friends were listed accordingly. On August 10, 1792, Germaine managed to finance Narbonne's departure for England along with her friend count François de Jaucourt (1757-1852) whom apparently she helped escape from prison. When the Convention replaced the third and dying assembly on September 21, it proclaimed the Republic and created a 'comité de surveillance'. Robespierre's domination sent ripples of horror throughout the city. Louis and his family were taken from the Tuileries to the Temple. Bailly left the mayorship. Amidst rumors that the clergy motioned to leave Paris, the massacre of two hundred priests had taken place on September 2 in Parisian convents. The first republic of France was born in a bloodbath.

Salons closed. In near hysteria, Germaine paid for a safe-conduct of her coach through dangerously crowded streets, and left for Coppet. She moved to the town of Rolle where on November 20 she gave birth to her second son, Albert, Narbonne's child. She had found the atmosphere at Coppet intolerable. Her parents sharply objected to her affair with Narbonne. She etched their criticism in her letters to him. Much to parental disarray, she left for England. She returned in June, having felt Narbonne's cool reception. Letters poured questions, threats, adoration and reproach. Replies were few and interspersed with promises and pretexts.

"You are the most cruel, the most ungrateful, the most barbarous of men!" she cried.[6] Ironic, she added that "one would like to know everything that you do not wish to divulge."[7] After disappointment in marriage, disillusion now affected Germaine's capacity to reflect. But she rallied: "I am taking charge of being yours without bondage . . . you must look after your happiness and security."[7] The latter was a priority then, for aristocrats returning to France faced the death sentence, even Necker. Germaine chastised Narbonne for wanting to go to Paris—out of vanity, she said—to defend Louis at his trial. The execution of the king on January 21, 1793, filled Narbonne with grief. Momentarily, Germaine's sympathy invigorated the fragile bond. But at the end of her near-monologue, Germaine admitted credulity, and reflected that the abandoning of herself to excessive feeling may have alienated her love-god.

Perspective widened, and darkened:

> One needs the happiness of those whom one loves . . . One would like to carry the crown of the world, that of one's garden also. One would like this, but one cannot.[8] One suffers because all ideas evolve around a dominating one . . . perhaps this immobile feeling helps in the recognition of oneself.[9] . . . Such a feeling is just that which helps us face our misfortunes. . . . I now know that my passion is my genius.[10]

Like her family and friends, Germaine experienced shattering sorrow from the trial and death of Louis XVI. She could neither concentrate nor read, nor write, she said. Some like Narbonne, who had been ministers to the king, felt guilty for not having better supported their master. Though a bourgeois vulnerable to court discrimination, Jacques Necker's sadness was similar, doubly so for his having been closer in Louis's affection than possibly the ministers, and known him well. Necker's despair in his 1797 *De la Révolution française* is unmatched in severity:

> Parisians, you were quiet witnesses to the most horrible sacrifice; . . . your tyrants suspected you. They feared Louis's last desire . . . to speak to his people. Drums were made to roar, and the king was not heard.[11]

Thousands from the nobility and clergy were assassinated, Robespierre and Marat rivaled each other in castigations, and now Louis de Saint-Just infected the Convention with blood-thirsty speeches. Germaine saw the full significance of the word 'Terror': law had been ousted. It was too late for any law-abiding counter-plan, even though a new Constitution was decreed June 24, 1793. Condorcet had bravely presented such a plan on behalf of the Gironde.[12] But like Condorcet, Germaine did not anticipate the latter's full demise. The Gironde fell in the summer of 1793. Robespierre, Marat and Danton brought armed rioters into the Convention and ousted the Girondins. There were arrests and executions. The solitary, vengeful assassination of Marat whetted Robespierre's anger. Danton's newly created Revolutionary Tribunal sprang into action. "We are in a sea of incertitude," Talleyrand wrote to Germaine on July 30, 1793.[13]

Aghast, Europe enlarged its coalitions, joined this time by England. In Holland, General Charles Dumouriez (1739-1823) was defeated after a heavy Austrian push. He resigned, accused the Convention of tyranny, and defected to Austria. Spain and Prussia joined the latter in preparation for an invasion of France. Harassed by the frightened populace, the Convention fell into anarchy. Its police force imposed civic certificates; it looted, and suppressed clubs and banks. Robespierre decreed the Law of Suspects. Harsh and hard, with strident oratory, he flattered the populace, lulled it with luxuriantly ornate and strangely sedative ceremonies of worship to a 'Supreme Being'. Mad with power, Robespierre led a massive purge, denying to every accused person a proper defense.

Germaine had returned to her desk. She had been working on a long essay called *On Passion's Influence on the Happiness of Individuals and Nations* (*De l'influence des passions sur le bonheur des individus et des nations*). She had followed the events scrupulously. But now, her heart ached for the unfortunate queen whose demise signaled the collapse of Versailles' resplendent house of cards. Since Marie-Antoinette's arrival in France in 1770 and thereafter, parties, intrigues, favors, glitter and pleasure accumulated within increasingly loose management. Adulated for nearly twenty years, and now hated for her lifestyle, nationality, and suspicions of contacts with Austria, on October 16, 1793, the daughter of Empress Marie-Thérèse of the ancient monarchical world was taken from her prison in the Conciergerie and drawn by cart to her final destiny. "The executioners have used every kind of torture . . . for this woman made famous by her misfortune," Germaine wrote to Narbonne on October 25, "yet Marie-Antoinette was able to give her name without horror."[14]

Marie-Antoinette's quiet denials of treason, extravagance and immorality had been her only defense. Germaine's remark of October 25 was a thoughtful justification, to say the least. She did more than this. Early during the interrogations she published an anonymous defense of the queen: *Reflections Concerning the Trial of Marie-Antoinette* (*Réflexions sur le procès de la reine*). To affirm the impartiality of her reflections, she stated having had few personal contacts with the queen. She had met Marie-Antoinette during presentations at court and had noticed the queen's exquisite courtesy in the midst of pressing crowds, but Germaine had been irritated by the queen's cool treatment of her father when Louis cancelled an order of exile against him. All that was forgiven now. Thomas Jefferson was not as forgiving as Germaine. In his opinion, the queen was "proud, disdainful of restraint... eager for the pursuit of pleasure."[15] In Germaine's *Reflections* the line of defense changed into a sharp attack on the envious press and the flighty character of the populace who at the words 'The Austrian woman' (l'Autrichienne) rallied in fury. Reproachful, Germaine reminded her readers that having left Versailles for the Tuileries with Louis, the queen stood by him to boost his self-confidence. Turning to the revolutionary leaders, Germaine showed how in their eagerness to "tie firmly their own cause to that of the people" they identified with the latter in their acts. Such a psychology condoned excesses all of which were "a sickness of the soul. The French should be ashamed of the queen's defenselessness," she added. "There will be no glory for the armies of France, nor for the new generation, if the terror which reversed the first promises of the Estates General persists in its ferocities."[16]

From the newspapers and directly through her correspondence, Germaine learned that more Girondins had been imprisoned, and thirty-one had been executed following Marie-Antoinette's death. That Robespierre pounded derisively "against men and ideas"[17] must have struck her as a downward path into mental disease. Her thinking about Robespierre in this pathological context made her reflect that the rule of one could be fatal for a nation in the circumstance of political upheaval. She was informed that carnage and plundering spread to more churches, that Philippe d'Orléans, who had voted "death" at Louis's trial, was executed, that the journalist Manon Roland, who ardently supported the Revolution during its early stages, died at the guillotine, after which Jean Marie Roland committed suicide. Having escaped from prison for only an instant, devasted morally and physically, Condorcet took poison. Fifty-eight, then sixty-eight more members of the Gironde died before the year ended. Saint-Just now led the Convention. Thousands perished, including scientists like Antoine de Lavoisier, merchants, artisans, laborers, and poets like André Chénier.

Jealous fury consumed the top: Danton's execution in April 1794 led to that of Robespierre himself, then of Saint-Just in late July 1795.

By an unprecedented twist of fate, military France was reaping victories against Austria and the Netherlands. Another victory bore a special significance: while supporting the oppressed Girondins, the southern city of Toulon had allowed the English to overtake the port. In December 1793 Toulon was besieged and captured. The victors were Paul viscount Barras (1755-1829), who had activated Robespierre's fall, and the young artillery brigadier general Napoléon Bonaparte (1769-1821).

Germaine also knew these events, but other preoccupations oppressed her: Her own patriotic relief could not do more than shelter émigrés. Distressed by the bloodshed, she searched for solace. She considered writing fiction and literary criticism, but personal anxiety held her back. The marriage with Eric had failed. The liaison with Narbonne that had resulted in two pregnancies had ended. Narbonne had gone to Germany. Jacques and Suzanne Necker caused continual concern. By early 1794, Germaine's relationship with her mother had deteriorated to the point of reciprocal silence.

Graceless yet still handsome, Suzanne's inflexibly Calvinist faith contrasted with her eclectic literary tastes, her love for Rousseau, and her encyclopedic knowledge, all of which as we know shone in the Necker Paris salon when Germaine was a child. That Suzanne suffered from emotional difficulties was long evident to Germaine. Now she became visibly upset during Germaine's joyful banter with her father. Suzanne's despair on hearing news of the Terror turned into bitter criticism of France. This became an obsession. Nor could she bear Germaine's longing for Narbonne, let alone the second pregnancy. She constantly lamented. "I cultivated her memory and her mind . . . During thirteen years, the best of my life, I seldom lost sight of her . . . my self-esteem transferred itself onto her."[18]

Suzanne was an enigma. Perhaps Germaine could not fathom the character contradictions. Being at war with oneself—the Calvinist moral rule—could not blend with the notion of perfectibility espoused among others by Buffon, Madame Necker's close friend and confident of many years. Suzanne's admiration for Rousseau was shared by Germaine, particularly on the subject of Héloïse. But now, Suzanne was writing an essay on divorce where virtue and abnegation in marital life were strongly reiterated. "My mother," Germaine wrote, "out of a bizarre insensibility . . . fears that I rather than she may animate society around us."[19] Germaine discovered the prickly side the enigma—jealousy. Whereas she had supplanted Suzanne in her Paris salon, now she supplanted her in the difficult art of comforting the politically despondent Necker.

In spite of ongoing publications, Necker's voice was no longer heard. "He laments," Germaine wrote to Narbonne in mid-July 1793, "he wants to save his fortune, he hates to compromise his reputation, he fears me, consults with me, is angry, and softens . . . presenting me with a character drawn in illusory regions."[20] Suzanne's death in May 1794 left Necker morbidly distraught. Germaine stayed nearby, agitated by his grief. She had witnessed passionate conjugal love. The images survived in her writing. Germaine's personal comment on her mother came ten years later: "She had sought the ideal man, she found him, and spent her life with him . . . She has deserved such happiness more than I."[21]

From Germaine's critical perspective regarding France, tumult and terror now pointed to a void. Searching for the nation's opinion seemed impossible. She saw her friends waver between old Jacobin ideas and self-centeredness. As events fluctuated, all were anxious for the future. Therefore she was far from alone in this political stress. Since her 'constitutional' days, Talleyrand, Narbonne and La Fayette had been regular visitors to her salon. Now, pro-Girondin encouragements enriched her intellectual ambiance and created new friendships. Finding a refuge for Mathieu de Montmorency and others gave her the impetus to recreate a salon wherever she eluded government agents—Coppet, Surrey, Mézery, Nyon, and Lausanne. Montmorency had returned from the American War of Independence to become a deputy in the Tiers Etat. Now a pursued émigré, he joined Germaine's entourage. Gentle, and religious, he listened to her republican views, and though clinging to a royalist loyalty became her lifelong advisor. The loss of his mother and brother to the guillotine left him a melancholy man.

After the birth of Albert, Germaine as we know lived in Surrey from January to May 1793. She reunited with other political friends including Alexandre de Lameth (1760-1829), who had been a member of the Assemblée Constituante. Talleyrand was there before his short sojourn in America, and there was Narbonne. Germaine went to the theatre, enjoyed Shakespeare, read English literature, attended a parliamentary debate between William Pitt the Younger and his adversary Charles Fox. She met Fanny Burney (1752-1840), author of *Evelina*, and the two became friends. In March 1793 Germaine commented wistfully to Fanny: "At this time, who can allow oneself to be occupied by the self?"[22] Mainly political, writing was a routine during the stay at Juniper Hall in Surrey. Germaine listened to readings, presented ideas that would evolve into her own essays, and conversed with her usual salon energy.

The return to Coppet via a careful itinerary that took her from Dover to Brussels and Cologne made her decide to shelter her friends in Nyon. Charles-Victor Bonstetten (1745-1832), the bailiff of Berne assigned to oversee émigrés in his region, joined Germaine's entourage. He too had writing in mind, and was interested in pedagogy. Swedish political exiles were protected at Coppet, including Louis-Adolph de Ribbing (1765-1843). That year, Eric de Staël spent several months in Coppet. His contacts with Gustave III's successor, the Swedish regent, made him resent Ribbing's presence.

Germaine spent the spring of 1794 in Nyon. She returned to her desk. Nearby, at Neuville, she met the publisher-printer François de Pange (1764-1796) who agreed to publish her new essay *Reflections on Peace addressed to Mr. Pitt and to the French Nation*. Germaine was sensitive to Pange's views. "Philosophy," he wrote, "has not led the revolution that she had prepared, nor will it end it either."[23] Pange's death from tuberculosis saddened Germaine. Friendship revived at that time with the old family friend Jacob Meister of Zurich. Immersed in philosophical writing, Meister drew from his experiences as editor of Grimm's popular *Correspondance littéraire*, from his reverence for Diderot and d'Holbach whom he had known, from the German poets Goethe and Wieland as well. He became Germaine's advisor on Swiss matters. Her affection for him held through the years of her life.

In May 1794, Geneva experienced political violence. Germaine was told to stop sheltering foreigners. Nevertheless from mid-June to early September, Ribbing stayed near her. In December, Benjamin Constant joined the group of exiles. This was definitely a 'group'. Bonds had formed during the extraordinarily stressful years from 1791 to 1794. Germaine exercised a magnetic hold on everyone. Affection, intellect, energy expended in finding security for all, financial assistance and lodging for some were gratuitous elements no one could resist. Relationships fluctuated. Only a few ended abruptly, as in the case of Narbonne after his short appearance in July. Most of these relationships lasted in spite of political circumstances that affected her friends' whereabouts.

Germaine's circle continued widening. Her magnetic hold on others flowed from her vitality in conversation and letters, frankness, limitless affection, and "an incessant need for intellectual activity counter to the necessity of reclusion for writing."[24] Not yet thirty years of age, Germaine had developed a social pattern and a manner consistently warm.

She responded quickly to esteem, to encouragement regarding her writing and to sympathy during periods of despondency.

As if it were another person, veritable and affective, France had become Germaine's ultimate political concern. She had reached an understanding peculiar to herself in this epheral relationship. She reflected that if social reform troubled the populace, then the idea of 'equality' had to be better understood. To her, it was the nation as a whole that needed reform. More than anything else, it needed to respect liberty. Germaine's *Réflections sur la paix adressées à M. Pitt et à la nation française* reiterates this. In this context, she paid tribute to England. "It has the right to speak for itself in this great world debate," Germaine stated, "its constitution being a masterpiece of reason and liberty."[25] In France, Germaine added, the only discernible general feeling now was a fear of invasion abetted, ironically, by its own emigrants. It had its soldiers and the produce of its soil; these were its real possessions. But France had made enemies; it had to decide its destiny by itself. "We must bring France and the world with it back to order and virtue and reflect that they link with true liberty."[26]

Germaine commented on those who came in and out of the public limelight; their presence in the midst of a confused public was tragic. In that blurred light, peace could have been viable only if it had come from reason. Germaine's essay pleaded for a general uplifting, reminding her readers, including Mr. Pitt, that "everything in nature tends toward repose."[27]

Mr. Pitt did not favor war. He had looked at the early months of the Revolution with approbation, particularly during the opening of the Estates General. He propounded neutrality during the emerging European coalitions. However, the British "national impulse" reacted to French violence, and in 1793 he was "forced into a policy repugnant to him."[28] Germaine's plea was rich with notions expounded by Montesquieu. This could only please the British prime minister. It could not, however, produce the desired effect, for it came one year after the declaration of a war that would last a full generation.

Germaine missed the gentle Condorcet, one of her treasured salon visitors. She questioned the existence of the contrasting, terrorizing character of Robespierre. But she cast aside political despair, and held on to Condorcet's belief in the perfectibility of human nature. She did sense Europe's nervousness and Pitt's reticence as she wrote the *Reflections on Peace*. But if France had to be entangled in war, it would have to do so as a free nation.[29] Hence she held on to the republican principle of liberty. In 1795 Germaine wrote a second *Réflexions*—this time on interior peace. François de Pange cautioned her not to publish it. The breaking up of the legislature into two chambers augured a government intent on restraining the press and political reunions. In her long essay, Germaine lamented that bloodshed had ended the French monarchy, defiance had followed suit, then suspicion and persecution. Could monarchy ever return without the stain of despotism, she asked. After 1789, while trying to cope with a fallen monarchy, the public did desire liberty, it did hope for a constitution and it showed readiness to support this, but desire, hope and readiness were twisted by "murderous scoundrels. Yet another revolution was now furthest from our minds. . . ."[30]

Anger and pessimism are a rare occurrence in Germaine's writing. She was impelled by a near despair of ever envisaging true liberty. She yearned for men of virtue, but with an ironic twist:

> In the state in which we are now, we can by the course of things arrive at liberty. The people's fatigue serves this purpose; otherwise it would have to revolt. Sadly, by having been made to suffer . . . it is now disposed to receive a free constitution, and not to interfere with it.[31]

For having been made to seek exile, Germaine and her friends did not find relief from emotional trauma and in Germaine's particular case, from the failure of a true republicanism. Melancholy engulfed them; remembrances of Louis, Marie-Antoinette, Condorcet, Bailly, Brissot, Manon Roland, Malesherbes and the many more brought to the guillotine found dark recesses in their minds and hearts. Against the mobile government's oppressive caution, Germaine wrote the poem *Epistle to Misfortune* (*Epître au Malheur*). She addressed France—the leitmotiv of her oeuvre:

> France, among your destinies, the horrible memory
> In all regions tears open burial spaces,
> Your storm obscures the azur of peaceful skies,
> The blood you poured has stained your crystal waters . . .[32]
>
> Germaine de Staël, *Epître au malheur*, 1795

6.
PASSION ANALYZED

> ... Europe must listen to the friends of liberty.... Let us combat, in France, vanquish, suffer, die in our affections, in our most treasured inclinations, and recover; perhaps the world will be amazed, and will admire....
>
> Germaine de Staël
> *De l'influence des passions sur le bonheur des individus et des nations*, 1796[1]

Germaine returned to Paris accompanied by the Swiss political writer Benjamin Constant in May of 1795. The self-imposed exile had lasted two and a half years. Her heart filled with excitement, apprehension and anguish. Though so bloodied by revolutionary terror, the capital still affected her as one of the great loves of her life. It exercised an irresistible hold on her, as it did for her friends, all their circumstances agreeing with the excitement of being there. Germaine's *Reflections on Peace Addressed to Mr. Pitt and to the French Nation* had been well received. In England, the young prime minister's Whig opponent Charles Fox (1749-1806) quoted from Germaine's text during a major parliamentary speech on March 24. He too did not favor war between their two countries, nor did he approve of England's using emigrés in the conflict. Germaine had pleasant memories of a meeting with Fox during her stay in Surrey; now, she appreciated the statesman's public approval of her work. In the *Gazette française*, P. Roederer (1754-1835), editor of the *Journal de Paris*, also complimented her.

However, Germaine could not over-exult. At that time, the Convention was feverishly preparing a new constitution, and though Germaine attended its sessions scrupulously, the dying Comité du Salut Public distrusted her energetic presence and her equally energetic salon. Unabashed, Germaine entertained members of the government themselves, newly returned emigrés, writers, diplomats, and aristocrats. Views enunciated in such an ambiance were not all friendly toward the Convention. The newspaper *Nouvelles politiques et étrangères* soon accused Germaine of counter-reactionary opinions and even of royalist support. Apprehensively, in the same paper led oddly enough by her family friend Suard, Germaine published a formal 'profession of republican faith':

> I sincerely wish to see the French Republic established on the bases of justice and humanity. . . . In present circumstances, only a republican government can offer calm and liberty to France. . . . I express this wish as the wife of the Swedish ambassador to France . . . against all new suspicions and old hatreds conducive to anarchy. . . . Friends of a just and free Republic need the support of enlightened French patriots. . . .[2]

Germaine's statement was published in early June 1795. Barely two months later, she was criticized once again, her former butcher having spoken against her at the Convention. That her salon guests included the politician Jean-Jacques Cambacérès (1753-1824), the 'conventionnels' Jean Lambert Tallien (1767-1821) and Barras, her friend Sieyès, Roederer, and the old friend and literary critic Jean de La Harpe (1739-1803), poses the question of indifference. Roederer, Suard at times, and even the distant Narbonne had praised her writing. Constant, her new companion, praised her *Epître au Malheur* in the *Journal littéraire de Lausanne*. The Convention's suspiciousness held on. Some said that Germaine's deportment was at fault, that she "smothered the politically ambitious Barras with attention while evidently determined to be influential."[3] This could not but exert fear among self-interested acquaintances and some of her friends.

On October 15 1795, Germaine was formally accused of royalism. Nothing could be further from the truth. The convention did not understand her rapport with emigrés; she reproved anyone motivated by royalism. She was given the first official order of exile, and left for Switzerland. At the end of the year, Constant joined her. Weary yet wanting to resist the offense to her republicanism, Germaine lamented that the work of her destiny tormented her.[4]

Germaine's poem *Epître au Malheur* is the touching story of Adèle and Edouard, a young couple living in hiding during the Terror and haunted by fear. When Edouard is found out and taken to be executed, Adèle does not hesitate to follow him, and dies with him at the scaffold. The poet accuses misfortune for its blind cruelty, for tearing away from life everything that has been loved. Nature pursues its course; she accuses it of implacability. Yet the soil trembles, the poet adds, and "woe to whoever dares to agitate it."[5] Germaine ended her epistle with foreboding indeed: do not touch France, do not interfere with this country as it is. Her fear of political destruction has revealed a part of her own character: in the motion of love, whether the object be the personalized, beautiful France or an unfortunate young couple like Adèle and Edouard, melancholy, much assertion, and impending menace ensue. More than the characters she created in her poem, the deepest object of her love has been France itself.

Assertion and morbidity had been part of Germaine's letters to Narbonne whose ungratefulness she could not forget. Though equally brief in time, the affair with Ribbing was even more intense. It possessed a certain elegance in the association of ideas, as if it had a style of its own. Tempestuous as it was bound to be on Germaine's part, and inasmuch as it was constantly expressed, love challenged Germaine's femininity. Her response to this was genuine. In this respect, this may have been the most complete love of her life.

Louis-Adolf de Ribbing was a seductive, military aristocrat. Similarity with Narbonne ended here. Swedish, of an ancestry going as far back as the Vikings, Ribbing at age twenty-seven had participated in the assassination of king Gustav III in 1792. This was the monarch to whom Germaine had sent political news after her marriage to Eric de Staël, and in whose honor she learned the Swedish language. Not visible at first, surely not to Germaine, Gustav's gradual fall into despotism discontented the republican-minded Ribbing and peers in the nobility who shared his views. Exiled from Sweden for life, Ribbing traveled to Denmark, Germany, France and in 1793, Switzerland. Political convictions formed during years of military and naval assignments in France, the country he came to love deeply. Respect for the Gironde paralleled his growing disdain for the Swedish monarchy, so much so that his part in the coup was definitely genuine. In so doing, he said, "I have wanted to serve all my compatriots and not a certain social class."[6]

Germaine met Ribbing in Nyon in 1793, when news of the Terror increased everyone's anguish near her, and in her particular situation increasing disillusion with Narbonne. To Germaine, the handsome neighbor appeared too solitary in his exile, emotional, proud, and nostalgic. In his own quiet manner he was helping Swedish émigrés and shared with Germaine and her friends feelings of disenchantement and horror over news of the Terror. Germaine quickly perceived Ribbing's contrasting sensitivity and forcefulness, which in his few letters to friends Ribbing called his instability. He admitted a weakness: he did not like writing letters.

Germaine had just published her eulogy to Marie-Antoinette, she was reviewing her story *Zulma* and working on the *Influence of Passions* gestated before the months of refuge in England. Ribbing too loved English literature, but most of all he shared Germaine's advocation of political liberty. Hating the traditions of royal absolutism and aristocratic privileges—for he had renounced his—Ribbing once exclaimed wanting "to see a magic power raised in the name of liberty. . . . When I hear that word . . . I feel a violent heart-beat and my blood rushing in my veins."[7]

Ribbing's sentiments were not unique in time and nationality. Well acquainted with publications originating in England, Germaine's friends had strong predilections for English philosophical thinking —John Locke and David Hume among others—and now publishing continued with renewed vigor not only in England but in France and Germany. Among the many that flourished in England were Edmund Burke's *Reflections on the French Revolution* (1796), his sharp criticism of the events being publicly refuted by Benjamin Constant; William Godwin's recent *Enquiry Concerning Political Justice*, in which he defended the Revolution; William Blake's *Songs of Experience* (1794) where the Revolution was given ecstatic praise; Edward Gibbon's *History of the Decline and Fall of the Roman Empire, also the Memoirs* (1796); Thomas Paine's recent *Age of Reason*. In France, equally abundant publications included François René de Chateaubriand's *Report on the State of France* (1793); M. J. Chénier's words to the theatre's *Song of Departure*; Félicité de Genlis's recently published *Chateau Evenings* (*Veillées du Château*). From Germany, there came Jean Paul Richter's *Maria Wuz* (1790); Frederich Schiller's *On Aesthetic Education* (1795); J. G. Herder's *Letters for the Furtherance of Humanity* (1793-1797); F. W. Schelling's *Of the World-Soul* (1798). Works by J. G. Fichte and Immanuel Kant were being translated between 1794 and 1797, therefore available to French and English readers.

Not that Germaine and her friends read everything in sight; they read nearly constantly, nevertheless, and imparted their experiences to each other. Where German texts had not yet been translated, knowledge of the language, for instance and soon, Constant's came to everyone's aid. Germaine and her friends became aware of conflicting judgements concerning the Revolution. Historical and philosophically oriented texts raised important questions such as 'What have we done, we Europeans?' and 'What must we do now?' Just as political self-consciousness had to be admitted, a door had to open into the future. The double perspective answered to the malaise Germaine and her peers had only just experienced. Destiny, one's own, and every nation's, became the primary question among serious authors and readers. Germaine had already felt this intellectual pull in relation to herself and to her writing. She kept the primary question in mind within the wider periphery of her great love, France. This became her most important mission as a writer.

As always, Germaine was unusually susceptible to love. Characteristically, one of her loves was love itself. In 1794, however, the feeling materialized once again. She marveled at Ribbing's "extraordinary feeling" for her, and his political sympathy. "He is one of us," she said to Narbonne in March 1794.[8] Later that Spring, Ribbing became her new love. Terrorist violence had penetrated in Geneva. Ribbing's attentions relieved Germaine of restlessness. Energy revived. In Lausanne, Nyon or Kirchberg, Germaine was happier, pouring out the idyllic experience in her letters to Ribbing. Alternately candid and aggressive, the letters move and sway, propelled by feeling. She admitted being curious concerning his character, and impatient over his absences. When Ribbing, a man of several past attachments, felt obligated to tell her that his "heart was forever closed to love," she immediately questioned his stance: "Between my duties and my faults, where do you expect me to place this new bond?"[9] The pen softened: "Each day I am more and more attached to you; there are treasures of kindness, pride, nobility in your character." Then came a faint accusation of reticence: "The more you are yourself, the less you are eager to show yourself." Then introspection: "What do you really think of me," she asks. She offered a resolution: "There is but one remedy here, we have to see each other often; the soul develops gradually."[10] For Germaine, a future spent with Ribbing was a natural association. She made plans for his joining her in Paris. Naively, she did not attach much importance to his having gone to live in Denmark whereas for him, this was the reverse. He had acquired property while thinking of his own future.

In time, Germaine's love letters manifested a scruple she attributed to men's behavior toward women. "Do realize that in my opinion," she wrote, "an honest man must be as truthful and faithful to a woman as he is to his companion at arms . . . and when I am reduced to isolation and abandonment, let me preserve the cult of your character to raise myself in my self-esteem."[10a] This was written in mid-April 1795, six months before the end of the affair. The biographer Simone Balayé offered a helpful rapprochement between Germaine's letter to Ribbing and the chapter on love in the *Influences of Passions*, where the phrase 'companion at arms' is repeated.[10b] Our interest sees a difference in emphasis concerning the male bonding—strong in Germaine's letter, less so in her text. The latter considers that love is women's unique passion, whereas with men, love is an episode. She attributes this imbalance to the "opinion of an unjust society (so that) . . . the laws of morality itself seem suspended in the relationships between men and women."[10c] That Germaine completed the *Influences* approximately one year after her comment to Ribbing indicates that reflection and possibly bitterness made her enlarge her focus of attention, and the manner with which she presented it. This imbalance later became a vital part of her novel *Delphine*.

Germaine attempted to alleviate her loneliness with a melancholic complaint: "When my soul, easily abandoned to painful sentiment, is left on its own, it can only wander among ruins, yet it still sees you there, consolation incarnate against the storms of life." Indeed, Germaine looked to Ribbing as a friend past, present and future. "I will consider you my tutelary angel," she added later. For her, the definition of unhappiness was absence. "I detest it, it is arid and calm, devouring and monotonous."[11] More with Ribbing than with Narbonne, there often followed the command of a return, and the reproach of indifference to a sensitive soul, finally the desire to be left alone in her sadness. But this time, Germaine imputed to her lover his "solemn responsibility" toward her for having made a promise.[12]

Political arrests and killings spread to Switzerland in 1794. Germaine continued helping friends, in some cases with well-organized disguises and the use of secret routes. Ribbing and Mathieu de Montmorency were made to leave Switzerland by the Secret Council of Berne. In September, Germaine and Ribbing parted tearfully. He gave her assurances of his love. They would meet briefly a year later. Ribbing never fulfilled her wish of a life together. She became lonely, self-pitying, and sleepless. One month after their parting she wrote to Ribbing: "This evening I have met a highly spirited person whose name is Benjamin Constant, not good-looking, but fascinating."[13] From Denmark, Ribbing seldom wrote, reminding her of his indifference to letter writing. Germaine saw complete indifference. Yet, longings and her vision of a career for Ribbing continued.

Certain elements in Germaine's letters during the year 1795 pointed to a new emotional stability. She was in her thirtieth year. Between laments and thoughts for his future, she expressed understanding of Ribbing's courage and political predicament. Afraid of being misjudged, she asked for his trust. His absence from August 1794 to August 1795 caused her to reminisce rather than to strike with anger. Moreover, as the pen relaxed, she described to Ribbing her project on *The Influences of Passions*. She would honor him within the text and call him the most unique of friends. There were complaints, questions, some morbidity, but in a diminishing quota. To counter the fact that Ribbing now owned a property in Denmark, the pen projected a mischievous claw: "If you don't need me, don't come . . . I am no longer necessary to you. I fear the generosity of your character, your perfect kindness. . . ."[14] Besides, she added, had he not professed deep love for France, should he not rather settle there? The claw retreated. Germaine mentioned her responsibility to her father and her children. She was weary, knowing that her tendency to dominate others was a character flaw, but still, passion was her genius, as she had acknowledged to Narbonne.

For some time since the age of twenty, Germaine had examined the ebb and flow of passion in herself and in others. The letters to Narbonne and Ribbing attest to this. She did so in several publications as well. The various and simultaneous forms this took in her craft are astounding. Between *Zulma*, started the year of her marriage (1786) and *On the Influence of Passions on the Happiness of Individuals and of Nations* completed ten years later, there had come the *Letters on Jean-Jacques Rousseau*, her fashionable tale *The Madwoman of the Forest of Sénart*, the idealistic *Sophie* and *Jane Gray*, a melancholy story called *Pauline*, the eulogy for her old family friend M. de Guibert, two short plays, the article for the Suard newspaper, letters to Gustave III, finally, as we know, the essay on Marie-Antoinette and the essays on peace. Soon there would come an essay on fiction. The impulse to write held fast throughout. It is inconceivable that during personal and political agitations that were emotionally overwhelming, energy did not seriously fail. She felt committed to one or more of her works concurrently, reading excerpts to her friends even during the heat of writing. In time, both the short monologue on passion, which is *Zulma*, and the long essay on passions anticipated later creativity in the great nonfiction essays and the equally great adventures in fiction.

"*Zulma* belongs to my soul more than any other work.[15] . . . In order to portray love, I have wanted to offer a picture of unhappiness in a person of passionate character. It seemed to me that this would happen with intense energy particularly when the unruly soul concerned had a cultivated mind; the faculty of judgement can alleviate pain, when it has not diminished one's power to feel."[16]

Zulma is doomed to execution for having killed her lover. She presents her own defense before the young man's mother, describing the past self-sacrifice and tenderness of her idyll in the seclusion of a refuge. Fernand had been accused of dealing with enemies of his homeland. Exonerated, he had left for dangerous missions, which his countrymen later glorified, though Zulma experienced pain and anxiety in his absence. Zulma had a premonition of Fernand's death on the battlefield; this would signify her own death. But the forethought had been wrong. Fernand returned, pricked by the enemy's deadly poison. Zulma sucked it away, proud and sure of her love for the man she was curing, not suspecting his attachment elsewhere. She saw Fernand with another woman in the forest, and killed her lover. 'I have lost the identity, the memory of existence,' she laments. Fernand's glorious exploits are still pure, and her heart, she exclaims, is her own defense—her judgment. Though exonerated, Zulma kills herself. 'Had he lived,' she cries, 'his inconstancy would have been justified.' For existing 'so forcefully' in herself, Zulma had to inflict this self-punishment.

Germaine considered publishing *Zulma* along with the *Influences of the Passions,* but she did not do so. Her yearning for conjugal love was strong at the time of writing this work, and she confided her feeling in her *Journal*; however, *Zulma* projected the yearning briskly, if not violently. This may have made her put the story aside, troubled by the clearly autobiographical projection. Nevertheless, her last literary child did not disappoint her readers in 1794. And now, in 1796, she could transfer the analysis of passion from one vehicle to another, from fiction to nonfiction.

At age thirty, Germaine's political trauma, the deep personal anxieties, the recent experience of love and separation from Ribbing shook her creative anima. She reflected while writing. She entertained political visitors like the liberal deputy Charles, Count Lameth, Emmanuel Sieyès whom she had known since adolescent years and who returned her affection by complimenting her on her élan, then the erudite peer-compatriot Benjamin Constant who had come to live with her. Constant's vivacious, skeptical and ironic intellect affected her; she felt encouraged to write with her own impetus, insight and feeling. While richly consistent with her character, these qualities became congenial to her art, as modus vivendi. They were bound to steady her pen within luxuriant avenues.

Germaine had a motive for writing *De l'Influence des Passions*. Calumny had hurt her. Now she felt a need to be judged by her writings. She says so in the foreword written in Lausanne, July 1st, 1796. "One has to reflect on the nature of individual and political happiness.... Let us put aside the monstrous events of the last few years ... for how else can we reconcile a hope for the future with the execration of the past?" She questions the effects of human passions on personal well-being. Passions influence destiny as much as they do political governments. Ranging from love for glory to self-serving excesses and crime, passions are impulsive "forces that thrust man independently from his will. There is the real obstacle to individual and political happiness." The government's problem, Germaine continues, is "to know to what degree it can excite or restrain these passions without compromising public well-being."

What is happiness? "Hope without fear, activity without anxiety, glory without calumny, love without inconstancy, imagination which embellishes, exaltation of that which is moral, good triumphant." Germaine then places the notion of happiness within the wide public context of nations. Governments, whether free republics or "calm" monarchies, can bring happiness thanks to "the emulation of talents, the silence of factions, military spirit abroad and respect for the laws within, all with a view to preventing misfortune and giving proper guarantees of that happiness."[17]

Lovingly, Germaine refers to Montesquieu. She derives from his *Causes of the Greatness and Decadence of the Romans* the idea that nations are raised by their governments as children. Montesquieu inspires her to suggest that a government can affect events for having instilled in its public "a conception of the social order."[18] On this, she adds, depends the destiny of the human race. She does not hesitate to compliment England on its organization of powers, to stress its representative quality and the "public tranquility" dependent on this intelligent combination.[19]

France must continue on, Germaine adds; there is hope thanks to its constitutional accomplishment in spite of its presently tumultuous situation. It has been soiled by intolerant and fanatical beings, but these cannot sway the philosophically minded who are outside France.

Germaine's analysis of passions reaches the rapport between individuals and their governments, starting with the love for glory which was detrimental to cities like Rome, Venice, and Berne. Psychologically perceptive, she then examines ambition, vanity, vengeance, and partisanship. Human nature dialogues with itself during such behaviors, supposedly succeeding for a time and eventually losing. Examples from history are given: kings, cardinals, men and women alike for whom self-interest has destroyed dignity in the very midst of the approbation and envy they have raised. "The acclamations of a crowd move the soul.... Excitement ensuing, the animation of such glory transports one's own hopes and enflames one with emulation."[20] Germaine could not forget the sight of Mirabeau at Versailles, nor that of Robespierre at the Convention.

"Nothing enslaves one more than vanity. In a person's character the combination of this passion with pride causes immeasurable pain . . . particularly among women for whom everything within themselves is either love or vanity. When women are prone to a kind of success in rank and fortune, it can feed their vanity and destroy the dignity of their sex. The true strengths of women come from nature's gifts. But busying themselves with pride and ambition, they destroy the magic of their charms. . . . Committed to such passions, they only animate against themselves the passions of those who only wanted to love them."[21]

Germaine cautions her readers that human beings are wrong to think that all have experienced love. This is the rarest of passions, for "it is the least egoistic." Different from "common affections," it leads to melancholy, and impressions are vague and cheerless. Literature has attempted to present love in all its force, as in *The New Héloïse*, in moments of Racine's *Phèdre*, in parts of Ovid and Ossian, in *Werther* as well, but writers who present love in the guise of voluptuousness, frenzy and a veritable malady "have failed to present this passion truthfully."[22] For Germaine, "here, all is sacrifice, all is the forgetting of oneself in the exalted devotion of love . . . all is kindness." Such an exceptional experience is otherworldly. Death itself is of no consequence.[23]

Having admitted to the melancholic consequences of love, Germaine now addresses the "veritable importance of attachments of the heart,"[24] and this is what men and women must consider. To the writer, this is the ultimate truth of the human situation. Germaine speaks from experience, with respect to her predilections in literature as well, and to history's examples. Concluding wistfully, she transposes her precept of consideration into the nation's domain. Unhappily in 1795, such considerations did not seem to be there even though, ironically, the Convention in May of that year organized a festivity called 'In the name of love' (fête de l'amour).

Irony of a different kind had come from the pen of François de Pange, whose death deeply affected Germaine. Morose and succinct, Pange's statement reproves the Convention for its inability to end the nation's restlessness:

> After five years of misfortune, our public spirit has only acquired three or four ideas. Those of the inconvenience of anarchy, abuses of freedom of the press, the danger of popular clubs, the absolute necessity of protecting our citizens and their dwellings at night. Such is this slow and painful education! [25]

In the summer of 1795 Germaine attempted to re-open her salon, but public criticism made her return to Coppet. Once more, the press spread rumors of a royalist conspiracy. The untruthfulness put Germaine in distress. She still helped friends to safety, but again, thoughts of destiny were her utmost concern. France was fighting abroad, its armies turning to pillage. Peasants, merchants, workers were discontented, schools in disarray. A bureaucracy had risen, rampant dishonesty at its core. It had availed itself of church holdings. As Pange had intimated, the "whole mechanism of socialization" lay broken.[26] And within this ruinous state of affairs, a lost sense of religion, indeed a potential killing of religion the legacy of which could not be but "sanguinary." [27] A hybrid religiousness had appeared. The dark mood of the populace stirred by massive celebrations at the Champ de Mars bred a strange return to primitive beliefs for a time. It had erupted out of fear. It subsided when fear calmed. Sooner or later, people were bound to reach for devotional comfort as a relief from fear.

By the end of the summer of 1795, what remained of the Girondins had regained seats in the Convention, including Sieyès. New committees emerged; schools of higher education opened. Many who considered entering the political arena published their ideas unhesitatingly. Brigadier-general Napoléon Bonaparte wrote to the government, stressing the nation's need for a stable, central authority. In 1795, he was a patriotic republican.

Paris recovered its zest for private festivities. Feminine elegance replenished itself. Juliette Récamier, wife of a prominent banker, opened her salon. Joséphine Tascher, widow of the military viscount of Beauharnais, guillotined in 1794, set the tone for a new taste in fashion—flowing and opaque. Just returned from America, Talleyrand found a niche in the Department of External Affairs, close to the Convention leadership of viscount Barras. The latter, having seen Bonaparte in action at the republican liberation of Toulon, placed the young man in charge of the Convention's defense.

The French armies had reaped victories abroad, but attempts at peace settlements with Prussia, Spain and Holland were failing. At home, the central and southern regions suffered from retributive massacres of Jacobins. Therefore, externally and internally, France was still in danger of regressing. The government ordered the army to act against citizens at the least provocation. In June, Bonaparte entered the War Ministry. But within the dying Convention, antagonisms fluctuated and fed the fear of violence. This has been called the White Terror. Ironically, the poet M. J. Chénier, member of the Convention, distributed three thousand copies of Condorcet's text on human progress.

The time had come to re-examine the Constitution. Two legislative chambers were created—a five-hundred-member council and the Council of Elders (Conseil des Anciens). In October 1795 the Convention died. A new Constitution was declared, and in November the Directoire was established with five leaders, Sieyès at the helm for a time. The event took place at the Luxembourg palace, which Germaine attended. A last insurrection, royalist this time, was quelled by the newly made commander of the Army of the Interior, Bonaparte. Political intrigues proliferated even though the membership was avowedly republican. Across the country, there subsisted disruptive Jacobin elements fearful of a return to privileges. Financial crises ensued. Barras' leadership was plagued by suspicions of embezzlement. His receptions at the Luxembourg attested to newly acquired wealth, which was the case with some other conventionnels. Thirty-two theatres poured out melodramas and romances, cafés opened, vendors, and gambling filled the Palais Royal. Publishing offered romanesque tales that grew in popularity.

In the midst of this flurry, Germaine's *De l'Influence des passions* was criticized for having been too personal. However, some grasped its originality, its input on the variegations of feeling among men and women, thereby its contribution to literature.[28] The relative success of her book may have been instrumental in the removal of her exile in December of 1796. However, Germaine's publisher-friend Roederer felt that her style had too much pathos and that corrections had to be made.

"What is style?" Germaine replied, "is it not the color and movement of the ideas? I do not believe that I lack eloquence, sensibility or imagination. . . . A work that has been thought need not be read like a novel. You mention 'obscurity' . . . I only see that which comes from this word, and not from the nature of the subject and the meditative turn of mind."[28a] Germaine agreed to some corrections. Later editions respected her style and restored the original 'qualities of color and movement.'

Germaine knew of other reactions to those fateful five years, for example J. de Maistre's *Considerations Regarding France* and Louis de Bonald's *Theory of Political and Religious Power*. However, the latter's suggestion that monarchy and Catholicism should be revised went against the grain of Germaine's convictions. She wanted her *De l'Influence* read abroad and asked her parents' Swiss friend J. H. Meister, still director of Grimm's *Correspondance littéraire,* to send her text to the German writers Goethe and Wieland. Goethe returned the compliment by sending her his just published *Apprenticeship of Wilhelm Meister*. Helpful advice came from the family friend and critic Suard. As we know, Germaine had written for his newspaper. Simply and directly, he cautioned her to write with "less tumult of feeling."[29] Here was more than affection for Germaine: Suard's life was endangered during the Terror; he may have been saved by Germaine's opportune warning. 'Tumult of feeling' were harsh words. Germaine's love for love itself and her irrepressible imagination during the experience of love[30] had misled her twice with men whose ambitions and independence rejected the notion of a single attachment.

Her letters to them flowed with such feelings. The pen needed taming. Much as the *Influence* presented a methodical structure, she did not refrain from concluding with her usual patriotic cry. Nevertheless, Suard did not understand Germaine well. Her powers of perception, logic and reflection were immense and steady qualities. She could apply her 'meditative turn of mind' at will. She was bound to prove this in her future writing years.

That Germaine was open to influence is incontestable. This time someone conquered her through her intellect. As we know from one of her letters to Ribbing, she met Benjamin Constant late in 1794 at the home of mutual Swiss friends. At that time republican views had pulled her away from the idea of a constitutional monarchy. Constant's political beliefs had evolved like hers. As with Ribbing, the principle of liberty was uppermost in his mind, but his inclinations were those of a scholar. He had studied in Great Britain and in Germany where he decided to consider entering politics but most definitely, the writing profession. His judgment regarding people and events was perspicacious, his character prone to cynicism. Fluent in English and German, Constant brought to Germaine a perspective attached to his classical education. Whenever the liberation of the individual was discussed, he gave first attention to the element of political power. Constant had attended the Convention sessions, admiring Sieyès and in his conservative manner rallying to the need for order, tempered oratory and the rule of law. At Coppet, he urged Germaine to be less outspoken with her views. While he published articles on republicanism in Suard's newspaper, he nevertheless held contacts with Parisians of every political stance. Perhaps unsure of himself, it seems that he may have been open to more than one political affiliation.

Still, no one could foresee the future. General malaise continued, suspense possibly abetted by the frenzy of festivities, the loosening of mores and hurried acquisitions of wealth. Writers attempted to address the question of the future, whether out of self-interest or consideration for the good of the nation. For some, writing and publishing became a form of escapism. In 1796 M.-J. Chénier wrote a tragedy, *The Nuns of Cambrai* (*Les Religieuses de Cambrai*). Writers with a scientific bent and rooted in the tradition of the Enlightenment continued on, like P. Laplace, whose *System of the World* (*Le système du monde*) (1796) associated the sun with a primitive nebula. Close to Germaine's circle, Madame de Charrière, long an intimate friend of Constant, published a critique of contemporary society entitled *Three Women* (*Trois femmes*). Newspaper articles flourished, notably the *Spectateur du Nord,* for which Germaine's peer Charles de Villers (1765-1815) soon contributed his *Idea on the Destination of Writers having left France and living Abroad* (*Idée sur la destination des hommes de lettres sortis de la France et séjournant à l'étranger*).

At the end of 1796 Germaine was told that she could return to France. She stayed at Benjamin's newly acquired property near Luzarches. Comings and goings fluctuated between his lodgings, her salon in Paris, and Coppet. Her relationship with Constant also fluctuated. His tantrums, her demands for promises and devotion, her frankness and his secretive manner presented a strange contrast with happy, exhilarating dialogues, and noticeably mutual encouragements on writing. In time, with possibly more than just affection, the rapport held for more than twelve years.

One would think that these commotions, not to say emotions and the now continual array of visitors, would interrupt Germaine's writing. This did not happen. One could say that she was as close to her desk as she was to her guests. As the century neared the end, Germaine challenged the infectious malaise. She was now certain of her patriotic, republican feeling. "I am French from the heart, closest to the Republic by my enthusiasm and movement of my blood, by everything that is in me, besides, where can one find one's happiness if not in one's homeland if this be but where one feels and reflects?"[31] Germaine's political certainty never left her, all the more so because she had seen the French nation torn to pieces. The bond was strong; she had been raised in an intellectual ambiance of extraordinary open-mindedness, starting with the presence of Diderot, the impressive and affectionate friend of her parents.

Germaine sent her *De l'Influence* to the new king of Sweden, and requested an improvement in her husband's situation. Eric de Staël had never had a passionate rapport with Germaine. He constantly expressed disapproval of her relations with emigrés, yet he showed a willingness to help her obtain passports for her friends. But through the revolutionary upheavals, he vainly tried to retain his ambassadorial position. The Convention greeted him ceremoniously, but left it up to him to form diplomatic ties abroad, sometimes with near success, sometimes not. Bitter, often ill, and short of funds due to an unruly lifestyle, a number of times he came to Coppet where Necker greeted him affectionately. Germaine wrote a considerable number of letters to Eric, enjoining him to build, then rebuild his failing career. Finally he lost his diplomatic status. In September 1796, Staël stayed at Coppet for an extended visit. Failings were overlooked. The couple reached a pleasant entente.

Having returned to Paris with Eric, Germaine gave birth to her fourth child in June 1797. Eric and Germaine called the little girl Albertine. That Eric was Albertine's father has been open to question. For some, the baby's red hair brought Constant to mind.

Happily, Germaine stayed on in her beloved Paris. In the new year, the word 'exile' vanished from her mind. She participated in Constant's Constitutional Circle, and re-opened her salon. La Fayette's homecoming from the Olmutz prison greatly pleased her. She had participated in bringing about his liberation through her extensive correspondence. Still, all was not well in governmental quarters, nor in rural France. The year 1797 saw a surge in royalist unrest, more danger of enforced changes within a Directoire plagued with antagonisms, and ensuing repression. Germaine observed, listened, conversed, and continued guiding her pen with a 'meditative turn of mind.' However, her friends counselled her not to publish her most recently completed text, or at least not too soon. An adverse wind had swept into the chambers of the Directoire.

> How can we, the first friends of liberty, we who are designated authors of the first Revolution, maintain an equilibrium between the Republic and a recurring monarchy? How can we pride ourselves on being stronger than two fanaticisms? Is it not more reasonable to ally with the Republic . . . to graft onto it justice and humanity, to be better founders than those who made it . . . ? There is a great calling for us now.[32]
>
> Germaine de Staël
> Letter to Alexandre de Lameth
> November 24, 1796

Part Two
TYRANNY

7.

CONFRONTATION

> There are moments when our destiny, either from the bond with society, from obedience to nature, or from its having started to make us what we are, suddenly turns from its first ties, like a river abruptly changing its course. . . .
>
> We authors, small prodigies of a prodigious era, who dare communicate our thoughts to future peoples, we do not know where posterity rests . . .
>
> François René de Chateaubriand
> *Essay on the Revolutions* (*Essai sur les révolutions*), 1797

Writing had become Germaine's full raison d'être when, at the end of 1796, she expressed her anticipation of political action to Alexandre de Lameth. However, beyond the periphery of her enthusiastic self, things were not peaceful. In government circles, elections manifested three potential dangers to the post-revolutionary republic: financial corruption within the Directoire, royalism among the new 'conventionnels', and in the army, Jacobinistic passions prevailing. The young general Bonaparte had embarked on the Italian campaign; at that time he was one with his soldiers in their pro-revolutionary ardor. Germaine's comments to Lameth on fanaticism, he being part of the government, were relevant to the political situation; they reproached the Directoire for not heeding to such dangers.

Yet things were relatively peaceful at and around Germaine's desk. Writing complemented the animation of her salon and her extensive reading; she drew from both with relish and respect. Some of her friends maintained contacts with German writers. With help, she published the *Essay on Fictions* written when attachments to Narbonne and Ribbing disentangled themselves, also when Constant's erudition and that of other guests awakened her cosmopolitan disposition. Germaine sent the essay to Goethe, who complimented her, and promptly translated it.

When Germaine divulged to Lameth her wish to see a place for herself and for her friends in a revitalized republic, she was also nourishing a literary project. The uplifting conversations on literature with François de Pange had become a part of her. At the end of 1796 she began writing *On Literature Considered in Its Relationships with Social Institutions* (*De la littérature considérée dans ses rapports avec les institutions sociales*). Her writing impetus was working in parallel lines: literary criticism on one hand, political criticism on the other. The tenuous situation in the Directoire and its effect on Germaine will be our first consideration.

The shock brought on by more than three years of bloodshed, unhappiness and revolutionary twists and turns were so clear and vivid in Germaine's mind that she was bound to seek explanations if not a judgement concerning the Revolution. Her father and countless other writers did the same. Our generation is doing so today. She too addressed the dying century's malady. She did so in the second text she was advised not to publish, the first having been the *Reflections on Interior Peace* of July 1795. Or else, her friends now cautioned, the Directoire would act severely, not only against herself but to her friends as well. In 1797, government officials, and public opinion in general, considered her a meddlesome political activist. But they did not know her well. Most only glanced at her writing, repeated Staëlean phrases to each other and made these into clichés. They were not sensitive to her particular kind of idealism, warm and unbloodied. Nevertheless, Germaine acquiesced, and put aside her text *Actual Circumstances that can End the Revolution and the Principles that Must Found the French Republic.*

"We, the young, Germaine cried out, "and you, the old, we the weak ones, you, the powerful, which among us would dare claim a state of happiness! . . . The future has no precursor. . . . We err through life as if thrown into a strange element, habits, feelings and hopes, all in confusion. Only pain can help man recognize himself, constant suffering is the only day to day bond."[2] This is not the time for reproaches, the author stated at the outset, nor for apologies. We must unite, and appease, within our country, for no outside force can do this for us. The word "liberty" proves this. In our own circumstances it must be clearly seen that the crimes of the Revolution are not by nature connected with the glorious principles of 1789. Robespierre's reign, Germaine continues, inflicted total inequality through terrorization. It fed on ignorance, loose mores and egoism. But now, how can we project for the future and create an opposite to our society's demise? Somehow, she adds, we must "adapt political equality to man's happiness," we must look at "the immediate consequence of political equality, at the right of every citizen to concur with the formation of his laws. Executive power being delegated, organized legislative power could constitute a pure democracy."[3]

Germaine admits to the difficulties of representation for a country of thirty million, for stability in the institutions where the nation's interest is of the greatest importance. Yet, the capacity of one person to delegate his powers of judgment and even his wisdom to another is the pure point of departure for representative government. What guarantees the protection of this judgment when it is placed in another's hands? The enemy is just those "personal advantages" of the someone else and that are "distinct from those of the nation." The choice of the 'delegated' is crucial. Correct representation respects "the interest and will of the nation," whereas despotism will override these two principles, "neither defending nor listening to them."[4]

On the matter of choice of representatives and their organization, Germaine states that the characteristics of a nation have to be taken into account. Circumstances such as the size of a country, the character of its inhabitants, the size of its army, the need of some nations for gradual input in arts, commerce, tranquility, and the need of others who are ardent and ambitious for stability—these have to be considered. Some nations need frequent elections whereas others, eager to maintain a high political profile, need a strong executive power. In the case of a naturally belligerent nation, the legislative force must be put in evidence.

Some circumstances in the history of nations have caused passions to override reason—the imposition of slavery, religious superstition, hereditary issues. Germaine anticipates that the latter will be abandoned. But "when prejudices fight against one another, war will never end . . . time can exhaust a war, but it can also revitalize one. . . . Considering the progress of the human mind, only a principle can triumph against prejudice. . . . That of equality, magnificent as it appeared in 1789, needed to rest on the nation's morality, particular and public, and this failed to happen."[5]

Germaine's examinations of royalist beliefs, the press, power, the Revolution's laws and Constitution, and what she called political virtues and crimes gave her ample opportunity to address the newly created Directoire. Cautionary as she tried to be during the writing process, she stressed that hatred for prejudice and love for equality had been the Revolution's underlying principles at the beginning and should still be deeply respected. Eagerly she analyzed political ambition and the influence a single individual can have on a populace. Mass psychology was to her a syndrome that she found difficult to reconcile with the basically good nature of human beings. How can one evil person, she asks, sway a large number of citizens into approving his murderous directives? Robespierre was still very much on Germaine's mind. Her interest in national differences of circumstance is a Voltairean characteristic. It is also a precursor of the psychology of national politics, as it was in Voltaire. More than this, Germaine's consideration that different nations have differing leadership needs has the quality of modern political science. Even so, the tone is Voltairean, starting with the hatred of fanaticism born from prejudice. But the vocabulary is Germaine's. She did not say, for instance, "political strengths and weaknesses" but "political virtues and crimes." Her language is moral; eagerly, she lifts examples from history, and speaks with the voice of Condorcet when appealing to the progress of a nation's spirit since the day of the first printing press.

Racine, Voltaire, the Greeks and Latins are the gods "whom nothing can tarnish." Poor taste is at the gates, however; it can trample imagination with "a daring that would make virtue itself blush."[6] Writers owe their nation a service. In fact, they possess much more than this. They have strengths that guarantee their being its intellectual leaders.

The 'power of reason' is the last section of Germaine's text. There again, her verbs are colorful and vivacious, just as she must have been in conversation. Except for the opening pages, this lengthy work is disciplined and definitely without "a tumult of feeling." This happened with one exception. Germaine gave in to anger on the subject of the press, and castigated it for its outrageously unjust and vicious calumnies. Aside from this, her discipline indicated a psychological realism congenial to her old sense of logic and quality of perceptivity as a writer. Her old respect for Montesquieu is visible: he insisted on our looking at circumstances in terms of their "actuality" rather than as absolute concepts. This has been pointed out by the scholar Lucia Omacini in her recent introduction to the *Circonstances*.[6a] Altogether then, Germaine's composure and quiet certitude based on her old gods and solid rationale held strong.

Germaine considered herself a political leader only in the intellectual sense. She believed in reformulating the Republic in terms of the principle of liberty as she saw it, as Condorcet had seen it. She yearned for this, as her text showed. With her, thought and feeling were always interchangeably earnest and ardent. Her doubly energetic presence attested to this. It troubled those who were placed—or had placed themselves—in high political echelons. In December of 1797 a new, energetic presence in both the Directoire and the Paris salons attested to fortuitous circumstances totally unlike Germaine's.

After his victorious Italian military campaign, the thirty-year-old Napoléon Bonaparte had every reason to be proud. Hard work, recognition of his talents, military strategy and courage had brought him to that point in time. Pride was natural to him. At age twelve a letter to his father, Charles Bonaparte, is evidence of this. He demanded better financial support at the Brienne Military Academy; his business acumen was devoid of emotional dependence, for he explained that he desired a better standing among fellow students. Not from a need to spend, he said, "but from a need to show that I have means, no matter what.... No, father, no. If this cannot be, take me out of Brienne, give me a training in mechanics." He expressed weariness from the insults of schoolboys whose fortune was their only advantage over him. They, he added, "are not up to the noble sentiments that animate me...."[7]

His family had come to Corsica from Tuscany. It had some claim to nobility but was poor. For the second son and his twelve siblings, the future was uncertain. Corsica had just been annexed by France at the time of Napoléon's birth in 1769. There were signs of political unrest. Napoléon was sent to military school in France with the help of a family friend. He became artillery lieutenant at age sixteen. Writing a history of Corsica, he longed to return home, nostalgic for the carefree childhood years. He was an expressive adolescent, with melancholic echoes of Rousseau:

> As I am starting to experience unhappiness, nothing is a pleasure for me, nothing is prosperous.... What shall I find in my country, where my compatriots tremble?... You have not only taken our island, you have corrupted our mores![8]

Napoléon graduated from the Paris military school at seventeen. At nineteen, he was made bitter by General Paoli's failure to liberate Corsica. His country was now disdained, and overburdened with taxes. This, he said, "is the most cruel torture for a people who have sentiment at heart."[9]

An avid reader enamored at first by the writings of Rousseau, then *Ossian* and *Werther*, Napoléon was often solitary and generally silent in society. He showed strength in mathematics. Wherever he was posted as a military, he sensed restlessness. From his perspective the egoistic society seemed confused, even though spectacles and books exuded at the time a semblance of sociability. Patriotic, idealistic at the time, he took military leaves to return home but felt disillusioned over the island's state of oppression.

Stationed with his regiment at Auxonne in 1788, he reflected on his situation as a military in France. At twenty, on August 23rd, 1789, he took the oath of fidelity "to the Nation, King and Law"[10] and gave his signature at the opening of the General Assembly. A year later he expressed his "adhesion to the revolutionary principles."[11] He had become a republican. At that time the Lyon Academy opened a pedagogical contest: if taught, it said, which truths and sentiments can best lead to happiness? Napoléon responded: "Happiness is not compatible with violent passion which destroys sentiment and natural reason . . . ambition, this immoderate desire to satisfy conceit, for being disorderly . . . only dies with life, having consumed it."[12] The Academy did not grant a prize that year.

Napoléon still gave moral support to his Corsican compatriots, particularly during his leaves of 1791 and 1792. However, events precluded other returns home until later. He witnessed crowd silences, and massive rituals such as the celebration of the 'Supreme Being.' He saw religion's transformation into a political instrument. Worship was dying. No one had foreseen the gigantic gatherings at the Champ de Mars and the festivities held in churches where pseudo-religious sentiment mixed with patriotic frenzy. Soon came the roaring approvals of inflamed oratory in the persons of Danton, Marat, Robespierre, and Saint-Just. Paris was shedding blood; violence was spreading into the provinces. A young military like Bonaparte could not but feel the urgent need for order in the streets and within the argumentative Assembly. Self-interest and hot-headedness were rife. In May 1792 he was sent to Paris from his garrison in Valence. Three months later he assisted in the taking of the Tuileries.

Always an avid reader, Napoléon was aware of the change in mood in the world of publication. Works that had flourished before the Terror exuded optimistic ideas of reform, for example from A. de Lavoisier, L.-S. Mercier and Sénac de Meilhan.[13] Some had looked outwardly, like C. Volney in *Travels in Egypt*, but now, while manners were loosening, sentimental novels appeared, like Bernardin de Saint-Pierre's *Paul et Virginie*. Escapism spelled distress.

Perhaps the most unsettling realization where Napoléon was concerned was the disintegration of the French army and consequently France's weakened military status. The emigration of aristocrats opened high-level military positions at home, moreover, military émigrés posed a danger to France; they had gone off to enemy troops. Soon, danger faced France from forces concentrated just outside its borders following the European Coalition's Treaty of Pilnitz in 1791. European armies had grown; fear of foreign attacks became a general obsession. Germaine's *Reflections on Peace* addressed to the young English Prime Minister William Pitt exemplified this fear.

When Napoléon took a fifth leave for Corsica, events affecting him personally drew him away from the island forever. The end of his support for General Paoli forced a quick departure, in fact, an escape with his family. In June 1793 the Bonapartes moved to Toulon. That same month the Montagnard insurrection gave Robespierre full power in the Convention. "Citoyens!" he shouted, "Stay firm! The dangers of our country are making your stand a supreme law!"[14] Robespierre's intention to raise a large French army was soon put into action. A million men were enrolled. It was then that Bonaparte saw the English siege of the port of Toulon. He went to Paris, met members of the Comité du Salut Public and obtained the artillery command against the siege. Barras, then in charge of the Mediterranean front, witnessed Bonaparte's quick success. He promoted him to brigadier-general. He had discovered the unmistakable qualities of military leadership: perspicacity, precision, steadfastness.[15]

Napoléon's ascent continued. In the spring of 1794 the success of the French armies signaled a war that would engulf a full generation of men. At home the brutal hysteria of execution ended with the deaths of Robespierre and Saint-Just. Many who had been sent on military missions were arrested, including Bonaparte. He was soon freed for having been promoted general of the army of the west. He opted to work in the War Ministry in Paris where the bureau of topography fascinated him. Then in October 1795 he helped defeat the royalist insurrection against the Convention. As this had been in response to Barras's request, he became chief general of the army of the interior.

Bonaparte's marriage to Joséphine de Beauharnais took place in March 1796. Soon after, as commander-in-chief of the army of Italy, he led prodigious victories—Montenotte, Rivoli, and the capitulation of

Mantua after the triumphant entry into Milan. For many years the names Lodi, Castiglione, Bassano and Arcole would ring in French citizens' ears and sustain their patriotism. His proclamations rang in his armies' ears:

> Soldiers! I know that you are deeply affected by the misfortunes threatening our homeland. But it will not run into real danger. The same men who have made it triumph against the European Coalition are with us. As we stand now, mountains separate us from France, but you will reach the other side with the rapidity of eagles to uphold the Constitution, defend Liberty and protect the government and the republicans.[16]

Bonaparte was proud of his men, he knew how to speak to them and with tenacious oratory share his triumphs with them. He never forgot those field battles and the glorious ceremonies of enemy surrenders—arms, standards and all. He was sensitive if not in a soldiery closeness to his armies' feelings for him. "I have been greeted by the army with demonstrations of joy and confidence," he wrote to the Directoire, "and one which I hope to have deserved in your eyes as well."[17]

The situation in the Directoire was far from glorious. Candidates vying for positions brought constant changes, depending on the ever-mobile polarization of political stances. Elsewhere, the peasants and laborers were poor, many refusing to join the army. Brigands banded on the roads. England's commercial blockade and its aid to royalists as well as Austrian intelligence added to the Directoire's harassments. Surveying the frontiers, Barras gave Bonaparte the command of the army of the Rhine. The attempted treaty of Loeben with Austria failed. Military pillage festered. In Paris, signs of fresh, immense personal wealth were in evidence, and as we know among members of the government. Lavish lifestyles emerged.

A different France appeared, with hunger and dissatisfaction on one side, a greedy race for acquisitions on the other, and monarchists in between, attempting a return to power. Salons came alive, at Germaine and Constant's Club Constitutionnel where Talleyrand met Benjamin Constant, Sieyès attending, as well as some of Bonaparte's generals like Jean-Baptiste Kléber (1753-1800). Around them, in such a dislocated society, an organized police intelligence was born.

Torn by factions left and right, the Directoire turned to the army for continued protection. The middle political strata of monarchists gradually solidified. It proclaimed a moderate stand but demanded better professionalism in the government, better finances, a return to religious ritual, and the eradication of thievery. But not all of these monarchists were moderates. Germaine's Club disliked the extreme monarchists even though she agreed on the need for those reforms.

As we know, Germaine had come to Paris from Coppet in mid-1797, after the birth of Albertine. She glowed with the success of *De l'Influence*. As always, she thoroughly enjoyed the stimulation and support of her intellectual friends. A correspondent asked her how she felt about her situation in France. She was angry, she replied, because of constant accusations against her of involvements with royalist emigrés. With Talleyrand, for instance, though she considered him a friend, she did not completely trust him. Until his impending appointment as foreign secretary, he had depended on her for financial support, but this was not an important factor in her rapport with him. Germaine was generous with all her friends. Much as she had been close to him during her self-exile in Surrey and before his journey to America, now she discerned through his prodigious activity, including his attendance at royalist meetings, a lack of principle. His conversational charm made her breathless in his presence, but now she became wary of his presence, as she did in fact of Barras. Talleyrand, Barras, and all who came in her salon unanimously admired her intellect, her drive, warmth, and inspiring manner equal to a "brilliant intelligence."[18] But politically, there were cautious opinions of her.

In Germaine's personal life, these were relatively peaceful months, thanks in part to Benjamin who helped her in the many daily activities and contacts. In return, she urged him to form a republican party, at least, she suggested, to address the Directoire. He did so, with a speech on *The Tree of Liberty*. Together, they attended government sessions at the Luxembourg and supported changes that followed moderate views. Benjamin was at his desk as much as she. His *Reactions and Effects of the Terror* is thought to have been written with Germaine. The call is for a forceful, stable government in the face of current arbitrariness and confusion. The nation's institutions and interests had to be re-examined. The idea of equality had erupted, Constant argued, but it had become unfamiliar now and needed to be addressed accordingly.[19]

Constant's complex personality disturbed Germaine. He was tortured by hesitations in love. Gambling made him lean on her financially and this harmed the relationship, particularly later, when Germaine wanted his help in establishing a dowry for Albertine. Yet, above discord, Germaine respected Constant's knowledge, his intellect, and she had certain powers over him. After barely four months of intimacy with Constant, Germaine exacted a written promise of loyalty, and made it mutual:

> We promise to devote our lives to each other, we declare that we consider ourselves bound indissolubly, that our destiny in all respects is one, that we will not form other attachments, and shall strengthen those that bind us, in our power to do so.[20]

Official, as in a marriage contract, the tone was firm though emotional, and based not on passionate love but on a passionate understanding unlike any of its kind. One can sense Germaine's desire for trust, moreover, pathos in her wish to cast away past disillusions. Imperiousness permeated this contract; it reflected her character.

Germaine was not easy to live with. Ever sensitive to criticism, she was most upset on hearing that some considered her unstable in her political affiliations. As someone said, "No sooner has she opted for one direction that she changes it in order to help a friend . . . she is too much a woman . . . too kind to be political."[21] The criticism was harsh and showed a poor understanding of her republicanism, including the statement that for her 'things' mattered more than persons. But the comment reverberated in the press. Accusations of intrigue multiplied; they reached the ears of Barras and of his entourage, that is, Bonaparte. Germaine suffered from the press attacks, not realizing for a time how far the reverberations would go, and could go. Yet she was determined to work at conciliating opponents, verbally and in writing. This was her political manner of being. Danger lay in her pushing this too far.

Basically, there was no complexity in Germaine's character as such. Loyal, confident, persuasive, energetic, and of course enthusiastic, this was the Germaine intimate friends knew. Her cousin and childhood friend Madame Necker de Saussure describes Germaine's gloom and boredom for being "made" to live away from Paris, one of her incessant needs being "intellectual activity."[22] With those whom she loved, except with Necker whom she revered, Germaine could be overbearing.[23] She sympathized with Necker in his loneliness, and his disappointment when the press cruelly commented on his text on the French Revolution. Her respect for him never wavered, even when he scolded her for her lavish expenses though he, secretly, helped both Eric and Benjamin with occasional financial help. Germaine and Necker were amused to hear that Bonaparte, sitting near the Egyptian pyramids, was reading *De l'Influence des passions.*

In her manner with men, Germaine may have acted on a strategy, at least it seemed so initially. From what we have seen of her rapport with Benjamin and previously with Ribbing and even Narbonne, her brilliant captivating conversation led to her emotional hold on her lovers. This disoriented them. If there was a conscious pattern of behavior, which some of the love letters imply, Germaine's later soul-searching may have confirmed it in her private judgment; not ours.

In late 1797, Germaine had a change of mind concerning her function as a writer, and accordingly, her publishing ventures. Abruptly, the parallel lines of literary and political criticism broke. Her political publishing activity ceased for an indefinite period, not that the impetus vanished from her salon and from communication with friends, in fact, on the contrary. That which did not flow in the public arena continued pouring in private letters. But politically speaking, the pen's public performance quietened. In print, the bifurcation became the following: temporarily silenced politics on one hand, and on the other, increasing and flourishing literary criticism and fiction. But the literary thrust hid a private subterfuge: protected from censure for over a decade, Germaine's pen interspersed political dreams, appeals and substances directly involving political principle within works of literary nonfiction and fiction itself, if not at their very heart. Coming from an essentially political person, nearly every stroke of the pen pointed to the political subterfuge. This happened in *Delphine, Corinne, On Germany*, and in *Ten Years in Exile*. In Germaine's masterful last work, *Considerations on the French Revolution*, the bifurcation closed ranks.

While Germaine's resounding name provoked press attacks and the unpleasant innuendo of caution in late 1797, the Directoire's need to repress the royalist faction had caught Bonaparte's attention. Corresponding with Talleyrand, he opined that the rightist press should indeed be suppressed and much of the administration regrouped. This attention was his mental entry into politics. On the government's part, profound gratitude flowed in his direction. When General Louis Berthier of the Grande Armée and the mathematician Gaspard Monge presented Bonaparte's signed Campo Formio Treaty of October to the governing body, the compliment highlighted the young general's strength. It specified that "true glory arouses the nation's gratitude."[24] Realistic and suave, the forty-four-year-old Talleyrand, now minister for foreign affairs, perceived Bonaparte's interest in politics. Yes, he wrote to Bonaparte, the recent repression of royalists "has cleaned the Directoire enough for us to feel that if the Constitution has been abandoned momentarily, we have returned to it once and for all, I trust."[25] The "once and for all, I trust" had to be held tightly. Bonaparte's relationship with Talleyrand and Barras was valuable to all concerned. Also, there was absolutely no doubt in anyone's mind that the twenty-eight- year-old military leader was the national hero of the day. The Republic would be safe in his hands. That is what every republican felt. When Bonaparte returned to Paris from the field on December 5, 1797, his first visit was to Talleyrand. The latter held a lavish reception for him five days later. Baroness de Staël-Holstein was present.

The event of December 10 was elegant, glittering with jewelry, color and candelabras. Germaine was full of animation, admiring, and like everyone else, curious. Her wide beautiful eyes were bright with the desire to please. This was the essential social Germaine, as in Jean-Baptiste Isabey's pencil portrait drawn that same year—with long, powdered curls, the open neckline and flowing gown. But neither time nor place allowed a conversational prelude to captivity. Her reputation prevented capture. She felt Bonaparte's reluctance to engage in conversation, to establish a preliminary rapport.

She well knew how and why the Directoire refused to give her their trust. But in her participation in the government's and society's concerted welcome to Bonaparte, she could not but allow her admiration of him to hold long enough for her to say, two years later, that he was "worth an army . . . his destiny is invincible!"[26] Admiration held long and deep with Germaine.

For Napoléon, destiny widened the military field deep into the European continent and later beyond its limits. The gates of the political arena were ready to open. He was poised, just on the edge of the Directoire's decisionmaking. When they met, both he and Germaine shared republican ideals. His altered, then vanished, while his attitude toward her hardened. Her republicanism kept its solidity thanks to her passionate belief in the principle of liberty. Undoubtedly, for all to see at Talleyrand's reception, here were two forceful beings, high in intelligence, extraordinarily talented and energetic, moreover still young in age. Germaine was poised, also. Maintaining an idealistic republicanism that no one could ever touch, particularly before an ambitious, realistic, and determined predator, she was ready to embark on the long and arduous journey that led her to the masterpieces of her oeuvre.

> . . . What is needed is a just mean, which in France is nothing but a passing so rapid that it barely serves as a transition from one excess to another. . . .[27]
>
> Germaine de Staël
> Letter to J. H. Meister, April 22, 1797

8.
IN THE COMPANY OF GODS

> When one writes to satisfy the soul's inner inspiration, one divulges . . . even unwittingly, every fiber of one's being and thought.[1]
> Albert Sorel, *Madame de Staël*, 1907

By the year 1795, Madame de Staël had set the precedent for lively intellectual give-and-take among her guests at Coppet. She enjoyed this to the full. She also had the talent of creating for her friends and herself the ambiance needed for serious writing. She orchestrated conversations that led to this on schedule and in the comfortable seclusion offered to all.

A visitor to Coppet described Germaine's evenings at the time of her writing *De la littérature dans ses rapports avec la société et ses institutions sociales*. Discussion centered on certain aspects of the text being written. The visitor named four examples: the influence of Christianism on literature; *Ossian*'s influence on northern poetry; the poetry of the north and its dreaminess; poetry of the 'midi' and its sensuousness.[2] The next morning, Germaine was at her desk in self-imposed confinement.

Until 1801, writing became for Germaine an oasis of literary criticism, a revitalization as it were of the creativity that had dominated her *Letters on the Writings and Character of Jean-Jacques Rousseau*. During that earlier period Germaine's style was airy and quick, if not impatient. It has been compared with her own "tumultuous manner of thinking."[3] Fifteen years separate the *Letters* from *L'Essai sur les fictions*, the latter being Germaine's first formal piece of literary criticism and preceding *De la littérature* by only a few years. At that point Germaine was reaching for inner inspiration. Her style flowed accordingly.

The world outside, the 'entire universe', as Germaine called it in her *Fictions*, was far from calm. It did not invite the peacefulness condusive to writing. The Directoire's increasing malevolence toward Germaine and the recent imposition of a momentary exile from France caused her much anxiety. This was not the only cause for worry. Unusually sensitive to signs of political fanaticism, Germaine grasped the degree to which renewed royalism agitated against the government's dictatorial repression. She observed the political scene with trepidation and puzzlement. The first connected with the fear of repeated orders of exile. Bonaparte's presence impacted surprise on the new stage of events, hence Germaine's puzzlement. Alert, questioning, she nevertheless kept to her decision to keep her distance from political writing and write in another genre. Against fatigues of coach travel to and fro Paris, toothaches, frustration and boredom from being away from Paris, Germaine's energies replenished. Her decision brought her to that oasis. It already sheltered the essay on fictions, and in 1800 it bore fruit with Germaine's text on literature.

The *Fictions*, written in 1794 and published in 1795, came before Germaine's intended separation from political writing. But it is not a political piece. Germaine did not work in a linear manner. Different genres intermixed, as we have already seen. The *Fictions* had probably long been on her mind and were therefore something apart from the pen's political concerns. However, one can say that the *Essai sur les fictions* prefaces the wide literary output of ensuing years in non-fiction and fiction.

According to Germaine, fictions are either creations of fantasy (le merveilleux) and allegory, or they are historical, or invented if not imitations where nothing is true yet resembling reality (où tout est vraisemblable). The first offer amusement. They do not seriously capture "the motions of the heart (la seule peinture des mouvements du coeur) or a character's ultimate power (la toute-puissance du caractère)." Nor does the marvelous provide an "impact of expressed feelings (l'impression des sentiments)."[4] Germaine is against the play of hazard. Granted, she adds, there are exceptional beauties in ancient literature, for example, Milton's depiction of Satan who is a reality—a man. She finds that the Greek hero Achille has character, but the imaginary opens itself to exaggeration. Why add to the beauty that we find in reality, including virtue's own beauty? Moreover, some literary strategies harm the thought process, and allegories can impede the understanding of ideas. Qualities of thought like finesse and subtlety stand above imagery and should be let free "to bring out a moral truth (faire ressortir une vérité morale)." Without this, "the picture (tableau) has no dramatic effect."[5]

Germaine wearied of Fénelon's *Télémaque* and Spenser's *Fairie Queen*, though she loved them for their poetic beauty. When one has to struggle through prolonged allegories, she writes, "one tires and barely manages to comprehend their philosophical sense . . . (On arrive à la fin tellement fatigué de la partie romanesque . . . qu'on n'a plus la force d'en comprendre le sens philosophique)."[6]

Whatever the genre, fiction can produce an "absolute" effect only when it contains "in itself alone that which gives the reader a complete impression."[7] In historical fiction, when tableaus depict heroism, the enlargement of the subject does not disfigure it; morality is intact. But in the final analysis, feelings are what matter most. Such motions change, early impressions of pure relationships are forgotten. In other words, attachments go toward different objects, they become other passions. Writers must seek these out and "extend the subjects of their novels to those new affects (c'est à ces nouveaux intérêts qu'il faudrait étendre les sujets des romans)."[8] While history does not explain private passions like ambition, pride and vanity, nevertheless it must reach into inner feelings and reveal such motions. Then, through fiction, it can incite to action.

Germaine considers that the world of fiction in an empire, with imagination as its source. This is how she projects forcefulness into her subject. Charm, seduction, these are powers congenial to the fiction writer's talent, but, Germaine specifies, the writer has a far greater responsibility. At best, the latter equals the writer's deeper powers. This is Germaine's argument for the moralizing potential of fiction. Whichever category or class fiction belongs to, its moral utility is of utmost importance.

The language of Germaine's argument is steady. It is also flecked with images unusually sensory and realistic. For example, when she brings the concept of happiness into her picture early in the essay, a satisfying simile arises. Happiness is vague, it does not lend itself to examination. This would destroy the concept, just as "the brilliant images formed in vaporous light disappear the moment one traverses them."[9]

Steadiness also supports recurring and salient references to virtue. Because virtue has its own beauty, there is no need to adorn it. Finesse and subtlety of thought are sufficient. Thought is the writer's tool. This gives his writing the desired dramatic quality. Respect for ease during the reading experience should apply. A reader's energy has its limit. Comprehension needs that ease once the first impression has been made, the movement of impressions from one to the other being free and thereby allowing inner feelings to be found out.

Germaine's argument never leaves the notion of virtue, that is, depicted virtue. She proposes a connection between thought and feeling in this depiction. For her, this is fiction as it should be. She admits to the mobility of feelings. She urges writers of fiction to pay attention to this, to make the effort to reveal feelings in their innermost spaces. This revealing is exactly that which will make fiction incite to action. Thus the argument supports the initial premise that fiction is an empire, and virtue is its rule. The arrival at active virtue is Germaine's political subterfuge. Much as it is quietly expressed at the end of a logical argument, it is climactic.

Germaine perceptively encourages the writer seeking near-reality in fiction. Children, she writes, "already know" the irregularities of reality.[10] Her remark concerning a reader's satisfaction is also psychologically sound: "when feelings depicted are completely natural, the reader believes that the writer is addressing him personally."[10] Thus the moralistic tone is softened and devoid of pedagogical 'inconvenience'. In the masterful novels of Richardson and Fielding, she adds, life is shown as it is in reality thanks to "an exact following of the gradations, developments, and inconsequences of the story of human nature even though the events are invented."[10] For Germaine, an author's constant return to virtue's 'advantages' allows that personal impression to be made.

Germaine's give-and-take in the writer-reader rapport came as a relatively new offering to the French reading public, particularly in the manner of her argument. Courses on literature like La Harpe's were published in 1799. In Germany there followed J. G. Herder's *Letters for the Furtherance of Humanity*, Jean Paul Richter's essays on imagination, and soon, Augustus W. Schlegel's lectures on literature and art. Schlegel (1767-1845) had founded with his brother Friedrich (1772-1822) the *Athenaüm* review. Its non-judgemental policy caught Germaine's attention via her German friends. But she wanted more than open-mindedness. For any author, literary edification had to be supplemented with knowledge of one's function in society 'as' author. Because this was the final point of her brief essay, Germaine was bound to propose a vision of literature's own proper function.

Germaine did not forget to focus on the 'take' element of the writer-reader rapport. With an original stroke of the pen, she paid a melancholic tribute to the 'good' book. It is "a restful, pleasant retreat from vain efforts against deception, when, far away, the entire universe is troubled. . . . But here, a tender and eloquent piece of writing stays nearby like the most faithful and understanding friend. Such a book serves the best part of human beings."[11]

How had writers of the past fared in this respect? The question came most naturally to Germaine. She was bound to identify other deities who have given such friends to succeeding generations, and reflect on their performance.

The essay that so pleased Goethe had resounding effects. Starting with *Hermann und Dorothea* (1797), wherein the German poet depicted heroism within the category of historical fiction, *Sur les Fictions* has had a long life. Stendhal's writings on sentiment and his novels became a realistic echo of Germaine's treatise. Generations of nineteenth-century and twentieth-century novels fluctuated from and beyond her innovative thrust.

In 1800, Germaine embarked with zest on her *Literature in Its Relation to Society's Institutions*. Significantly, she chose the following epigraph for the first edition's title page: "The memory of times passed, their comparison with my present state, everything elevated my heart to lofty notions."[12] This was taken from count Volney's *Ruins or Meditations on the Revolution of Empires* (1791). The "elevation of the heart" subsisted, having come from the essay on fictions and carrying the notion of responsibility. Now, the political thrust is overt, purely and simply.

What a republic of letters should be and republicanism itself intermingle in this work. Just as literature has the duty of "indicating the important qualities that the republic can one day expect to see in her citizens, no matter who they are,"[13] so the government has the duty of "directing that irresistible force caused in human beings by their moral nature, just as within their physical nature there exists the principle of motion."[14] Intellectual progress has been slow, though continual. To Germaine, the virtue of pity, feelings for glory, liberty, then intellectual beauty and happiness are just those powers that literature can capture. Impressed, the reader can therefore perfect himself, for "human nature is serious."[15] There are pitfalls. A people may collapse from an enlightened state into a period of uncertainty, "the Hades of the lukewarm,"[16] as Dante put it, and one in which admiration has vanished. Old prejudices and factious tyranny can strike at literature's capacity to "paint the soul's energy in its entirety."[17] This is Germaine's elaboration of the phrase 'the complete impression' in *Les Fictions*. But pitfalls can affect literature along the historical path.

The most ancient Greek literature, she explains, captured nature in its confounding energies, catastrophies, and human contrasts. In those far-away ages heroic beings and gods met within splendid imagery. With Homer, language became music and poetry all in one, resplendent with nature. Friendship in love (l'amitié dans l'amour) was not visible here. With Aeschylus and his peers, the duty was to impress masses of spectators with godly powers and their terrifying forces. If anything softer than calamity came on stage, Germaine opines, it took the form of mythological dreams; still, everything on and outside such spectacles depended on the will of the gods (la volonté des dieux). Superstition, a grotesque fear of the unknown (l'inconnu et l'inexplicable), held introspection at bay. Nevertheless, the Greeks gave our world vivid literary and artistic impulses. Equally unforgettable are the analyses by Aristotle and those of the Greek historians who opened the vistas of human knowledge.

Intimate sentiment, reflection, and patriotic devotion (ce sentiment intime, cette volonté réfléchie . . . ce dévouement patriotique)[18] rather came with Roman literature. Thus Germaine sharply delineates the Romans from the Greeks. To her, each nation had its cultural character. The Romans were consistently willful, realistic, evaluative of ideas, solemn and dignified, whereas the Greeks were enthusiastic, high-spirited, talent-oriented and jealous of their reputation. Stoïcs and Epicureans left a philosophical legacy. With Virgil, Horace and Ovid, sensitivity illuminated the stage.

While Germaine respects national characteristics and describes them, she honors specific authors. To her, Tacitus and later Shakespeare, Montesquieu, Voltaire, and Rousseau speak for themselves, each a deity of his own. She brings into relief how they reacted to the political and religious pressures affecting their societies and themselves, each in his particular era. With some authors Germaine is comfortable, as with old friends like Seneca, who according to her penetrated further into the heart of man (il pénètre plus avant dans le coeur de l'homme). She also has a predilection for monastic and northern writers, the latter being particularly attractive to her because of their melancholy and sadness. Though frank about her tastes, Germaine is mindful of her initial search, as one commentator has said, for "the literary accomplishment of a complete impression of the movements of the heart. At the same time she maintains a belief that human reflection inherits time (la réflection hérite du temps)."[19] Logically, she supports the ideal of perfectibility, particularly as it looks toward the future:

> If Bacon, Machiavelli and Montaigne have ideas and a knowledge infinitely superior to those of Pliny [and] Marcus Aurelius . . . is it not evident that human reason has progressed during the interval separating the lives of these great writers? The most remarkable genius never rises above the enlightenment of his century, he only does so to a degree.[20]

Looking at her world, however, Germaine laments on the situation of human reason. The Revolution has sickened it. One cannot escape from such a realization, from this happening, its execrable misdeeds (ces forfaits exécrables)[21], the despotism that preyed on superstition, sullied morality and cut short the Republic's young achievements. Her lament is possibly the most personal of her political statements so far. She cannot put away memories of the Terror. Moreover, the romantic notion of destiny plays a part in her reaction to the despotism that in the person of Robespierre literally strangled the young republic. For having killed so many and having fatally stung even the tenderest of beings, Condorcet and young poets like André Chénier, revolutionary fanaticism muddied the path of a perfect destiny.

But still, seeking consolation from the reality of the Terror, Germaine wishes to comfort her readers. The legacy of European literature is perennial and refreshingly variable. With an innovative turn of mind, Germaine invites philosophical interpretations of the human capacity to feel. A history of love, for example, should be based on what the writer has experienced (de ce qu'éprouve l'écrivain qui l'exprime). Feeling finds different expressions in different countries. What may seem bizarre to one nation is of natural interest to another; imagination, language, and climate all bearing on this. That which binds men and women—courage versus weakness in Shakespeare's *Othello,* for instance—withstands analysis from the same comparative vantage. An author like Shakespeare may portray madness (quand la tempête de la vie surpasse ses forces)[22] partly from osmosis or from vaguely distant, gross and ferocious eras somehow connected with him; another, solitude and the countryside, with its meditative impact. So may tranquil domesticity be portrayed, as in parts of English literature; or elsewhere, sensibility exacerbated by the torments of passion, as in Goethe's *Werther.* Here, eloquence is German literature's richest literary characteristic.

Characteristics abound. Among French writers, reflections concerning the need to please are abundant. To a certain extent this has blocked serious thought, yet superficiality has met its challenge with Jean Racine (1639-1699). His cult of moral beauty is unsurpassed in eloquence and poetic perfection. Voltaire's witticisms against prejudice, ignorance and superstition are invaluable sources of emulation, so is Montesquieu's engendering of a political science per se. Should the study of society reach "the certitude of a science one day," Germaine adds, "in its principles and application, the first steps will have been taken by Montesquieu."[22a] Her exploration takes a tangential path: she contrasts French literature with northern, eastern and southern literatures, but returns to Voltaire's dramatic poetry where, from her general perspective, even elegance is secondary to the quality of universality. Voltaire's poetry reminds us of our commonality, and affects us accordingly. His prose has a pervasive influence of its own in the domain of philosopohy: "When philosophy progresses, everything marches along with it."[23]

It can be said that to a degree Germaine's text anticipates comparative literature, but for the time being mainly through her veneration of Voltaire. She respects his forays into English thought and his appreciation of the same. Her exploration of English letters is more source-oriented, particularly on the subject of Shakespeare. When she glances back at the homeland, the tone is neither ironic nor critical, but rather affectionate, and concerned. Hers is a personal, emotional journey.

The 'here and now' of literary creativity and its connection with experience are as important to Germaine as traditional values, perhaps even more so. In this sense she continues on where Voltaire left off, respecting the circumstances and needs of her time. Because her manner is frank and assertive, the 'here and now' is political. Segments on literary figures are interjected with statements like the following: "Only in a free political state can one unite the genius of action to that of thought."[23a]

The periphery of Germaine's exploration is mobile. Subjects in Part II of the text, for example, are an enlargement of social institutions to the point of becoming thematic. Emulation and eloquence are two themes in themselves. They are favored subjects. The third is the situation of women writers. All three will be treated extensively in later works, but here, the first impulse is strong. The 'here and now' projects an outright, general claim: "the existence of women in society is still uncertain. . . ." Narrowing her claim in order to consider women as writers, Germaine allows that women's education might improve, but for the moment, she argues, women writers are "neither in the natural order nor in that of society" so that their attempted ascendancy reaps criticism if not oppression. Germaine raises a question she will attempt to answer later: as men seem to forgive women's lapses in domestic duty, they do not forgive a woman who attracts attention with "a distinguishing talent." This is a "singular problem." Why then are they content to be with women of less than high intelligence and talent?

The tone is not ironic. It is deeply serious. Germaine does not rest her claim. Rather looking at the Revolution's social consequences, she laments that contrary to the respected accomplishments of women in past history—their humanity, generosity, and "delicatesse," post-revolutionary society fails toward women by blocking pleasantness and wit, filling itself with mediocrity and mindlessness. Germaine is motivated by what she has seen—the loosening of mores, youth's idleness, avidity for pleasure and wealth among the older generation. Nevertheless, because she believes in perfectibility, she proposes a guideline for the future:

> To enlighten, to instruct, to seek perfection in both women and men, nations and individuals, this is still the best secret of all reasonable aims, for all social and political relations if we wish to assure a durable foundation.[23b]

Germaine's guideline is characteristic of her consideration for the future. At the same time, her choices of particular authors reflect the development of her personality. They are the mirrors of her youth, adolescence and young maturity. All the eclectic stimuli are there, intermingling: Richardson with Racine, La Fontaine, Montesquieu, Voltaire and Rousseau. Suzanne Necker's legacy is there: Shakespeare, Milton, Fielding, Swift, Sterne, Gray, *Ossian*'s ubiquitous inventor Macpherson, Lessing, and Goethe. Suzanne's eclecticism stretched into modern times, including Buffon and Diderot. Germaine's eclecticism is a parallel of her mother's.

Diderot's conviction that human feelings should be described dramatically surely lingered in Germaine's memory alongside the first trip to London, when she first heard Shakespeare 'in situ'. Germaine's theatrical propensities during childhood also deserve attention. Reciting poetry outdoors fitted her "perpetually vivacious nature"[25] and pleasure came from the plays written and performed in Necker's garden at Saint-Ouen. Dramatic sensitivety had not changed when Germaine filled *De la littérature* with her august panoply. Naturally, then, Racine held court with Voltaire and Shakespeare. Germaine expressed her enthusiasm for Racine, for his heroes, their grandeur and will, for his affective choice of words and their rhythm, and his eagerness to present moral beauty at its best. Racine's dramatic poetry touched Germaine's theatricality since her early creative years close to her mother's salon. The old friends F. La

Harpe and J.-F. Marmontel had encouraged her pride in the art of recitation.[26] That in subsequent years Germaine identified with Racine's Phèdre, recited and acted out her model before friends and hosts, manifests at its source an extraordinary fiber of her personality.

From the chosen epigraph on to twenty-nine chapters, Germaine's memories, knowledge, predilections and concerns are composite parts of her intellectuality. Wistfully, in the end, she felt that the path of her "literary existence was already deeply traced."[24] Wistfulness had a strong opposite. She was convinced that the writer must give of himself to the utmost, must captivate, and move his readers toward new domains of thought and feeling.

De la littérature was a success. Germaine attended to a second edition in 1801. After the *Fictions* and *De la littérature*, she was ready to reflect on the path she had taken. She would write a novel.

> Look into a crowd ... can't you see facial features where a friendly expression, gentleness and kindness reflect a soul yet unknown which would hear yours? ... That crowd represents the nation. ... Forget what you know, what you fear. ... Give yourself to your thoughts ... and sail full sails, and ... you will get there, you will carry with you all those free affections, all those minds still free of the imprint of tyranny.[27]
>
> Germaine de Staël, *De la Littérature: On Eloquence*, 1800

9.

IN THE COMPANY OF MEN AND WOMEN

> This *Journal des Hommes libres*, thrown at me only because I am the friend of a man who has spoken independently on a government regulation! . . . Have we returned to the furors and intolerances of the Revolution's most terrible epoch? Will it start over again, forcing into despair the government's own friends? Are kindness and friendship dead? . . . Is a simple opinion a crime, not only for Constant but for me as well?[1]
>
> Germaine de Staël, Letter to Roederer, January 9, 1800

From the end of 1799 to that of 1802, the life of Germaine de Staël can only be described as perpetual motion. Qualitatively, it fluctuated from positive to negative poles. Quantitatively, agitation and exhilaration alternated from climax to anti-climax in degrees humanly unimaginable. This went from the consequences of Bonaparte's Coup d'Etat of November 1799 to the gestation and emergence of Germaine's new literary child, her first novel *Delphine*.

In 1799, Eric de Staël left the rue de Grenelle Swedish embassy. He no longer lived with Germaine. In Geneva for the rest of the winter, Germaine often saw her favorite cousin Albertine Necker de Saussure. Having returned to Paris in April against the wishes of the Directoire, Germaine had completed *De la littérature* begun in October 1798. Meanwhile Benjamin Constant published *The Consequences of the Counter-Revolution of 1660 in England* where he presented a criticism of the constitution already in its formative process. Repressive, the Directoire urged Germaine to leave Paris, which she did until November. Her salon suffered from the effects of this edict. Sieyès and Barras both turned away from her. Clubs were silenced, Jacobin riots broke out. Germaine's misgivings were correct; the ambiance was menacing. However, Bonaparte's late summer return from Egypt and French military feats in September altered this mood. The nation had kept its trust in Bonaparte.

Bonaparte's attitude to both the Directoire and the nation was quite another matter. Before the Egyptian adventure, the image of the lavish court life he had seen in Milan was on his mind. To his aides, he spoke of the Directoire as an equal, and as for the French, "they need glory," he said, "and the satisfaction of vanity. As for liberty, they do not know its meaning."[2] On November 9-10, the council of five hundred was dispersed, and Lucien Bonaparte assisting, a Coup d'Etat eliminated the Directoire, replacing it with a Consulat. On Christmas eve, Bonaparte was named first consul. The same day, the new government formed a consultative assembly called the Tribunat. Sieyès helping, Benjamin Constant became one of its members.

Germaine had managed to return to Paris just before the coup. It was suggested that she quietly stay in Saint-Ouen. But political excitement and the presence of Bonaparte in the atmosphere of swift change were propitious for Germaine, even if for only a moment. She re-opened her Paris salon. Around her, elation sustained the feeling that the Republic was safe.

Germaine entered her thirty-fifth year in the new century. She may have felt aged, as she said in *De la littérature*, and weary from political harassments that she considered odious, but personally, her vim and vigor were intact. She had made several journeys to and fro Paris, Coppet and Geneva. She fretted over Staël's failure to retain his ministerial functions. As he constantly incurred debts, she felt it necessary to separate from him. Elsewhere, Constant's political status pleased her, and the translation into English of her *Des passions* delighted her. A new edition of her text on Jean-Jacques Rousseau appeared. Now she could continue helping her aristocratic friends and use her salon to conciliate republican views with contitutional monarchism among the returning emigrés. She entertained lavishly, flirted with higher-ups, and instigated nominations among her friends in the new government.

But worry haunted Germaine. The Directoire's creation of the so-called Helvetic Republic and its financial impositions added to her concern that the French government would not pay the two million francs owed Necker. Germaine had written to Barras, defending the

Swiss peasantry whom, she said while quoting Montesquieu, "paid more to nature than to any other country to its government. They are country-loving protestants," Germaine added, "their mores are clean, they cannot bear the thought of being immersed in war."[3] Germaine's illusory trust in Barras can be seen as a precursor of changes in her feelings for Bonaparte. Moreover, French troops invaded Switzerland. However, Necker's privacy was respected by occupying forces. Another concern complicated Germaine's situation. Anxious to see her children study Latin, German, English and music, she needed tutors for them, Necker himself, Germaine and Mathieu de Montmorency having attended to this so far. A young tutor was found.

Then, on January 5th, Benjamin Constant made an unwelcome speech in the Tribunat. The latter should be independent, he said, otherwise it would be but "servitude and silence, a silence that all of Europe would hear."[3a] Promptly, Joseph Fouché attacked Benjamin in the *Journal des Hommes libres,* and blamed Germaine for having influenced him. Fouché suggested that Germaine return to Switzerland. She stayed, but her salon suffered from this. A 'simple opinion' was considered a crime indeed. Germaine was also publicly criticized for having 'abandoned' her husband. Talleyrand held receptions without her. Though Bonaparte closed the list of émigrés and a triumphant plebiscite ratified the new constitution (Year VIII) drawn at the time of the Coup, Germaine felt the sting of governmental manipulation of the press, much of its republican elements having been repressed. Worse still, criticism came from the literary world.

The writer Stéphanie Félicité de Genlis (1746-1830) intrigued against Germaine, obviously wanting to harm Germaine's prestige as the recently published *De la littérature* was gaining success. Years back, Germaine had met Madame de Genlis in Suzanne Necker's salon. Genlis described young Germaine's emotional comportment during a reading: "The child cried, exclaimed, kissed my hands and embraced me,"[4] Genlis wrote, disapproving of such demonstrations and the presence of a child in her mother's salon. Education was a formal, professional matter for Madame de Genlis who at the time had the charge of Philippe Egalité's children at the Palais Royal. Her texts on education drew praise in spite of their overtly moral tone. Her novelettes were successful. A fine musician, Genlis was witty, but her graceful style lacked intellectuality; it did not rise above the bourgeois mentality of the day. Her *Manual for the Traveller* (1799) briefly compared France and Germany, but she did not have the feeling for literature as a mission. She was envious of Germaine, who in turn praised her, but the stings of 1800 were offensive, nor could Germaine accept remarks concerning Suzanne Necker:

> That Madame de Genlis should attack my writing and myself are of no concern to me. The former are there to be read, the latter to be loved or feared. But my late mother has only me in the world to defend her! . . . I will not allow any outrage to come against her.[5]

De la littérature was widely read. François de Chateaubriand's remark that Germaine's claim of perfectibility was an obsession disappointed her. Here was another child of the Enlightenment, bright, talented, and enthusiastic. Born in 1768, he too experienced the trauma of the Revolution, having lost a brother to the guillotine. Raised in the provincial aristocracy critical of royal power, he had tended to his estate near Rennes, went to America during the Terror, joined the army on his return, was wounded, and opted to live in England where he taught French. In the summer of 1800 he came to Switzerland where he met Germaine. He too worshipped Bonaparte as a hero. As Germaine complimented him for his *Atala*, he returned the compliment by proclaiming her the friend of liberty. He was torn by timidity. "I was still quite rustic, I dared not look at the woman surrounded by admirers."[6] But Chateaubriand came to Germaine's salon and later to Coppet where he took an affectionate interest in Germaine's eldest, whom he called 'mon petit Auguste'. In December he dared oppose Germaine on the subject of perfectibility in his publishing avenue, the *Mercure de France*.

They differed in their view of the future. Hers was positive, his not. For her, belief in perfectibility championed progress.[7] "How could the human mind be forced to retrograde! One cannot resist progress!" she exclaimed in *De la Littérature*. When Chateaubriand published the *Genius of Christianism* in April 1802, Germaine noted the chapter title 'Virginity and its poetic rapports.' "Our poor Chateaubriand," she remarked, ". . . in these unhappy times, are our readers able to take this seriously?"[8] This was Germaine's manner with fellow writers. Favored, Chateaubriand was forgiven.

Wherever, in Saint-Ouen, Paris, Geneva, Lausanne or Coppet, more anxiety came Germaine's way. Eric de Staël' dejection made her request his return to Sweden. Formally separated from him, the children would remain with her, she said. As for Benjamin Constant, Germaine's displacements were his as well. But his ambivalence exasperated her. In spite of the solemn promise of 1797, he had attachments elsewhere. Evidently loyalty to her was more intellectual than not; their minds seemed surprisingly attuned to each other, their republican passion one and the same. A complex man, Constant had difficulty explaining to himself the nature of his attachment to she who evidently was not the only ideal woman. Nevertheless, Constant stayed with or near Germaine ten years longer, assisting her, never hesitating to pay tribute to her work.

Germaine did not fail to see the star of republicanism wane in government circles, particularly in the circle surrounding Bonaparte. It became dangerous for Germaine to challenge this change. In June, Talleyrand forbade her from attending the celebration of the victory at Marengo. This broke the rapport between Germaine and Talleyrand.

But new friendships evolved. The German linguist baron W. Humboldt (1767-1835), impressed by Germaine's publications, joined 'constitutionals', deputies, poets and journalists in her salon. He marvelled at her startling intellectual power, and offered to introduce the German language to her. Still, old friendships suffered. Sieyès no longer came to rue de Grenelle. Through the revolutionary turmoil, the idealism of this 'abbé' from Chartres had responded to Germaine's, and hers to his. With mutual friends like La Fayette, they had conversed on the subject of the constitution, on the ideal of representative government, and together they had revered Condorcet. They grieved over the latter's misfortune. The brutal turn of events deeply affected Sieyès. Though leading governmental debates up until November of 1799, he became less open, less confident, and worked privately at a constitutional plan that focused on the nation's working levels and would offer a jury protective of representative powers. He was aware of the machinations of renewed royalism, of the government's financial difficulties also. He attempted to maintain the public's respect for the Directoire. But on November 9 and 10, 1799, barely five months after Bonaparte's return from Egypt, the general's military, political and personal aides carried out the Coup d'Etat (Brumaire VIII). Sieyès' personal expectations of constitutional representation evaporated. They had never become public. The Coup produced a triumverate—Bonaparte as leading consul, J.–J. Cambacérès as second consul, who as we know had been minister of justice under Louis XVI, and as third consul Charles Lebrun (1739-1824) who had also assisted Louis XVI.

Ideally, Sieyès struggled with the problem of establishing "compatibility between the nation's sovereignty and the need for representation."[9] Sieyès posed the following question to the first consul: should the governing power be considered as the true representation of the nation? The unwarranted faux pas received the laconic reply: "the day on which the happiness of the French will rest on excellent organic laws, all of Europe will be free."[10]

Germaine was losing one who well understood her political anima. She may have sensed Sieyès' loss of dynamism and his alienation while attempting to finish his illusory plan. Undoubtedly, Sieyès overlooked the force of the nation's adulation for its military hero while republican armies triumphed abroad. The young, middle-aged Jacobins and old Girondins idolized Bonaparte. Germaine understood this and for some time still shared this kind of patriotism, though hurt by governmental criticism.

Talleyrand gave other receptions. The personification of courtesy, discretion and astuteness, the man who once officiated as bishop of Autun grasped the reins of political ascendancy. His insensitivity toward Germaine seems illogical considering her financial generosity. In the presence of Bonaparte Talleyrand may have spoken ill of Germaine. The consul read her works assiduously, for good or ill.

Coming so soon after the Egyptian adventure, the coup surely benefited from the latter's cultural success. Countering military and maritime disasters, Bonaparte's assignments to the sixty-five archaeologists, scholars, artists and engineers who accompanied him opened ancient Egypt to the modern world. However, now, at home, the growing British blockade, England's alliances and its eventual coalitions with Austria and Turkey, war having resumed with Austria who suddenly took Naples and Milan, all had to be faced with a firm hand. Commerce and industry needed strengthening. Nevertheless, the coup spared the young Republic from bloodshed.[11]

Military victories increased. European powers had no resource but to accept the coup. Hardened by the Egyptian experience, Bonaparte determined to hold his position. "One must secure the anchors," he said, "and bank on the imaginations of the nation (jeter les ancres, et s'appuyer sur les imaginations de la nation)"[12] Characteristically, he would not tolerate critical interference. This attitude held to the end; his course of action went accordingly. Immediately after the coup he concentrated on the interior pacification of France, reorganizing the administration, forming a network of 'préfectures' designed to maintain order, and lavishing honors right and left. He visited the Institut and returned the ministry of foreign affairs to Talleyrand. "His ancestry makes up for everything," Bonaparte said of him.[13] Attention was given to the police system; the former montagnard Joseph Fouché (1759-1820) who had terrorized Lyon took its direction.

Bonaparte called Germaine and her friends ideologues. He wrote anonymous articles disparaging them. He systematically castigated Germaine, and showed distrust of the Tribunat. For some time he valued the presence of Cambacérès and Lebrun. What may be considered the clearly equitable epoch of his rule, unaffected by contempt, still free of the illusion of conquest even though the personal political plan was already in his mind, Bonaparte invited fresh young talents in the administration, worked arduously at the daily agenda, astounded and drove his aides with the wide grasp of organizational priorities and needs. He closed the list of emigrés. The regaining of Piedmont and Lombardy removed the threat of another Austrian invasion. A plebiscite of three million ratified the new constitution. The new century opened propitiously for the first consul. Germaine had a similar estimation: "All nuances except the philosophical are employed by the government.... This nation is hard to govern ... and there is plenty of government at hand.... Bonaparte, who is surely a very great man ... will do extraordinary things either in war or in peace."[14]

Abroad, a fervent admirer of Montesquieu became president of the United States of America. Had Thomas Jefferson returned to Paris after his eleven-year absence, he would have seen different street names, changes in mores and idiom. Fashion created a relaxed deportment, festivities filled Paris with pleasure-seekers. The salon of Joséphine, Bonaparte's wife since 1796, gathered an ethnic and cultural mixture of guests. On her part, Germaine orchestrated old revolutionaries, former emigrés, royalists, writers, generals, and Russian, German and Austrian diplomats. Salons intellectually sympathetic to Germaine's had thrived abroad—Adèle de Flahaut, Talleyrand's future wife, who formed a cosmopolitan group near Hamburg. In Florence, Louise countess of Albany, a friend of the poet Alfieri, did as well.

Germaine heard echoes of Bonaparte's comment that her conversations had the tone of opposition. Her father wrote to consul Lebrun. Germaine's language, he said, was only "the effect of a vivacious imagination ... coming from a wide expansion of character."[15] Germaine wrote to a new friend, Joseph Bonaparte, hoping that "so kind and amiable" a person as the first consul's brother would help pacify the critic.[16] Joseph became an intermediary, but verbally only. Thrown into situations and responsibilities alien to his mild and passive character, the elder Bonaparte's only possible gifts to Germaine were kind words.

During a last encounter at a reception, Germaine tried to fathom Bonaparte's fixed look of concentration. She sensed antipathy. Her patriotic hero-worship broke. If Bonaparte's swift and admirable reorganization of the government baffled her, so did his severity. She was intrigued. To her, the new administration had an aura of transience about it:

> Bonaparte has felt with reason that a government not based on institutions had to be so at least on its men, and he is keeping them. No one however considers this stable, because France is like a life annuity on his head and this idea does not displease him. He fears the dangers of this visibly enough, but he would not want to make himself less necessary: after him, not the deluge . . . but chaos.[17]

One can assume that with her quick intelligence Germaine could not help but connect Bonaparte's not wanting to make himself "less necessary" with the invincibility she attributed to him earlier. Therefore Bonaparte was bound, in her view, to hold the helm of his ship for a much longer and deeper journey.

And now, Germaine had to reconsider her situation as a writer-citizen. She had been hurt. Yet it was out of question to reiterate the self-defense she had written in the unpublished *Circonstances*. A personal statement would only incur more criticism. "I have not hurt anyone," she had written. "For a moral reason perhaps, and out of pride, I have not acted out of resentment . . . and have used all the means nature has given me to be useful to the unfortunate."[18] Moreover, Germaine was proud of her *De la littérature*. Constant published a fine critique of her text. The historian Pierre Daunou (1761-1840) complimented her in the *Clef (Key) du Cabinet des Souverains*. She met the philosopher J. M. De Gérando (1772-1842) whose favorable article appeared in *Le Citoyen français*. There were criticisms that led her to present a second edition of her text, but privately, her *Littérature* signaled personal glory. Elsewhere, however, Bonaparte could not but have felt the arrow in the text's chapter on emulation. The "unenlightened warrior," she had said, "does not grasp the imagination of others; there always remain in them feelings that he has not captivated, and ideas that will judge him."[19] Oddly, Bonaparte accepted an invitation to visit Necker while in Geneva. Both exchanged courtesies. Necker had recently published his *Course on Religious Morality*. To Bonaparte, he appeared to be just another ideologue. Necker found "nothing imposing . . . nothing transcendent . . . in the young Caesar."[20] This was as close a rapprochement as possible between Bonaparte and Germaine; it was indirect, and it ended.

New friends besides Daunou and Gérando came into Germaine's life as she was about to embark on a new project. She was buoyed by their learning and support. She corresponded with Charles de Villers (1765-1815) whose passion for German culture impressed her. Villers had just published *The Philosopohy of Immanuel Kant.* A self-exiled novelist, he was eager to impart German thought to French readers. He communicated the extraordinarily wide range of Kant's thinking to Germaine, including the caution that the real and the imaginary had to be kept apart during observations on human nature. Having written on the power of the imagination in *De la Littérature,* it seemed impossible, now that she had learned from Villers the thrust of Kant's *Observations on the Sublime and the Beautiful,* "to not have the feeling that there exists in us a power that modifies what sensations transmit to it. Is this not the soul . . . this unity?"[21]

Other relationships evolved. Feminine acquaintances became friends and joined Germaine in her salon, moreover often visited her at Coppet. Baroness Julie de Krüdener (1764-1824), a vibrant Russian woman whom Germaine met in Geneva in 1801, brought an aura of mysticism to Coppet. A friend of Bernardin de St. Pierre and Chateaubriand, Krüdener also spoke of Jean-Paul Richter, whose romantic *The Titan* had just appeared. The Danish poetess Friederika Brun (1765-1835), a friend of Léonard Simonde de Sismondi (1773-1842), was introduced to Germaine by the family friend Bonstetten. Friederika and Germaine sympathized at the first encounter. They shared predilections for music, Italy, and the theatre. Friederika often came to Coppet.

When Necker sold his Paris house to the banker Jacques Récamier, Germaine went to visit the handsome 'hôtel particulier,' as stately houses were then called, in order to meet its new owners. Juliette Récamier (1777-1849) never forgot that moment:

> She was wearing a little flowered hat. . . . I was struck by the beauty of her eyes and by her gaze. . . . I had just read her *Lettres sur Jean-Jacques Rousseau* and had deeply loved that reading. I expressed how I felt more with my eyes than with words.
>
> She intimidated and attracted me all at once. Immediately one felt that here was a person perfectly natural in manner yet superior by nature.[22]

In Germaine's estimation, Juliette was the essence of femininity. Discretion and intelligence controlled Juliette in harmony with her physical beauty and grace. "How do you govern as you do the empire of beauty?" Germaine once asked Juliette. "One gladly honors you with that empire, because you are eminently kind, and it seems natural for a soul so gentle to have such a charming visage as the expression of itself." [23] The loyal, mutual affection of Germaine and Juliette lasted nearly twenty years. The spirit of their conversations led Constant to remark that "the rapidity of one in the expression of new ideas matched by the rapidity of the other to seize these and judge them, this male and strong mind opening up every thought and that delicate and refined mind which understood it all, this union of minds was touching and most pleasing to the observer."[24]

In April 1800, Germaine started to write her novel *Delphine*. That summer spent in Switzerland was relatively peaceful. Correspondance had its place in the daily routine in a parallel with the new project. Germaine addressed government officials like the secretary to Fouché, Claude Fauriel (1772-1844), a critic of southern French literature whose compliment of the *Littérature* pleased her. Necker published the *Cours de morale religieuse* to lukewarm reactions, but Germaine treasured this work.

In Paris, the first consul's increasingly military ambiance betrayed eagerness to hold on to the 'anchor' as tightly as he had intended. Now in the city for the winter, Germaine intensified the contact with Joseph, with Lebrun, and she reached Bonaparte's close friend marshal Louis de Berthier (1753-1815) as well. When the separation from Eric de Staël became official, Germaine was criticized for having 'abandoned' her husband. Dismayed by this untruth, she left Paris in the spring of 1801 and returned to her project. Bonaparte's signing of a Concordat with Rome also distressed her, for this went against the republican notion of separation of church and state. By the end of 1801, changes in the government intrigued Germaine still. Military personages entered the Senate, some were given diplomatic posts. Germaine sensed further degradation of social mores in the midst of an ebullient theatre. The press labored under Bonaparte's iron hand. In addition, Germaine suffered more criticism from Madame de Genlis. That winter, Germaine changed her mind concerning the government and particularly the first consul.

Constant criticized the early draft of Bonaparte's civil code. In January 1802, he and eighteen associates were expelled from the Tribunat. He returned to writing. The moral and political sciences were suppressed from the Institut. Dictatorship evidenced itself. To Germaine, Bonaparte's lavish Easter promulgation of the Concordat seemed ridiculous. That spring, her salon gathered the 'constitutionnel' Camille Jordan (1771-1821), Gérando, Fauriel, Juliette, Constant, and some of Bonaparte's marshals like Jean Bernadotte, who became a friend. At the

Tuileries, Bonaparte held audiences; there were glittering military reviews and receptions. Germaine expressed her opinions carelessly.

In early 1802, Staël became ill. In vain, Germaine tried to have the young Swedish king take charge of him. She paid his debts, and decided to bring him to Coppet. Eric died en route. Germaine's regretted not having found a Swedish pension for the husband whose diplomatic career had opened with a measure of success. During the Terror, as we know, Eric helped with passports for her and her friends. An eight-year liaison with an older woman incurred costs, and Staël's situation steadily deteriorated. Under the veneer of elegance and courtesy, stubbornness and indolence became visible. Staël was never able to adjust to Germaine's temperament and intellectual prowess. Germaine was distraught by his death. There had been tender moments with this child of the 'ancien régime' thrown into a fulgurant world he could not understand. But for her, and forever in her melancholic heart, marriage had failed.

In early August 1802, Bonaparte became consul for life. A plot against him failed; Bernadotte was implicated. Bonaparte was aware that Bernadotte knew Germaine. He was angry with Necker who criticized the new constitution and insisted on parliamentarism. He decided to impose the order of exile. In early July, he sent word to Germaine that she must not return to France. At this point in life, Bonaparte had said adieu to what he called "the romance of the Revolution." Reality came first, it excluded hypothetical ideas.[25] Such an attitude matched the hero's comportment. The epoch following the Coup brought internal peace and order. Now it was time to look beyond the nation's borders.

Exile was bound to affect Germaine's disposition. Fortunately at this point, her devotion to her father, family and friends and the hours spent in her study held despair at bay. Publications by old and new friends enchanted her. Works issued from a brilliant, ebullient, idealistic generation, most of them her peers. Among these were G. Cabanis' *Physics and Morality,* Villers' essays in the *Spectateur du nord,* Louis de Bonald's *On the Natural Laws of the Social Order,* Chateaubriand's *René* and the *Génie du christianisme,* Juliette's friend Pierre Ballanche with the *Sentiment Considered in its Relation to Literature and the Arts,* Sismondi's text on Tuscany, and Constant's *Principles of Politics.* Similar phenomena came from neighboring countries. In Germany, the names F. Shelling, F. Novalis, L. Tieck, and I. Kant among them, then J. Herder, F. Schiller, F. Schlegel, A. Wilhelm Schlegel, and Germaine's friends Humboldt and Goethe held sway.

English writers like W. Godwin and Jeremy Bentham were familiar to Germaine, and now Wilberforce. In Italy, Alfieri radiated in a salon known to her. From the idealism of Shelling and Kant's transcendentalism to the utilitarianism of Bentham, let alone Alfieri's picture of heroism, every claim, every argument spurred discussion at Coppet, and left its mark. For having published successfully, Germaine experienced a commonality with those writers, whether present or distant. All affected her with their originality, lucidity and open-mindedness. She endeared herself further to persons like Villers, and encouraged Daunou and Gérando as she had done with Chateaubriand.

Récamier and Krüdener came to Coppet. Germaine wrote a play for evening pleasure called *Agar dans le désert*. She was attentive to Villers' suggestion that she read Aechylus and Euripides, whom German writers admired. She admitted to self-consciousness to Villers for not knowing the German language well, expressing the desire to go to Italy, England, and Germany which now especially appealed to her.

Devotion to Necker and the enjoyment of her children checked Germaine's desires. Like her new friend Sismondi, Necker advised her against exaltation. He worried about her. "Poor dear," he wrote to her, ". . . though filled with the spirit of centuries you are but a child in character."[26] His absences from Coppet upset her. "Without you," she wrote, "my inner being falls into a state of disorganization."[27] Nevertheless, calming in the privacy of her study, Germaine continued with her project. Exercising the talent she knew she possessed made her call "on all the resources, all the effects of the natural motions of the soul."[28] Two and a half years had passed since her cry to Roederer. She now knew that kindness and friendship had not died. She would reiterate this. Beyond the oasis in which the *Fictions* and *Littérature* were born, now onto the open sea, a new and different urge to write lifted Germaine's sails. She completed her first novel. In December 1802, *Delphine* was published. This was Germaine's literary Coup.

> Lift your head . . . don't allow anyone, no matter how powerful, to trample upon you . . . ![29]
>
> Jacques Necker to Germaine de Staël, 1802

10.
SAILING, FULL SAILS

> I am making a novel, I am looking for a subject amenable to tragedy, at the outset I want a literary career for myself, countering what is happening now ... I shall go into the domain of the imagination. Then we shall see what I will become.[1]
>
> Germaine de Staël, 1800

Delphine at twenty is the wealthy aristocratic widow of Monsieur d'Albémar, whom she had dearly loved. Her native province is the Languedoc, where she yearns to return one day. This is Paris in the year 1790. Delphine enjoys a warm correspondence with Louise d'Albémar, her sister-in-law who lives in a convent in Montpellier. Louise offers kind counsel, for the young widow is ambivalent toward Paris. Intellectuality is precious to her, but she abhors prejudice and gossip, religious superstition, and political shallowness. She is making arrangements for the dowry of her young cousin Matilde de Vernon, who is engaged to Léonce de Mondoville, a gentleman of Spanish and French ancestry due to arrive soon.

Matilde's mother, Sophie de Vernon, is Delphine's closest friend. Feelings of fascination and inhibition alternate in Delphine's attachment to Sophie. Though intelligent and pleasing in conversation, Madame de Vernon does not encourage emotional display. She is authoritative, secretive, and she gambles at cards.

Thoughts, feelings, and observations fill the letters between Delphine and Louise, Matilde and Delphine, Sophie and Delphine. Louise is eager to have Delphine come to join her in convent life, while Matilde insists that Delphine should abide by religious ritual and most certainly exercise restraint in expressing political opinions. Sophie repeats her daughter's injunctions. Delphine would be wise to convert to religious belief. In her more private letters to Louise, Delphine reveals a reverence for the Supreme Being. This is said with effusion; and accordingly, she rejects the Roman Catholic worship. Yet, trusting in Sophie's knowledge and experience, Delphine questions her on her convictions. Sophie is flatly noncommittal.

Delphine's character is visible to her close friends, but to the Paris society filling Madame de Vernon's elegant salon she appears to be a young, wealthy woman; a striking blond beauty; spontaneously generous; and an intellectual. Certain elements in that society are sarcastic toward her. Madame du Marset and the elderly Monsieur de Fierville are appalled by Delphine's expressed approval of the Revolution. Fearless, Delphine maintains her political conviction, unaware at first that her deportment is a declaraction of war against the opinion of her aristocratic society. Unfortunately, she often abandons herself to exaltation. She is aware of this. Monsieur d'Albémar had taught her the art of self-analysis. Distressed, she considers that propensity a character flaw.

As the story of Germaine's first novel *Delphine* unfolds, Thérèse d'Ervins becomes a protégée, since Delphine feels indebted to the young woman for her solicitude during an illness. Thérèse is mistreated by her husband. The latter had been saved by Monsieur de Serbellane, a Tuscan supporter of the Revolution. Thérèse has fallen in love with Serbellane. Léonce's preceptor, Monsieur Barton, meets both Matilde and Delphine in Sophie's salon. He realizes that his young pupil should rather marry Delphine. He shows her a letter he has received from Léonce. She is moved by the young man's intellect and sense of conscience, as she puts it. On the road to Paris, Léonce is attacked and wounded in the chest. Barton rushes to help his friend, choosing Delphine as his continuing correspondent.

Visiting Delphine, Sophie meets Serbellane and on hearing of Léonce's unhappy accident considers Serbellane a good "replacement" as husband-elect for Matilde. This change of mind startles Delphine. Reading another letter by Léonce, she is moved by his nobility of heart and his ancestral pride. She realizes that he is impetuous like her, that with him reflection blends with sentiment, something she admires in a man. She finds his melancholy endearing. She shares his disdain for religious superstition. Aided by her imagination, Delphine surmises that Léonce is open to love.

Delphine has decided to offer her home as refuge to Thérèse and her child. Soon, she meets Léonce in Sophie's salon. He is enchanted by her. He perceives her vulnerability through her seductiveness and wishes to be her protector. He hears her speak vehemently against religious prejudice and is surprised by her independence of mind. Personally, he has respected public opinion enough to never allow himself to be outspoken. Their first conversation centers on Léonce's puzzlement. Never missing Delphine's actions, verbal or otherwise, Sophie sees that this new relationship will hinder her plans for Matilde. She holds Delphine to her financial support of her daughter and has the formal contract between Léonce and Matilde quickly arranged. Delphine is agitated.

When Serbellane accompanies Delphine to Sophie's concert soon afterward, Delphine sings a lament from the opera *Dido and Aeneas*. She notices Léonce's somber reaction to the applause. At another reception, Delphine's brilliant dancing performance of a polonaise accompanied with harp and wind instruments fills the audience with ecstasy, but not Léonce. He is distraught with jealousy. His chest wound reopens and he collapses. Rushing to his aid, Delphine compromises herself.

This is the first love crisis for Delphine and Léonce. Others follow as their love progresses. New personages appear, new events unravel and coalesce in their sequences: Serbellane's secret meeting with Thérèse at Delphine's home; d'Ervins' untimely arrival and death in a duel with Serbellane; gossip implicating Delphine; her departure for her estate at Bellerive; journeys to Cernay where she finds solace with new friends, Elise and Henri de Lebensai; chance meetings with Léonce in Paris, his love coming to light. Unaware of Serbellane's care for Thérèse, Léonce errs and accuses Delphine of dissimulation. Thérèse will leave, and Delphine agrees to raise her child. Cleared of Léonce's suspicions, Delphine nevertheless suffers from society's relentless malice and new acts of perfidy on Sophie's part. But Sophie is fatally ill. Léonce's declarations of love do not assuage the pain of Delphine's situation. She has promised the dying Sophie to respect Matilde's marriage bond with Léonce. She will be tied to this promise.

Paris, Bellerive, later Switzerland, and in the distance Languedoc are the salient atmosphere for this tapestry of character and love. Delphine's soft and flowing garden; later, the severe, overbearing Alps; the south appealingly warm and bright, these are the variables of an ambiance moving in accord with the development of a passionate relationship. Hues and shapes pale against darker colorings of its deepening.

Rumblings of the Revolution are distant; the fears of Delphine's aristocratic milieu are only beginning. Léonce's act of duty in the Vendée at the story's finale is the only historical event. As fiction, the story unfolds in a realistic and psychological manner in spite of the theme of love, which could otherwise place it in the category of romance. This is so because with Germaine de Staël a love story's primary focus is the delineation of character. Delphine and Léonce are hurt by discrepancies of character throughout their experience of intellectual and emotional rapport. Their passion develops in the midst of a cold and tortuous society. Only a few exceptional friendships provide solace. They too are part of the reality of life.

Kindness is Delphine's principle of action. Every fiber of her being moves accordingly. She has one purpose, one desire: "to be loved by those with whom I live." She projects her desire into society itself, wishing "that each one be free of interference during the search in their conscience for a way of life best suited to their character."[2] Youthfully enthusiastic, she speaks of her wish only to those whom she respects for being capable of reflection. But she reproaches herself, for in the midst of the society she lives in she easily gives in to the charms of conversation "with men of distinction." While they have drawn her "into listening, responding, letting me give way to high spirits . . . this displeases other women . . . who are at the game table."[3] Malicious criticism hounds her. But her love for Léonce finds nourishment as if by magic in his "elevation of feeling."[4] Self-examination deepens melancholy, the uncertainty of human destiny troubles her, "the tiredness of life"[5] darkens her fantasies. Standing before the painting of a tragic scene, Delphine feels as if she were "in the middle of the sea, exposed to danger, and far off onto the waves there appears a mysterious, ominous shipwreck."[6]

Delphine's fortitude counters melancholia for a time; it will not allay her terrors. Generous and enthusiastic, beautiful inside and out, she has one particular wish for Léonce: she wants to impart her enthusiasm to him. "It is a principle of life," she tells him. "Some are fortunate to have received it as a gift, others, for lacking it, do not question their existence. . . . Yet it is as necessary to love as it is to virtue."[7] Léonce has sensed her force of character. But she is young, he feels, he being barely five years her senior. Will she be strong enough before the storms of life? He is impressed by her easy giving in to enchantment.[8] But her speaking of virtue seems too personal, as if "it were the only air her generous soul can breathe, and . . . there is in her look something sensitive and trembling that invokes help. Who will defend her from the evils of men!"[9]

At a concert, Delphine sings once again. The lament from Marmontel's *Dido* fills her with the music's power more than ever, though it has long been familiar to her. Her song expresses her love for Léonce. He has heard her sing. What is love, he exclaims, but another life within life! Expressing her impressions of him, she tells him that his qualities and faults belong to a proud soul, that he needs the approbation of himself more so than that of others. He replies that he could not bear the loss of his self-esteem, nor that of love. "Do you feel as I do," he asks her, "that the universe and its centuries have wearied of the talk of love; yet once in thousands of chances, two beings respond to each other with all the faculties of their mind and soul . . . ?"[10]

Several months later, nearly one year after their first meeting, Léonce fully acknowledges Delphine's independence of mind, but with a critical point:

> You love liberty as much as you do poetry . . . and all that which can exalt humanity; ideas that one would think are foreign to women conciliate somehow with your amiable nature..But I have heard others quote you on the subject of the Revolution. It seems to me that a woman needs aristocratic backing in her opinions. . . . [11]

Delphine will be careful to avoid giving opinions displeasing to him, but she adds that "even if I were a man it would be impossible for me to not love liberty . . . to close my heart to generosity . . . to all pure and real sentiments."[12]

Mobile and logical, their love dialogue buoys their thoughts and feelings as if on a sea alternately sun-filled and somber. On bright days Léonce tells Delphine that she inspires and animates him. He sends her a quotation from the English poet George Lyttleton:

> . . . Her eloquence was sweeter than her song,
> Soft as her heart, and as her reason strong;
> Her form each beauty of her mind express'd,
> Her mind was Virtue by the Graces dress'd.

Léonce adds that "no woman before you has ever merited this portrait."[13]

Into the second year of their attachment for each other, Delphine has dark forebodings. Now twenty-two, she is ill. Exaltation has wearied her, as if her soul were losing its mobility. "Are the memories, is happiness itself illusory?" she asks. "Have I lost happiness too soon?"[14] She knows that her powers of reflection are troubled. The unpredictability of her situation clouds the moments with Léonce. "Motions of the soul cannot be fathomed," she reflects, "yet moralists never cease to meditate on passions and character."[15] She is too vulnerable, too exposed to the relentless prejudices of a society where rank is god, calumny its messenger, and the creating of impressions its rule. Vanity and ostentation are this society's habits. Truths and kindness are absolute unknowns. Delphine is distraught, for she has failed to conquer society.

Léonce has been advised to seek solitude, for he too is pursued by the perfidy of gossip, notwithstanding the fact that he has married Matilde and has been attentive to her needs. Matilde has succumbed to tuberculosis. Léonce is free to marry Delphine. Much as he has listened to public opinion, for a moment he sheds his respect for it. "Consider our earth from a high vantage point," his friend Henri de Lebensei tells him. "Do you not feel that all the miseries of society lie at the level of its city fogs, and never rise higher? Believe me, constant rapport among individuals troubles the mind and stifles the soul's principles of energy and elevation."[16] Léonce will go to the Vendée nevertheless, and will be killed in action.

Society had refused to protect the bond between the lovers. It never sanctioned it. Though the lives of women start and finish with devotion to others, the novelist continues, though the happiness of others is indeed women's major vocation, outside that sanction there is no haven for women. Society controls and engulfs its women, making them dependent on others and incapable of forming independence of mind.

Delphine knew very few women who dared challenge society and its tenacious conventions, this being during the two brief years of her relationship with Léonce de Mondoville. Elise de Lebensei, divorced and protestant, though calling herself an ordinary person, explained to Delphine that she used her reason to break social rules. She had liberated herself from conjugal violence through harsh public criticism and alienation. She and Henri de Lebensei, her second husband, moved away from Paris society and to Cernay, where Delphine first meets them. Delphine witnesses how Henri, disdainful of opinion and deeply interested in advocating freedom of religious worship, stands by his wife like a shining knight. The couple's tenderness, sensitivity, order and shared moral and political attitudes reveal a marriage in which friendship is the most precious component. Delphine considers Elise's circumstance the antithesis of other marital situations. It is natural for her to decide that only in a marriage such as this can a woman find happiness.

Elise's confidences are gloomy at times, if not dramatic. She warns that flaunting opinion is dangerous. Should Delphine really want a love relationship, Elise says, the man she chooses has to possess courage to confront objections to feminine outspokenness and impetuosity. Léonce never fully exemplified that courage.

Thérèse d'Ervins' idyll had ended because of her overbearing religious beliefs. Society had hounded her with the illicitness of her rapport with Serbellane. To Delphine, the young woman's decision signified that religion could be a solace. Louise d'Albémar's contentment seemed a better example of such decisionmaking. Louise became a favored counselor on moral and sentimental issues to all and particularly to Delphine. But there had been misgivings concerning the very young Matilde de Vernon; when newly married she constantly occupied herself with religious devotions in the presence of a priest. This ruined the possibility of frankness in marriage. Elsewhere, Delphine saw idleness, a many-hued persiflage, gambling. Her moral sense was most offended, however, by the more general circumstance of women confined by their dependence on men.

Madame de Vernon had tried to assuage this kind of predicament. She once told Delphine that "there is a way to grasp the character of men, and women must find it, if they wish to live in peace on this earth."[17] From Delphine's perspective, Sophie's argument represented a nefarious adaptation. Though rooted in necessary resignation, the compromise was dangerous, for in Sophie's case, intelligence built a cold reserve, habits of dissimulation and manipulation. It took time for Delphine to discover these; for many, the discovery would never come.

Observing the lives of women during her carefully guarded idyll, Delphine reached a conviction congenial to her character: married love was the only solution, the only ideal that could offer happiness. The opposite, a loveless marriage, ultimately "degraded character, destroyed beauty and made glorious old age an impossibility."[18]

Delphine's later guilt and despair attest to her misgivings. She will struggle with her own moral self-support; disillusion will sap her strength, her youthfulness, and hopes regarding the future. Though fatally ill, she will bear the influence of Léonce's morose aunt Madame de Ternan and agree to enter convent life. Her decision, before a painful reunion with Léonce in the fall of 1792, is tragically inconsistent. She is full of a self-pity unlike what she had expressed earlier in her travel journal, where courage overcame disarray:

> Having reached the mountain top, I found my way into the wood. I walked to the edge of the precipice. Morbidity beheld me. Leaning over the dark rim, I held the last, slight branch. . . . Must I admit to weakness? I pitied my youth, held back, and continued on.[19]

Delphine's 'continuing on' was definitely congenial to her character. But was it not most unnatural for her to take the monastic vows? Had she not been heroic before the temptation of suicide?. To all intents and purposes in the art of novel-writing, Delphine weakened to the point of losing her courage under the influence of an older woman. She met death in illness, like Matilde, and before them, Sophie.

So much for the action of the novel. Coincidentally, in a sixth, anticlimactic part of the story, the French government's disestablishment of monastic orders had allowed the lovers' idyll to resume. But there is far more than action such as this in Germaine's novel. Socio-political colorings support Delphine's heroism from the beginning. Her abhorance of prejudice and malicious talk sets both tone and mood. Her rejection of these finds strength and continuous solace in her first desire in life, which is "to be loved by those with whom I live."[20] This is Delphine's principle of action. Matilde must accept the offer of financial help without embarrassment, without considering its effect on others, but rather for what is good in the action itself.[21] However, Delphine is not without qualms in her relationship with Matilde's mother. From the start there is affection, but it is "impossible to discuss thoughts and feelings with Madame de Vernon."[22] Delphine realizes where her inhibition comes from : Sophie's passion for success in social intercourse and her total disinterest in "the principle of human nature's conduct"[22] is just that source. Delphine's inhibition is morally motivated.

By revealing the character of her heroine in such a manner, Germaine has broached the subject of relationships, and immediately, Delphine's goal in life, that is to say her practical, moral precept. From then on, the portrait emerges in thick, arresting strokes of the pen. Delphine may be inhibited before the powerful, calculating Sophie, but elsewhere she is outspoken and argumentative regarding her personal opinions, much to the surprise of men and women in the Parisian society that surrounds her. She reveals convictions that go against the grain of religious convention and aristocracy's disdain of early revolutionary principles such as liberty. She will be sensitive to reactions coming at her and against her. Her abandoning of herself to exaltation will bring on a first crisis. Not without anguish, Delphine will exercise self-analysis.

Differences from Léonce add to the portraiture. His respect for public opinion, his credulity, therefore, before the gossip enveloping Delphine, mar his enchantment with her from the beginning. Like the edges of an uneven chiaroscuro, his conformity and the jealousy stirred by her musical success conflict with his desire to protect her from exaltations that will stir public criticism. Their relationship evolves accordingly.

Léonce does not meet Delphine's idealism. As she expresses her thoughts concerning liberty and enthusiasm, he is impressed. Her intellectuality appeals to him. Her hatred of mediocrity and ordinariness fascinate him, but he does not share her contempt for religiosity. His Roman Catholic upbringing forbids this. He becomes aware of Madame de Vermon's manipulations, for one, and grieves for Delphine in her suffering. In sentiment, Léonce comes close to Delphine, but he remains a mobile part of her life, seeking, admiring, loving, and confounded.

Identifying Delphine with an English poet's portrait, "Soft as her heart, and as her reason strong,"[13] Léonce's anxieties conflict with his admiration. He sees pride in her anger with public criticism and worries over her "continual need to please."[23] Too respectful of public opinion, he cannot grasp the motivation that draws Delphine to others. He has not discovered the 'motion of her soul'—a phrase favored by Germaine, which is Delphine's desire 'to be loved by those with whom she lives.'[20] Her aid to emigrés such as M. de Serbellane, for one, has no other motive but generosity.

Léonce's first letter to Delphine comes well into the novel's second part. It is haughty and brief. He has believed prickly gossip. The letter establishes the author's distress concerning the France of 1790; it was far from an ideal society. The young Revolution had offered chances to redress it from the niceties, prejudices and discriminations of the ancien régime, but the chances vanished. Both victims of that society, character differences between Léonce and Delphine can only bring them anguish.

On her part, Delphine is the link between all components of the novel. To Louise, Matilde, Sophine, Barton, Thérèse and later Léonce, Elise and Henri, Delphine narrates her experiences and expresses feelings all in one. Her letters are often monologues filled with self-analyses and at other times, calls for responses that engender action. Beneath their courteous formality, dialogues flow. The stiltness of letter-writing is only apparent. In a moment of exaltation, she even addresses Léonce within a letter to Louise, her major confident. The Barton and Lebensei letters are liaisons between the lovers. To an extreme, Sophie's letters reflect the older generation's immorality. Dying, she confesses her loveless control of the world she has created, therefore her failure in happiness.

Germaine once described her prescription for style to her journalist friend Roederer. She obeys her dictum. *Delphine* offers a movement of ideas, a passionate tone, imaginative resources such as Delphine's blond beauty, her songs and dances, her garden, her fright before a somber sea, and calm before an Alpine lake. From the novel's dedication on—"A la France silencieuse," she provides a political coloring to her ideas. The words have a double connotation. Aristocratic France lived in silent fear from 1790 to 1792, when the novel takes place. From the author's perspective, France was also silent at the time of her writing —from 1800 to 1802, trepidating under the thumb of a man for whom many reluctantly shed their hero-worship.

Germaine also realized that society had changed. Mores had loosened, journalistic criticism of every hue had become the norm. Calumny will be Delphine's opprobrium. It invents false truths, twists truths out of proportion to itself. Delphine's every gesture, be it outspoken resistance to convention at a reception or toward individuals, even against her exaltations, is a struggle against the malice that has invaded society. She is therefore in conflict with society in general, her entourage, and herself. Her struggle with such a reality will be her tragedy. Agitations change her. Illness overtakes her. She knows then that love out of wedlock will not offer happiness.

With respect to love, Germaine's novel is autobiographical. Three months after having announced to Adelaide de Pastoret that she was 'making' a novel, she further confided that she still "needed years to completely repress her heart." She was continuing on with the novel, she said, adding that it "had become the history of women presented from diverse rapports."[24] She has referred to herself, and to characters in her novel: Thérèse d'Ervins, Elise de Lebensei and Matilde, Léonce's wife. Thérèse has suffered from abuse; Elise, after her divorce, has found love in marriage; Matilde, dominated by religious superstition, cannot enjoy a frank relationship with her husband.

The marriage relationship of Elise and her second husband Henri is ideal. Theirs is friendship itself and independence from public opinion.

According to Henri, whose political orientation becomes the author's mouthpiece, the Revolution failed to bring political liberty to its people, let alone the knowledge of what liberty is. The great danger to a nation, Lebensei writes to Léonce when terror is manifest, "lies in the attempt to impose political institutions on a people by force . . . this can only break a nation's spirit . . . indifference and a kind of corruption happen . . . yet we each have a conscience tending toward liberty. . . . In the world's great debate, there still is not a French nation; only misfortune can form a true public spirit in this country."[25] In the name of friendship. Henri advises Léonce against joining the army of émigrés, but Léonce follows his conscience as an aristocrat, and meets death on the battlefield.

Much as Germaine has anticipated her novel to be a work of the imagination, she gives in to pathos. Her Galatea comes from inspiration, and intentions. "The author and I, we are two,"[26] she had written to Roederer in 1796. Inadvertently, her comment belies her particular creativity. Once immersed in her subject, Germaine does check the autobiographical urge, but it eludes her on the subject of marriage because of the anguish concerning her own failed marriage. Yet more often than not the impetuous brush paints ideal feminine beauty inspired by the desire to counter the ugliness of a society that has shed its mores. Submitting to the domination of an older woman a second time and taking monastic vows, Delphine has failed to conquer society. Regarding herself, she assuages her guilt and resists the idleness imposed on her. She will leave the convent, and regains hope in future good deeds. But she is too ill to find this liberation.

Even the reunion with Léonce cannot free Delphine of her qualms, a fortuitous circumstance being that revolutionary laws closed monastic orders at that time. Delphine's intense self-analyses have taxed her last strength. "I am weak, I pity myself! So many men and women walk assuredly on the road traced for them and content themselves with regular, monotonous days, whereas I . . . weary from exaltation, fail to quieten the pulse of life . . . as if I were guilty."[27]

Germaine's intentions as author and herself are the weaponry of this novel. She specifies that the positions of women and men in society are without balance. Under the "proscription of opinion, a woman weakens, but a man rises; for having made the laws, men are free to interprete these, or flaunt them."[28] Consequently, Germaine argues, society dictates that only one happiness is allowed women: love in marriage. Such prejudice must be reformed. Using Lebensei's voice, Germaine questions the nature of morality. It is universal, detached from circumstance, it is above an unnatural religion where beings subjugate each other while conscience must not be made subject to the decision of others.

While Léonce has felt it impossible to marry a woman who in the eyes of society is a former nun, Delphine, on the other hand, has held on with consistency to her principle of generous action and until her illness, to that of enthusiasm. These constitute her victory in her personal conflict against exaltation.

A critic of Madame de Staël has said that *Delphine* "is an ambitious work coming early in the author's life."[29] *Delphine* would not be the end of Germaine's literary career. As in *L'influence des passions, Les fictions* and *De la littérature*, the vivacious pen was bound to seek other boundaries, and continue on.

> Philosophy is not the only source of ideas such as liberty. . . . there is such a thing as generous enthusiasm, which embraces you as do all noble and proud passions, and dominates you imperiously.[30]
> Delphine, letter to Léonce,
> Part III, XXXIII, 1791

Part Three
TALISMANS

11.

THE TEST OF SORROW

> Undoubtedly there have always existed romantic temperaments and sensibilities in the sense that passion predominates reasonableness, strangeness attracts, the present is unsatisfactory and suffering is delectable.[1]
>
> Henri Peyre, *Qu'est-ce que le romantisme?* 1971

Five years separate *Delphine* from *Corinne or Italy*. They were the years when the deepest sorrow in Germaine's life met new and powerful emotional and intellectual excitements. *Delphine* appeared in December 1802, when Germaine was thirty-six. The *Journal des Débats* called her novel dangerous and antisocial. It has been thought that the criticism came directly from Napoléon's pen. The *Mercure de France* echoed this, unfortunately from the pen of Germaine's friend Roederer. What was she addressing, they asked. Divorce? Religion? Politics? Journalistic opinion missed the emotive thrust concerning marriage and affection within the latter's fold. Nor did that opinion grasp the novelist's implication that the impending trauma of the Revolution had been poorly understood by the aristocracy.[2] *Delphine*'s spiritualism connected with that trauma in her anguished anticipation of what was to come.

Much as Germaine had endeavored to use her novel *Delphine* as a vehicle for ideas, and particularly where the principle of enthusiasm applied to one's rapport with others, she felt that she had much more to say. She wrote *Reflections Concerning the Moral Purpose of the novel Delphine*. Perhaps out of provocation, or from another autobiographical urge or the desire to clarify the subject of feminine love, where her Galatea was concerned, Germaine maintained the following:

> Women are sovereign at the beginning of a love relationship, and one cannot exaggerate, even in novels, all that which passion inspires in a man afraid of being unloved. But when a woman's tenderness is obtained, if the sacred bond of marriage does not give to feelings a new character and depth, if this is not so, a man's heart is the first to turn cold: men do not have as we do the imperious need to be loved; their destiny is too independent . . . they do not suffer the secret terror of isolation pursuing women endowed with a brilliant destiny.[3]

Nonetheless, Germaine was relieved by her friends' encouraging comments. The old family friend Suard published extracts of *Delphine* in *Le Publiciste*. On reading the four-volume genevese edition, Germaine's relative Rosalie de Constant exclaimed: "Never since *Clarissa* have I felt such a complete illusion; the least details are given perfect care, they produce real magic."[4]

In her salon, Germaine entertained political personalities, arguing that a moderate republic was the only true solution to the present state of affairs. But this was to her detriment. Benjamin echoed her views in his articles and speeches. Eager to see a more considerate representation during elections, he advocated what he called elective liberty, much to Napoléon's irritation. Controversy over *Delphine* continued. From the consulate came criticism against the novel's dedication "to silent, enlightened France" which, of course, aimed at "the tyrant who forced her to be silent."[5]

Napoléon's displeasure over *Delphine* came specifically from her praise of Protestantism. He had signed the Concordat with Pope Pius VII on July 16, 1801, whereby France and the Holy See agreed to reinstate the Roman Catholic ritual. Clearly, Germaine had attacked the Roman Catholic Church and the impositions it inflicted on its worshippers. In *The Woman Philosopher* (1804) Madame de Genlis parodied Delphine, if not Germaine herself, but to no avail. France read *Delphine*.

Concurrently, Necker published his *Last Political and Financial Views*. He denounced Napoléon's ambition outright. He too dedicated his text to the nation. He still idolized British parliamentarism; it was the best guarantee to political liberty. Otherwise, he stated, the alternative was tyranny. The trickery of elections already pointed to this, he added. The "old ideologue" had gone too far. The *Mercure de France* attacked

Necker, calling him vain and ignorant. The consular grudge was bound to snap back and slash from father to daughter. Germaine felt personally threatened. Grief over Eric de Staël's death added to her fears.

At that time, Napoléon had made Austria fall back on several fronts. Now England was bristling and becoming aggressive. European hostility grew. At home, Bonaparte made the surviving aristocracy accept civic institutions that took away some of its possessions. The police kept things in order. The first consul's deskwork became monumental. Each day started with the review of Fouché's police reports. Among the new cabinet members stood the handsome Narbonne, now aide-de-camp to the consul. In early 1802, on the subject of civil powers, Napoléon was heard to say that "As First Consul, I am governing, not as a military, but rather as a civil magistrate."[6] Before the disbanding of the Tribunat, Napoléon dominated four assemblies: the Council of State, the Tribunat, the Legislature, and the Senate. In the latter, gradually more and more members came from his own choosing.

Bonaparte paid close attention to his brothers Joseph, Lucien, Louis, and Jérôme. Soon he appointed them to prestigious positions in European countries which, from one victorious entry after another, he termed either republics or kingdoms. For a time scholars and scientists were welcome in his increasingly courtly entourage, musicians and artists also, especially Denon, Greuze and David. Every day, month, and year, the aura of his command widened, became more variegated, and the physiognomy of France changed. Merchants prospered; mills opened; professional vocations bloomed; bourgeois bought property. An assassination attempt tightened Bonaparte's hold. Deportations ensued. A new generation of military and administrative elites emerged. Considering her republican conviction, Germaine observed this with trepidation. Materialism and opportunism worked their brand of realism together. But concerns regarding religious belief subsisted elsewhere in the French society, for it had fractured itself. Writing on Christianity as a kind of rebirth, Chateaubriand understood this, and he approved of the message given by Delphine-Germaine. To his mind and to those of Germaine's intellectual friends, the frenzied idolizing of a Supreme Being, the spectacle of its murderous parallel in the early 1790's, had left a trauma: a sense of the tragic, a feeling of the nation's vulnerability. From the internal perspective, the malaise could certainly be attributed to "the difference in status between men and women,"[7] which Germaine had pointed out.

Readers like Chateaubriand appreciated Germaine's description of feminine independence of opinion, of Elise and Henri de Lebensei as well. Personally, Chateaubriand had reservations and one fear regarding Germaine's novel. "With scissors," he said, "I would make myself a Delphine of my own. . . . I don't like Léonce. . . . what charms me though is your depiction of unhappiness, so much so that I tremble for you. . . ."[8] As his *Génie du christianisme* appeared shortly before *Delphine,* Germaine returned the compliment: the *Génie* was very long!

Napoléon's Concordat of July 1801 was sheer political strategy. Rome being detached from the European monarchs, now came the opportune time to woo it into an alliance. However, in line with this prestigious peace treaty, church officials were to be named by the consul. Thus, church and state bonded within his hold. With Machiavellian determination, he continued recreating a government in his own way, with energy, intelligence, and astuteness. Notwithstanding the overtly political moves, in the minds of others organizational feats offset his rapidly growing despotism. We remember that at the start of his administration, again the most admirable, he let it be known that whoever wanted to work with him would be hired, aristocrats if need be, bourgeois, republicans, even moderate royalists. But now, cautious scrutiny grasped everyone. The Council of State, Legislature, and Senate continued on. He was still careful to content the Senate with prerogatives and to please his military heroes with strategic as well as honorary positions. Nevertheless, visiting diplomats who witnessed the military displays saw a change in him. His military blood was up. The extraordinarily democratic hour vanished. For one, Napoléon's interest in Constant's political acumen altered, particularly when he fired the Tribunat.

Distrust had turned to disdain, and now anger with the arrogance of its members. Napoléon's repression became manifest in individual and public domains. As Germaine and Constant were one in political aspirations and particularly in republican conviction, the consular eye followed them closely. This applied to persons in their entourage; aggravation grew. A more general, politically pregnant field of attention paralleled this: crowds now came regularly to the Tuileries, formally seeking audiences. Considering his character, the circumstance of adulation was bound to affect him. Ambition made him envisage a monarchy of his own. He acted accordingly. Receptions, celebrations, decorations honoring ongoing military victories, extravagance, pomp, and glitter engulfed his attending society. Thus his monarchical machine was born. He pardoned emigrés, returning fortunes to some, but swiftly deporting anyone connected with conspiracy. He instigated a plebiscite toward a consul-for-life nomination. It succeeded on August 2 1802. "Our enlightened bonds," he declared, "are property and commerce."[9]

Did sentiment survive from the adolescent years? Though he had formed strong attachments during his military upbringing, loved his army and his men, and had bonded with his older brother Joseph, still, from our perspective today, attachments have been difficult to fathom; strong to all appearances, they seem chameleonic. Only one person used the familiar 'tu' with him, Jean Lannes, who supported him unreservedly until his death in battle. By the end of 1803, Bonaparte the republican citizen had metamorphosed into Napoléon the ruler. The assertive public phase of his life impacted an inexorable, irreversible change from the first entry into politics. Character had not changed. It had hardened. He controlled journalistic opinion. Holding a grudge against England for its support of Bourbon agitation, he ordered recruitments, arrests were made, and war fired into the heart of Europe. Electric, subject to tantrums, he excused his excesses of temper by saying: "France is at war."[10] A voluminous, mechanistic set of regulations took hold of France; this was when Napoléon gave the official order of exile to Germaine de Staël.

Conspiracy returned. On hearing that Louis de Bourbon-Condé duke of Enghien (1772-1804) planned a return to France with military aides, Napoléon ordered the capture of the young duke in Germany. Louis's execution in March 1804 angered royalists both foreign and national. Even non-royalists shuddered at the bluntness of the act. Chateaubriand, for one, resigned from the diplomatic post Napoléon had given him in Italy. As with Germaine, Chateaubriand's feelings changed. A wound had been inflicted on Europe. It pointed to a syndrome. The consul "for life" refused to see Bourbon blood usurp his position; he had to destroy every such challenge. Facing restless European monarchs, he would indeed have to create a new monarchy.

In early April, 1804, Germaine wrote to her father that "for sure, the death of the duke of Enghien has produced much reaction. Politically speaking, a shame bound to inhibit alliances will come out of this. . . ."[11] Germaine's initially emotional reaction to the younger Bonaparte's presence, her hero-worship, her admiration, all vanished. Her perspicacious observations, her disappointment over the growing despotism upset her sense of liberty nearly as much as the order of exile. Psychological fascination with the consul as person held, but Germaine's political anima was bound to experience bitterness. As she exclaimed to her correspondent Charles de Villers, "How rare manliness is! And how far from astonishing it is that despotism can establish itself in the midst of so many who are so well suited to serve it!"[12]

The last thread of Germaine's respect broke a month later. On May 18, 1804, with Cambacérès, his school friend Louis de Bourrienne, his brother-in-law Joachim Murat, and Joseph at his side, surrounded by his senate, and with Joséphine at his feet, Napoléon proclaimed himself emperor. This happened barely one year after Germaine's order of exile. "I think that Bonaparte finds that I have too much existence . . . and without having done anything to diminish me, he does not want to see me standing . . ." she reflected, vowing to never stop writing as a friend of the Revolution.[13] The tone may seem gingerly, but the words are trenchant. She was deeply humiliated. The present was strange for her now, and most unsatisfactory. She wrote letters to Joseph Bonaparte, pleading for an end to her exile, for counsel concerning her eldest son's education, and for a return of the Necker fortune, the debt never having been paid. She suffered this exile for ten years.

Only frantic activity and miraculous literary success could assuage such unhappiness. At first, Germaine applauded the publications of her friends Camille Jordan and Louis de Fontanes—*The Real Sense of the National Vote on the Life-Consulate* and *Parallel between Caesar, Cromwell, Monk and Bonaparte,* respectively. She had supervised Camille's work, having appreciated his gift of a translation of Friedrick Klopstock's *Odes*. As ever, her friendships were open, exuberant, and growing. They offset the near hysteria often caused by police surveillance. Commuting between Coppet and nearby Geneva, she entertained her guests and organized soirées. Soon, these refuges became less and less bearable.

Escape to another territory, into strange lands and places, was not in order. Still, the temptation of going to Germany attracted her. Moreover, Germaine had changed. Something in her had amplified. In contrast to her ideological friends who relied greatly on experience, Germaine always found greater value on sentiment. Her state of duress and possibly a clarification of her thinking on the subject of feeling during the writing of *Delphine* now brought sentiment into relief. If there were to be any further writing, she would want to rely on this part of herself. Friendships and literary predilections eased some of her despair, but resilience now came from that part of her character. Besides, a part of her most congenial to sentiment "desired to fully live the instant, to enjoy it as a pure moment of existence."[14] This was her passionateness, her strength. It would come into her next major work. Meanwhile, she comforted friends who were also receiving the order of exile. Constant was near her much of the time, though his feelings for her were ever in turmoil. He had offered her shelter at his property near Paris before the exile was made clear in mid-October, 1803, at first away from Paris, then France. Germaine had accepted his offer. Now, restlessness made him despondent. He wanted an end "to this long and bizarre dependence."[15] He was disgusted with politics. His own *Principles of Politics* published in 1802 had brilliantly reminded French readers of Montesquieu's *Spirit of Laws*. He turned once again to his old project on religion. He still could not tear himself away from Germaine.

Constant responded to Germaine's own plans. Very soon after the formal order of exile they left together for Metz and on to Frankfurt, Weimar, Berlin, Leipzig, and Weimar once again. The German adventure thrilled Germaine. She relaxed enough to entertain her hosts with readings and recitations. Considering her propensity to give in to high spirits, Germaine cannot but have appeared a perplexing phenomenon to her German hosts. In retrospect, this does not seem to have impinged on her reputation. The reason is simple. Upon her arrival and stay in the culturally rich town of Weimar, she was already known and respected as an author. This is what keenly interested her new German friends. Her passionate enjoyment of reading excerpts from Racine's *Phèdre* before the Weimar court can only have been contagious. Her elocution was clear, her manner endearing. As it had been for her during her youth, the emphatethic interpretation of *Phèdre* was thorough, if not mesmerizing.

In mid-November 1803, Germaine's meeting with her correspondent Charles de Villers in Metz also lifted her morale. So far, theirs had been a most pleasant epistolary rapport. He too was an ardent friend of political liberty. He loved her *Delphine*, and said so. This time, and in person, they discussed his publications, and more than anything else his adulation for the philosopher Kant. She felt inspired to write on Germany, on its literature and philosophy. A Kantean precept stayed with her from that period on, like a bloom found on a new shore inviting creativity:

> Two things fill my heart with admiration and veneration ever renewed, ever increasing whenever reflection touches upon them and applies itself accordingly: the starlit sky above, the moral law within me.[16]

Germaine and Constant stayed in Weimar until March 1804. In spite of the excitement of the German adventure, the reality of exile itself, the thought of it every day affected Germaine. This became evident to those closest to her. She found solace in reading. Villers offered her Jean-Paul Richter's *History of My Future Life*. Reading her old family friend Suard's *Medley of Literature (Mélanges)* felt like a return to lands fully known. Shortly before Christmas, knowing that her father was ill, she wrote lovingly, expressing her self-portrait, as she put it, saying that pseudo-happiness consisted of the absence of pain. What is pleasure, she mused in her letter, if not "love, Paris, or power... each is essential to my heart, my mind and my activity, everything else is metaphysical where enjoyment is concerned, but real in suffering if those elements are lacking."[17]

At last Germaine met the eminences of German poetry: Christoph Wieland, her senior by thirty-three years and ardent francophile; then Friedrich Schiller, her peer, and finally Goethe, older by seventeen years. Weimar, then called the German Athens, benefited from the tutelage of the duke of Saxony-Weimar, Charles-August. The town enchanted her, as did her hosts. Study of the German language continued. She read Goethe's *Apprenticeship of Wilhelm Meister* with Constant. She felt inhibited in the presence of the poet himself, even though he had expressed admiration for her work and had indeed translated her *Fictions*. His comment about her visit is superlative, with a touch of mischief:

> Of all the creatures alive whom I have met, she is the most mobile, the most apt to combat and the most fertile in words. But hers is the most cultured mind... she is the most spiritual of women.[18]

Intrigued that her new friends did not live in the midst of a lively society, Germaine felt that this certainly would not suit her. On the other hand, she thought, seclusion might have been the key to their literary genius. Getting to know Germany and the Germans, Germaine felt confident. A prose translation of Goethe's ballad *The Fisherman* fascinated her. She sang, played the piano and danced for her hosts, enjoying their not seeming to mind what she called her bizarreries.

The bond with Schiller was instantaneous. He quickly perceived her sensitivity. "You have a solitary soul,"[19] he said. This pleased her immensely. They conversed for hours, inexhaustingly on her part, somewhat less so on his. Understandingly, Schiller's contemporaneity pleased her, whereas with Goethe the seniority and self-possession impeded immediate adulation. Strangely enough, there were similarities in their comportment as writers. Goethe too could have moments of "uninhibited display of self," he too was magnetic and he also wrote from feeling. Like her, he was concerned over the "problematic of feeling."[20] Such concern is part of their literary greatness. But there had been differences in background, upbringing, and early effervescences. The Goethean introversion could never meet Germaine's ebullience. But his tribute to her was gallant.

On April 18, 1804, Germaine heard of her father's death. His last advice had insisted on caution, to stay out of politics and live by one's intellectual tastes. Now, her greatest friend and mentor had gone. "What does the universe mean to me," she wrote to Claude Hochet on May 9, "as I cannot discuss it with him now! . . . All my thoughts have lost their aim. . . ."[21] In the public eye, Necker had fared poorly since July 1789. Indifference had deeply hurt him. During the solitary years at home he had written diverse political essays which, as we know, were met coldly. He had long lost his audacity and resoluteness. Literally, history has been unkind to him, not to mention those who have polarized his qualities and faults, thus only staying on the surface of this warm personality. Germaine had a very different view of him. She saw his idealism, the analytical strength, intelligence, and unceasing eagerness to examine French political society from the point of view of its "governability."[22] Germaine would ever remember her father's strengths. She had observed him closely, worried about his despondencies, and rejoiced on seeing him occupied with writing. She had once written in her journal: "how good it is that in the act of writing, a statesman can detach himself from political interests that have agitated him mercilessly! What boundless consolation his mind offers him then in his desire to help fellow beings."[23] At the time of her remark Necker was writing *De l'importance des opinions religieuses* (1788) which became her favorite among his writings.

Germaine had thrived on and benefited from Necker's unending affection, and returned it in kind. Nearly forever in her young lifetime, they had lived side by side as writers. Early on he teased her, calling her 'Monsieur de Saint-Ecritoire' (Mister Holy Writing Desk). But he had seen the quality of her work. Admiring, inspiring each other, theirs was a thorough writers' interior, but while respecting her intellect, he fretted concerning her ebullient character. He had witnessed comings and goings at Coppet with some grumbling and astonishment, but with patient generosity. He helped redress some of Eric de Staël's finances, he bore Constant's furtiveness, and agreed to welcome Bonaparte at Coppet largely to excuse Germaine's political impetuosity. Necker helped with the care and early education of his grandchildren. His impact on Auguste de Staël was fruitful. Later, Auguste entered a political career.

Germaine returned to Coppet, by coincidence one day after Napoléon's self-coronation. Her publication of her father's manuscripts and her biographical essay appeared in February, 1805. Suard praised her commemoration in *Le Publiciste*. She described Necker's moment of political triumph with filial adulation. Madame de Genlis attacked the essay in the press. Constant defended her eulogy.

On the Character of Monsieur Necker and of his Private Life reveals Germaine's talent as historian. This was particularly so where she described Necker's favored project for provincial administrations. Germaine pointed out the positive reactions to this among what she considered as France's two major classes: "the enlightened class, and the ailing class, that is to say, those who esteemed the public good, and those who suffered the effects of its lack."[24] This was only one example of Necker's moral strength. It became a permanent part of Germaine. Quietly, firmly, without ostentation, and like Necker's own religious beliefs, it permeated her oeuvre.

Further in her eulogy, Germaine expressed astonishment with Necker's calm deportment during the crises surrounding 1789. "I stayed close to him at the time of his exile. How calm and serene he was! Letters would come predicting the court's desire to have him back, others contradicting this.... He waited through this confusion with a security that I have witnessed so long as his heart and conscience were unaffected."[25] Ever present in her political, literary and now historical outlook, Germaine's interest in a person's character is a valuable component of her oeuvre. Along with this, reflections concerning the trauma of the Revolution and its impact on the French nation remained with Germaine the rest of her life. Their metamorphosis emerged at the end.

Germaine quietened, publicly and privately. Juliette Récamier, Montmorency, her cousin Madame de Saussure, Sismondi, Bonstetten and Constant were near her, urging her to come out of herself. To allay the emptiness that had struck her on the return to Coppet, they conversed with her on writing and on current publications: Madame de Genlis's *New Moral Tales*, Madame de Krüdener's *Valérie*, E. de Senancour's *Obermann*, Schiller's *William Tell*, Villers's *Essay on Luther*, Sismondi's *History of the Italian Republics*, and from yet another friend, J. De Gérando's revision of his *Comparative History of Philosophical Systems* (1804).

Solace came from nature. In *Delphine*, nature accompanied suffering with a dramatic visual impact that had a sterling quality. Now, it was as though Germaine imposed on herself the enjoyment of nature with a 'this, or else' discipline. Schiller was right. The solitary soul had acted. "I am still sad, but calmer, for nature has regained its beauty, like a music replenishing the soul's harmony.... Only in an ideal existence can one find a refuge these days. If there were no more music, no greenery, no moon during Springtime, we would not be able to understand how those feelings originate inside us, so very different from those among Napoléon's courtiers...."[26] Unhappiness gives a melancholic sting at the end of this reflection.

In early December 1804, Germaine, her children, and their new tutor departed for Italy. Constant and Sismondi met them on the way. Sismondi had long encouraged her to make this journey. The new tutor was an exceptionally fortuitous discovery, someone to whom Germaine had been introduced during the journey in Germany. Immediately she had sensed that Augustus Wilhelm Schlegel (1767-1845) would be right for her boys now approaching adolescence, and for Albertine now aged seven.

Her premonition was right. Schlegel became a stable member of Germaine's entourage for thirteen years, that is, for the rest of her life. He had read Germaine's *Passions* in a German translation seven years before the meeting in Berlin in March, 1804. He was born in Hanover in a family imbued with intellectuality. Interests in everything from theology to medicine surrounded him. He opted for theology at the university of Göttingen, later wrote a dissertation on Homer and was encouraged to translate Dante and Shakespeare into German. He became a tutor in Amsterdam, and a literary critic for the *Athenaeum* founded with his brother Friedrich. When this review ended in 1800, Wilhelm went to Berlin where he taught literature, which he had also done at the university of Iena. Known as critic and scholar to Goethe, the latter had suggested a meeting with Germaine.

Wilhelm had also been schooled in Greek, and besides Dante and Shakespeare he had translated Calderon, Italian and Portuguese literature. He had espoused as well a veritable cult for aesthetics. Granted that his eclecticism and francophile affections impressed Germaine, his prompt gesture of acceptance pleased her even more. There is scant indication that for coming into her family he fell in love with Germaine. Three aspects of his personality are known to us: at age thirty-seven, clearly, he opted to leave academia and start a new life in an environment entirely different from his own. He loved Coppet. He never deviated from the contract Germaine imposed at the outset—to help her with her children, to assist in her study of the German language, to be her secretary. Germaine gained a faithful friend, and the security she had long sought for the education of her children. To a large extent she had tutored them so far, her father and Montmorency had helped indeed, and there had been a previous tutor, but now the situation needed regularity. Friendship ensued on all parts. Most probably, except for Constant's gyrations, Schlegel's presence during the next thirteen years offered Germaine a balance within the ever-exuberant ambiance she created. This was so even though her 'joie de vivre' was contrary to Schlegel's morose character and at times caused him distress. Now, an excellent tutor provided attention and affection to her children.

Wilhelm's reaction to his new lifestyle was positive. Comfort, the freedom to study and meditate, a horse, swimming in the lake, and access to the Coppet library "near a woman with rare kindness and openness of mind... are an epoch in my life,"[27] Schlegel wrote to a friend in Germany on May 25, 1804. Conscientious regarding his assignments, he admired the fact that Germaine continued giving translation exercises to her children.

Bonstetten and Sismondi were often at Coppet then, while Constant's presence manifested nothing short of jealousy toward the new tutor. But as in the recent past, Coppet became a modus vivendi of writers given to literary and philosophical research. When Wilhelm's brother Friedrich came for a month's visit, Germaine appreciated his 'metaphysical' talent, as she put it, but she preferred Wilhelm whose knowledge astonished her. After the return from Italy, if not during the journey itself, Schlegel experienced momentary rebelliousness, perhaps even a love-crisis. However, allowing for Germaine's displeasure over this, in October, 1805, Schlegel pleaded for her tolerance of him strictly in terms of the original contract. Germaine remarked to Friedrich on Wilhelm's melancholia which, she added, "he attributes to me but is the effect of the country in which we live, and he can be assured that for ever, I love him as a brother."[28]

The journey to Italy lasted from the end of December 1804, to late June, 1805. From Torino they went to Milan, Bologna, Rimini, Rome, Naples, Venice, and Florence with returns to Bologna and Rome where once again she met Humboldt, her mentor of German studies. The party met Lucien Bonaparte, the Portuguese ambassador's son Pedro de Souza, the military count Maurice O'Donnell who accompanied Germaine during her tour of Rome, and the poet Vincenzo Monti (1754-1828). Her meeting with Caroline Bonaparte Murat irked Napoléon. Germaine exulted in the Italian experience. She engaged in a sentimental correspondence with Souza, O'Donnell, and Monti. In Rome, the Italian Academy of Letters (Arcadia) honored her, and applauded her declamatory prowess. She was given the name Telesilla Argoica, the Greek poetess who led the city of Argos to victory against Sparta.[29]

Travels also took Germaine to Ferrara, Padua, Verone, Venice, and once again Milan and Torino. Describing her state of mind to Suard, she explained that "perhaps unhappiness gives one's thinking a cruel activity. . . . I have felt the impact of nature more than elsewhere. . . . I will write the kind of novel that will be the frame of my Italian journey and I believe that many thoughts and sentiments will find their place there."[30] On arriving in Naples, Germaine agreed with Chateaubriand that the city did calm one's soul, but to Monti she added a critical innuendo: "In Naples, I felt as if enthusiasm came from the air, nature's perfumes and marvels . . . But a nation so favored by the sky and so degraded by its government . . . where physical life is beautiful and the moral narrow, such a nation only likes the superficial: it needs tableaus, wanting to see rather than feel and think."[31]

Italy alleviated Germaine's grief. At this point in her life, aged thirty-eight, with her vitality intact, she passed the test of sorrow. Returning to Coppet, Germaine was poised to write the second novel. This became her first resonant retort to exile. It countered darkness—a talisman, as it were.

> She is all one piece. Nothing is false, nothing morbid, which means that in spite of the enormous difference in our natures and way of thinking I am comfortable with her. . . . She represents French culture in its purity . . . her handsome intelligence rises up to the level of genius. . . . She will not accept the obscure, the inaccessible; regions that she cannot capture do not exist for her.[32]
>
> Friedrich Schiller, 1804

12.
THE TEST OF SUCCESS

> Do you know this country, where the sun
> Caresses orange blossoms so lovingly?
> Have you heard the melodies
> Celebrate the gentleness of nights?
> Have you inhaled such perfumes,
> Luxuries of air pure and soft?
> Strangers, where you have come from, tell me,
> Is nature as beautiful and generous?[1]
>
> Germaine de Staël, *Corinne or Italy*, 1806
> Corinne's Capitoline improvisation:
> Mignon's song.

The setting is Italy in 1795, on the eve of Napoléon's Italian campaign. Throughout the seventeenth and most of the eighteenth centuries, Spain and Austria had dominated Italy. Though physically intact, the old magnificent cities had lost their political powers. The story, *Corinne or Italy,* therefore takes place during the ancient country's last breath.

Corinne is a young woman of genius, poetess, musician, actress and declamatory improviser all in one. She speaks directly to her audience, inviting all to enjoy life with her in their exquisite physical environment. Her vivacity and beauty, her language and knowledge are magic to the melancholic military traveler, Oswald, Lord Nelvil, the Scotsman who will love her. To him, Corinne's qualities are like the jewels of a necklace, there to be discovered and cherished one by one. Corinne is touched by Oswald's sensitivity. His reserve troubles her. She reflects on her destiny. Is destiny the pursuit of glory, she wonders, or that of love?

In spite of Oswald's reserve and opposition to her outspokenness, "in their souls mysteries and emotions point to a secret kind of resemblance."[2] Corinne's mind is mobile, like the novelist's own state of mind during the act of writing. This double introspection often arrests the story's flow. Each pause manifests the writer's solitariness, and her own story. With each return to her heroine, the flow resumes. Corinne's ambiance emerges, warm, imaginative, and far too content with aesthetic enjoyments to submit to social compunctions of any kind.

Oswald comes from a conventional society ruled by elders like his father and now the old family friend Madame Edgermont. For a moment, love breaks through his old attachments. Corinne respects his dignity. Their quiet feeling of happiness is indeed like that resemblance of soul. Intimacy comes not from Oswald, but from seductive Corinne. She has taken the first step, and firmly decides to make Oswald remain in Italy.

Though for some time he cannot bring himself to reveal his sadness over the loss of his father, Oswald declares his love. Corinne comforts him, understanding that his sense of duty connects with a morality existing in a society different from hers. She has experienced that kind of society before coming to Rome, for she was once part of the Edgermont family—a secret she will divulge in time. The relationship develops, but not without unevenness. Corinne's powerful imagination, the pleasures it creates for her, distress Oswald to the point of his displeasure.

Oswald is never on firm ground in his new attachment. Italy is not his firm ground. He is a transplanted soul. That he reproaches Corinne for abandoning herself to joyfulness in the presence of others, that he is moody and forbidding, and goes so far as to demand that she sacrifice her public successes, agitate Corinne. Ebullience is an integral part of her character. She resists, dancing at festivities and giving poetic improvisations. When alone with him, she attempts to contain exaltation. Inexorably, one's anxiety alternates with the other's remonstrations. Corinne gives a splendid performance in *Romeo and Juliet*. Oswald, frantic in his possessiveness, admits his jealousy: ". . . no matter what advantages or gifts he owned, he could not equal hers, and this idea inspired fears concerning the duration of their affection."[3]

Moments of shared sentiment before the art and ancient beauties of Italy bring a respite. These are calm uniformities of mood in the novel. But Corinne and Oswald possess judgements that are too mobile, too incisive. However, a new tenderness overcomes Oswald when he realizes that Corinne's poetic success is vital to her. Learning that her social standing within the Edgermont family is being questioned, he decides to help her. He leaves Corinne. Once in his native environment, Oswald sways from his duty to Corinne. His late father had selected Corinne's half-sister Lucile for Oswald's bride. The elder Lord Nelvil's domination subsisted beyond death. Oswald becomes interested in Lucile who, in appearance and manner, is the antithesis of Corinne. Prodded by Lucile's mother, respecting his late father's memory, Oswald marries Lucile.

On hearing the news of Oswald's marriage, Corinne becomes inactive and reclusive. Her creativity has been shattered. Returning to Italy, Oswald laments over Corinne's fatal transformation. His speech, his whole being suffers from the counteraction of pain against vanished happiness.

> This beautiful Corinne whose animated features full of life were destined to portray happiness, this daughter of the sun, marked by a secret suffering, resembled flowers still fresh and brilliant yet fatally menaced by a dark spot.[4]

Sad reconciliation comes in the presence of Oswald's child. Corinne dies. Oswald's love for Italy succumbs. So does the rule he had once given himself: "in happiness and unhappiness, one must be at peace with oneself."[5] Hounded by unbearable thought and feeling, he wanders away aimlessly.

Germaine's novel presents a new heroine who creates her world in complete harmony with her physical surroundings. She is vigorous, naturally responds to beauty, and acts accordingly. Compared with Delphine, Corinne is flesh and blood, living on the soil she has chosen for herself. She is therefore more human.

The novel takes place in a setting known to many, but poetic sources far outweigh it: Petrarch, Ovid, Virgil, Tasso, Plutarch, and Tacitus. They are Corinne's gods. Shakespeare is there, whose Juliet Corinne will impersonate. Her mind draws from her gods, and from site to site she makes surrounding antiquities her own through ecstasy. Corinne is also sensitive to natural beauty. She is another Mignon, whom Goethe extolled during his Weimar years (1775-1786). Her improvisation of the nostalgic young girl enchants Oswald. But Corinne is also modern-minded. She respects the renowned Alfieri, Metastasio, and Kant. During discussions with Oswald she draws from Jacques Necker's *Course on Religious Morality* (1800).

Which is to say that *Corinne or Italy* is autobiographical. It can be said that the novel's heroine and much of her love story spring from the author's personal fantasies. Young women with imagination and emotional depth often create their ideal selves in daydreams, intensely so if their society and even their own weaknesses inspire such an effort of mind. Destiny, success, and affections come naturally during these fantasies. In rare cases, as with Germaine de Staël, the mind creates in writing or in art a lifelike fantasy, body and soul combined. Love is a logical projection, for the writer's ideal is a woman eager to love and vulnerable to it all at once.

Germaine's first journey in Italy brought forth not only what she saw—hence the descriptive elements of her book, but friendships that stirred new affections. Germaine is like her creation, eager to love, and exceedingly sensitive to male affection. In the novel, Corinne's similar eagerness reaches Oswald. How, then, does Germaine present a new hero who will respond to Corinne's appeal, and possibly with a sensitivity superior to that of Léonce toward Delphine? Where is the prototype, in Germaine's own life? Could it have been the Italian poet-friend Vincenzo Monti? No, for Monti does not have any of Oswald's characteristics. Monti possessed Corinne's charm. The transfer may have happened. "That beautiful sky is in your eyes," Germaine wrote to Monti in mid-June, 1805, and its climate is in your soul." Just returned from Italy, Germaine was readying for her novel. "You cannot know how much life you bring to life," she added.

> If existence is a good thing, you double it when one converses with you. Your eloquence and mobility, the latter dangerous to whoever loves you, exude charm and diversity. . . . You are Italy to me, its marvels and its charms.[6]

Monti visited Coppet in October 1805, when Germaine had started her novel. A few months before, Napoléon requested from Monti the historiography of Italy; Monti had to leave Coppet. That same fall, Germaine now immersed in her novel, there came to Coppet the young writer Prosper de Barante (1782-1866), whose father was the local prefect. Prosper fell in love with Germaine. The description of Corinne's intimate rapport with Oswald evidently reflected this attachment. Prosper eventually distanced himself, respecting his father's wishes.

Constant's propensity to exaltation and his hesitancies may have etched themselves into Oswald's character. Years of enthusiastic conversations between Germaine and Constant on history, ancient and modern literature may have inspired the novel's dialogues, and even the painful efforts Oswald made to understand Corinne. Like Oswald, Constant had past commitments toward his father and these troubled him. Jealousy, hesitation toward Germaine inflicted agitation on both parts. Always Germaine's intellectual counterpart, Constant worshipped her superior mind, admired her authorship, and faithfully published reviews of her work. In part, Oswald is Constant.

But Benjamin Constant was not a northerner, nor military. Adolf de Ribbing fitted these traits. Memories of Ribbing's gentlemanliness lingered in Germaine's mind. He may have partly entered Oswald, minus the latter's morbidity and social prejudice.

If Corinne is a fantasy flecked with autobiographical caprices of the pen, it can partly be seen as a romantic effusion. Aesthetic enthusiasm, nostalgia, yearnings for affection, thoughts on destiny, ecstasy before classical ruins, love for nature, and pathos, these are all components of the romantic psyche. They meet in Corinne, in her gestures, language, voice, and physical force. Born in 1805, Corinne is the first of her kind in French literature. However, she is more vigorous than her younger sister of the nineteenth century—George Sand's melancholic and consummate musician Consuelo. Corinne's rusticity will not transcend into her romantic descendants. She is too attached to her chosen soil. Though tragic, her temperament is not soft and lamenting, and she is never sentimental. She is after all the Enlightenment's child, where eloquence incites to action, and philosophy and religion are revered together. But again, she is also a post-revolutionary emblem of Italy, where past, present, and future meet. She does cross the bridge into the romantic era while carrying the beauties of her favored antiquity, but she points toward the future.

Corinne or Italy was published in the summer of 1807. Success greeted the novel. From afar, Goethe complimented Germaine. Napoléon's *Le Moniteur* grumbled that while being overly descriptive, the novel did not compliment France, the fatalistic and erudite character of Erfeuil being unpleasant. But Napoléon's marshals read *Corinne*. All of Europe read *Corinne*. All received the message of Italy's glory. In the final analysis, "art, grandeur and enthusiasm" form an equilibrium with "ruins, death, melancholia and consolation, all being themes that amplify" in the novel's progression.[7]

Much as Germaine's Italian readers liked her description of their landscapes, her representation of nature's interplay of light and shadow, clouds and wind was but a sensory accompaniment to the story. With Germaine, characterization came first, and in conjunction with it, differences in disposition toward society. Her composite priority served the action and mood of her novel. It was its steady focus, as in *Delphine*.

Germaine had long reflected on the opinion of men concerning women of exceptional talents. In the *De la littérature*, two years before *Delphine* and seven before *Corinne*, Germaine anticipated the fates of her two heroines:

> ... Is she not an extraordinary woman? men will ask. No more need to be said. Such a woman is abandoned to her own strengths, and left to suffer on her own.... She must continue in her singular existence ... within classes that are not hers ... and who consider her a class of her own....
> She is an object of curiosity, perhaps envy, and one deserving pity.[8]

No one could escape from Germaine's priority. Napoléon's marshals may have sought respite from the battlefield, aristocratic and bourgeois readers unknown to Germaine may have been enamoured with the novel's cultural and emotive substances, but these were not the only incentives for reflecting, reading on, and considering *Corinne* a welcome talisman. In 1807 and on into 1809 Europe was in turmoil.

In the late fall of 1805, when Germaine started writing her novel, Napoléon had captured Vienna. His victory at Ulm on October 20, 1805, and his defeat at Trafalgar the next day gave everyone a quiver. Ugly counterblows followed. Bloodshed at Austerlitz forced Austria to relinquish its Italian possessions. England decided to create a blockade from Elba to Brest. When Napoléon imposed on German princes the signing of a Confederation of the Rhine, the Holy Roman Empire vanished from everyone's mind. As pressure mounted, coalitions among the European nations accumulated, and Prussia mobilized. Further French victories at Iena and Eylau in November and February were not enough for the mobile emperor. Triumphant at Friedland against Russia in the summer of 1807, he invited tsar Alexander I to Tilsit and staged a dramatic peace treaty. He had humbled Austria. Now he flattered her capital with a lavish military court.

All eyes opened. Russia became agitated. Napoléon's subjugation of Spanish princes and his armies' entry into Portugal preluded massive bloodshed. In January, 1808, his armies invaded Spain all of which suffered murderous confusion and devastation for five years. European fear turned to indignation. More troops overran a country bereft of its prisoner-monarch Ferdinand VII. Made king of Spain, Joseph Bonaparte ruled minimally, ignorant of guerilla warfare.

Spain was Napoléon's tactical error. Europe had wearied, it distrusted his treaties and was insensed when Pope Pius VII was forced to reside in Fontainebleau. The fifth attempt at a coalition broke after Napoléon's victory at Wagram. Europe became angry. In December, 1809, Russia abandoned the Tilsit agreements. Arthur Wellesley duke of Wellington (1769-1852) came to the Iberian peninsula. England had entered the arena.

Privately, political exile anguished Germaine. Humiliation, surveillance and the incessant capture of her mail made her frantic and sleepless. "Exile," she wrote when depicting Corinne's first departure from England, "is for sensitive beings a torture more cruel than death; the environment becomes unpleasant, life in general also, even details of one's life.... One only knows the pleasures of one's country for having lost them."[9]

At the time of the treaty of Tilsit, Germaine reconsidered her situation. Perhaps she could go to America, and her eldest, Auguste, might benefit from such a plan as his studies had weakened. Would Thomas Jefferson welcome her son in America? Dated April 25, 1807, Germaine's letter to the president of the United States stated her request; she also expressed her opinion of the French emperor: "... Against the judgement of men ... the one who disposes of everything will perhaps decide how to end the debate between power and virtue...." Jefferson replied affectionately on July 16, 1807: "The grandson of Mr. Necker ... will find a sincere welcome at Monticello."[10]

Germaine's plan did not carry through. She had to oversee the printing of *Corinne*. The novel's reception cheered her. Except in one particular case, friends close to her were filled with admiration. Constant gave a positive review. Remembering their walks together in Rome, Humboldt complimented her on her cosmopolitanism.

From slightly further afield, the Swedish diplomat baron Carl von Brinkman (1776-1847), who knew Germaine since 1800, loved Corinne, but not the pseudo-hero of the story. In his opinion, Oswald could not match Corinne, considering her strengths. Brinkman overlooked three contextual elements: Corinne's reason for choosing Oswald; the nature of their bond; Oswald's internal conflict. Germaine had written that it is easy to understand "how a woman devoted to the arts and letters can love a man with differing qualities and tastes. Such a woman tires of herself, and cannot be seduced by a being who resembles her: harmony of feeling and character oppositions are needed so that love can arise out of both sympathy and diversity."[11] We may recall that in an earlier chapter, Germaine prepared the reader for the above argument by referring to the mystery that can be part of a love relationship: "in spite of differences . . . there was a secret soul resemblance supposing a similar nature, though circumstances modified this nature differently."[12] Germaine's argument holds once she alludes to 'kindred souls', for this spurred the lovers' particular bond. Earlier still, Germaine defined Oswald's behavior with verisimilitude: "Lord Nelvil's mind was . . . penetrating, but he only looked at himself in terms of the past. He viewed actual situations with confusion. Easily carried away, easily remorseful, passionate and timid, conflicting elements within him prevented him from understanding himself before events themselves occurred."[13]

Monti also praised Germaine's book. The exception was Prosper de Barante, who expressed strong misgivings. As we know, he had been close to Germaine when she started to write *Corinne*. Yes, he said, Corinne is real. "But you have locked me inside Oswald, and I cannot defend myself. You have known how to mix imagination and reality . . . and made Oswald dejectable. . . . He has come too close to the truth. . . ."[14] Later, Prosper bitterly reproached Germaine for having thus used their intimacy.

Germaine's close friends did not object to seeing their accomplishments praised by Corinne—Humboldt, Monti, Goethe, Sismondi, the brothers Schlegel, Friederika Brun, the actor Talma, and Juliette for her portrayal of the famous 'shawl' dance of the day. Publicly, *Corinne* overshadowed the novels of romanesque entanglements that were popular at the time, such as those of Ann Radcliffe. Names like Genlis, Tensin, Cottin, Charrière, Meulan, and Edgeworth did not have Madame de Staël's muscle and fire.

Against the exile, success sustained Germaine only to a degree. Constant's novels *Adolphe* and *Cécile* brought renown, but Germaine was troubled: her possessive and domineering character traits were manifest in *Cécile*. In fact, Constant's absences and Germaine's reproaches complicated the two lives that had so bonded more than fifteen years. Constant had secretly married. He 'cloistered' himself, to use his own words, where no one could reach his interior self, for "my life is nowhere but in myself."[15] Now, Constant thoroughly distressed Germaine. Her attachment to him had become instinctive, and filled with the illusion of his undying affection. Beyond intimacy, their paths separated, even though Constant's presence at Coppet was felt now and then.

New friends came to Coppet. The dramatist Elzéar de Sabran, for one, and in the winter all participated in theatricals honoring Voltaire. Germaine wrote *Agar dans le desert* for such an occasion. In April 1806, she was allowed to journey as far as forty leagues from Paris. With Souza, Montmorency, Juliette, Jordan, Hochet, Sabran, Prosper and Constant as well, she went to Auxerre and Rouen. It was here that *Corinne* was completed. The poetess Friederika Brun honored Germaine in a text on Geneva. Germaine reviewed their mutual friend Bonstetten's text *On Nature and the Laws of the Imagination*. Germaine stole into Paris at the end of April, just before the publication of *Corinne*. She was promptly made to return to Coppet. Juliette and Prince Augustus of Prussia—nephew of Frederick the Great—were Germaine's guests. The artist Elisabeth Vigée-Lebrun came as well. Her painting of Germaine as Corinne seated at the Cap Misène came from that period. Germaine thanked Elisabeth, admitting to the picture's idealization of herself.

Chateaubriand became a welcome visitor. He advised Germaine to give more time to the enjoyment of her countryside. He had published a controversial essay on the Revolution in *Le Mercure*. "Napoléon is a false man," he wrote, lamenting that the murder of d'Enghien, the war in Spain, and the poor treatment of the Pope revealed "a nature foreign to France."[16] Discussions on spiritualism with Chateaubriand, Gérando, and Schlegel softened Germaine's restlessness.

But Germaine's 'joie de vivre' was affected. Was her talent intact, she wondered. She reproached herself for what she called her flighty conduct (légèretés). Writing to Gérando in mid-July, 1807, she confided that the best she hoped to have accomplished was "the education of my children . . . so that they can honor their grandfather."[17]

That summer, Germaine gave more thought to the idea of a text on Germany.

Does one dare compare France with Germany, she asked herself. What is the German psyche? A second journey to Germany began in November of that year with Albert, Albertine, and Schlegel. Recently, the hospitality of Germany's honored poets had been exhilarating. Now, in Munich, Weimar, and Vienna, she sensed a generally sharp and overt disdain for France. This vexed her natural cosmopolitanism. She felt that the idea that Germans have good sense and the French have wit could be "modified in a thousand ways. Surely . . . the most enlightened in both countries can understand that spirited thinking is but reason applied to new objects . . . the mass of the two nations will always be in opposition; but at the summit, everyone meets in a common language."[18] From 1807 on, the thought of writing on Germany allied with this conviction. Earnestly, while traveling, she continued with studies of the German language and literature.

The party had reached Vienna in mid-January 1808; they opted to stay mainly there until the end of May. They traveled to points nearby, to Bohemia and Moravia. The care of her children included playets that, like *La Sunamite,* were not only meant to entertain their hosts but to act as educational diversions. They allowed ten-year-old Albertine to appear on stage. Germaine saw Maurice O'Donnell, who had been her companion part of the time in Italy, and Sismondi, who stayed nearby until Germaine's return to Switzerland. Correspondence filled the days and evenings, but Germaine well knew that her letters were being opened. Serious thought effervesced. *Corinne* had been an embrace of Italy. It had made an impact. If, in harmony with the sculptural relief of its heroine Germaine had caught the spirit of Italy, then could one attempt to embrace Germany as well? Germaine felt that France did not know this neighbor, which Napoléon and his soldiers were trampling upon. Now she was determined: France should know Germany. Goethe wrote to her, enjoining her to speak well of his people. The project was innovative even for this reason alone.

In Vienna, Germaine had met Charles Prince de Ligne (1735-1814), Necker's peer, a former Austrian marshal. His was the voice of the Old Régime, of its military upbringing, knowledge and experience. Cosmopolitan and aristocratic to the extreme, Ligne had pleased sovereigns and men of letters by his conversational charm. He had met Voltaire and had given sympathetic accounts of visits with Rousseau. Though having proclaimed himself a Frenchman, he had come to loathe the Revolution and its despotic aftermath. A prolific writer, he was eager to publish memoirs in which he accused Napoléon of being a sorcerer, "a man whom some call a god and others a devil, but never a man. . . ." Ligne added that "only by losing the war can Napoléon acquire the reputation of a great man, though he ruined this by being only a good captain and the torment of the world."[19] Such was the cry of the old world. When Germaine published a preface to the section on letters in Ligne's memoirs, he was grateful, but still could not respond to her republicanism.

At that time Germaine met the thirty-five-year-old Clemens von

Metternich. His anger against Napoléon presented a harsher front: starting with Prussia, a new coalition had to be aligned against the self-proclaimed emperor. His belligerence, the royal seats he instituted in Holland, Westphalia, Naples, and Spain, the gluttony of spoils, the incessant battles, the resulting commercial atrophy of Europe, all of these ills had to be addressed. Metternich's elder Goethe had met Napoléon in early October, 1808, after the Erfurt Conference, and said, in his typically laconic style: "Napoléon *is* something, and one can see by his looks that he is; that is all."[20]

This time, Germaine's theatrics did not enthuse Vienna. Ostensibly exiled though now a well-known author, she sensed suspiciousness in the Habsburg circle. She felt the hatred for Napoléon, and the nefarious effects of political intrigue. But the encounters with Ligne and Metternich remained in her thoughts. If she were to write on lands east and north of the Rhine, she would have to be cautious and impartial. She did not know at the time that she had greatly impressed Metternich's associate and historian Frederich von Gentz. His remarks would have cheered her.

> I found her easy to be with, very clear, never leaving the subject, organized, coherent, really great and engaging as no other woman in society. . . . Nowhere else have I found such universality and depth of soul.[21]

Napoléon hated Gentz, knowing that he was a political agent yearning for a stronger Germany. The emperor was aware of Germaine's travels, contacts, and ascendancy in public opinion. Surveillance continued abroad.

Germaine returned to Coppet, her coach filled with books and gifts. She studied scrupulously. Schlegel gave readings from Lessing and Goethe. Julie de Krüdener came, creating a mood of pietist mysticism. With Montmorency, Sismondi, Sabran, and Vigée-Lebrun, she enjoyed a shepherds' feast at Interlaken. The economist baron Kaspar de Voght visited Coppet. He imparted his knowledge of Prussia to Germaine. Voght applauded her work: she would "win battles that would decide the fate of a nation."[22]

The exile reached its eighth year. It caused Germaine to fail the test of success. She worked in earnest, her creative powers were intact, but she had qualms concerning her future as a writer. She had anticipated Corinne as much as she had Delphine, she presented them both, and set them free into the public's embrace. Now, she would look at old Germanic Europe, its people, and try to capture their character, struggles and hopes. Wistfully, she wrote to Ligne: "One must offer something,—a legacy."[23]

True thinking and generous sentiment, are they not what this world needs from beings capable of carrying them out? Should each woman and man not open a path according to her or his character and talent? Or should they imitate the bees, where hives fill with activity without progress?[24]

                                        Germaine de Staël, *Corinne ou l'Italie*, 1806

13.
THE PATH TO GLORY

> ... My dear Sir ... You have seen the first days of the French Revolution and I remember that at my father's house you were saying to the revolutionaries present that their demagoguery would bring despotism to France. Your prediction came true. ...[1]
> Germaine de Staël to Thomas Jefferson, November 10, 1812

Germany is the homeland of thought, Germaine expressed at the beginning of her text *De l'Allemagne*. But the country is not yet formed as a nation, she continued. It is a disparate medley of states not even bonded in a federation, and they are oppressed by war. How can one generalize on peoples some of whom are northern, others southern, yet enough to support such a claim? Germaine admits her difficulty. She quickly finds her recourse: she will speak of character in the circumstance of solitariness, most certainly so in comparison with France:

> The clearest contrast can be seen between minds that have developed in solitude and those formed by society. Impressions coming from outside oneself versus meditations of the soul ... action versus theory, all offer strongly opposite results. The literature, arts, philosophy and religion of the two peoples attest to this difference.[2]

The air people breathe; their soil; local governments and events; the countryside, tastes, and mores the roots that, unlike those of the Latins, tend toward self-analysis and melancholy, all have to be taken into account, the impacts of wars and ecclesiastic power also. Germans have a Gothic spirit; memories of chivalry linger. Within the mores, good-naturedness (bonhomie) and domestic affections are evident. If oppressed, which is the present circumstance, Germaine adds, submission is strong. They work hard, are respectful, but they hold to their customs, charters and legends. Climate connects with states of mind. Northern fogs and frosts are kin to people of powerful imagination, and music is in their blood. They are worriers, and have formed cumbersome class separations that are passively repeated. Education is serious, love is serious, more so than marriage which can readily be dissolved by divorce. Religious faith is deep. Protestantism has been facilitated by the natural spirit of analysis. Luther, Germaine remarks, has the most German character—rustic firmness, conviction, courage, and eagerness in the study of abstract ideas.[3]

Although Germans lack the vivacity and social charm of the French, they have benefited from their vigorous spirit of analysis. Their way of seeing things and feeling has guided them toward those "diverse regions of the soul" which Goethe, their most talented poet, has delineated.[4] Solitary labor and its corollary independence have given Germany great writers indeed—Lessing, Klopstock, Goethe, and Schiller. With one, literary criticism flourishes; with the other, a patriotic spirit is born. With Goethe magnificent poetic vistas are opened, from the youthful *Sorrows of Werther* to the world-weary *Faust*. With young Schiller there is genius, a naturalness "identifying with everything that is beautiful and true over and above any country, any century."[5]

Germaine maintains her grasp of the German psyche beyond the great writers; she enters the religious and philosophical domains. It is a tour de force. She is at once historian, critic, interpreter, translator. Schlegel has been supportive, but Germaine's memory of her association with Villers has also greatly helped. Her admiration of Schiller's sensitive creativity is personal. He had translated Racine's *Phèdre*, Germaine's favorite play, this being just previous to his premature death in 1805. Germaine treasured their meeting, regretting his disappearance. In her enjoyment of German thinking, she realized that her own convictions regarding morality in writing were more solid than before. The enthusiasm described at the end of her book has just that personal significance. It is not just an extroverted exuberance, a panache. It is vivacity of mind, its home is the open mind; its enemy is mediocrity, the sleep of mind. Such vivacity is aesthetic experience per se.

Besides having met some of the writers whose works she describes,

Germaine had visited places, attended plays, and witnessed traditional events in situ. The simple life-style of the Moravians moved her. She may have remembered the freedom festivity in Switzerland's Interlaken, when she sat next to Elisabeth Vigée-Lebrun, "so animated, so full of genius" that the artist felt inspired to represent her companion as Corinne.[6]

Germaine knew that Immanuel Kant's thinking had been a subject of controversy in both Germany and France, and had continued on after his death in 1804. His complicated style and vocabulary puzzled readers eager to understand this new philosophy. The position he took against some previous and contemporary thought disgruntled admirers of Locke, Leibniz, and Jacobi. For Locke, sense experience is the source of knowledge; for Leibniz, the understanding of one's destiny, if at all possible, is a single, individual motion; for Jacobi, religion is the only avenue to truths beyond those given by experience. In Germaine's understanding of Kant, over and above the senses and individual conjectures concerning destiny, over and above belief also, conscience and the feeling of duty it creates are the only viable sources of human thought, of the application of reasoning and of aesthetic judgment. Kant's precept that conscience is "the spontaneous activity of the soul"[7] could not but appeal to Germaine. Her search for "movements of the soul" during the experience with fiction agreed with this.

She had embraced Goethe's notion of the 'regions of the soul'; now she readily connected with the moral philosophy of the solitary man of Koenigsburg. As she began her *De l'Allemagne*, intellectual Europe was bewildered by the three Kantean *Critiques* of 1781-1787, 1788, and 1790. From Kant's point of view, here was a challenge to the Enlightenment's praise of human accomplishment, but minus religious morality affected by dogmatic, mystical or evangelical precepts. His entire work, from the short essay on the beautiful and the sublime, which Villers introduced to Germaine, up to the final text which in his words placed 'religion within the limits of reason alone,' every Kantean moment of thought constituted a call to arms against self-centeredness and interest. Spontaneously, Germaine understood this call. Her moralistic fiber had been touched when Villers showed her Kant's reflection concerning "the stars above and the moral law within." Her republican ideal of liberty met with this reflection in a Rousseauesque, Christian manner. She too was a moralist, though not with a philosophical frame of mind. Hers was a naturalism imbued with the inimitable romantic enthusiasm that she possessed and hopefully projected onto others.

Lengthy and variegated, *De l'Allemagne* reveals much of Germaine the writer. At times one must allow thought to rest, she muses. One must shake the imagination, aspire to know the human heart, and inspire curiosity on the notions of philosophy. Her words are fresh and psychologically sound but the style is poetic. When she adds to "the language of the soul" that along with this, music, art and poetry can be made to develop in others,[8] she is at the heart of pedagogy and aesthetics combined. Metaphysics, the analysis of ultimate reality, has to be rethought. One has to dig (creuser) deeper down into the self. She is a true Kantean here. If there is such a thing as perfectibility confronting society's hypocrisy—which she has described in her novel *Delphine*, and failure in this, then we are far from the goal of moral perfection.

In the second part of her text, Germaine places herself in the minds of ordinary people: " Do they really know this earth," she asks, ". . . does their heart not beat on hearing echoes in the mountains, do they understand the diversity of countries, accents and foreign idioms, popular songs and dances that reveal the genius of others . . . do they not have such sensations and memories. . . ? Can nature possibly be felt without such enthusiasm?"[9]

The exile's noose tightened. Chateaubriand shared Germaine's anguish: "A thousand details of Napoléon's oppression are scattered to the winds in the story of his tyranny. The persecuted dreaded meeting their friends for fear of compromising them; the latter did not dare visit them, for fear of aggravating their demise . . . one lived in fear of the despot."[10] In February, 1810, a new governmental department controlled printing, librairies, and it enforced censure. Germaine immersed herself in a private printing of *De l'Allemagne*. An editor named Nicolle assisted her in this in Tours. A semblance of respite came during a five-month stay at Chaumont near the Loire, and later at Fossé. She rented these chateaus, invited her friends, and corrected proofs of her text. This ended abruptly when she, Juliette Récamier, and Mathieu de Montmorency were ordered out of France by the police minister Rovigo. She had made the dangerous error of sending her book to Napoléon along with a letter pleading for an end to the exile, and for a chance to have her children educated in Paris. She was not listened to, Chateaubriand wrote on her behalf, nor was he, nor were many others. Nor did Napoléon like *De l'Allemagne*. His henchmen censured it, then proceeded to seize and pillage the manuscript. Fortunately, a copy had been put into the safe hands of Germaine's son Auguste and sent out of France. A year later, Schlegel arranged for the security of the proofs in Vienna; it was published in French in London three years later.

Your book is not French, the duke of Rovigo said. She was beside herself with anger, frustration, and now fear. *They* had not seen that France, its vivacity and genius were present in her text, comparison and contrast juxtaposing France with Germany, whether openly or in innuendo. No one could dispute the presence of Voltaire's genius at the root of French vivacity and the cultivation of good taste even though the Revolution had torn the country's spiritual thrust to pieces, if not morality itself. But these qualities had not vanished. The censurers did not understand this message. Germaine's desire to have two great nations know each other was not heeded. Worse still, Germaine herself, her text, and her political status and renown precluded any understanding at the top. The tyrant, as Chateaubriand put it, "saw the arrogance of an uncontrolled self-esteem"[10] in Germaine's independent venture.

Despondent, Germaine abandoned herself to new attachments: the young Russian diplomat count Piotr F. de Balk; Camille Jordan, now member of the Académie; and again, Maurice O'Donnell. She wrote to Talleyrand, now viceroy; no answer came. She thought of getting married. Coppet became the scene of theatricals, literally and figuratively. The stage actor Talma came. Scenes from Racine's *Phèdre* and excursions near Coppet gathered all guests. Sismondi, the German playwright Zacharias Werner, and Schlegel worked at their projects. Schlegel's manuscript on *Dramatic Art* reached serious proportions, and with Adalbert Chamisso, a guest acting as translator, he was able to complete it. Adalbert was a young German poet whom Prosper de Barante had brought along to Chaumont. He started writing *Peter Schlemihl* there.

Once everyone returned to Coppet, Chamisso became quite enamored with his hostess. Germaine wrote short comedies for her visitors—*Capitaine Kernadec, Signora Fantastici, Mannequin*. A new prefect named Capelle took his post in Geneva; he was unpleasant, and this weighed heavily on Germaine. She became feverish. The children were growing up. An English governess became part of Germaine's household. Frances Randall also acted as secretary. She liked Coppet, adapted herself to Germaine's lively routine, and became a lifelong friend. Her presence was a pleasant happening. More readings filled the evenings, musicales with harp, guitar, and piano accompaniments.

Germaine's friends noticed her anguish. "She is a tragic personage," Chamisso wrote: "she will perish in this exile."[11] Germaine heard that her publisher Nicolle was ruined by censorship. Surveillance intensified, coming from the new prefect.

In November 1810, having settled in Geneva for the winter, Germaine met a young Genevese hussard named John Rocca. Wounded and ill with tuberculosis, he had come home from the Spanish front. He had published a paper on the campaigns of Walcheren and Anvers and was writing an autobiography called *A Country's Nostalgia (Le Mal du pays)*. Aged twenty-three, this descendant of the old Swiss Calvinist aristocracy was charming, impetuous, and smitten. At age forty-five, Germaine's health had weakened. The exile which tormented her, she lamented, "condemns one to survive oneself . . . adieus, separations, everything is the same as the moment of death, yet one is present with the full strength of life." [12] Still suffering from insomnia, she resorted to opium. Soon, Barante and Villers were also hit by the order of exile from France, then Schlegel from Coppet. Germaine now turned to her desk, starting the *Reflections on Suicide*. She wrote articles for Michaud's *Biographie universelle,* including one on Cleopatra, and a brief tragedy called *Sapho* where, in poetic stanzas, difficult feminine relationships are delineated.

The *Reflections sur le suicide* reveals how mentally, Germaine did continue working under the strain of the political noose. Though she constantly expressed emotions in her letters, she did not let events such as the loss of dear ones, separation from close friends, and incessant attacks on her status as a writer affect her genuine respect for life:

> There is a future in every form of occupation, and what human nature needs at every moment is a future. When our abilities find no scope for action outside ourselves, they devour us like the vulture of Prometheus. Work exercises and directs these abilities. When one has some imagination—and most people who suffer have a good deal—one can always take new pleasure in the study of the greatest works of the human mind.[13]

Her friends' publications pleased her. Chateaubriand's *Itinerary from Paris to Jerusalem* brought him a seat in the French Academy. Then came J. de Maistre's *Essay on the Basic Principle of Political Constitutions;* Sismondi's lectures on literary Spain which followed his *Literature of Southern Europe* and paralleled her overview of Germany; Benjamin Constant's *Wallstein*; Maine de Biran's *Relationship Between the Physical and the Moral in Man*. Lord Byron's *Childe Harold's Pilgrimage,* Jean de Müller's *History of the Swiss Confederation,* for which Germaine wrote a preface, Goethe's *Faust Part One* and *Elective Affini-*

ties, Monti's translation of Homer, these and works by F. Hegel, H. von Kleist, C. de Saint-Simon, P. Prud'hon appeared in that second decade of the new century. Still, tension filled the atmosphere. Schlegel published a comparison of the two Phèdres—Euripides' and Racine's. Discussions on these works filled the atmosphere, but political tension coming from the outside left its mark. Germaine's staunch Roman Catholic friend Montmorency was jailed, her playwright friend Louis-Elzéar de Sabran also. For security's sake, Germaine had to insist that Juliette keep her distance from Coppet. All letters were being opened. In February, 1811, surveillance became unbearable. Germaine considered leaving Switzerland, but she hesitated. In May, Schlegel was in Vienna where he placed the *De l'Allemagne* manuscript in good hands. Germaine opted to spend the winter in Geneva that year. She wrote a piece on education in which she polarized circumstance and innate morality, following Kantean precepts. Then, coming from a preoccupation entirely her own, she addressed the problem of the irreconcilability of the passion for glory with conscience.[14] She had completed the essay on suicide, and started writing *Ten Years in Exile.*

Who were with her still, in Coppet? Sismondi, who lamented over the noisy theatricals, Bonstetten, Germaine's childhood friend Catherine Rilliet-Huber, the children, and Rocca, to whose steady presence Germaine became increasingly sensitive. Chamisso left, peeved by Rocca's attentions to Germaine. At the end of the summer of 1811, secretly, Germaine and Rocca were married. Did this union give Germaine a chance to live the conjugal love so well described in *Delphine*? The reply to this could only be complex, desires mixing with circumstance. In April 1812, a child was born, named Louis-Alphonse. Within the privacy of the family he was called "The Little We" (le Petit Nous). He was taken to the pastor of Longirod near Nyon, for the first years of infancy.

At the time of Germaine's marriage, Napoléon was at the peak of his power. The world had changed. Europe had become the stage of coalitions countering his military push—Austria, England, Prussia, and very soon the northern allies Sweden and Russia. The emperor had made himself king of Italy. A press bureau now scrutinized publications. Military recruitment intensified. Thus, internal and external fronts were bound together. Joseph Bonaparte half-heartedly ruled in Spain, Louis became king of Holland, and Jérôme king of Westphalia. In spite of his brisk, electric manner, family tradition and loyalties were still in Napoléon's blood. Strategies meant to please and maintain them were his way of tightly keeping those bonds. Yet, affection had been there at the outset. As far back as 1795 Napoléon had said to Joseph:

> We have lived so many years together . . . that our hearts have become one, and you know more than anyone else how mine is entirely yours. My emotion in saying this is intense. . . . This has not happened often in my life.[15]

But ten years later, concerned over the Spanish resistance, Napoléon wrote to Joseph:

> I fear that you are misleading me on the Spanish situation, and are misleading yourself. . . . There is energy among the Spanish. You are dealing with a new people with the courage and enthusiasm of men still immune to political passions. . . . Don't look after your interests . . . I will look after them. . . .[16]

Aside from changes in personal relationships, Napoléon could well reflect on the positive implementations he had brought about. The spirit of industrial enterprise flourished. Military schools filled up, so did the Université de France where mathematics, physics, and natural science were honored. Monumental building projects began. Routes were built through the Alps. The modern international world was being born, a steady hand cold as the bayonet's steel on one side, and old, confused, monarchical elements on the other. "France seemed content. She was paying in money and in blood for her glory, her domestic tranquility, and the fascination of her military might."[17]

Agitated, Russia attacked near the Danube. Napoléon's attempt at negotiation failed. He ordered deeper conscription. Mindful of the appearance of power, he instructed family and aides to maintain their lavish lifestyle. As Prussia mobilized, it was joined by Russia in a new coalition. Following Napoléon's victory at Jena, Weimar was sacked. From Berlin, a blocus was decreed against England, forcing Holland's adherence to this.

Momentary incoherence and latent paranoia became evident to Napoléon's aides. He suspected them, especially Talleyrand in the latter's rapport with Tsar Alexander I of Russia. Talleyrand had to relinquish his lucrative ministry. The imperial entourage narrowed. Though difficult, the victory at Eylau early in 1807 had spurred the emperor on toward Russia. Napoléon distanced himself from friends and foes alike, rising above the nebulous fray while constantly on the move with his armies. He requested from the artist David a large painting of his 'coronation'. This was the new Napoléon.

Not far from the disastrous adventure in Spain now fed by eighty thousand more French troops, discontent within the French populace and hunger paralleled imperial diversions. The iron grip weakened. Conscription became a nightmare. Pseudo-diplomacy gyrated. Napoléon's obsession with power far exceeded ordinary ambition. His closest aides, Berthier and Lannes, feared the worst. Recalling Talleyrand, Napoléon posed the question of an alliance with Austria. Talleyrand's thoughts were elsewhere: he concerted with Fouché on the notion of a future without Napoléon.

Fatally wounded at the battle of Fessling (1809), Marshal Jean Lannes warned Napoléon against engaging in further aggression. Austria joined the coalition against Napoléon. After his victory at Wagram a few months later, Napoléon imposed another peace treaty on the defeated. Returning from Vienna, he astounded everyone in the Senate by ordering it to pronounce the terms of divorce from Josephine. He wanted a son. Looking at the dying European dynasties, he felt it opportune to create one of his own. Four months later he married young archduchess Marie-Louise of Austria. Daughter of the Germanic Francis II who had fought against the Revolution and Napoléon, Marie-Louise had consented when Metternich negotiated the startling 'tour de force'.

The "man who is," in Goethe's words, exerted fear by censoring, if not policing, every critic. State prisons were built, the old penal code reinstituted. Inside the administration, new confidants came into view such as the banker G. Ouvrard. Open to flattery, Napoléon unburdened tensions by calling out to his soldiers that military valor, theirs and his combined, would take them further and further on, from battle to battle. Affection subsisted in his army. At court, he ordered more festivities and asked his new aide de camp, Narbonne, to maintain the lavish tone. If Spain, England, and now Russia were obsessions, so was criticism.

Because of her influence as a writer, Germaine had become a higher risk to herself and to her friends. She was in the tyrannical web. Policing became her nightmare. Gloomy, she wrote the *Ten Years of Exile* (*Dix années d'exil*) in a swift, terse prose unlike anything she had written before. Recalling the first orders of exile of 1802 and 1803, she recorded her first journey to Germany, the death of her father, her disconsolate escapes into Italy, her attempts to obtain relief via Joseph Bonaparte, her returns to France and secret wanderings closer to Paris. The first part of her text recapitulates the years up to 1804; the second, coming after a gap in time, describes the years of work on *De l'Allemagne* subsequent to stricter impositions of exile after 1807, including the ban on travel. She relates her stay in Chaumont, then the final escape from exile in 1812.

Dix années was later edited by Auguste de Staël and published posthumously. Fully autobiographical, the recollections alleviated Germaine's trauma. Germaine's perceptions of Napoléon are most salient:

> Emperor Napoléon, whose character reveals itself completely in each phase of his life, has persecuted me with meticulous care... and inflexible harshness, and my relations with him taught me to understand him long before Europe had discovered the key to this enigma, and while it was allowing itself to be devoured by the sphinx, through inability to understand it.[18]

Napoléon was "quick to discern a person's weak points,"[19] Germaine continued, and he acted upon this. Hers, she added, was her hatred of boredom. Thus, their perspicacities matched each other; he acted on his accordingly. He was able to use Talleyrand's knowledge of "the ways of old regime society"[20] to his own advantage, she continued. Perspicacity also acted in his manner toward the French, where imagination had to be fed. He confused old Europe with "his barrage of simultaneous threats, promises," celebrations; it believed him when he uttered the word "peace" while undermining its governments.[21] He published outlandish arguments that were "swallowed whole," such as "to oppose the nation's representative is to oppose the nation—a sophism that suited French selfish interests."[22] For Germaine, such tyranny evoked the noise of machines in a mint:

> He makes thousands of men perish, with the remorselessness of those wheels striking iron, and most of his agents are equally unfeeling, the invisible propulsion of these human machines comes from a will both violent and methodical, which transforms moral life into a servile instrument.[23]

Germaine's feelings spiraled during the prolonged exile. They were not directed at herself, for she had opted to challenge rather than resign herself to it. Angry, she rather castigated those who were gullible during the travesty of monarchy at home and abroad. She felt disgust toward gaping crowds, surprise also over such naivety, even though she well perceived the fear at its root. Her exasperation speaks for itself, indignation and disillusion feeding each other. But the loss of privacy undid her. The first escape to Germany had not alleviated those feelings. Sadness engulfed her after her father's death. The description of how she rushed to Coppet, made herself work, put his writings into safe-keeping and published some, manifest her deep veneration. To us, catharsis during the writing of her filial admiration alleviated the Napoléonic syndrome.

Germaine reminds her readers that in her 1804 essay on her father she had described his coming to Paris at age fifteen, serious and talented. Success in banking was not her focus, but rather his kindness. That so soon after his second speech and public acclamations he suffered the calumnies of Mirabeau and then exile was a full reversal of destiny. She laments that he refused to fight ruse with ruse and so sadly accepted defeat. Public indifference to his writings was incomprehensible. For her, Necker's *Importance of Religious Opinions* was a great work. She imparted its ideas to her children and ever upheld its moral quality. "The presumptuous," she said, "who mistake defects of character for profundity of thought, must still be taught that if there is sometimes cleverness in immorality, there is genius in virtue."[24]

Germaine felt that both France and Necker were dishonored by the Revolution. The feeling is a leitmotif in both her short biography of him and the *Dix Années*. It would animate the last substances of her oeuvre. At the time of writing on her exile, France had been dishonored once again, and Europe was still under the Napoleonic spell. Germaine's tone is now militant. "We must not fight that man with any of his weapons. He must fail only because mankind has a conscience and the universe has a God."[25] Germaine's political anima and Christian faith coalesced in this simple outcry.

On May 23, 1812, Germaine took her smallest coach and went for a quiet promenade with Albertine. Near Berne, a large coach having been readied, Germaine was met by Schlegel. Rocca and Albert joined them further on, a cook as well, and the most extraordinary journey began. The decision to escape to England required nerve, acumen and unflinching organization. It all happened: Zurich, the Tyrol, Salzburg first, then Vienna for a sixteen days' rest. Germaine met Ligne, Gentz, Balk, Humboldt, O'Donnell. Suspense was high as Rocca's papers were not in order. Germaine requested help from Metternich. The police reported all moves—from Brünn in Moravia to Olmütz, Teschen, Landshut, Lvov, and

Brody in Galicia. By July 14, Germaine had driven safely into Russia. During the two months in Russia, the travelers were in Kiev, Orel, Toula, Moscow and Novgorod until they finally reached St. Petersburg.

Carefully planned correspondence gave Germaine a chance to have pleasant encounters with foreign dignitaries and aristocratic friends. In spite of fatigue, Germaine found respite and comfort during her long escape. She was pulling away from the "sphinx" and by 1812 she was rushing just ahead of him in Russia. Her meetings with Tsar Alexander I were most ingratiating. They gave her the relief she had long sought in higher echelons of European thinking, and because they were political, possibly more exciting to her than with the Prince de Ligne, whom she had grown to respect. She discovered that modesty blended with sagacity in Alexander, who was eleven years younger and not yet embittered by political life. He described his impression of Napoléon during the Peace of Amiens of 1802 when, ratifying the French capitulation in Egypt and speaking of a "victorious" peace with England, he "upset the balance of power of Europe. And the curtain was gone." Alexander remembered what he thought then: "Now Napoléon will be the most famous of tyrants in history."[26]

Germaine never forgot one of her conversations with Alexander:

A.: I regret not being a great captain. . . .

G.: . . . But a sovereign is rarer than a general! Your example is sustaining the nation's public spirit, now that is the greatest of victories, is it not?

A.: Yes, I love my country. I know what it is capable of becoming. I do desire to better the lot of the peasants. . . .

G.: Sire, your character is a constitution for your empire, and your conscience its guarantee. . . .

A: Even if that were the case, I would never be more than a fortunate accident.[27]

In mid-August 1812, to everyone's distress at Alexander's court, the news came that Smolensk had been captured by marshal Michel Ney. The Russians set fire to their city, as they would later to Moscow. Germaine could hardly believe these consequences of the Napoleonic invasion. Before the exhausting flight toward Stockholm, Germaine visited a convent. She was surrounded by students. A young girl greeted her, and recited pages from Necker's *Cours de Moralité religieuse*. The battle of Borodina raged on the eve of Germaine's September 8 departure from St. Petersburg. This old Russian city could not have made a better gesture toward Germaine.

From Thomas Jefferson to Germaine:

> My dear Madam and friend . . . of what scenes has your native city been the theatre, and with what havoc has it overspread the earth! . . . It is by millions that Bonaparte destroys the poor, and he is eulogized and deified by the sycophants even of science. . . . Bonaparte will die, and his tyrannies with him. But a nation never dies. . . . I sincerely pray that . . . the mediation of the virtuous Alexander . . . may produce just peace.[28]
>
> The United States of America
May 28, 1813

Part Four
LIBERATION

14.
THE PRICE OF GLORY

This woman has been for me a veritable vision of the world. . . .[1]
                                                    Dorothea Schlegel, 1812

. . . You have subjugated everything, and your successes echo as far as Copenhagen, the charm of your presence is irresistible. . . . This is something I certainly could not doubt.[2]
                                                              Ribbing, 1812

In mid-September 1812, a fishing vessel left the Finnish port of Turku (Arbo) for Sweden, arriving there on September 24 after a dangerous storm near the Archipelago of Aland. On board were a frightened Germaine accompanied by Albertine, Albert, and Schlegel. Napoléon had just won the battle of Borodino; his police had not won Germaine. In the early October light, Stockholm rose before them, beautiful in its inlets and waterways. This was the harbor of freedom.

She heard that all the potentates of Europe, the English and German included, were now not only allied in their hatred of the French emperor, but ready to act. Their alliance represented an unbeatable coalition. The news had come at the end of September that Moscow was burning—Russia's statement of its hatred. The Moscovites had left their city. Everyone knew what was in store for the Grande Armée of nearly seven hundred thousand men and their thousands of auxiliaries once Napoléon started the inevitable retreat: winter was coming.

Excitement overwhelmed Germaine. She closed the portfolio of the

Dix Années just as the last unfinished sentence reiterated her fear of boredom. Even this evaporated. As someone reported to Ribbing, "Madame Staël fell like a bomb on Stockholm."[3] The endless, silent pine and birch forests of Russia and Finland vanished from her mind. Warm welcomes dissipated the sensation of northern winds that had chilled her frenzied escape. Now she could prepare for the final lap, reaching for shelter in England and perhaps even, later, in America. But first, occupations had to be found for the two boys. Auguste arrived in Sweden with Benjamin Constant. As she said in *Dix Années*, "I was determined to arrange for the return of my sons to their father's native land by putting them in Sweden's military service."[4] A commission among the hussars was given to Albert. Auguste became an aide to Bernadotte, and Schlegel secretary to the latter. Dinners and receptions greeted the little family; partying continued on for eight months. Germaine read excerpts from *Delphine* and *De l'Allemagne* to her hosts, and as always, from her favorite classic—Racine's *Phèdre*. She had developed a good acting stamina; she thoroughly enjoyed being center-stage, even during a reading.

Reversals plagued Napoléon between the late fall of 1812 and the early spring of 1813, starting with the retreat after a month in fire-torn Moscow. Mud, ice, desertions, and enemy skirmishes broke the army's back, death ensuing. The emperor spoke of courage in his proclamations, soldiers still idolizing him. "There isn't anyone among yourselves who does not wish to return to France by any other road than that of honor," he said to them.[5] During the retreat the Beresina and Nieman rivers were crossed but then, in early December, Napoléon silently left his army. He quietly reached Paris, intent on forming a new army, and started clearing his papers. By February, Prussia freed itself of his control and declared war. He ordered the conscription of younger men. All of France abhorred this. He fought again, at Lützen against Russia, Bautzen against Prussia. Then Metternich broke the alliance with France.

In early 1813, history's perennial play with surprise and coincidence now paralleled the weakened perspicacity of its most conspicuous personage. Patriotism rose in Germany, this psychological phenomenon making its first appearance there. A new fighting breed emerged, desiring to free itself of the French presence.

In Stockholm, Germaine was greeted by her friend and peer Jean Bernadotte. He had become Prince Regent to Charles XIII of Sweden, thanks to the support of many in this country. Ironically, Napoléon had consented to this earlier. He had originally promoted Bernadotte from marshal in 1804 to Prince Pontecorno in 1806, wanting this distinguished leader's support far from the fray. But Bernadotte's opinion of his former superior had changed. He broke ties with Napoléon in 1809, opting to stay in Sweden where personal ambition matched the esteem of his subjects. Therefore, Germaine was now seeing not only an old friend but in fact the impending monarch of Sweden, for by election this happened that very same year. An intelligent man, the new Charles XIV of Sweden was suddenly thrust into the role of one among many potentates in the international situation. Now he was no longer far from Napoléon's 'fray'. He saw a valuable political aide in Germaine, listening to her views and being open to her influence. He did not hesitate to help her. His popularity in Sweden impressed her. She knew of his military valor. His part in the battle of Leipzig was well known. She reflected that this excellent head of state could become a leader in France. She strongly supported his having Sweden join Europe's sixth coalition.

Young Albert had broken military orders to go gambling. He was reprimanded, and shortly after, all three, Albert, Auguste, and Schlegel, left with Bernadotte on the military campaign that soon countered the French invasion of Pomerania. Impressed by the young man's seriousness, Bernadotte promoted Auguste to aide-de-camp. Germaine was proud of Auguste. Now twenty-two, he had completed his studies at the Paris Polytechnic School. While in Paris he made countless errands for his mother, assisting in her efforts to help emigrés. He had found a way of meeting Napoléon in December 1807, pleading on Germaine's behalf, but this had failed. Now, he exercised a touching, filial protection over her. In 1810, he had helped save the original manuscript of *De l'Allemagne* from capture, as we know, Albert having also taken part in the adventure. Auguste's wise counsel, compassion, and loyalty to Germaine were qualities reminiscent of Jacques Necker. Auguste's letter to his mother of June 1812 attests to this: "... one must guarantee oneself against emotion; only look before you ... dear angel, we are living at a time when one must stifle one's soul as it can be a disturbance. ... I hope that ... you will see that it is not possible to love more than I love you. ..."[6]

Germaine's rapport with Albertine, now sixteen, was excellent and pleasantly tinged with camaraderie. In her letters, Germaine expressed pride and admiration concerning Albertine. She wrote of the adolescent's beauty and agreeable manner even though impetuosity could occur. Though religiously pensive, Albertine joined her mother in salon theatricals. But Germaine was anxious. Charming in her view, Albertine was at a marriageable age. Rocca's illness also caused anxiety. His attitude vexed Germaine when he expressed fears that one day she might love him less. She had the marriage to him confirmed legally, and they never parted. But someone was missing; near the end of her stay in Stockholm she expressed her loneliness from Constant: "I often look at your letters to me, for I have them with me. . . . I would love to receive more. My father, you and Mathieu (de Montmorency) are in a corner of my heart, closed forever. . . ."[7] Germaine was longing for Constant's "admirable spiritedness" and looking back with nostalgia.

She fretted over Schlegel's absence also. "I cannot go on without your company (entretien)," she wrote; "it seems that I am without ideas since we have said goodbye. . . . Do not forget that we are your family."[8] Germaine had firmly welcomed Schlegel into her family circle, the gesture was acknowledged, but resolve was tested as Schlegel disliked Rocca. He was moody, he lamented the loss of youth's poetic inspiration, and his own vain pursuit of esteem from others. He was a difficult man, but his affection, knowledge and intellect were precious to Germaine.

The fact was that Germaine missed her men. She returned to her travel-desk, and to ever-present reflections concerning the Revolution. Somehow, once and for all, the trauma of that period had to be made to dissipate. Germaine embarked on a new work—*Considerations concerning the French Revolution*. This was the real Germaine, living full tilt socially, and writing, respecting her solitary soul's vocation. Her mind calmed in the midst of the excitement spurred by her escape from exile. It seldom stilled. Carefully, lucidly, the pen was put back to work. Thoughts about the Revolution had become an osmosis, and very much alive because of their emotional complexity. She would gather all the threads. She would write her own history of the event and include those questions so very congenial to the direction of her thinking since her first publications: what had happened? What of France's fate? This last now had a double meaning, for Napoléon had retreated from Russia.

Germaine's Swedish friend baron Carl von Brinkman, ambassador to Berlin, wrote to her at that time. He praised *Corinne* and spoke of posthumous glory for its author. Glory for a woman, she had said in *De l'Allemagne*, "can only be the brilliant passing of happiness (le deuil éclatant du bonheur)."[9] Her contemplation of the notion of glory had been purely personal. Replying to Brinkman, she looked at it differently:

> My young years were tempestuous and often merited blame, but now, any justification has to be political, for I believe that one cannot be man

without the cult of liberty, and thought in me is manly. Should I hope
for glory it would be through this liberty's virtues counter to the ills of
despotism.... That is my claim to posterity....[10]

Brinkman's effusive letter had pleased Germaine. Her reply is precise, the point of view at once intellectual and psychological, coming from the fully developed political persona. Self-analysis had crystallized in the response to the Swedish admirer.

On June 18, 1813, Germaine, Auguste, Albertine, and Rocca left for England. That spring of 1813, Napoléon heard Chateaubriand's speech on liberty at the Institut. He was angered. News of the French evacuation from Madrid, of Joseph's defeat by Wellington at Vittoria, of further French departures from Spain, of the military setback at Kulm, then Switzerland's rejection of the title Federate Republic, all added to imperial detestation. Louis de Narbonne, the aide-de-camp whom he had made ambassador to Vienna, died just as Austria joined the enemy coalition. Where had the fourteen years of high administration and military power gone? Napoléon had reached his goal of building a monarchy, but allegiance pulled away from him. Patriotism vibrated within the enemy.

Napoléon's second German campaign began in September 1813. A month later, Napoléon suffered a heavy defeat at Leipzig; Bernadotte had contributed his Swedish contingent. At Hanover and again at Liège, Bernadotte conferred with Constant; the subject was the creation of a new French government. All of Europe was on the alert for massive change. Now Germany was lost to Napoléon. Russia and Prussia prepared to enter Paris. Austria approached Lyon after its invasion of Switzerland, and England came from Portugal to Toulouse, thus facilitating the former Spanish king Ferdinand's recovery of his status. As Prussia and Sweden occupied Holland, Westphalia destituted Jérôme, and Joseph suffered his downfall. At home, the Legislature condemned the war and the suppression of political liberties. In January, Napoléon's king of Naples, Joachim Murat, defected, attempted to leave the Mediterranean coast, and was executed.

At Chatillon-sur-Seine, near Paris, the French emperor rejected the terms of peace offered by the Allies. It was now early March 1814. He quarreled with the Legislature and continued fighting, this time inflicting bloodshed on French soil. Secret communications fluctuated between the Allies, the French government, and the police. Heads and minds turned. At the end of March, Paris fell to the Allies. In the middle of this disarray, crowds jubilated. Alexander came to meet Talleyrand. Napoléon's ministers relegated to Blois, enjoining Marie-Louise and her three-year-old son to do the same.

Germaine had opened a salon in London. Her zest astounded her English aristocratic friends. Walter Scott pronounced her "the hurricane in petticoats."[11] Lord Byron, who lived near the estate she had rented, complimented her as the most eminent of ladies. Germaine showed signs of nervous exhaustion. But her need to shine was irrepressible. She was painfully unsure of her political fate. Suddenly, in mid-July, not long after the news of Louis de Narbonne's death, Germaine was told that Albert had died during a gambling duel with a Russian soldier. Heart-broken, shunning the social flurry, she became silent. She returned to her desk. From Germany, Schlegel wrote an affectionate eulogy: "Albert had an unlimited confidence in his strengths and agility."[12] The letter described the twenty-one-year-old's feat of valor in Hamburg: during battle he crossed the lines to reconnoiter the enemy position, then impassively returned to his position. Byron comforted Germaine. "With all the world at your feet," he said soon after the tragic news, "my praise is only the feeble echo of more powerful voices. . . ."[13] Auguste came close by, working at the Swedish delegation. In October, John Murray published *De l'Allemagne;* a new friend named James Mackintosh praised it in *The Edinburgh Review.*

The battle of Leipzig of October 1813 signaled the definite blow to Napoléon's empire. Germaine agreed to meet members of the Allied coalition who gathered in London, including the duke of Wellington. She realized that drastic changes would affect France, far from least the coalition's political force. She tried to adjust to the idea of a Bourbon return, if only it were constitutional. The alternative, international occupation, made her shudder. Was a liberal monarchy possible, as her father had wished? Ever filled with republicanism, she was conscience-stricken. She had always hated the political machinations of the royalists.

In late December she renewed contact with Benjamin Constant. He was then publishing an essay called *On the Spirit of Conquest and Usurpation.* With irony, he called Napoléon's empire a hazard and lavished praise on the coalition. Privately, Benjamin thought that the contact with Bernadotte could lead to political opportunity in a new French administration. Fate was not ready to open this avenue for Constant, not quite yet. Meanwhile, Germaine remonstrated him for his panegyric of the coalition:

> We must not speak ill of the French, when the Russians are in Langres. May God banish me from France rather than have foreigners bring me to it![14]

By January 1814, Germaine decided to accept a Bourbon return. She became acquainted with Louis XVIII at Hartwell. As comte de Provence having emigrated in 1791, he was prepared to negotiate a treaty with the Allies on condition that the French frontiers of 1792 be maintained. This reassured Germaine. Extraordinarily, as events moved precipitously, she felt empathy for Napoléon. "I hate him now," she wrote to Constant, "but after all, forty battles could be considered a claim to nobility . . . enough to make me want to wish him success."[15]

In her extensive correspondence Germaine expressed horror at the very thought of a foreign administration of France. As a political activist, famous and persuasive, and one whose ebullient conversation charmed many though it alienated others, she found it in her heart to pity the despot who tyrannized more than ten years of her life. Only those who knew Germaine very well—Constant, Schlegel, and Auguste—fully understood her "rare kindness," as Schlegel called it. While Napoléon faced a recalcitrant government, the warmer thread of Germaine's old ambivalence tugged at her sensitivity. But greatly fearing external political interference, she had to accept the Bourbon return—the very antithesis of her republicanism. One can say that the motive for her change of attitude was practical, the alternative being danger to that which was as deep in her heart as liberty itself: France.

Early in April 1814, the Senate, Legislature, and marshals voted for Napoléon's abdication. The emperor's secretary Berthier stood among these. The tsar acquiesced, Austria and England did also. Two weeks later, at Fontainebleau, Napoléon abdicated. Standing before his army, he did this, he said, in favor of his son. Berthier signed the Senate's declaration of defeat. A constitutional charter was adopted. Foreign minister once again, Talleyrand arranged with Metternich the terms of the armistice. Fouché entered the Senate. Marie-Louise and her child left for Austria. Young Napoléon II never returned to France. On May 20, Napoléon left for the Island of Elba. A few aides accompanied him.

France was no longer silent. "A considerable change took place in the public mind. From absolute submission and the silence that had reigned during the empire, suddenly a singular vivacity of sentiment and language occurred. While . . . the surprising idea of a Bourbon return to power began to spread, and the Bourbons became popular . . . a bitter quarrel erupted among political opponents. The press was recovering its liberty."[16] The Allies flooded Paris. So did the nobility and clergy returned from exile. In some quarters the feasting emitted sounds of absolute monarchy. Inconsistency ruled: Louis honored marshal Ney for his military valor during the Russian and European campaigns, and Berthier received the royal accolade. Beyond his role as secretary to Napoléon, he had long been a personal friend to the emperor. That he should have had to sign the order of abdication must have been a tenuous experience. Soon after Napoléon's departure, the count of Provence became Louis XVIII. Louis attended a mass at the cathedral in memory of his unfortunate brother Louis XVI. By the end of May the Treaty of Paris reaffirmed the French frontiers of 1792. Louis replaced some ministers and censured the press, thus inheriting problems contingent on moderate rule.

One third of Napoléon's army had defected. His brothers were silent, including Joseph. Favored, yet irresolute and apathetic in the high responsibilities Napoleon had given him, particularly the Spanish throne, Joseph left a now bloodied and devastated Spain. Outwardly, Napoléon was no longer necessary to France. But personally, he was still full of fire. Surrender was foreign to him.

Germaine's sojourn in England lasted nearly a year—from mid-June 1813 until May 8, 1814. She was therefore in England during the disastrous battle of Leipzig, when the Allies entered Paris, and when Napoléon abdicated at Fontainebleau in April 1814. The circumstance of Germaine's second visit to England kept her away from the continental flurry, and it offered the satisfaction of returning to her desk. This happened with more endeavor than during the festive stay in Sweden. Political anxieties could now be mastered, and 'letters' seriously attended to during restful weeks in the English countryside. The periphery of friendships widened. Yet, the loss of young Albert left a deep, silent gash in her heart. Countering personal tragedy, her London salon balanced with the welcomes in country homes where the ambiance enchanted her. The return to writing may have owed much to the weeks spent at the estate of the statesman lord Henry marquis of Lansdowne. Germaine became acquainted with British liberal thinking 'in situ'. She met the whig parliamentarians lord Charles Grey and William Wilberforce. "Here I am," Germaine wrote from lord John Darnley's estate at Cobban Hall in the summer of 1813, ". . . in the most beautiful habitation in the world . . . a large park, most noble hospitality . . . prayers in common in the morning and after dinner. . . ."[17]

Thoughts concerning the future of France gained emphasis and focus. Germaine's republican mind made her a difficult and at times obstreperous conversational guest, but it became evident to all that her respect for English parliamentarism was sincere and deep. Nevertheless, some were "shocked by her persistence in wanting to be heard as a political exile; hence they held in check their admiration for her as a writer."[18] Those who met her for the first time were not aware that this traveler, thin and pale, suffered from ill health. The long and complicated escape from the noose had taken its toll. At the end of the ordeal, Germaine had lost a son. Albert may have most resembled his mother in temperament and manner. His death struck deeply, much as the presences of Auguste, Albertine, Schlegel and Rocca sustained her. Political freedom buoyed her. Wellington not only impressed her, but the victor of the Spanish campaign felt affection for her. Like Jacques Necker, he reprimanded her for her outbursts and advised against indiscretion. On meeting Germaine, the poet Byron expressed an ambivalent though equally affectionate reaction: "Her works are my delight, and so is she herself—for a half hour. I don't like her politics . . . but she is a woman by herself and has done more than all the rest of them together, intellectually; she ought to have been a man."[19] Germaine responded to the kindness of women friends like Elizabeth Foster, duchess of Devonshire. It was she who introduced Germaine to politically sensitive members of English society and there, Germaine discovered that she was far from alone in her thinking. The fate of France was on everyone's mind.

Germaine's exile was lifted on April 30, 1814. Paris! Auguste returned first, then Germaine, Albertine and Rocca on May 12. Germaine reopened her salon at rue Saint-Florentin. Juliette Récamier and baroness de Krüdener did the same, and Talleyrand now invited Germaine regularly. Montmorency and Barante shared her triumphant return. Glory was uppermost, but she was unwell. The complicated journey had been costly. She wanted to retrieve her father's two million francs from the government, and Constant owed her a large sum. She worried about Rocca's illness. Then marriage arrangements for Albertine became the priority. Constant published an essay on constitutional monarchy. There came Alexander, La Fayette freed from Olmütz, Humboldt, while Schlegel spoke of his soldierly adventures. Bernadotte had come, but hesitation made him return to Sweden. Alexander and Wellington were assiduous visitors. Germaine and Alexander visited the ailing Joséphine at Malmaison, the first and flamboyant stronghold of young Bonaparte's rule.

Germaine was pleased with the success of *De l'Allemagne*. Publications rekindled: J. Philippart dedicated his memoir of Bernadotte's campaign to Germaine; Chateaubriand wrote on Bonaparte, the Bourbons, and the need for a legitimate royalty; Rocca's account of the Spanish campaign was well received—Wellington complimented him. Then came Byron's *The Corsair.* Admiring Wilberforce's humanitarianism, Germaine offered a preface to his translated article on the treatment of blacks. She published an appeal to the capital's sovereign visitors to follow the example of Wilberforce's 1807 parliamentary act, when England abolished slavery.

On March 1, 1815, the unimaginable happened. Napoléon landed on the southern French coast. He had escaped from Elba with a few aides. Arriving in Grenoble, then Lyon, he knew that he was free to act on the presumption to return to power. A thousand soldiers, then more, had amassed alongside him. He reached Paris, ready for action. He astounded the entire nation.

"He destroyed the energy of public spirit with this ghastly landing!"[20] Germaine exclaimed. She feared that whatever muscle was left in the nation would turn soft. Her diagnosis was correct. More soldiers flocked toward him, including old comrades at arms. Politicians living on opportunism and self-interest turned to him. "If he triumphs," Germaine added, "that will be the end of liberty in France; if he is beaten, there goes our independence."[21] Chateaubriand shared her feelings: "suspicion has turned to fear . . . his inclinations have altered, they no longer hold his . . . qualities."[22] Respect for France collapsed within the Congress of Vienna. It broke up in mid-March, verbally outlawing the renegade emperor. Troops sent to block his approach to Paris joined him. Louis XVIII departed for Belgium, royalists fled.

For one hundred days, Napoleon returned to his desk, to his men and his dreams. For just such a moment in time, he held France in the palm of his hand. At the Tuileries, proclaiming citizenship for himself and all who listened, he spoke of appeasement and proposed a new imperial constitution. Drawing funds from the banker Ouvrard, he called on former enemies he deemed qualified to draw this new charter with him: the former 'constitutionnel' and military strategist Lazare Carnot, Cambacérès, and . . . Constant.

Benjamin wrote the *Appendice to the Imperial Constitutions* (*l'Acte Additionnel*). His appearance on the scene was peculiarity itself. He had published a strong criticism of the emperor in the *Journal des Débats*. He had hesitated, left Paris, returned, met Fouché and Joseph Bonaparte, then suddenly became Napoléon's counselor of state. From her retreat in

Coppet, Germaine greeted this comportment with irony; moreover, she rejected advances now made by Fouché and Joseph. Evidently Napoléon wanted enemies near his grasp. Napoléon's ministry flattered Germaine, wanting her to come to Paris, but she desisted. She saw through Napoléon's subterfuge and was disconcerted that her friend Sismondi had rallied to him. New supporters had to be made, blatantly and with financial gifts. More war was envisioned, arsenals, a cavalry, and frontier protection. But distrust inside and out spread its venom.

A ceremony at the Champ de Mars barely lifted the public's silent stare. Then, Napoléon left for the battlefield. On June 16, 1815, his army met the Prussian general Gebhard Blücher at Ligny near Waterloo. During the battle's first day, glory lasted one historical moment. On the next day, Russia invaded the region, Wellington arrived, and Blücher renewed the battle supported by the allies massed at Waterloo. On June 18, the Bonaparte adventure ceased. The emperor was made to abdicate on June 23rd. Brought to the British ship the Northumberland, he thought of his son, and of a journey to America. But he was a prisoner of war. He was taken to the Island of St. Helena.

Napoléon lingered six years at St. Helena. Like blown leaves glittering with spoils, his family left for Italy. Joseph went to America. Irresolute, the elder brother had shown sympathy for Germaine, but had not forcibly helped her. Napoléon used Joseph as intermediary and once asked Germaine "what it was that she wanted," to which she had replied: "what I *think* is rather what matters."[23] For more than ten years, the self-made emperor held Germaine in his implacable grasp. Nevertheless, there, at St. Helena, her pleading letters were found in his portfolio.

For many, opinion battles with the enigma of Napoléon. Opinion prolongs the enigma, for it is ambivalent. It continually separates a public's hunger for hero-worship from the private cynicism of others. Parts of Napoléon's administration function today, and buildings attest to his glorification. But ironically, years before the end of his life, he himself had youthfully expressed his eulogy. We will recall that in the Lyon essay of 1791, aged twenty-two and barely out of the Brienne military academy, he wrote that "ambition . . . this immoderate desire to satisfy conceit . . . only dies with life, having consumed it."[24] In 1815, Napoléon's desire for a Europe conquered, organized, and submitted to his rule shattered before his coalesced enemies.

During her young political years, Germaine was impressed by descriptions of Bonaparte's courage, clear thinking, and self-control on the battlefield. Her hero-worship was genuine. Fascinated and puzzled by his politics step by step, she reflected on the consul's ambition. She grew to hate his oppression, and finally him as well. She understood his presumption to reach absolute power at home and abroad. She remembered Rousseau's counsel that the study of character is vital to one's estimation of a ruler. The drama of 1815 was bound to further Germaine's study of character. Napoléon's transformation from romantic hero to consummate despot is at the center of the history he created. This is Germaine's history too; she perceived his transformation, became his outspoken critic, and suffered from the exile he inflicted on her.

> "Why would you destroy the destiny of a woman who . . . has never harmed anyone? Why would you force a mother to seek elsewhere but in France the resources for the education of her children? . . . From the height of your position, why could you not turn to me from a sentiment of protection and benevolence?"[25]
>
> Germaine de Staël
Letter to Napoléon, September 26, 1803

15.

THE TESTAMENT

> It is a remarkable thing that when one looks in depth at the thinking of all human beings there is not one enemy of liberty. . . . From one end of the world to another, the friends of liberty communicate through that subsistence. . . . Be it the abolition of slavery, the liberty of the press, religious tolerance, Jefferson thinks like La Fayette, La Fayette like Wilberforce, and those who have preceded them are in that same great harmony of political opinion.[1]
>
> Germaine de Staël
> *Considerations concerning the French Revolution*, 1816

In early 1816, Germaine faced a difficult situation. She needed the full recovery of the previous monarchy's debt to her father. Constant was also indebted to her. She hoped that his payment would help toward Albertine's impending marriage to the young duke Victor de Broglie. Constant did not comply.

Formerly secretary to Narbonne, the serious-minded Victor de Broglie had captured Germaine's interest and Albertine's heart. Besides his excellent education, Victor's liberal views coincided with Albertine's, and Germaine's as well. Victor and Auguste succeeded in obtaining a dispensation from the pope concerning Albertine's protestant faith. The ceremony was scheduled for February 20, 1816, in the city of Pisa. Germaine could well be pleased. Victor, Auguste, and Albertine shared spiritual sympathies. This continued for the rest of their lives.

Both Rocca and Germaine suffered from increasing ill health. Yet, she continued working on her *Considerations concerning the French*

Revolution (*Considérations sur la Révolution française*). Sometimes she returned to a 'composition' on Richard the Lion-Hearted. Her friends continued publishing—Chateaubriand, now in the second Restauration's Upper Chamber, Schlegel, and Sismondi. Goethe translated Byron's *Manfred*. Her old rival Madame de Genlis began her memoirs and published *Henri IV*. Germaine's major occupation became the *Considérations*. She did maintain a steady correspondence with the Allies now occupying France, including Arthur Wellesley, duke of Wellington. Her letters to him are affectionate and full of concern for the fate of France. Seeing Prussian soldiers settle in the Tuileries filled her with dismay. She wanted such uninvited forces appeased and sent away. Halfheartedly at first, whether in Paris or Coppet, along with Auguste and Victor, she supported international conciliation. She finally came to terms with the Bourbons provided the monarchy would be liberal and constitutional.

She did not dislike Louis XVIII, having had the occasion in England to perceive his moderation. Louis re-instated the French Academy, but he had his hands full. Pillage continued, vengeful ultra-royalists led a 'white Terror' in the south, and the entrenched occupation was costly. Louis took the duties of foreign affairs himself. Talleyrand and Fouché were disgraced. Louis's prime minister, Armand duke of Richelieu (1766-1822), was a friend of Alexander. The latter's prestige stood high among the Allied occupation. Armand helped quell the southern unrest. Concerted efforts softened Frederick-William of Prussia into allowing France to maintain its old frontiers. In turn, Frederick-William was a friend of Wilhelm Humboldt, Germaine's unwavering admirer.

However, another foreign dignitary had come to Paris with intentions far from moderate. Metternich wanted to impose a heavy indemnity plus a seven-year occupation of France. Wellington offered to arbitrate on this insistence. Richelieu aiding, the contribution was lessened, and the occupation reduced to 1820. Louis's position was definitely constitutional. Germaine was right; she had repeated to the king that any hardening on the part of the Allies would alienate the French from him. A temperate ministry emerged. The striving for peace subsisted in spite of actions that troubled public opinion, one of these being the execution of marshal Ney. The government did not forgive his allegiance to Napoleon. Thoughts turned to the establishment of elections by direct suffrage. Germaine was gratified when Victor de Broglie entered the Upper Chamber and worked toward this new electoral law.

In late December 1815, Germaine, Albertine, Rocca and Schlegel left Coppet for Lausanne, then Rome and Pisa, preparing for Albertine's marriage. From Pisa in early January, Germaine wrote to Thomas Jefferson that she was "not eager to return to France so long as strangers are its masters . . ." but, she added, "I am going to marry off my eighteen-year-old daughter to the duke of Broglie. He is a peer of France, grandson of the marshal of Broglie, moreover a friend of M. de La Fayette, which tells you everything concerning political opinions. Our family is still a small intellectual island where Franklin, Washington and Jefferson are revered as in their own country. . . . May you be assured of my attachment for you."[2] Replying on September 6, Jefferson expressed his understanding of her political reluctance. "Your feeling is worthy of you," he added.[3]

At the time of the letter to Jefferson, while in Milan, the poet Monti invited Germaine to present an article for the first issue of his *Biblioteca italiana*. She complied and wrote *On the Spirit of Translation* (*De l'esprit des traductions*). "If every modern nation reduced itself to the esteem of its own treasures," she wrote, "it would always be poor. . . . One must tend toward the universal, if we desire mankind's betterment." Germaine's phraseology is idealistic, moralistic, and appealingly simple. "One must always seek new nourishment for the mind, besides, genius escapes the monotomy of style and form locked in one nation's tradition. . . . To translate a poem such as the *Iliad* is not a matter of using a compass and copying an edifice's dimensions, but rather of animating with the breath of life a different instrument. . . . A. W. Schlegel has translated Shakespeare with such exactitude and inspiration that this poetry is now perfectly congenial to German readers."[4]

Germaine's eclecticism was daring. Her emphasis on German accomplishments ruffled Italian feathers. She apologized. More than ever, at this stage in her life, she was imbued with the cosmopolitanism of her fellow writers. She may have remembered the serious correspondance, encounter and friendship with Charles de Villers lost two years earlier. His labors toward a Franco-German literary and philosophical rapport had influenced her. Surely, such commonality could be extended to other countries.

From Pisa Germaine revisited Florence until early May, working on her text. After the return to Coppet she greeted English visitors—Lansdowne, Byron, also her cousin Mme Necker de Saussure. The attractive chateau had become a center of intellectuality warmed by her hospitality.

The pleasant, natural ambiance aiding, conversation, meditation and writing were sought by all in what has come to be called the Group of Coppet—in addition to the above were Juliette, Sismondi, Bonstetten, Schlegel, Krüdener, and Chateaubriand quite often, then Montmorency and still Constant.

France transformed itself. The hard-working young bourgeoisie sought stability and order, more so even than religion. Except for Christian convictions that were sincere and echoed Germaine's in a traditionally humble and discrete manner, Victor, Auguste, and Albertine were all for political sensibility. For Germaine, the principle of liberty had to be respected above everything else.

Thanks to Louis XVIII, Jacques Necker's two million francs were reimbursed. Germaine continued writing the *Considérations*. More British friends came to Coppet, including the reformer Henry Brougham, whose knowledge of English legislative methods interested Germaine and her children, then the scientist Sir Humphrey Davy and his wife. Byron stayed at a villa nearby. Germaine understood his marital problems and his need for solitude. He appreciated her esteem, and teased Rocca whom he called 'Monsieur l'Amant'. Sismondi having returned, the Napoleonic lapse was forgiven.

By the fall it was time to return to Paris in order to supervise Albertine's pregnancy and confinement. Germaine's salon at the rue Royale attracted lords, Italian and German aristocracy and her political luminaries, the "superior men" as she called them. Montmorency soon became minister for foreign affairs. Germaine reconciled with Constant and urged him to write, as always, but this time on the tenuous position of the monarchy. The France of 1816-1817 was not ready for a fully liberal government. A parliamentary monarchy would have to maintain internal appeasement, to which both Germaine and the foreign dignitaries earnestly agreed.

As in the past, Constant complied with Germaine's insistence and continued writing on political matters. His article, "The Doctrine That Can Unite Political Views in France" countered Chateaubriand's "On Monarchy According to the Charter." Wellington came to Germaine's salon. He advised patience. He had reprimanded her on her petulance during her hesitations concerning the Bourbon presence.

On October 12, 1816, now aged fifty, Germaine wrote her testament in the following manner: "I commend my soul to God, who has been generous with me . . . in the hand of my father, to whom I owe what I am and what I possess ... in spite of my having strayed from his principles. ... My advice to my children is to remember the conduct, virtues and talents of my father, and to try to imitate him with the best of their character and strengths. ... I now pronounce as legitimate my marriage to Albert Jean de Rocca and the birth of our child Louis Alphonse de Rocca. ..."[5]

Germaine's intellectuality animated her correspondence. Always, observations and statements allied with feeling. Possibly in her last letter to Wellington, she regretted having been reprimanded by him. She could not bear this from a person she so admired. Her intention of writing on Richard the Lion-Hearted probably connected with her feeling toward the English statesman whose character strengths she had observed. She counted on him to aid France, knowing that he had his own mind regarding France and would never be an instrument to others on this subject. On December 16, she wrote:

> I was right when I dared tell you that your presence would be good for Paris. It is most unfortunate that we should depend on foreigners; but genius is cosmopolitan and I firmly believe that, though English and the first among the English, you would be generous towards France. ... You are recalling France' errors....
> ... It is like a changeable stream ... but France remains and it wishes to follow England's example.[6]

Mutualities of feeling comforted Germaine. She sought this comfort, particularly at the apex of her writing career as the foreign presence continued to distress her.

Early in 1817, she lamented on this in her last letter to Thomas zJefferson:

> France is so far from the lights shining around you. Shall we ever be free in this country of ours? Twenty-seven years of efforts brought us only tyranny and conquest. Yet at the bottom of this mass there is a desire to find the fruits of suffering, a confused idea of liberty floating above our heads. ... I am going to publish a work that I recommend to your interest. It is called *Considerations concerning the French Revolution*. ... You will find your name in it, with the good sentiment it always inspires in me. ...[7]

In spite of considerable fatigue, Germaine returned to her desk. In heart and mind, she considered France a human being, someone deserving pity and reproach for indifference to its faults. This was the personal mood of her *Considerations*. The major thrust of her work held throughout: the fundamental cause of the cruelties perpetrated by the French during the Revolution was "the absence of happiness, which leads to the absence of morality."[8] Her text describes the opposing forces that developed side by side and finally clashed, fragmenting the country, perhaps irreparably.

From one political period to another, Germaine sees a movement of self-centered powers pitting themselves against those who, gradually freeing themselves from financial servitude, united and demanded "certain rights."[9] Fatal to the possibility of entente, there came rulers who, like Louis XI, held executive and legislative strength in their own hands. For a moment, a genuine consciousness of what a nation is and should be made a person like Henri IV publicly recognize demands such as the right to religious worship. Cardinal Richelieu's oppressive despotism, Germaine continues, caused deep inroads into the French character, taking away its originality, loyalty, candor, and independence. Political degradation combined with the cardinal's insistence that Paris be the center of influence, allowed French pride to let itself be flattered by an extravagant court and the clatter of wars. Louis XIV "never knew what a nation should be,"[10] thus frank communication among human beings was deprived during the long establishment of his "house." After the revocation of Henri's Nantes Edict in 1685, personal and public royal abuse became constant, affecting the great personalities Pascal and Racine, among others. At his death, Louis XIV left the country in financial disorganization. Louis XV's expenses met resistance; indeed, the eighteenth century saw a reinvigorated public opinion. It found argumentative agreements in the minds of enlightened aristocrats. But soon, opposing forces diversified, multiplied, and clashed. The century ended in a human cataclysm.

Characteristically, the substances of Germaine's text are opposites. The kindness of Louis XVI met recalcitrant privileged courtiers, his timidity met a discontented populace; his hesitations met massive, fatal distrust. The ancient courtier Maurepas blocked the efforts of Malesherbes and Turgot eager for political and financial reforms. Necker's attempts to redress discrepancies in food supplies and taxation, his efforts to boost provincial administration met opponents who took financial privileges for granted.

In time the nation saw itself carrying the privileged class on its shoulders. It expressed horror; it read; it learned to speak of equality and liberty. Once the concept of absolute monarchy—that is, total obedience to the monarch—fell into disfavor, popular conviction and action took new directions. The nation's spirit had metamorphosed. Respect died. Mirabeau and Sieyès played their characteristic parts: one spoke with the fire of ambition; the other wrote thoughtful answers to the question "What is the Third Estate?" The populace no longer listened. Recalling the explosive crowd and troop movements of July 14, 1789, Germaine asks:

> How could minds of that caliber possibly pronounce themselves on the affairs of a great people? Were they prepared against the dangers they had provoked? Were there ever really such men, rejecting reason, unable to agree on their hold on force itself? [11]

Uncontrolled oratory, roars and acclamations, vandalism, exhausting harangues, insult, conspiracy, such was the storm that unleashed tumult and made it reign. There is in a nation "a certain mass of feelings that must be checked like a physical force," Germaine comments. Speaking in the language of political science, she adds that "necessarily, a constitution that opens itself to the humiliation of either the sovereign or the people will be made to fall by one or by the other."[12]

Describing the shattering events before her self-imposed exile to Coppet, she points to the impediments in the work of the first Assembly, the animosities, press attacks, troubles in the provinces, factions coming to the surface, then Louis's arrest and imprisonment. So many ills, she reflects, suffocated "this famous Assembly which had united so much light and so many errors, with some durable good and immediate misfortune." Always, she looks at simple, basic human elements:

> Those who suddenly found themselves possessing boundless power had never exercised political right. It would take a long time to learn that their injustice on one citizen would fall on everyone else. [13]

Among many, Germaine had emigrated in September 1792. She identifies with this large exodus. All suffered guilt and pain. For some, nostalgia deepened their patriotism, but all were horrified on hearing of the Terror. Germaine's definition of this as a nation's reversal of fortune carries the implication of infection: "we saw the hope of a free constitution reversed, and the most genocidal events take the place of salutary institutions."[14] She describes the poverty, the swaying of mobs with pikes held high, "enough to alter forever the respect that the human race should inspire,"[15] and at the other end of the spectrum, political fanaticism. She compares the meeting of the two extremes after Louis's execution and the fall of the Gironde to a descent into Dante's hell, "circle by circle, further and further down . . . obliterating with blood everything that remained of human nature's capacity for greatness and generosity."[16] On the edge of one circle, there appeared the figure of Robespierre, a man she had once met in her father's house and had deemed to be enjoyably envious and mean, such being the contradiction of a complex character. Now, on that edge, he embodied hypocrisy and political evil.

According to Germaine, Bonaparte's entry on the heels of three struggling administrations signaled the end of hope for a representative government. His ascent brought the end of respect for political doctrine and republican principles, therefore to the Revolution's best initiative.

> . . . He exerted fear . . . by the simple effect of his person on others . . . intimidating, calculating, not at all amenable to sympathy. . . . I felt that his soul held a sword cold and cutting . . . that he despised the nation . . . and acted naturally in only one circumstance: that of command.[17]

Concerning France, Germaine has painful regrets. The nation is that being whom she loves enough to scold as one would a child full of genius yet disgracefully behaved. Her text now becomes an emotional appeal to the nation's sense of fairness. She enjoins it to understand that liberty originates in a domain deeper than tolerance, that its principles are rather in the soul."They are part of us . . . they are the source of human character, and the only means of freeing ourselves from tyranny."

Ultimately, Germaine envisions the soul where, above prejudices, "those principles ennoble character. . . . Here, virtues and ideas form the golden chain once described by Homer. . . ."[18] Germaine's philosophical tone is naturalistic; literally, she claims that the principles of liberty "come from nature." [18]

As a historian, Germaine does not hesitate to attribute the loss of political liberty to those who imposed despotic rule like Richelieu and Napoléon. Concerning the latter, she asks: Would it not be . . . a great lesson for humanity if we took into account his actions beyond the Rhine and the Alps, the Allied invasions of Paris, the three million Frenchmen who perished from Cadiz to Moscow, Liberty's demise

> followed by inveterate aversion? An enlightened nation's worse error has been to put itself in the hands of one man. . . . If the French nation . . . in spite of all her faults, had constituted herself and had respected

the lessons given by ten years of revolution, that nation would still be the light of the world.[19]

Written during several years, and possibly begun soon after Necker's death, Germaine's political history vibrates with a nervous anxiety that alternates with calm reflection. This must have depended on moments of self-imposed concentration. One senses that she courageously reminds herself of her faith in human nature. Why a nation has taken a certain direction is always open to argument, she writes, but what matters in an examination such as this is rather "the nature of feelings in the hearts of human beings.... This sacred fire will never die though only in broad daylight can it reappear."[20] Thus Germaine's history amalgamates feeling and action.

Undoubtedly, Germaine's last oeuvre marks the end of a lifelong political thrust. Reflections on Jean-Jacques Rousseau's intellect and personality were its genesis. Years of writing flowed from this,—explorations, experiments, and creations conquering both substance and public. She tapped the basic problems of human relationship in its private and public aspects—possession versus liberation, indifference versus understanding, everything alternating in respective spheres, whether the human beings were fictitious—Delphine-Corinne, Léonce-Oswald—or nations among themselves. But the culmination of her art is here, in the *Considérations*, where the political spiral reaches her timeless, spaceless vision of liberty.

As it has shown in its opening statement, the *Considerations* wishes to tame the problem of brutality—incomprehensible to her, and just as reprehensible. Hence her effort to recollect as with a clinical eye what she witnessed and experienced. While writing, she ached for France. Knowing that many others felt the same, she tried to pull out the substances of her trauma once and for all. As her children might benefit from her text, and because of illness, she may have considered this her final testament.

The narrative swiftly pulls together events, causes, catastrophes and their consequences. For example, the aftermath of Louis XV's death presents "words, actions, virtues, passions and vanities, and the public mind . . . as tending toward the goal" of redressing disorder and establishing individual rights.[21]

Segments on Germaine's father—his character and deeds, and those related to England—its history and political evolution, can be seen as beacons projecting light against France's revolutionary terror. These segments contrast with disorder and cruelty, one pointing to kindness and the other to sanity, hence their optimistic quality. However, the tone is suspenseful: Germaine is pleading for the fate of France before the foreign negotiators who are in its midst.

Much as Germaine's text is a testimonial, she is a historian just the same. A recent re-edition of the *Considerations* by Jacques Godechot (1983) points to Germaine's subjective manner, yet the critic ranks her highly in the domain of political sociology. He praises her for having held together the totality of the Revolution from 1750 to 1816.[22] Godechot commends to attention Germaine's statement that the era was more than a series of events, but "one of the great epochs of the social order. Those who have considered it an accidental event have not looked at the past . . . attributing to actors of the moment what centuries had prepared."[23]

Godechot agrees with Germaine's decision to view the Revolution with respect to the passing of time. This is an entry into political science, he adds, and for having this quality, the book is "more than a history."[24] In 1979 the noted Staëlean scholar Simone Balayé emphasized Germaine's "deep belief in the great notions of the Enlightenment, particularly that of perfectibility."[25] In our opinion this belief authenticates Germaine's position as a historian. The idealism that never left her made her treasure that era's brilliant emphasis on religious and political independence of thought congenial to perfectibility. We have seen that Germaine did her utmost to highlight this independence in her essays and novels. For being a most articulate and 'engagée' witness of her time, she is an accredited historian even for this reason alone.

In the *Dictionary and Critique of the French Revolution* (*Dictionnaire critique de la Révolution française*) (1988), Marcel Gauchet compliments Madame de Staël for having shown the "mutual antipathy" among the ancien regime's classes.[26] Indeed, Germaine's enumeration of the conceits, irritabilities, jealousies and humiliations that fed antipathy up to and through the Revolution's tortuous journey is startling. Poisonously, they tore apart initial republican principles that were pure and genuine.

Germaine describes other maladies: the fanaticism of some, self-interest within the upper class, personal resentments among assembly deputies—all infections fatal to the nation's hunger for well-being, therefore to a working republicanism. Politically failing, the Revolution increased the already deep misery of its people. The populace became cruel. "The absence of happiness leads to the absence of morality."[27]

And again, character is an important part of Germaine's representation of human relationships. One particular trait, the "art of deceiving others . . . which Machiavelli called an accomplishment,"[28] struck her as the most dangerous politic of all. As we know, Germaine met Robespierre in her parents' home before her marriage. On the day of her second encounter with him, September 3, 1792, news of the princess of Lamballe's murder had a devastating effect; the death of Marie-Antoinette's closest friend augured more cruelty. That day, Germaine had decided to leave France. Her carriage was stopped, she was taken to the Hotel de Ville where Robespierre sat at the Commune's desk. She confronted him silently. Fortunately a writer-friend member of the Commune interceded and led her back to the Swedish embassy. During ensuing hours the royal family was taken to the Temple prison, a large number of political prisoners and priests were massacred. Germaine soon escaped from France. The image of Robespierre's impassive face never left her. She read his speeches extolling the equality of fortune and rank, and found them incoherent. She knew the corruption, genocidal sang-froid, the impersonal, mysterious manner, and she considered his ritual of the 'Supreme Being' a religion "arranged for himself."[29] But she could not fathom Robespierre's viciousness.

Germaine did fathom Napoléon's rise, his rule as well. A change succeeded his entry into politics. Buoyed by military success, he exercised a business sense that camouflaged personal interest. This was visible to Germaine long before Napoléon's errors of later years. She explains his mastery of the European continent through his persuasive manner of negotiating with other powers, his humiliating and injurious words in private confrontations, these being oratorical opposites that perplexed and confused others. Germaine remarks that his candor before the senate on the eve of his 'coronation', and his impatience with Paris high society where pleasantnesses could prick, pointed to both hypocrisy and fear of moquery. From the perspective of the exiled political victim, Napoléon's calculating 'rule of one' placated the nation, everything and everyone was known to him, and liberty died.

As with Robespierre, Napoléon's despotism was based on dissimilitude. Germaine saw incoherence in both rulers, for it is a trait "distinctly recognizable among those who do not think out of respect for the law of duty."[30] According to her and where post-revolutionary years were concerned, Napoléon used the will of the French. They misread his cause, which was far from being theirs. Pathologically, the French imagination attached itself to him out of weariness from a doubly oppressed past. The fateful attachement was history's own irony. Germaine saw that Napoléon had his own opinion concerning imagination; he used the public's, and said so.

Deep into her text, Germaine diagnosed the French nation of 1789. In ancient times, spirit and force emanated from publicly admired individuals. Despotism came, and by the eithteenth century tax-free privileges and religious intolerance had ingrained themselves into the nation. In spite of philosophical outcries, these institutions afflicted the populace. They totally ignored its mind. Ruled by financially ruinous monarchies, the poor became miserable, more so during periods of famine. According to Germaine, the nation had patience, it knew of its military valor, but it did not *know* liberty. When the third estate first met, revolutionaries facing political responsibility had learned nothing concerning political virtue. Among some, anger was virulent. Concurrently, the upper class of society was far from ideal. In our understanding of the *Considerations'* final pages, men and women who use their talents, who practice "self-sacrifice, exalt honor and greatness of soul"[31] are the ideal that a society should nurture. On the eve of the Revolution, this had not been so. Consistent, Germaine's thinking connects directly with her novel *Delphine*. Here, character cameos portray a society fragmented by prejudices. In the same circumstance of time, Germaine describes relationships among men and women where instances of marital happiness are rare, particularly among the older generation. In only one case is there an example of a husband respecting without concern for his self-esteem his wife's political and religious independence of mind. Within marriage, this respect is the only guarantee of mutual amicability, if not happiness.

In Germaine's estimation, the France of 1816 still suffered from social instability. According to her, the returning nobility were pockmarked with selfishness, old revolutionaries wearied of ideas they had profaned—such as the idea of liberty, while others were jacobinistic creatures lacking political conscience. Germaine is wistful: "Whereas for so many centuries generous souls have loved liberty, the greatest deeds have been inspired by it ... now, new ideas and sane judgements can only emerge if young men will become men by looking after their country, believing they are its citizens, and being useful to it."[32]

Public conscience needed invigorating. Renewed efforts depended on the nation's "originality of character, its loyalty, and independent spirit,"[33] those authentic qualities lost in the past. When Germaine extols "this energy of independence which knows how to resist everything on earth,"[34] she has touched the French nation's nerve.

In late February of 1817, Germaine's pen lay still on the desk. Energy vanished. Great ideas, enthusiasms, and affections now reigned only in glory, her body paralyzed. Lucid, she rebelled against the illness. Albertine's little Pauline was brought to her bedside. Chateaubriand and Louis XVIII visited her. In early May, Germaine dictated a last appeal to Wellington to end the occupation of France. On July 14, her children, Frances Randall and Schlegel received her final adieu.

> ... I have a real cult for the beauty of your soul. . . .[35]
> Wilhelm Schlegel, letter to Germaine de Staël
> Berne, December 26, 1810

> ... I have lost the object of my cult and of my passion, of my respect and confidence, the one whose voice ever thrilled my heart.[36]
> Albertine duchess of Broglie
> Coppet August 14, 1817

CONCLUSION

> Madame de Staël's name still rises first to the lips when we are asked to mention a woman of great intellectual power.[1]
>
> George Eliot, 1854

In her second preface to the essay on Jean-Jacques Rousseau, Germaine presented her profession of faith in her calling. "Writing," she said, "is a consolation for the sorrows of life . . . it develops one's mind . . . along with an ever-renewed hope that the ordinary course of life does not offer."[2] Germaine's eagerness to reach excellence combined with the feeling of melancholy. Both feelings remained with her throughout her artistic pilgrimage. Since the youthful confidences entered in the *Journal*, she examined her strengths and weaknesses as a writer. She learned from self-analysis that writing can appeal to sentiment, and be powerful thereby. She developed a habit of confrontation and questioning into a veritable technique. She put her intellect to the task.

Thus for Germaine, the intellect is primarily kin to sentiment. Each is nearly at a constant to the other. One has only to review her convictions in their developmental trajectory to realize that here is a conscience-oriented philosophy: feeling can be a source of ideas and develop along with these; 'attachments of the heart' can be assessed in a scientific manner; one must hold on to the 'feeling of the self', for it is identical to one's moral existence. The call for such an assessment is psychological. Madame de Staël's perception of human behavior, particularly in the relationships between men and women, moves with a clinical eye. This is evident in the novels *Delphine* and *Corinne ou l'Italie,* also in the long essay *The Influence of Passions.* Sentiment subsists throughout. One senses Germaine's autobiographical feeling for her two Galateae. Sentiment permeates the depictions of love relationships that end pathetically, relentlessly so in spite of momentary enchantments.

As I have pointed out, Delphine lives in a society 'which controls and engulfs its women, making them dependent on others and incapable of forming a complete independence of mind.' The predicament is the psychological key to the novel. According to Germaine, very few women could 'challenge society and its tenacious conventions.' For one, dominated by her desire to be loved, the tender-hearted Delphine fails to tame society. Around her, a world fragmented by social, religious and political prejudices barely offers examples of marital happiness. Prejudice has seeped into the fabric of marriage itself where, for example, a man's tenacious concern for his self-esteem prevents him from recognizing his wife's intellectual qualities. While such qualities are evident in both Delphine and Corinne, relationships with Léonce and Oswald respectively end in tragic failures.

Germaine questioned the problematic of women endowed with talent and high intelligence in the society of equally talented and intelligent men. She keenly felt that a woman risked her happiness by allowing personal glory to flaunt society. A woman of superior talents and intelligence, Germaine wrote in *The Influence of Passions,*

> ... might feel free of others's enmity, and think of herself in the company of the most famous of men, but she would never attain to their calm and cool headedness. Imagination is always the first of her faculties. Her talent might increase, but her ... feelings would be troubled. Her mind could bring glory, and such greatness could enlighten others, but it would fail in personal relationships.[1]

Did Germaine have intuitions regarding this portrait? This does not seem to have been so. She once confided to her friend Julie de Krüdener that she did not possess "the completeness of feeling which honors you. I see the pros and cons of everything, my desire at the time is the only stable part of me. I have seen your self-confidence, even in the face of human evil. This has left me ... with a painful disposition even in my highest thoughts."[8] There is no mirror image in the portrait. Feelings moved quickly with Germaine, and seldom to their completion. It was in her nature, then, to let past experiences of painful feelings leave her. Only a faint, vaguely sad reminiscence remained. Moreover, 'highest thoughts' did not concern herself. As she grew older, they drew away from herself, and lodged elsewhere—the problems of evil, liberty, freedom from tyranny, and more than anything else, the nation.

Nevertheless, within the variables of society, male and female differences troubled Germaine. Undoubtedly, they engendered her two novels where she could create two specific case studies, so to speak. From her perspective, such differences were both general and particular. Generally, the female mystique differed because of an all-embracing sensitivity, let alone a powerful imagination. However, according to Germaine, men and women shared equally potential talents and intelligences. Yet at the same time, human nature possessed the unpredictable if not elusive component of character. This was so for all concerned. While one might alienate oneself from society (Delphine), another might continue asserting oneself (Corinne). Well aware of these complexities, Germaine offered her diagnoses, then strongly upheld a women's education nourished and maintained with trust in each one's personal judgement. Her offers and her call were inspired by her 'enlightened' upbringing where, irrespective of sex, the independent perfecting of one's mind held court.

During the years of preoccupation with her novels, Germaine expressed political anxieties in the long essay on *Circumstances that can end the Revolution*. Tension from constant surveillance had changed her lifestyle and left her restless. Enervations caused nearly continuous travel, yet they did not separate her from her pen. Hence the 'oeuvre' progressed from the literary genre to a political science of her own devising. Mathematical calculation must be applied to politics, she wrote. While curiously psychological, the pronouncement agrees with her pedagogy, for she believed that human nature's moral and physical forces were comparable, both being equally open to direction.

Though complex, Germaine's intellectuality took her on a rigorous journey. It was sustained by the belief that human nature is open to perfectibility, therefore must move foreward and progress. Around her, brilliant writers responded to her views, some in agreement, some not, particularly on the subject of perfectibility. But in person and in writing, they respected her and eagerly discussed common concerns such as the ideal political society, for one, and France's destiny, for another. These confidences nourished her socio-political thinking early on, as the two essays *On Internal Peace* indicated.

Indeed, elders like the physiognomist Johann Lavater, count Hippolyte de Guibert, and later Charles-Victor de Bonstetten, then Johann Wolfgang von Goethe, Thomas Jefferson, baron Kaspar de Voght and Arthur Wellesley duke of Wellington responded to Germaine with affectionate encouragement. All wanted to realize Voltaire's dream of a just and therefore ideal society. They were as youthful as Germaine in their idealism. Among her peers, talented scholars, publishers, poets, journalists, writers and government officials also gave her confidence: Benjamin Constant, for one, and others who, though critical at times, did not waver in their respect for her quality of mind: François de Pange, Wilhelm von Humboldt, François de Chateaubriand, Charles de Villers, Claude Fauriel, Friedrich Schiller, Simone Sismondi, J. M. De Gérando, Camille Jordan, Mathieu de Montmorency, Friederika Brun, Henry lord Lansdowne, finally Wilhelm Schlegel, the companion of later years.

Thoughts concerning an ideal society and France's destiny deepened. In her diagnostic manner, Germaine attached kaleidoscopic emotions to the nation, and attempted to resolve problems of unreasonableness, self-interest, and most of all cruelty. Her creative relationship with France intensified. As critical powers matured, she saw that the fate of France and that of liberty were conjoined, and at stake. Thus France and liberty became major themes in the 'oeuvre'.

When Germaine published *De la littérature* in 1800, she added a minor yet no less important theme to the bond between France and liberty: that of the writer's duty of leaderhip toward the nation. Her precept connects readily with the Enlightenment's belief in progress. With Germaine, progress is political, moral, and intellectual. For the remainder of her writing career, she energetically challenged writers to overcome the trauma of the failed revolution with reflection and understanding, and ever reminded them of the importance of hopefulness in the light of intellectual of progress.

Sooner than many of her peers, Germaine perceived the hypocrisies of Robespierre and Napoléon. As we have seen, the punishment for her outspokenness dramatically affected her, but she acted on her convictions until the end. Her disdain did not cause bitterness. It rather added to her increasingly evident melancholy.

We must also remember that in private encounters, Germaine was truthful. This was part of her charm and pleasantness. At Coppet, respect for truthfulness became her little society's modus vivendi, affection aiding. Frankness and enthusiasm are youthful characteristics. Whereas some great minds isolate themselves in self-adulation, on the contrary, in the 'oeuvre' and the numerous letters, Germaine opened her mind and much of herself to others. Some unhappy consequences ensued. Her eagerness to share extended from things of the mind to excessive financial kindnesses. Concurrently, the emotional possessiveness that countered kindness made her lose her first loves—Narbonne and Ribbing.

Jacques Necker well understood his daughter's intellect and character. He sensed danger when she went too close to the center of the political arena. Necker did not look at Germaine with a public eye. Public ambivalence tilted increasingly toward negativity and the press pursued her like a beast. Germaine's extroversion and unconventionality caused calumny and gossip. This distressed Necker, but in his mind's eye Germaine was a shining example of intellectual strength. However, he did not hesitate to express his concern over her ambition. "Calm your ambition," he wrote to her, "until you will be in a country where you will be able to say and write what you will. . . ."[3] Germaine's defense of Marie-Antoinette (1793), her call for peace with England (1794), her texts on fiction and the influence of passions (1795-1796) and the book on literature (1800) confirmed her strengths. Success was undeniable. A letter from Samuel Constant praised her erudition. "You are extending the boundaries of human thinking,"[4] the letter said. But Necker's pride did not blind him to the fact that her political criticism would even raise suspicion of conspiracy. "Poor dear," he wrote to her shortly before the first order of exile from France, "here you are in the open sea, and my thoughts are following you, for though filled with the spirit of centuries you are but a child in character. . . ."[5]

Fears allayed when Necker realized that his daughter had become a respected author. Near the end of his life, he gave her the ultimate compliment: "It is a fact that you are the most amiable and high-spirited (spirituelle) person in the known world. From this, how can we possibly contribute to your happiness?"[6] Necker's accolade still showed concern for Germaine. He sensed that glory would come in the way of her personal happiness.

Germaine's style tightened during the search for ideas on the world at large, but she never abandoned the belief that ideas have color, as she once said to the critic Pierre-Louis count Roederer. Ideas also have movement and often seek the support of history. The preface to her *On Literature* offers such an example: "We cannot foresee the limit of human thinking," she wrote, "but then, why is so-called perfectibility unleashing every imaginable political passion? What relationship does perfectibility have with such passions?"[9] At the time of writing, in 1800, the future seemed unclear. Her questions were meant to jolt her readers out of complacency, look at their government, and address the issue of liberty with questioning. She reminded them that in the early months of the Revolution such questions had not been asked, in fact, in the public's mind the notion of liberty was new and vague. She reiterated that for her, perfectibility of mind did not imply a superiority of modern over ancient thinking. While the latter subsists, she added, "the mass of ideas of all kinds increases with each century . . . and civilization progresses in all classes and in all states."[9] No one, no government or religion can possibly reject the notion of perfectibility. Only the despotic can negate it; it is they who condemn human spirit. The lies and superstitions on which despotism feeds degrade human nature, she continued. "We need a more enlightened government that respects public opinion . . . and refrains from the moment's strongly agitated personal interests."[9] For Germaine, self-interest is the enemy and, philosophically speaking, the antithesis of perfectibility. In her *Circumstances that Can End the Revolution,* Germaine's reply to her own question on political passions directly attacked the government created by Bonaparte's coup d'état and his self-promotions. It is not surprising that Germaine's friends urged her against publishing the *Circumstances.*

Germaine's critics were wrong to speak of her subjectivity in writing. Against this, she confronted the dichotomy between perfectibility and despotism with logic and consistency. Where emotion is concerned, she had studied the subject as far back as her youthful *Journal*, where she attempted to confront emotion impersonally. One of her earliest experiments with fiction addresses emotion in such a manner: in the *Madwoman of Sénart,* the narrator and leading character vows to be open to emotion in every imaginable way. The slight encounter with the desolate, mad creature is a brief but sharp image of the dangerous and pathetic workings of unchecked sentiment. In another early fiction, *Sophie or the Secret Sentiment*, young Sophie also personifies emotion, but pathos has lightened. Sophie overcomes anguish thanks to the invigorating feeling of the self (le sentiment de soi), that is to say, emotional security. Pathetic workings of sentiment returned during Germaine's later fiction. The character struggles and entanglements of Delphine and Léonce, Corinne, and Oswald, added in no small degree to the destructions of their relationships.

In retrospect, *The Influence of Passions*, which Germaine calls a meditation, presents an impartial study of sentiment. The work is systematic, it aligns diverse passions, including ambition. Confronting the latter, the author describes an unimaginative being striving for power, locking himself in the present, and concentrating solely on his course of action. He is insensitive, wrapped in a pseudo-crushing of himself. The portrait is mobile: the personality dries itself out. Germaine's representation is not unlike that of Bonaparte's during a youthful essay in which he called ambition a consuming of the self. Was there perhaps a model other than Napoléon at the time of Germaine's 1796 meditation? It is tempting to reply 'Talleyrand', for she knew him well. If ambition, she adds, "distorts the heart: when one has judged everything in relation to oneself only, then how can one transport oneself into another?"[10] While Germaine's question is vital to the subject at hand, it also impacts the 'oeuvre' as a whole. It is part of her logical ethic. Germaine's reverence for Montesquieu often comes forth in the *Influence* where the humanitarian ethos is clear. Montesquieu, she once wrote, "seems to give life to ideas; at every line, he reminds us of the moral nature of human beings, yet this reminder comes in the very midst of the mind's abstractions."[11] Once again, we can appreciate the degree to which Germaine's intellectuality found inspiration in the Enlightenment.

In a writer's vocation, intellectuality applies not only to kinships and style, but to context as well. From this threefold perspective, one can say that in addition to the *Influence of Passions*, *Delphine* and *Considerations concerning the French Revolution* are Madame de Staël's greatest works. *Delphine* is the melancholy edifice of a society stiffened by prejudice and hardened to the point of cruelty to a young woman who is naïve and beautiful morally as well as otherwise. From the point of view of the novel's context, every element of Delphine's relation to her society is an instance of suffering—her love for Léonce primarily, and her near-subjugation to older women like Madame de Vernon, personifications of disillusion and bitterness. The novelist has transformed the problematic of the social rapport between men and women into a sociological sphere where only knowledge, tolerance and religious belief free of superstition could offer a resolution.

Next to *Delphine*, the *Considerations* represent a crumbling edifice: it is France torn by political passions through and beyond the Revolution. Only two elements are of a positive nature: Necker's teaching, and England's parliamentary example. Contextually, that is to say against the generally melancholic components of the picture, Germaine leaves the reader with the advisory hope that the young will pay attention to their government, and be their nation's conscientious citizens. Compared with the pathetic edifice of *Delphine*, the *Considerations'* answer to the question regarding an ideal society leaves the reader with an optimism that is at once political and pedagogical.

Germaine's unhappiness on seeing France occupied by foreign powers marred the last two years of her life. But she had done her duty as a writer and instilled provocative themes in the minds of many. That France was a child much in need of redressing and that its destiny was unclear countered her themes of perfectibility, liberty, and morality. Ever melancholic, she interspersed among these those human failings she most abhorred: mediocrity and the grim realities of hypocrisy, despotism, and genocide.

Since her time, some of Madame de Staël's pronouncements have been fragmented and have become clichés. What critics have said and repeated among themselves concerning her personal life has often been conjectural. Fascinating and adventurous as her life's story appears to be, such a perspective is tangential. The intellectual Germaine who wanted to stir her readers is she who needs to be known. Her voice and gestures may have vanished, but not the strong echoes of conversations and letters many of which transpired into her writing. The pen helped reverberate these echoes during her years of reading, reflection and concentration, whether in Paris, Coppet, or the large coach traveling across Europe, Russia, Poland, Scandinavia and England. Madame de Staël's writing is her reality.

Barring years of distress that left her wistful, there were undeniably bright phases in Germaine's life: her childhood, republican enthusiasms during the maturing years, a father's love fully reciprocated, literary success, the many orchestrated gatherings in her salons where eclectic attitudes and ideas were bound to meet, then probably most of all the great friendships that filled Coppet where again, intellects varied and challenged each other within conversational art itself.

Germaine may have been impetuous and overbearing, but for being youthful, her intellect was unstained. It had a moral basis. Its presence in the 'oeuvre' is steady and consistent. It never allowed personal motives to enter the line of thought. We are two at the task, Germaine once said. This cannot but have been the secret of such consistency, for in the dual relationship of author to person and person to author, each challenging and responding to the other, morality stayed pure. In writing, the intellect flourished with sentiment, and most of all love for mankind. In daily life, this translated into unreserved affection and generosity.

Germaine manifested a colorful writing impulse since childhood. In the garden at Saint Ouen, she delighted in writing and offering theatrical performances with her young companions. This was the nourishing ground of a boundless and passionate imagination, so much so that during mature self-analyses she considered imagination the staying power of a woman's mystique. One can say that if Madame de Staël as person and author cultivated the intellect to a high degree, nevertheless she never relinquished her gift of imagination, especially in her fiction. Imagination painted the physical portraits of Delphine and Corinne. Granted, the idealism and romanticism of these heroines are congenial to Germaine's melancholy. However, Delphine and Corinne are more than self-projections. Imagination practically brings them to life thanks to the extraordinary energy expended in Delphine's acts of benevolence and Corinne's passionate nature. Gestures and voices resonate. The art of the novel advances due to this masterful combination of self-projection and imagination, Moreover, Germaine offers a stirring example of her belief that beauty is truth. Imagination remained a companion to intellect along with psychology and this philosophical sentiment. It had given Germaine much happiness during childhood; it never vanished in memory's abandonments.

Germaine opted to return to non-fiction in order to face her political battles with everything that her intellect could provide. Variegated and even complex as her art became, Germaine loved and sought the treasured moments at her desk. Equally so, she held her family, her men, her numerous friends, Paris and glory in deep affection. She learned that glory overreached personal happiness. But contentment did come in later years. Away from adulation, in the quiet study at Coppet where "all ambitious ideas seem very small at the foot of mountains that touch the sky,"[12] calm reigned, and the energetic pen waited. Compared with military spirit . . . the art of writing

> is also a weapon, words are also an action, provided the soul's energy expresses itself fully, feelings rise to the level of ideas, and tyranny sees itself attacked by . . . generous indignation and inflexible reason.[13]
> Germaine de Staël, *De la Littérature*, 1800

Chateau de Coppet, a lithograph from an original drawing by Jean-Jacques Deriaz (1814-1890). Reproduced by permission of the Chateau de Coppet, Switzerland.

EPILOGUE

> Time does not change anything in this great emptiness that nothing will fill. But it softens those first impressions which human strength could not bear for long.[1]
>
> Auguste de Staël
> Letter to the duchess of Devonshire, September 30, 1817

Auguste, Albertine, and Victor published both the *Dix Années d'Exil* and the *Considérations sur la Révolution française* in 1818, one year after Germaine's death. Both texts met with considerable success. Critics agreed that in the *Considérations* her having positioned the Revolution's historical roots deep into France's past was an innovative and contributive entry into political science.[2]

Benjamin Constant, while finishing his project on religion, offered affectionate tributes to Germaine, to her character and writings. His appraisals were based on nearly sixteen years of companionship. Much as their relationship was far from even, and perhaps more so for this reason, his estimate is important. It has become evident that she valued his attachment to her, the qualities of his mind, and his literary and political counsel. These were the most, if not the only, steady facets of his rapport with her.

Constant's text on religion expounds a moral philosophy that clearly reflects Germaine's manner of thinking. In retrospect, one can see the marriage of their ideas. "Everything that morally excites tenderness and enthusiasm," Constant writes, "the spectacle of a generous sacrifice . . .

aid to the suffering, disdain for vice . . . resistance to tyranny, awakens and nourishes the soul's mysterious disposition. If the habit of selfishness causes one to smile at this exaltation, the smile, however, hides a secret shame; it is ironic because instinct warns that an offense is made to the most noble part of one's being."[3] Enthusiasm, generosity, pity, hatred of vice and tyranny, these were components of Germaine's morality. Selfishness, secretiveness, irony and shame were Constant's. Unconsciously perhaps, Constant thus resumed his sixteen-year dialogue with Germaine.

We know that Constant was exceptionally kind to Germaine in spite of his ambivalence. Reserve concerning his relationships with other women, his gambling and financial dependence created tension. Nevertheless, above all culpability, Constant admired, respected, and loved Germaine as much as, if not more than, any of her other and numerous affections. Acid comments in his novel *Cécile* go against the grain; they are a cry of exasperation caused by both his hesitations and Germaine's mobile temper. But Constant's final tribute is solid and clear-headed. Written some time after Germaine's death, it appeared in his *Mélanges de littérature et de politique:*

> Her two dominating qualities were affection and pity. Like all beings endowed with genius she had a passion for glory and like all souls of quality a great love for liberty. But these two sentiments softened when the happiness of those whom she loved was in danger, for something in the world was more sacred to her than success or even a political cause. . . . Her energy of character and the vivacity of her impressions often took her away from her writing . . . to help the oppressed . . . tirelessly. . . . Privately, her unique conversational talent acted like magic . . . even away from her one still heard her expressions . . . one held feelings in check in order to discuss them with her. . . . Her impartiality, the variety of her talents and universality of views transformed her from a political writer of the first order into an ingenious observer of human weaknesses and the faithful interpreter of sufferings of the heart.[4]

Constant's views on parliamentary liberalism led him to a position in the Council of State where he served until his death in 1830.

Attentive to Germaine's fifth child—Alphonse, the "petit nous"—Auguste and Albertine were saddened by Rocca's death in January 1818. A friendship had formed in spite of Rocca's youthfulness and the secret marriage with Germaine.

Auguste had grown up in Coppet, away from the revolutionary clashes and bloodshed. Educated in turn by his mother, Necker, the tutor

Gerlach and often, Mathieu de Montmorency, Auguste's gentleness was sometimes mistaken for passivity. Into maturity, his strong devotion to Germaine was touching. He shared her triumphs and sorrows, and expressed a need of her, calling this a durable interest in life. He helped Germaine with her financial affairs and the countless negociations she invented to recover the state's debt to her father and alleviate her exile. Auguste's encounter with Napoléon during one such mission impressed the latter. Barely aged twenty-one, Auguste wrote to Germaine that he "found happiness in playing the role of head of the family yet guided by a being so superior to myself, therefore being a protected protector."[5]

Auguste's publication of Germaine's works may have attenuated his grief, if not softened it. Having met Wilberforce during a visit to England, Auguste engaged in social work, published religious papers and political tracts in which he, like Constant and Victor de Broglie, expressed liberal views. He survived his mother by only ten years.

Albertine, now duchess of Broglie, published a *Journal on Education*. Her tendency to give way to somber exaltation made her turn to religious thinking. However, Albertine opened a salon. One of her first visitors was the marquis de La Fayette. Regular guests included the poets Alphonse de Lamartine and Alfred de Vigny, political thinkers like Alexis de Tocqueville and François Guizot. Albertine actively supported her husband's liberalism.[6] Fanny Randall, Albertine's former tutor, became her secretary and companion. Fanny and Albertine are buried side by side. Victor de Broglie paid tribute to Germaine at the Académie Française, reiterating that what Germaine was for her children would never be understood by any but those who lived within her intimacy. Victor's career reached the height of success. He became prime minister to Louis Philippe of France (1830-1848).

Victor and Albertine's daughter Louise, born one year after Pauline, married Joseph Othenin, count d'Haussonville, whose writings and careful study of the family archives initiated for him and for his descendants considerable research and publications that are descriptive as well as appreciative of Germaine. Besides the members of the Broglie family, those of Othenin himself—d'Andlau, Pange, and Luppé—greatly enriched his legacy.

Wilhelm Schlegel too had lived within Germaine's intimacy. His grief was shattering. He deeply respected Germaine and the feeling was mutual. As Germaine said to Goethe in 1811, "this is a man whom I am learning to love more every day."[7]

Before his departure for the universities of Heidelberg and Bonn where he taught literature and continued publishing translations of European classics, Schlegel protected Germaine's unedited works. An agreement soon followed with Auguste de Staël and Victor de Broglie whereby he embarked on the successful edition of Germaine's complete works from 1820 to 1821. Germaine's cousin Madame Necker de Saussure assumed the biographical task in this edition, thereby becoming the first official biographer of Madame de Staël. And so Schlegel distanced himself from Coppet after twelve years of devotion to Germaine and in full agreement with the contract originally formulated. A moody person, Schlegel's affection for Germaine was replete with tension, but loyalty prevailed. Later, he translated Germaine's *Considérations* into German.

Count Adolf Ribbing had long separated from Germaine, but a tender, admirative feeling remained. As we know, Adolf applauded Germaine's publishing successes. Most probably, his grief for her revived the republican exaltations that had initiated the romantic entanglement with her. Exile from his native Sweden ruined Ribbing morally and financially. He lived in Denmark, Belgium, and came to Paris to earn a modest living as journalist. He died a wanderer at age seventy-eight, longing for home.

Two who deeply mourned Germaine and to quite an extent had lived within her intimacy were Charles-Victor de Bonstetten and Mathieu de Montmorency. Older by a generation, Charles-Victor knew Germaine since her childhood. He was from Berne, and as bailiff for the region of Nyon had protected Coppet from military harm. Liberal, his views brought the order of exile. After the return to Geneva, Bonstetten became a steady visitor at Coppet. If the invitation included several days or even more, he accepted on the proviso that he lodge in the gardener's cottage, bring his valet, his cook, and his horse, to which Germaine agreed. She encouraged him in his writing and helped him publish philosophical and literary essays. He greatly admired her for her spiritedness, as he put it. It was he who introduced the poetess Friederika Brun to Germaine. Mourning for Germaine, Bonstetten turned to a work clearly reminiscent of both *Corinne* and *De l'Allemagne: L'Homme du Midi (South) et l'Homme du Nord, ou l'influence du climat* (1824). Bonstetten constantly complained of ill health. He died at age ninety-seven.

Mathieu duke of Montmorency was Germaine's peer. He had been tutored by the abbé Sieyès. Mathieu fought in America, returned home to serve in Artois' guards, and entered the States General as its youngest delegate. As we know, he was one of the first aristocrats to give up tax privileges. Germaine helped him escape from the Terror. His attachment to her caused him to also suffer the order of exile. He became deeply religious. Spending much time with Germaine's children at Coppet, he became a mentor to them, and particularly to Auguste. Germaine returned his affection with gratitude and respect. He survived her only nine years.

"There is nothing in the publications by Madame de Staël that comes close to the naturalness and eloquence of her letters. Here, imagination lends full expression to sentiment."[8] Chateaubriand's judgement of Germaine's epistolary style holds for posterity. He dearly loved her, though he did not live within her intimacy. Theirs was the solid affection of colleagues, companions at arms during the rugged years of political rebellion. They respected each other's talents. No pettiness had ever entered that sacred association of writer to writer. When Chateaubriand visited Germaine shortly before her death, he was greeted with "Bonjour, my dear Francis (in English), I am suffering, but that does not prevent me from loving you."[9] That summer day in 1817, Chateaubriand was struck by the feeling of general desolateness around him. Later, grieving over the loss of their mutual friend, Chateaubriand and Juliette Récamier visited Coppet and the dark wood at the end of the park where Germaine and her parents lay entombed. Chateaubriand became ambassador to Berlin, to London and Italy, and later minister of foreign affairs. He presented the *Etudes historiques* in 1831. His *Mémoires d'outre-tombe* often speak of Germaine. When her life ended, he said, part of his had ended as well.

In his meditative manner, Alexander of Russia too must have felt that Germaine's departure meant the falling away of a bright, sprightly era. There would be no more dialogues on character and destiny. He may have understood Germaine better than many of her political luminaries (les hommes supérieurs), as she called them, and certainly so on the international scene. Alexander most probably best assuaged Germaine's fears concerning the future of France. In a letter of February 1817, he predicted to her that ". . . if everything in France still does not come up to your expectations, I like to think that obstacles to a stable and conservative Restoration will soon be lifted . . . intentions will be purer."[10] Like Bernadotte, Wellington, and then Louis XVIII, Alexander admired Germaine's works, respected her as a writer and person, but he particularly expressed genuine concern and affection for her. He probably endeared himself to her more than Wellington. Alexander reigned until 1825, but the early liberalism that had so pleased Germaine did not lead to reforms.

His interests rather turned in the direction of mysticism. Friendship with Julie de Krüdener probably had some bearing on this change.

Julie, who was Germaine's peer, greatly influenced any who were open to pietist views. She impressed Germaine. Julie's disdain for the sect-oriented probably caught Germaine's interest. These have "dispositions to enforce in the minds of others methods and forms that are shocking to those who have something much more vast in the soul,"[11] Julie stated. Germaine's discretion concerning her religious beliefs could readily agree with Julie's comment. For Germaine, liberty detached from politics was congenial to belief. But her religious feelings were deeply personal even though they were very much part of her morality and generous manner of being. Julie probably touched a sensitive area of Germaine's heart. Moreover, she encouraged self-analysis. From Germaine's responses to her, one can see that such analysis brought Germaine's melancholic side into focus. The few who knew Germaine well saw how this character trait combined with affectionateness. But Germaine was also full of joie de vivre. At her death, this contagious feeling came to an end. It would be so for Julie Krüdener as well.

Germaine's affections for her women friends warmed her voluminous correspondence. Feelings were richly exchanged. Juliette Récamier's experience of grief after Germaine's departure was long and desolate. Theirs had been a rare relationship. Germaine called Juliette "la jeune soeur de mon choix" (the young sister of my choice).[12] She took great delight in announcing to her prospective guests that the most beautiful woman in the world would also be there, at Coppet. Since their first meeting in Paris in 1798, Juliette had steadily shared Germaine's thoughts, her activities and family life, literary success, social relationships and the sufferings of exile. Juliette could not but feel a deep sense of loss after July 14, 1817; friendship had lasted nineteen years. At the time of their politically imposed departure from Chaumont and the enforced dispersion abroad, Juliette was most compassionate, particularly during Germaine's agitations over the brutal censorship of *De l'Allemagne*. Germaine wrote to Juliette that everything was collapsing and she missed her: ". . . you were the gentle and tranquil center of our lives here, and nothing will hold together again. . . ."[12] Juliette submitted to exile because of the association with Germaine. She found it difficult to accustom herself, as she put it, to not being in Germaine's company. Conjectures have pointed to an abnormal rapport. They cannot be justified. Juliette was flirtatious, but only with men, including the lovesick

Prosper de Barante and for an infatuated moment, Auguste de Staël. But with and for Germaine, Juliette was a kindred soul. Desolate, she lost her closest friend.

The curtain has come down. Family and friends are fixed in mourning, many others standing by, equally still. The image is close to reality. The imagination brings to life the wide, crowded stage. The span of years has been 1766 to 1817. The curtain lifts, gestures beckon, and under the candlelight, one particular voice resonates with familiar phrases like "enlightened beings"(hommes éclairés), "beings whole" (hommes tout entiers), "motions of the soul," "the soul captured" (l'âme saisie), "society's movement." Consistent, harmonious, and tenacious, these phrases are the crystals of Germaine's writing. She comes forth, and warms the stage with her presence. "We must move with our century . . . we must correct our failings and acquire still more of the irresistible progress of our reason, our enlightenments."[13] As Constant had well understood, something more sacred than success impelled Germaine to speak—her kind heart, enthusiasm, and a brilliant mind eager to have us believe that against tumult, terror and tyranny, there is such a thing as perfectibility.

> . . . Her nature, at once ardent and sad, accessible to the most noble passions and ever ready to give of herself thereby, yet troubled by the feeling of the nothingness of life and tormented by the problem of destiny . . . this was the essential Germaine de Staël.[14]
> Count d'Haussonville, 1925

POSTSCRIPT

The lifespans of Madame de Staël's elders and peers offer astonishing contrasts. It is hard to believe that men of great minds like Necker, Condorset, Jefferson, and Goethe bore the shock of a murderous revolution; that soon after, military might sent tremors throughout Europe. Yet within this slice of history, writers respectful of the better things of the past sought to recover from political trauma and move society to even better heights. This was Germaine de Staël's generation. Despite anxiety and in a few decades of writing, she did her duty as a writer. She enlightened her peers in turn.

Denis Diderot	1713-1784
Jacques Necker	1732-1804
J.-B. Suard	1732-1817
C. Prince de Ligne	1735-1814
Suzanne Curchod	1737-1794
M. Marquis de Condorcet	1743-1794
T. Jefferson	1743-1826
F. Comte de Guibert	1744-1790
J. H. Meister	1744-1826
C. V. de Bonstetten	1745-1832
Gustave III of Sweden	1746-1792
F. Comtesse de Genlis	1746-1830
E. Sieyès	1748-1836
E. Baron de Staël	1749-1802

POSTSCRIPT

J. Goethe	1749-1832
C. M. de Talleyrand	1754-1838
V. Monti	1754-1828
Louis XVI de France	1754-1793
P. Roederer	1754-1835
Marie-Antoinette d'Autriche	1755-1793
Louis XVIII de France	1755-1824
L. de Narbonne	1755-1813
M. Marquis de La Fayette	1757-1834
W. Wilberforce	1759-1833
F. Schiller	1759-1805
Alexander de Lameth	1760-1829
Joséphine Bonaparte	1763-1814
François Joseph Talma	1763-1826
C.-J. Bernadotte	1763-1844
J. de Krüdener	1764-1824
J. C. Rilliet-Huber	1764-1843
F. Gentz	1764-1822
F. de Pange	1764-1796
F. Brun	1765-1841
A. de Saussure	1765-1841
A. Comte Ribbing	1765-1843
GERMAINE DE STAËL	1766-1817
C. G. von Brinkman	1767-1847
W. von Humboldt	1767-1835
M. de Montmorency	1767-1826
B. Constant	1767-1830
A. W. Schlegel	1767-1845
Joseph Bonaparte	1768-1844
F. de Chateaubriand	1768-1748
Napoléon Bonaparte	1769-1821
A. W. Duke of Wellington	1769-1852
G. M. de Gérando	1772-1842
S. de Sismondi	1773-1842
P. Ballanche	1776-1847
Juliette Récamier	1777-1849
Piotr F. de Balk	1777-1849
Frances Randall	1777-1833
Alexander I of Russia	1777-1825

M. Count O'Donnell	1780-1843
H.P.-F. Marquess of Landsdowne	1780-1863
P. de Souza	1781-1850
P. de Barante	1782-1866
Victor duc de Broglie	1785-1870
G. Lord Byron	1788-1824
Jean Rocca	1788-1818

Madame de Staël's Progeny:

Gustavine de Staël	1787-1789
Auguste baron de Staël	1790-1827
Albert baron de Staël	1792-1813
Albertine b. de Staël Duchesse de Broglie	1797-1838
Alphonse Rocca	1812-1842

From Albertine (1797-1838) and Victor third duke of Broglie (1785-1870):

Pauline de Broglie	1817-1831
Louise de Broglie	1818-1882
*Albert duc de Broglie	1821-1901
Paul de Broglie	1834-1895

From Louise de Broglie and J. Comte Othenin d'Haussonville 1809-1884:

Victor d'Haussonville	1837-1838
Mathilde d'Haussonville	1838-1898
Gabriel Othenin d'Haussonville	1843-1924

From Gabriel Othenin d'Haussonville and Pauline d'Harcourt 1846-1922:

Aleth d'Haussonville <LaTour-Landry†	1867-1946
Elisabeth d'Haussonville	1869-1967

*This is the only line of descendents remaining
†Names preceded by "<" are from marriage contracts (in-laws)

From Elisabeth d'Haussonville (1869-1967) and Jacques comte Le Marois (1863-1920):

Béatrix Le Marois <d'Andlau, Bonneval   1893-1964

*From Albert fourth duke of Broglie (1821-1901) and Pauline de Béarn 1825-1860:

Victor Fifth duke of Broglie	1846-1906
Maurice de Broglie	1848-1862
Amédée de Broglie <L. de Montebello	1849-1917
François de Broglie <Casteja <La Moussaye	1851-1939
Emmanuel de Broglie	1854-1926

From Victor de Broglie and Pauline de la Forest d'Armaillé 1851-1928:

Albertine <Luppé	1872-1846
Pauline Countess Jean de Pange	1888-1972
Maurice Sixth duke de Broglie	1875-1960
Louis Seventh duke of Broglie	1892-1987
Nobel Prize in Physics 1929	

The only remaining Broglie branch is from Amédée de Broglie & G. Soutzo.

AFTERWORD

Germaine de Staël was unquestionably one of the most important women in history. She did not exercise the power of Queen Elizabeth, nor achieve the saintly stature of Joan of Arc, but she was the first woman intellectual, or "mandarin" as the French would say. There had been women in politics before, of course; there had been noted women novelists, or travel writers such as Lady Mary Montagu, or historians such as Catherine Macaulay Graham; even, if one wishes, philosophers (Marie LeJars de Gournay). But Mme de Staël was the first woman to be all these things. Moreover she played an eminent role in all these activities. Napoleon is reported to have stated in exile on Saint Helena that in politics he had had only two enemies: England and Mme de Staël. For her stance in their epic struggle, as well as for positions taken in her writings, she must be considered a founder of the liberal tradition. Forced by Napoleon into near-perpetual exile, she gathered around her what has become known as the Coppet group, a set of thinkers from various nations whom she nurtured into productivity: Benjamin Constant, an important theoretician of liberalism and a pioneer in the comparative study of religions; Bonstetten, with his work on philosophy and esthetics; Sismondi, who demonstrated the fallacy of "trickle down" economics already in the early nineteenth century; Humboldt, with his theories on language and on biology; the Schlegels (Auguste was the tutor of her children) with their revolutionary theories in esthetics; Mathieu de Montmorency and Julie de Krüdener with their investigations of mysticism. Even this enumeration fails miserably to credit the breadth of her associations.

However, Germaine de Staël cannot be seen merely as someone who encouraged others to write and think. She herself contributed materially to the evolution of western thought and culture. We owe her much. To paraphrase Simone Balayé, the leading Staël scholar of our age, she combined much of what was best about the Enlightenment with what was best in Romanticism, as she lived through the transition from the one age to the other. While her literary career opened with an essay on Rousseau's works (1788), it culminated in *On Germany* (*De l'Allemagne*) (1810), which was to figure as a sort of bible of Romanticism on the European continent in the first half of the nineteenth century. Paramount in her political thought was her thoroughly French revolutionary cult of liberty, her opposition to tyranny and oppression, be it from individuals such as Napoleon or from institutions. She much admired English constitutional monarchy, encouraged nationalist aspirations, and hated the Revolution's Terror as much as she did Napoleon. However, on the subject of slander, of which as an active participant in political life she had often been the object, her cult of liberty became decidedly clearer. In that context, it was the responsibility of the press she advocated above all.

In view of this remarkable career, it is astonishing that Germaine de Staël should still be little known in English speaking countries, and it is to be hoped that the present biography by Dr. Dixon will renew interest in her and lead new admirers to her side. Indeed, there have been a number of valuable American scholarly studies of her works during the last thirty years—by Madelyn Gutwirth, Charlotte Hogsett, Marie-Claire Vallois and Nancy Miller—but these have usually been limited to some aspect of her writings, and often, understandably, conceived from an avowedly feminist perspective. In their treatments of Staël's relatively brief but stormy life, biographers have sometimes found it difficult to resist the temptation to dwell on its "scandalous" emotional and sexual turmoil, to the detriment of a due consideration of Staël's activism and literary achievements. As its title suggests, J. Christopher Herold's influential biography *Mistress to an Age* published in 1958, perhaps unduly emphasizes her rather picturesque private life. A half-century later, we are less prudish—or perhaps more inured—to this aspect of her story. The present study has the advantage of profiting from the very considerable Staël scholarship which has fluctuated in the last half-century, and particularly from the impressive work done by another American scholar, Beatrice Jasinski, in making available the very rich correspondence of Mme de Staël. This has allowed Dr. Dixon as biographer to envisage

Staël's life from within her own perspective than was formerly the case. Dr. Dixon's text also has the particular virtue of carefully placing Staël in her historical context, for she was not only very much a part of her age, but a major political figure in that period. It sometimes seems as if she knew everyone—her parents considered an engagement to Pitt the Younger, she was acquainted with Byron, with Alfieri, with Bernadotte, with Goethe, with the Duchess of Devonshire, and Czar Alexander, to name only some of the noted foreigners with whom her name can be more than passingly linked.

Intellectually as well as politically, Staël was a cosmopolitan, unlike many of her countrymen, open to foreign cultures for what they had to teach France. She wrote extensively about Italy in her novel travelogue *Corinne* (1807), and even more so about Germany, but also about Russia and England. She thought of fleeing to the United States after the Terror and corresponded with Jefferson. She held that each age and culture produced its own literature and ideas, and in a wholly original fashion, applied Montesquieu to esthetics and with her incessant contrasts among the literatures of France, England, Italy, and Germany, she created comparative literature. Perhaps even more important, she drew from classical esthetics. For Staël, there was not one ancient model to be imitated by all throughout the ages, whence her appreciation for Shakespeare, for Dante, for Goethe and Schiller. In ethics, the trials of the Revolution convinced her that enlightened self-interest was not a sufficient guarantee of moral conduct; rather, as Kant had predicated, man must turn to his innate conscience, to his transcendant sense of right, and of duty. This insight led her finally to her cult of enthusiasm, to the sense of the spirit within us, which could provide not only moral guidance but also the inspiration for true poetry and the creation of beauty.

Not only did Germaine de Staël address universal issues: she did not flinch before embodying the complexities of her experience as a woman while attempting to represent them in the fictions and plays she composed throughout her lifetime. Her novels, *Delphine* (1804) and *Corinne* (1807), eagerly read and exploited or deplored by women authors like Elizabeth Barrett-Browning, George Sand, George Eliot, Harriet Beecher, and Margaret Fuller, achieved a kind of cult status among women readers throughout the nineteenth-century. But women alone were not admirers ot Staël: the nineteenth-century male cultivation of the genre of the *Künstlerroman* that she employed so fruitfully in her *Corinne* owed much to her example.

AFTERWORD

If some of Staël's ideas now strike some as ethereal, it must be acknowledged that she lived them and applied them in a tumultuous historical context. Sergine Dixon here admirably performs the task of tracing the whole of Staël's career and analyses her multiple writings through the unfurling of that context. Here, the reader will learn much about Germaine de Staël, and, hopefully, will demand to know even more.

Frank Paul Bowman,
Professor Emeritus, University of Pennsylvania
Member of the Honors Committee of the
Société des études staëliennes,
contributor to the Société's Colloques de Coppet
in 1966-1970, 1988, 1991.

Madelyn Gutwirth
Professor Emeritus, Westchester State University
Member of the Honors Committee of the
Société des études staëliennes,
Contributor to the Société's Colloque de Coppet
in 1982, 1988, 1991.
Author of *Madame de Staël, novelist—Essence of the Artist*, 1978.
Contributed to the Cahiers staëliens of 1979,
and on Madame de Staël to
Essays on Nineteenth-Century European Women Writers, 1987,
also to *Research in the Humanities*
Vol. 86, 1983-1986.

ACKNOWLEDGMENTS

I am indebted to the late Simone Balayé, the admirable scholar who led the Society of Studies of Germaine de Staël (Société des études de Germaine de Staël) for her friendship, her support of my project and for the inspiration emanating from her numerous publications concerning Germaine de Staël. Friendship began in 1988 when Mlle Balayé and I met in her home in Paris. At once and without question she understood my eagerness to present Madame de Staël from the perspective of her 'oeuvre' and to Anglophone readers. Her encouragement never wavered.

My thanks go to Professor Paul Perron, former principal of University College at the University of Toronto, for his positive reaction to my project. His comments were thoughtful and constructive. I am grateful also to Professors Frank Paul Bowman and Madelyn Gutwirth, as well as the late Eva Friedlander, for their steady interest in this endeavor; to Anna Chapman, my copy-editor, for her sensitive assistance; and finally, to my editor at Prometheus Books, Steven L. Mitchell. During years of association with the American Friends of George Sand, I had the pleasure of knowing Georges Lubin, the editor of the Sand correspondence. He seconded my decision to portray Madame de Staël from the point of view of her authorship. Monsieur Lubin acquainted me with the Dosne-Thiers Foundation in Paris, both names being part of my family genealogy. Adolf Thiers' masterful biography of Napoléon (*Histoire du Consulat et de l'Empire*) has been a most resourceful aid. My debt extends to my husband, Julian Dixon, for his counsel, support and unlimited patience.

Sergine Dixon (née Dosne) 2006

NOTES

OPENING REMARKS

For the complete works of Madame de Staël, I have used the Lefèvre edition published in Paris (1858) in three volumes. The initial L accompanies each reference to this edition. The translations are mine throughout except where I have used the D. Beik English edition of *Dix années d'exil—Ten Years in Exile*. Texts referred to more than once are marked "ibid."

THE NURTURING

1. Denis Diderot, *Oeuvres philosophiques*, ed. P. Vernière Garnier: Paris, 1964, *De l'interprétation de la nature*, p. 175: Jeune homme, prends et lis . . . Come je suis moins proposé de t'instruire que de t'exercer, il m'importe peu que tu adoptes mes idées ou que tu les rejettes, pourvu qu'elles emploient toute ton attention. Un plus habile t'apprendra à connaître les forces de la nature; il me suffira de t'avoir fait essayer les tiennes. Adieu.

2. Béatrice W. Jasinski, *Madame de Staël Correspondance générale*, J.-J. Pauvert: Paris, 1962, I, 1 p. 12, Germaine Necker to Suzanne Necker ca. 1778: . . . ma principale envie est en m'instruisant de vous être plus agréable. . . .

3. Georges Solovieff, *Madame de Staël Choix de lettres (1778-1817)*, Klincksieck: Paris, 1970, p. 30: . . . ton style est un peu trop monté..Quand on a plus vécu, on s'aperçoit que la véritable manière de plaire et d'intéresser est de peindre exactement sa pensée et sans emphase. . . .

4. P. N. Furbank, *Diderot*, Knopf: New York, 1992, pp. 295-96.

5. Ibid., p. 102.

6. G. Soumoy-Thibert, *Les idées de Madame Necker* in *Dix-huitième siècle Montesquieu et la Révolution*, PUF: Paris, 1989, p. 360.

7. B. d'Andlau, *La jeunesse de Madame de Staël*, Droz: Genève, 1970, p. 31.

8. L, II, *De l'influence des passions*, ch. III, p. 119: L'amour de l'étude... a tous les caractères de la passion... L'esprit aime l'ensemble, il tend au but... il s'élance vers l'avenir... en avant de ses efforts et de son espérance.

9. M. Cranston, *Jean-Jacques Rousseau*, Universityof Chicago Press: Chicago, 1982, III, p. 86.

10. Diderot, ibid., I, pp. 9-10: ... il n'y a que les grandes passions qui puissent élever l'âme... Sans elles, plus de sublime... la vertu devient minutieuse.

11. Montesquieu, *Esprit des lois*, Pléiade: Paris, 1966, II, preface, pp. 229-30: Les hommes ne sont pas uniquement conduits par la fantaisie... chacun dépend d'une loi... générale (1748).

12. Voltaire, *Essai sur les moeurs et l'esprit des nations*, Editions Sociales: Paris, 1962, ch. Lxxxi, p. 53: Je voudrais découvrir quelle était alors la société... comment on vivait dans l'intérieur des familles... plutôt que de répéter tant de malheurs... funestes objets de l'histoire... de la méchanceté humaine.

13. Immanuel Kant, *Werke*, ed. E. Cassirer, IV, p. 169: Beantwortung der Frage: Was ist Aufklärung? And in E. Cassirer, *The Philosophy of the Enlightenment*, University Princeton Press: New Jersey, tr. F. Koelln & J. Pettegrove, 1951, p. 163.

14. Jean-Jacques Rousseau, *Emile ou l'éducation*, ed. F.-P. Richard Garnier: Paris, 1961, IV, *Profession de foi du vicaire Savoyard*, p. 361: Les plus grandes idées de la divinité nous viennent par la raison seule... Dieu n'a-t-il pas tout dit à nos yeux, à notre conscience... ?

15. A. Robert Turgot in Alexis de Tocqueville *L'Ancien Régime et la Révolution*, Gallimard: Paris, 1856, II, p. 166: La nation est une société composée de différents ordres mal unis..et où personne n'est occupé que de son intérêt particulier. Nulle part il n'y a d'intérêt commun visible.

16. Jacques Necker, *De la Révolution française*, Maret: Paris, 1797, pp. 5-7: J'ai occupé une grande place dans le gouvernement, et auprès du roi, à peu d'années des Etats-Généraux... où l'on pouvait découvrir les avant-coureurs d'une révolu-tion... réels ou prononcés... j'ai vu... la grande force de l'opinion publique. Elle m'avait singulièrement frappé.

17. M. Cranston, ibid., II, p. 272.

18. G. de Diesbach, *Necker ou la faillite de la vertu*, Perrin: Paris, 1978-87, p. 237: ... les sots ne pouvant... prendre conscience de leur sottise, jouissent d'un bonheur sans mélange... A l'inverse, l'homme de génie, appliquant à soi-même sa lucidité, ne connaît qu'incertitudes et tourments.

19. Jacques Necker, *De l'administration des finances*, II, in J. Starobinski, *Le Journal de Mademoiselle Necker*, Cahiers Staëliens: Paris nouv.série 28, 1980, p. 57.

20. Ibid., pp. 69-70: Si maman avait écrit . . . elle aurait acquis une réputation d'esprit, mais mon père ne peut pas souffrir une femme auteur . . . l'inquiétude le prend. . . .

21. Ibid., p. 57: . . . il est des mouvements qui perdent de leur naturel dès qu'on s'en souvient . . . l'on serait comme les rois, ils vivent pour l'histoire . . . malheur à celui qui peut tout exprimer . . . qui peut supporter la lecture de ses sentiments affaiblis. . . .

22. Ibid., p. 58: . . . la métaphysique qui s'attache à l'immortalité, voilà celle qui me transporte. Elle a pour but le calme de l'âme, les mouvements les plus sensibles.

23. Ibid., pp. 73-74: Ma mère dit à mon père: j'ai retrouvé dans ta fille la sensibili-té . . . de son enfance. Je crois, répondit mon père, qu'elle ne l'a jamais perdue.

CHAPTER 1: MOMENTS IN TIME

1. Simon Schama, *Citizens: A Chronicle of the French Revolution*, Knopf: New York, 1989, pp. 303-304. Sieyès's *Qu'est-ce que le Tiers Etat?:* Tout. Qu'a-t-il été dans l'ordre politique? Rien. Que demande-t-il? A y devenir quelque chose.

2. Furbank, ibid., p. 416.

3. E. Lever, *Louis XVI*, Fayard: Paris, 1985, p. 196.

4. F. Furet-M.Ozouf, *Dictionnaire critique de la Révolution française*, Flammarion: Paris, 1988, pp. 76-84.

5. B. Jasinski, ibid.. II , I, p. 255: Germaine de Staël letter to Gustave III of Sweden, September 4, 1788: . . . j'aurais appris avec plaisir à Votre Majesté la nomination de mon père, mais on lui remet le vaisseau si près du naufrage que toute mon admiration suffit à peine pour m'inspirer de la confiance.

6. F. Furet-M. Ozouf, ibid., p. 341.

7. G. de Diesbach, ibid., p. 318: Je reste, mais vous voyez ce peuple et les bénédictions don't il m'accompagne . . . Eh bien! Avant quinze jours peut-être, c'est à coups de pierres qu'il me suivra.

8. *Thomas Jefferson Selected Writings*, Random House: New York, 1944-93, pp. 401-402: letter to John Adams, August 30,1787: . . . never was a license of speaking against the government exercised . . . more freely . . . Caricatures, placards . . . have been indulged in by all ranks of people . . . mobs of ten, twenty and thirty thousand people surrounded the parliament house . . . even entered and examined members' conduct.

9. B. W. Jasinski, ibid., I, I, p. 228: Germaine de Staël, letter to Gustave III of Sweden, December 28, 1787: ". . . des brochures sans fin paraissent tous les jours, et le genre de libelles est tellement souffert que l'on dirait que maintenant la liberté de presse est permise tant qu'on ne parlera que des personnes. . . .

10. B. W. Jasinski, ibid., I, II, p. 274: Germaine de Staël letter to N. von Rosenstein, January 21, 1789: La France est au moment de donner un grand spectacle à l'Europe.... Ce qui est à craindre, c'est l'esprit de corps ... toutes les subdivisions qui donnent un autre centre que le centre commun. . . .
11. Germaine de Staël, *Considérations sur la Révolution française*, ed. J. Godechot Tallandier: Paris, 1983, pp. 140-41: J'étais placée à une fenêtre ... voyant pour la première fois en France des représentants de la nation . . . Quand le roi vint . . . j'éprouvai . . . un sentiment de crainte. . . . Les députés exprimaient plus d'énergie par leurs physionomies que le monarque . . . il fallait de la force des deux côtés.
12. G. E. Gwynne, *Madame de Staël et la Révolution française*, Nizet: Paris, 1969, p. 286: On sortait du silence d'un pays gouverné par une cour, pour entendre le bruit des acclamations spontanées de tous les citoyens.
13. P. de Lacretelle, *Madame de Staël et les homes*, Grasset: Paris, 1939, p. 36.
14. Germaine de Staël, *Du caractère de M. Necker*, Paschoud: Genève, pp. 69-70: . . . Rien ne peut égaler l'émotion que font alors éprouver les acclamations de la multitude.
15. B. W. Jasinski, ibid., I, II, pp. 325-26, Germaine de Staël letter to Gustave III of Sweden, August 16, 1789: . . . tant d'événements malheureux, glorieux, incroyables m'ont agitée . . . Je me demande si mille ans se sont écoulés depuis un mois. . . .

CHAPTER 2: GERMAINE'S WORLD

1. J. Starobinski, *Le Journal de Mademoiselle Necker: réflexion et passion.* Cahiers staëliens no. 28, 1980, p. 60: Qu'il m'en coûte pour me réveiller! . . . Ce n'est pas le caractère du bonheur que de craindre tant de commencer où tous les souvenirs vont rentrer dans le coeur . . . Non, le sentiment de soi subsiste encore et c'est lui qui caractérise l'existence morale. (1785).
2. Ibid., p. 71: C'est un homme parfaitement honnête. Incapable de dire ni de faire une sottise, mais stérile et sans ressort. . . .
3. Ibid., p. 75: J'aurais voulu être adorée de l'univers et tout sacrifier à un seul objet.
4. Comtesse Jean de Pange, *Monsieur de Staël*, Portiques: Paris, 1931, pp. 84-85.
5. B. W. Jasinski, ibid., I, I p. 167: Germaine de Staël to Eric de Staël, May 11, 1787: . . . vous aurez à vous reprocher d'avoir abandonné une jeune personne qui vous était confiée, et qu'il ne fallait pas éloigner sans retour quand son âme était restée pure et son coeur prêt à devenir sensible.
6. M. L. Pailleron, *Madame de Staël—les Romantiques*, Hachette: Paris, 1931, p. 33, quoted from count A.Fersen: Elle n'est pas jolie . . . mais elle a de l'esprit, de la gaité, de l'amabilité, elle est très bien élevée et remplie de talents.

7. Ibid., p. 33-34: quoted from count H.Guibert: . . . Ses grands yeux noirs étincelaient de génie; ses cheveux couleur d'ébène retombaient sur ses épaules en boucles ondoyantes; ses traits étaient plutôt prononcés que délicats; on y sentait quelquechose au-dessus de la destinée de son sexe.
8. Ibid., p. 38: quoted from Madame de Boufflers: Elle est impérieuse et décidée à l'excès, elle a une assurance que je n'ai jamais vue à son âge.
9. B. W. Jasinski, ibid., I, I, p. 248: . . . Si la femme qu'on a épousée parce qu'elle vous convenait par sa position et par sa fortune a des torts réels envers vous, il faut balancer dans le silence de sa raison et de sa conscience, le parti qu'on veut prendre. Mais . . . s'il lui reste assez de qualités pour vous inspirer de l'amour, le plus mauvais chemin à suivre, c'est celui que tu prends.
10. Ibid., I, I, p. 150: Je suis pure et je t'aime. Que t'importe après cela les défauts de mon caractère? Pourquoi t'atteignent-ils quand ils ne partent pas du coeur et qu'ils passeront avec ma jeunesse?
11. Ibid., I, I, p. 119: Il se livre un peu à sa gaieté avec moi: il s'amuse des lettres que je reçois. . . . Il me les arrache, et se plaît à me mettre dans des colères. . . .
12. Pange, ibid., p. 95.
13. de Lacretelle, ibid., pp. 30-31.
14. S. Schama, ibid., p. 257.
15. A. Sorel, *Madame de Staël—Collection Les grands écrivains français*, Hachette: Paris, 1907, pp. 16-17 and 28.
16. Germaine de Staël, *La folle de la forêt de Sénart*, Cahiers staëliens, No. 52 2001, p. 14: . . . je voyais tout avec émotion, et mon coeur attendri s'ouvrait à toutes les sensations.

CHAPTER 3: GERMAINE'S PEN

1. Germaine de Staël, *Sophie ou les sentiments secrets*, L, III, p. 697: Qu'il m'en coûte pour me réveiller! Ce n'est pas le caractère du bonheur que de craindre tant de commencer la journée, de retouter le moment où tous les souvenirs vont rentrer dans le coeur . . . Non . . . le sentiment de soi subsiste encore et c'est lui qui caractérise l'existence morale. . .
2. Ibid., *Jane Gray*, p. 628: . . . la vraisemblance est commandée par la vérité, et l'imagination, loin d'égarer la pensée, renouvelle à nos yeux l'expérience, et rend sensible à la génération présente la grande leçon des siècles passés. . . .
3. Ibid., p. 629: Je voudrais avoir pu faire éprouver l'admiration que j'ai ressentie pour ce rare mélange de force et de sensibilité. . . .
4. Ibid., p. 671: Les vrais maux des humains sont tous au fond du coeur. . . .
5. Germaine de Staël, *Lettres sur les écrits et le caractère de Jean-Jacques*

252 NOTES

Rousseau, 1788, L, I, Préface, p. 1: Il n'existe point encore d'éloge de Rousseau. J'ai senti le besoin de voir mon admiration exprimée . . . J'ai goûté quelque plaisir en me retraçant le souvenir et l'impression de mon enthousiasme. . . .

6. Ibid., p. 3: . . . il fallait que son coeur et son exprit fussent calmés pour qu'il pût se consacrer au travail.

7. Ibid., p. 4, . . . il lui fallait, pour choisir entre toutes ses pensées, le temps et les efforts que les hommes médiocres emploient à tâcher d'en avoir.

8. Ibid., . . . peut-être a-t-il trop souvent lié les arts aux sciences, tandis que les effets des uns et des autres diffèrent entièrement.

9. Ibid., p. 6: Il est remarquable qu'un des hommes les plus sensibles et les plus distingués par ses connaissances et son génie ait voulu réduire l'esprit et le coeur humain à un état presque semblable à l'abrutissement; mais c'est qu'il avait senti plus qu'un autre toutes les peines que ces avantages, portés à l'excès, peuvent faire éprouver.

10. Ibid., p. 8: . . . les hommes, faits pour la liberté, se sentent avilis quand ils s'en sont ravi l'usage, et tombent souvent alors au-dessous d'eux-mêmes.

11. Ibid., p. 10: Je me transporterai donc à quelque distance des impressions que j'ai reçues, et j'écrirai sur Héloïse comme je le ferais, je crois, si le temps avait vieilli mon coeur.

12. Ibid., p. 11: . . . son talent de peindre se retrouve partout. Et, dans ses fictions comme dans la vérité, les orages des passions et la paix de l'innocence agitent et calment successivement.

13. Ibid., p. 21: . . . si les femmes, s'élevant au-dessus de leur sort, osaient prétendre à l'éducation des hommes; si elles savaient dire ce qu'ils doivent faire, si elles avaient le sentiment de leurs actions, quelle noble destinée . . . !

14. Ibid., p. 1: Peur-être me reprochera-t-on de traiter un sujet au-dessus de mes forces . . . mais . . . qui peut oser prévoir les progrès de son esprit? . . . D'ailleurs, n'est-ce pas dans la jeunesse qu'on doit à Rousseau le plus de reconnaissance?

CHAPTER 4: THE RAPE OF UNITY

1. B. W. Jasinski, ibid., I, I, p. 180, Germaine de Staël letter to Eric de Staël, May 27, 1787: Je suis indignée contre ce vil Mirabeau. Apporte-moi cet abominable ouvrage, mais que mon père n'en sache rien. Il ne faut pas troubler ce calme étonnant que si peu dont le génie même égalerait le sien seraient capables.

2. Solovieff, ibid., p. 53, Germaine de Staël letter to Gustave III of Sweden August 16 1789: . . . moi qui voyais ce que j'ai de plus cher au monde au gouvernail pendant la tempête . . . une intrigue de cour . . . qui voyait tout le royaume dans Versailles et pensait qu'on détruisait la force du peuple en renversant dans M. Necker son plus fidèle défenseur, et . . . menée par M. le comte d'Artois, a tout fait. On a lié dans l'esprit du roi sa cause avec celle de la noblesse.

3. B. W. Jasinski, ibid., I, II, p. 328, Germaine de Staël letter to Gustave III of Sweden August 16 1789: . . . mon père a trouvé tous les pouvoirs anéantis ou confondus . . . une vieille nation retombée dans l'enfance plutôt que revenue à la jeunesse . . . la liberté obtenue avant que l'esprit public ne soit formé, enfin une incohérence dans les idées, un contraste entre les caractères . . . qui fait frémir.

4. S. Schama, ibid., pp. 339-43.

5. G. de Diesbach, ibid., p. 148.

5a. B. W. Jasinski I, II, p. 364n H. N. de Buffon: Jamais ministre n'est parti plus incognito. . . . L'indifférence des Français de Paris . . . est une des choses qui m'a étonné dans ma vie. Ni satires, ni éloges, rien, pas un mot pour le départ d'un homme adoré il y a quinze mois. . . .

6. R. Cobb-Jones, *Voices of the French Revolution*, Topsfield, Mass., 1988, and in Cahiers Staëliens No. 53, 2002, Simone Balayé, *Madame de Staël et la presse Révolutionnaire: Journal de la cour et de la ville février 1791*.

7. B. W. Jasinski, ibid., I, II, p. 486n : Observons qu'il s'agit plutôt d'un conseil secret, non d'une conversation de salon.

8. Ibid., pp. 489-90, Germaine de Staël letter to Gustave III, September 11, 1791: . . . Il est vrai que j'ai partagé l'espérance de mon père à l'ouverture des Etats Généraux. L'on devait se flatter qu'il résulterait de leurs lumières et des excellentes intentions du roi une constitution libre . . . L'ivresse de la nation a éloigné ce terme, mais pourquoi le parti des opprimés ne pardonne-t-il pas à ceux qui ont espéré?

9. L, I, *Mirza ou lettres d'un voyageur*, Préface, pp. 147-48: La grandeur des événements . . . fait si bien sentir . . . l'impuissance des sentiments individuels que, perdu dans la vie, on ne sait plus quelle route doit suivre l'espérance . . . quel principe guidera l'opinion publique à travers les erreurs de l'esprit de parti . . . ?

10. B. W. Jasinski, ibid., I, II, p. 441 Germaine de Staël letter to Eric de Staël June 1, 1791: Comme je ne connaîtrai personne dans cette nouvelle législature, je donne ma démission de la carrière politique . . .

11. L, II, *De la littérature: De l'émulation*, p. 354: Il ne faut pas ôter au people l'admiration. De ce sentiment dérivent tous les degrés d'affection entre les magistrats et les gouvernés. . . . Des milliers d'hommes peuvent-ils se décider d'après leurs propres lumières? . . . Une impulsion . . . animée doit se communiquer. . . .

CHAPTER 5: THE HYDRA UNLEASHED

1. Jasinski, ibid., I, II, p. 495, letter to N. von Rosenstein, September 16, 1791: Il y a une vie entière de réflexions sur le spectacle qu'a donné ces deux années, et j'ai besoin de lire mon extrait de baptême pour savoir que je n'ai que vingt-quatre ans.

1a. S.Balayé, *Lumières et liberté*, Klincksieck: Paris, 1979, p. 246.

1b. L, III, *A quels signes peut-on reconnaître quelle est l'opinion de la majorité de la nation?* (1792), p. 530: "Il n'est plus que deux partis, les royalistes et les républicains. Pourquoi tous les deux n'oseraient-ils pas se nommer? Quels sentiments condamnent les républicains à l'hypocrisie, et les royalistes au silence?

2. Jasinski, ibid., I, II, pp. 494n and 494: . . . du matin au soir ce sont des danses, des illuminations . . . le peuple se croit heureux, et met de la vanité à le paraître en présence de ses ennemis . . . Ce nouveau régime l'amuse . . . l'arrache à l'ennui. . . .

3. A. Mignet, *Histoire de la Révolution française*, Didot Perrin: Paris, 1824, p. 172.

4. Jasinski, ibid., II, I, *Lettres inédites à Narbonne* October-November 1792 pp. 49, 50, 54, 58: Moi qui ne cède qu'à une impulsion, qui n'ai qu'une idée et qu'un sentiment, je suis très facile à comprendre. . . . J'ai pris pour vous un genre de passion qui absorbe tout mon être . . . Les idées, les sentiments sont absorbés par ton image. Cet enivrement qui semble s'accroître par les événements, qui en apprenant à détester les hommes, font aimer celui qui a dépassé l'imagination. . . .

5. Lacretelle, ibid., pp. 57-58.

6. Jasinski, ibid., II, I, p. 24, letter to Narbonne, September 19, 1792: Vous êtes le plus cruel, le plus ingrat, le plus barbare des hommes.

7. Ibid., p. 68, November 18, 1792: . . . il faut savoir tout ce que vous ne voulez pas écrire. . . .

8. Ibid., p. 144, end-July 1793: On a besoin et du bonheur de ce qu'on aime, et de son plaisir. . . . On voudrait mettre sur sa tête et la couronne du monde et celle de son jardin. On voudrait, et l'on ne peut rien.

9. Ibid., p., 152, August 6, 1793: On souffre dans toutes ses idées autour d'une seule, si ce centre immobile de nos sentiments ne vous aidait pas à vous reconnaître.

10. Ibid., p. 206, November 11, 1793: Un tel sentiment . . . est le meilleur de tous les moyens contre tous les malheurs. . . . ma passion est mon génie. . . .

11. Jacques Necker, *De la Révolution française*, Maret: Paris, 1797, I, pp. 183-84: Habitants de Paris, vous avez été les témoins . . . du plus horrible sacrifice . . . Je ne vous juge point, car vos tyrans . . . vous suspectèrent . . . ils eurent peur que Louis . . . ne fut écouté . . . et par un ordre barbare ils s'affranchirent de toute inquiétude . . . dès qu'il eut prononcé 'Français!' . . . on commande aux tambours de rouler . . . et le roi ne fut plus entendu.

12. Furet-Ozouf, ibid., p. 297.

13. Jasinski, ibid., II, I, p. 148 n2, Talleyrand: Nous sommes dans une mer d'incertitude.

14. Jasinski, ibid., II, I, p. 193-94, letter to Narbonne, October 25, 1793: Les bourreaux ont épuisé tous les genres de supplice . . . pour cette femme célèbre par ses mal- heurs . . . Elle a pu nommer son nom sans horreur, elle a compté sur ses regrets.

15. *Thomas Jefferson*, ibid., pp. 95-96.
16. L I, p. 49, *Réflexions sur le procès de la reine* (August 1793): Mon nom ne pouvant être utile, doit rester inconnu; mais, pour affirmer l'impartialité de cet écrit... j'ai. eu avec cette princesse le moins de relations personnelles. Ces réflexions méritent donc la confiance de tous les coeurs sensibles, puisqu'elles ne sont inspirées que par les mouvements dont ils sont tous animés.
17. Furet-Ozouf, ibid., p. 382.
18. B. d'Andlau, ibid., p. 24. Also in Diesbach, ibid., p. 239, and in Othenin d'Haussonville, *Le Salon de Madame Necker* (1885), II, p. 35: J'ai cultivé sa mémoire et son esprit. Pendant treize ans les plus belles années de ma vie... je ne l'ai presque pas perdue de vue... et mon amour-propre s'était transporté sur elle.
19. S. Balayé, *Ecrire, lutter, vivre*, Droz: Genève, p. 33n, letter to Eric de Staël, November 15, 1790: Je lui suis entièrement dévouée... plus consacrée que je ne l'étais étant fille... Mais par une bizarrerie qui n'est pas sensible, elle craint que je n'anime la société de mon mouvement et non du sien....
20. Ibid., p. 32n, letter to Narbonne, July 19, 1793: Mon père soupire, veut sauver sa fortune... sa réputation, me redoute, me consulte, se fâche, se radoucit... m'offre sans cesse un caractère dessiné dans les nuages.
21. B. d'Andlau, ibid., p. 15 and in L, III, *Du caractère de M. Necker et de sa vie privée*, p. 538: Il lui fallait l'être unique, elle l'a trouvé, elle a passé sa vie avec lui... Elle a plus mérité que moi d'être heureuse.
22. G. Solovieff, ibid., p. 87, letter to Miss F. Burney Juniper Hall, March 8, 1793:... qui peut maintenant se permettre de s'occuper de soi?
23. Comtesse Jean de Pange, *Madame de Staël et François de Pange*, Plon: Paris, 1925, p. 254: La philosophie, qui n'a pas conduit cette révolution qu'elle avait préparée ne la terminera pas non plus....
24. O. d'Haussonville, *Madame de Staël et M. Necker*, Calmann-Lévy: Paris, 1925, p. 55.
25. L, I, p. 82, *Réflexions sur la paix adressées à M. Pitt et aux Français* (1794):... il y va de l'existence même de cette Angleterre, la gloire du monde et de la liberté.
26. Ibid., p. 71: Il faut ramener les Français et le monde avec eux à l'ordre et à la vertu. Mais pour y parvenir, on doit penser que ces biens sont unis à la véritable liberté.
27. Ibid., p. 79: La valeur et l'énergie que les Français ont montrées... relevant leur caractère aux yeux de toutes les nations... chaque jour, en renouvelant les triomphes... donne parmi les esprits faibles... un mouvement ascendant à leurs opinions.... tout tend au repos dans la nature....
28. B. Macaulay in *Encyclopedia Britannica*, New York, 1911, vols. 21-22, p. 673.
29. E. and R. Badinter, *Condorcet*, Fayard: Paris, 1988, p. 377.
30. L, I, *Réflexions sur la paix intérieure* (1795), p.100: On veut être libre, on espère une constitution, on se fait un devoir de la défendre... mais tous ces

mots ont été prononcés par des scélérats . . . ils ont servi à dévouer des milliers de victimes.
    31. Ibid., p. 100: Dans l'état où nous sommes, nous pouvons . . . arriver à la liberté. La fatigue . . . du peuple sert à ce but. Il faudrait qu'il se révoltat pour ne pas l'obtenir . . . et ce qui est triste . . . c'est qu'en lui faisant supporter le plus horrible joug, on l'a disposé à revoir une constitution libre, c'est à dire à ne pas s'en mêler.
    32. France, de tes destins le souvenir horrible
    Dans tous les lieux pour nous entr'ouvre des tombeaux;
    Ton orage obscurcit l'azur d'un ciel paisible,
    Le sang que tu répands teint le cristal des eaux.
Epître au Malheur L vol. 3, p. 621

CHAPTER 6: PASSION ANALYZED

    1. L, II, pp. 1-4, *De l'influence des passions sur le bonheur des individus et des nations*: . . . que l'Europe écoute les amis de la liberté . . . Laissez-nous en France combattre, vaincre, souffrir, mourir dans nos affections . . . ; renaître ensuite, peut-être, pour l'étonnement et l'admiration du monde.
    2. Jasinski, ibid., III, II, pp. 7-8, letter to the editors of the *Nouvelles politiques*, May 31-June 2, 1795: . . . je souhaite l'établissement de la République sur les bases sacrées de la justice et de l'humanité. . . . dans les circonstances, le gouvernement républicain peut seul donner du repos et de la liberté à la France . . . pour la femme d'un ambassadeur . . . et pour tous les hommes qui ne vivent pas de soupcons nouveaux et de vieilles haines . . . n'y a-t-il pas que les amis de la République . . . auxquels tous les Français éclairés et patriotes veulent se rallier?
    3. d'Haussonville, *Madame de Staël et M. Necker*, ibid., p. 46.
    4. Pange, ibid., p. 214.
    5. L, III, ibid., p. 627, *Epître au malheur:* Malheur à qui voudrait agiter sa patrie!
    6. Comtesse Jean de Pange-Simone Balayé, *Madame de Staël Lettres à Ribbing*, Gallimard: Paris, 1960, p. 19.
    7. Ibid., p. 19, Fragment from Ribbing's memoirs: Je voudrais reconnaître un pouvoir magique au nom sacré de la liberté; quand je l'entends prononcé . . . je sens mon coeur battre violemment et mon sang passer en tourbillon dans mes veines.
    8. Jasinski, ibid., II, I, pp. 246-47, lettres à Narbonne, March 12 & 15, 1794: . . . son extraordinaire sentiment pour moi . . . Il est devenu un de nous par ses qualités . . .
    9. Pange-Balayé, ibid., p. 43, letter end-November circa 1793: Pourquoi vous croyez-vous obligé de me dire que 'votre coeur est pour jamais fermé à l'amour'? . . . Entre mes devoirs et mes torts, où voudriez-vous que je plaçasse un nouveau lien?

10. Ibid., p. 46, letter December 1793: Tous les jours je m'attache à vous davantage. Il y a dans votre caractère des trésors de bonté, de fierté, de noblesse . . . et plus vous êtes vous, moins vous êtes pressé de le paraître. . . . A présent . . . mon inquiétude commence à se porter sur l'impression que je fais sur vous. . . . il faut nous voir beaucoup; l'âme se développe par degrés. . . .

10a. L, II, p. 62, *De l'influence des passions*: Les hommes . . . peuvent avoir reçu d'une femme . . . les marques de dévouement qui lieraient . . . deux compagnons d'armes.

10b. Pange-Balayé, ibid., p. 295, letter of April 18, 1795: Songez qu'un homme honnête doit être aussi vrai, aussi fidèle dans ses promesses à une femme qu'à son compagnon d'armes et laissez-moi . . . conserver le culte de votre caractère pour me relever à mes propres yeux.

10c. L, II , pp. 61-62, *De l'influence des passions:* L'amour est la seule passion des femmes . . . l'histoire de leur vie; c'est un épisode dans celle des hommes . . . tandis que les lois de la moralité même, selon l'opinion d'un monde injuste, semblent suspendues dans les rapports des hommes avec les femmes. . . .

11. Pange-Balayé, ibid., p. 67, letter of March 1794: Livrée à elle-même, mon âme erre dans les ruines, et vous y voit encore planer comme le génie consolateur . . . p. 281, letter of March 17, 1795: Vous viendrez à Paris . . . et vous serez sûr alors que je vous regarderai comme mon ange tutélaire. . . .

12. Ibid., p. 129, letter of August 1794: Sachez respecter sans la craindre cette solennelle responsabilité.

13. Ibid., p. 151, letter of September 18, 1794. from Monchoisi-Ouchy: J'ai trouvé ici ce soir un homme de beaucoup d'esprit qui s'appelle Benjamin Constant . . . pas trop bien de figure, mais singulièrement spirituel.

14. Ibid., letter of March 5, 1795: Si tu n'as pas besoin de moi, ne viens pas, je ne puis supporter l'idée que notre seul lien soit ma douleur.

15. L, I *Zulma* (1794) p. 206: Quand le malheur est irrévocable, l'âme retrouve une sorte de sang-froid qui permet de penser sans cesser de souffrir. . . . Cet écrit plus que tout autre appartient à mon âme. . . .

16. Ibid., J'ai voulu, pour peindre l'amour, offrir le tableau du malheur le plus terrible et du caractère le plus passionné. . . . Ce sentiment ne pouvait avoir toute l'énergie imaginable que dans une âme sauvage et un esprit cultivé; car la faculté de juger ajoute à la douleur, quand elle n'a rien ôté à la puissance de sentir.

17. L, II, *De l'influence des passions* Introduction, pp. 1-4: C'est dans ce siècle qu'on est conduit à réfléchir . . . sur le bonheur individuel et politique . . . La base est la même, la certitude de n'être jamais si agité ni dominé par aucun mouvement plus fort que soi. . . . Celui des nations serait aussi de concilier la liberté des républiques et le calme des monarchies, l'émulation des talents et le silence des factions, l'esprit militaire au-dehors et le respect des lois au-dedans. . . .

18. Ibid., p. 6: . . . les nations sont élevées par leurs gouvernements, comme

les enfants par l'autorité paternelle ... le destin de la race humaine dépend de la manière dont les peuples conçoivent l'ordre social.

19. Ibid., p. 9: ... En Angleterre ... la combinaison savante d'intérêts opposés mais qui se balancent répond de la tranquilité publique.

20. Ibid., ch. I, p. 19, L'amour de la gloire: Les acclamations de la foule remuent l'âme, et par les réflexions qu'elles font naître, et les commotions qu'elles excitent, toutes ces formes animées sous lesquelles la gloire se présente doivent transporter la jeunesse d'espérance et l'enflammer d'émulation.

21. Ibid., ch. III, p. 45, La vanité: ... c'est aux dons de la nature que les femmes doivent leur empire: en s'occupant de l'orgueuil et de l'ambition, elles font disparaître tout ce qu'il y a de magique dans leurs charmes ... Les triomphes de la vanité ... ne supposent ni estime, ni respect pour l'objet ... Les femmes animent ainsi contre elles les passions de ceux qui ne voulaient penser qu'à les aimer.

22. Ibid., ch. IV, p. 53, L'amour: ... représenté comme inséparable ou de la volupté ou de la frénésie, l'amour est un tableau plutôt qu'une passion de l'âme.

23. Ibid., p. 56: ... pour passer sa vie [avec l'être aimé malgré toutes circonstances] est une passion qui rassemble dans l'âme tout ce que le temps enlève aux sensations; une [telle] passion ... c'est dans la réalité des choses humaines qu'il existe un tel bonheur....

24. Ibid., p. 58: Il est des caractères aimants qui ... convaincus de tout ce qui s'oppose au bonheur de l'amour ... effrayés des chagrins de leur propre coeur ... repoussent par une raison courageuse et une sensibilité craintive tout ce qui peut entraîner à cette passion: c'est de toutes ces causes que naissent et les erreurs adoptées ... sur la véritable importance des attachements du coeur, et leurs douleurs.

25. Pange, ibid., p. 179: Après cinq ans de malheurs, notre esprit public a acquis trios ou quatre idées. Celles des inconvénients de l'anarchie, de l'abus de la liberté de presse, du danger des sociétés populaires, de la nécessité de rendre inviolable le domicile des citoyens. Lente et pénible éducation!

26. P. Gaxotte, *Histoire des Français*, Flammarion: Paris, 1951, p. 315.

27. P. Chaunu, *Le grand déclassement*, Laffont: Paris, 1989, p.158.

28. G. Fraisse, *Muse de la raison: la démocratie exclusive et la différence des Sexes*, Alinea: Aix-en-Provence, 1989, p. 128.

28a. G. Solovieff, ibid., pp. 147-48, letter to P.-L. Roederer, November 22, 1796: Vous, mon cher Roederer ... vous êtes donc d'avis que je ne sais pas écrire? ... Qu'entend-on par le style? N'est-ce pas le coloris et le mouvement des idées? Or trouvez-vous que je manque ou d'éloquence, ou de sensibilité, ou d'imagination? ... Je ne le crois pas. Direz-vous qu'il y a de l'obscurité dans ce livre? Quel est l'ouvrage pensé qui se lise comme un roman? Je n'apellerais obscurité que celle qui vient du mot et non de la nature du sujet et du tour d'esprit méditatif....

29. R. de Luppé, *Madame de Staël et Jean-Baptiste Suard Correspondance 1786-1817*, Droz: Genève, 1970, p. 19.

30. Pange-Balayé, ibid., p. 29.
31. Pange, ibid., pp. 246-47, letter to François de Pange, June 15, 1796: Je suis la personne la plus française par le coeur, la plus amie de la République, par enthousiasme, par mouvement du sang, par tout ce qui est involontaire... Où est le bonheur si ce n'est dans sa patrie... dans le pays où l'on sent et pense...?
32. Jasinski, ibid., III, II, p. 275, Lettres d'une nouvelle républicaine: Comment vous autres, premiers amis de la liberté, désignés comme les auteurs de la première révolution,... pourions-nous rester en équilibre entre la République et la monarchie de Condé? Comment nous flatter jamais d'être plus forts que deux fanatismes?... n'est-il pas plus raisonnable de se rallier à la République, de la diriger au lieu de s'y soumettre, d'enter sur elle la justice et l'humanité, d'être plus fondateurs que ceux qui l'ont créée, de faire aimer ce qu'ils ont fait haïr? Je vois là une belle place.

CHAPTER 7: CONFRONTATION

1. François de Chateaubriand, *Mémoires d'outre-tombe*, Pléiade Gallimard: Paris, 1946, I, pp. 382-83: Il y a des moments où notre destinée, soit qu'elle cède à la société, soit qu'elle obéisse à la nature... se détourne soudain de sa ligne première, telle qu'un fleuve qui change son cours... Nous autres auteurs, petits prodiges d'une ère prodigieuse, nous avons la prétention d'entretenir des intelligences avec les races futures, mais nous ignorons... la demeure de la postérité....
2. Germaine de Staël, *Des circonstances actuelles qui peuvent terminer la Révolution et des principes qui doivent fonder la République en France* (1798), Droz: Genève-Paris, 1979, ed. L. Omacini, Introduction, pp. 1-2: Nous jeunes, vous vieillards, nous faibles, vous tout-puissants, qui donc oserait se dire heureux!... Les uns sont agités, les autres sont aigris... L'avenir n'a point de précurseur. L'homme erre... Ses habitudes, ses sentiments... tout est confondu. La douleur seule encore lui sert à se reconnaître....
3. Ibid., p. 14: Il y a beaucoup de raisons politiques qui détournent des associations assez resserrées pour y établir la démocratie pure dans le pouvoir....
4. Ibid., pp. 19-20: ... il y a représentation, c'est-à-dire fidélité dans les procureurs fondés, là où règne l'intérêt et la volontéde la nation, et il y a despotisme partout où ni l'un ni l'autre ne sont ni défendus ni écoutés.
5. Ibid., pp. 25-27: Quand les préjugés luttent les uns contre les autres, la guerre n'est jamais finie... [Vu] les progrès de l'esprit humain, quand un principe a triomphé d'un préjugé, le pas en arrière ne se peut plus....
6. Ibid., II, IV, L'écrivain: ... il importe que l'accroissement de l'art ne soit pas avili par le goût exécrable qui... en abuse si cruellement!... En se complaisant dans des idées rebutantes, il a déjà renversé la barrière de l'imagination.... Déjà son langage lui a inspiré l'audace de ce qui fait rougir la vertu.

6a. Ibid., Introduction, p. LX.

7. Jules Romains, *Napoléon par lui-même*, Perrin: Paris, 1963, pp. 46-47, Bonaparte in a letter to his father from Brienne, April 5, 1781: Je suis las d'afficher l'indigence, et d'y voir sourire d'insolents écoliers qui n'ont que leur fortune au-dessus de moi, car il n'en est pas un qui ne soit à cent piques au-dessous des nobles sentiments qui m'animent... Non... si la fortune se refuse... donnez-moi un état mécanique....

8. Ibid., pp. 51-52, meditation, May 3, 1786: ... puisque je commence à éprouver des malheurs, que rien n'est plaisir pour moi ... Quel spectacle verrai-je dans mon pays? Mes compatriotes ... qui baisent en tremblant la main qui les opprime!... Français, non contents de nous avoir ravi tout ce que nous chérissons, vous avez encore corrompu nos moeurs....

9. Ibid., p. 62, letter to General Paoli Auxonne, late 1788: ... Accablés sous la triple chaîne du soldat, du légiste et du percepteur d'impôts, nos compatriotes vivent méprisés ... n'est-ce pas la plus cruelle des tortures que puisse éprouver celui qui a du sentiment?

10. Henri Peyre, *Qu'est-ce que le Romantisme?* PUF: Paris, 1971, p. 113.

11. J. Romains, ibid., p. 65.

12. Ibid., pp. 79-80, Le Discours de Lyon 1790-1791: Le bonheur est ... incompatible avec une passion violente, puisque celle-ci est destructive ... du sentiment et de la raison naturelle.... L'ambition, ce désir immodéré de contenter l'orgueil ou l'intempérance, qui n'est jamais satisfait ... est, comme toutes les passions, désordonné, un désir violent et irréfléchi qui ne cesse qu'avec la vie; comme un incendie ... il ne finit qu'après avoir tout consumé....

13. D. Roche, *La France des lumières*, tr. A. Goldhammer, Harvard University Press: London, p. 590.

14. Mignet, ibid., p. 391.

15. J. Romains, ibid., p. 89.

16. Ibid., pp.113-14: Soldats! Je sais que vous êtes profondément affectés des malheurs qui menacent la patrie; mais la patrie ne peut courir de dangers réels. Les mêmes hommes qui l'ont fait triompher de l'Europe coalisée, sont là. Des montagnes nous séparent de la France, vous les franchirez avec la rapidité de l'aigle ... pour maintenir la constitution, défendre la liberté, protéger le gouvernement et les républicains.

17. Ibid., p. 103, Report to the Directoire, March 28, 1796: J'ai été reçu à cette armée avec des démonstrations d'allégresse et de confiance que l'on devait accorder à celui que l'on savait avoir, pendant cinq mois, mérité ... votre confiance....

18. Dumont-Wilden *Vie de Benjamin Constant* Gallimard Paris 1930 p. 68.

19. F. Furet-M.Ozouf, ibid., p. 953.

20. G. Solovieff, ibid., pp. 153-54: Nous promettons de nous consacrer réciproquement notre vie, ... nous nous regardons comme indissolublement liés, que notre destinée ... est pour jamais en commun, que nous ne contracterons. jamais aucun autre lien, et que nous resserrons ceux qui nous unissent. ...

21. E. Gwynne, ibid., pp. 41-42, Gwynne also quotes A. Sorel, *Madame de Staël*, ch. I, p. 53.
22. d'Haussonville, ibid., p. 55.
23. Comtesse le Marois née d'Haussonville, *A l'ombre de deux femmes*, in *Revue des deux mondes*, no. 12, 1959, pp. 672-90.
24. J. Orieux, *Talleyrand*, Flammarion: Paris, 1970, p. 190.
25. Ibid., p. 187.
26. Solovieff, ibid., p. 164, letter to J. H. Meister, October 15, 1799: Quoi qu'il en soit, c'est un grand événement, et cet homme, de plus, vaut une armée. Il ne faut pas, pour son bonheur, lutter de voeux contre cette république; sa destinée est invincible.
27. Ibid., p. 152, letter to J. H. Meister, April 22, 1797: Vous sentez que mon patriotisme a beaucoup d'humeur... il me faut un juste milieu, qui n'est jamais en France qu'un passage si rapide qu'il sert à peine de transition entre un excès et l'autre...

CHAPTER 8: IN THE COMPANY OF GODS

1. A. Sorel, ibid., p. 5: Quand on écrit pour satisfaire à l'inspiration intérieure dont l'âme est saisie, on fait connaître par ses écrits, même sans le vouloir, jusqu'aux moindres nuances de sa manière d'être et de penser.
2. R. de Luppé, *Idées littéraires de Madame de Staël et l'héritage des lumières*, Vrin: Paris, 1969, p. 71.
3. G. Solovieff, ibid., p. 308.
4. L, I, p.130: *Essai sur les fictions*.
5. Ibid., p. 133.
6. Ibid., p. 134.
7. Ibid., p. 135:... une fiction, quelle qu'elle soit, ne produit un effet absolu que quand elle contient en elle seule ce qui importe pour que les lecteurs, dans tous les moments, en reçoivent une impression complète.
8. Ibid., p. 140.
9. Ibid., p. 128:... c'est l'anéantir comme ces images brillantes formées par des vapeurs légères, qu'on fait disparaître en les traversant.
10. Ibid., p. 139:... les enfants, sans pouvoir s'en rendre compte, savent déjà qu'il y a moins de régularité dans la véritable marche des événements.
11. Ibid., p. 147: Ce plaisir de la retraite... repose des vains efforts de l'espérance trompée; et quand tout l'univers s'agite loin de l'être infortuné, un écrit... tendre reste auprès de lui comme l'ami le plus fidèle, et celui qui le connaît le mieux... il sert aux meilleurs des hommes.
12. Germaine de Staël, *De la littérature considérée dans ses rapports avec les institutions socials*, Droz-Minard: Geneva-Paris, ed. P. van Tiechhem, 1959,

I, p. 2: C. F. Count Volney: La mémoire des temps passés, la comparaison de l'état présent, tout éleva mon coeur à de hautes pensées.

13. Ibid., II, II, ch. VII, p. 393: On veut qu'un homme, dans un état libre, alors qu'il se fait remarquer par un livre, indique sans ce livre les qualités importantes que la république peut un jour réclamer d'un de ses citoyens, quel qu'il soit.

14. Ibid., p. 427: J'ai tâché de rassembler . . . tous les motifs qui peuvent . . . engager les bons esprits à diriger cette force irrésistible, dont la cause existe dans la nature morale, comme dans la nature physique est renfermé le principe du mouvement.

15. Ibid., I, I, Discours préliminaire–De l'importance de la littérature dans ses rapports avec la vertu p25: Les ouvrages gais sont . . . un délassement de l'esprit, dont il conserve peu de souvenir. La nature humaine est sérieuse, et dans le silence de la méditation, l'on recherche les écrits raisonnables ou sensibles.

16. Ibid., p. 28: 'l'enfer des tièdes' chant III.

17. Ibid., p. 35: l'art d'écrire serait aussi une arme, la parole aussi une action. . . .

18. Ibid., ch. I-V, pp. 47-111.

19. Ibid., ch. VII, pp. 121-29.

20. Ibid., ch. VIII, pp.130-48: Si Bacon, Machiavel et Montaigne ont des idées et des connaissances supérieures à celles de Pline, de Marc-Aurèle . . . n'est-il pas évident que la raison humaine a fait des progrès . . . le génie le plus remarquable ne s'élève jamais au-dessus des lumières de son siècle, que d'un petit nombre de degrés.

21. Ibid., ch. IX, pp. 149-56.

22. Ibid., ch. XIII, pp. 193-207.

22a. Ibid., ch. XX, p. 280: . . . si l'art social atteint un jour en France à la certitude d'une science dans ses principes et dans son application, c'est de Montesquieu que l'on doit compter ses premiers pas.

23. Ibid., II, I, ch. XX , p. 282: Quand la philosophie fait des progrès, tout marche avec elle; les sentiments se développent avec les idées.

23a. Ibid., II, II, ch. III, p. 323: Ce n'est que dans les états libres qu'on peut réunir le génie de l'action à celui de la pensée.

23b. Ibid., ch. IV, pp. 331-38: Eclairer, instruire, perfectionner les femmes comme les hommes, les nations comme les individus, c'est le meilleur secret pour tous les buts raisonnables . . . toutes les relations sociales et politiques auxquelles on veut assurer un fondement durable.

24. Ibid., conclusion, p. 428: Mais dix ans après la route de l'existence est déjà profondément tracée. . . .

25. Comte d'Haussonville, ibid., p. 14.

26. J. A. Bédé, *Madame de Staël et les mots* in *Madame de Staël et l'Europe*, Klincksieck: Paris, 1970, pp. 319-28.

27. Staël, *De la literature*, ibid., II , ch.VIII, On Eloquence, pp. 412-13:

Jetez les yeux sur une foule . . . ne vous arrive-t-il pas de rencontrer des traits dont l'expression amie . . . vous présagent une âme . . . qui céderait à vos sentiments! . . . cette foule est la nation. . . . livrez-vous à vos pensées . . . voguez à pleines voiles . . . vous entraînerez toutes les affections libres, tous qui n'ont reçu . . . le prix de la servitude.

CHAPTER 9: IN THE COMPANY OF MEN AND WOMEN

    1. G. Solovieff, ibid. Staël letter to P.-L. Roederer, January 9, 1800, pp. 167-68: Ce *Journal des Hommes libres* lancé contre moi . . . parce que je suis l'amie d'un homme qui a prononcé un discours indépendent sur un règlement. . . .
    2. Furet-Ozouf, ibid., p. 220.
    3. G. Solovieff, ibid. Letter to Barras, January 22, 1798, pp. 158-59: Que veut donc le Directoire de nous?
    4. B. d'Andlau, ibid., quotes from Mme de Genlis, *Mémoires*, III, pp. 315ff.
    5. G. de Broglie, *Madame de Genlis*, Perrin: Paris 1985, p. 371: Je ne la laisserai pas outrager.
    6. Chateaubriand, ibid., II, p. 156: J'étais encore tout sauvage; j'osais à peine lever les yeux sur une femme entourée d'adorateurs.
    7. S. Balayé, *Ecrire, lutter, vivre*, ibid., p. 294.
    8. Jasinski, ibid., IV, II, p. 487: N'est-ce pas trop compter, même dans ces temps malheureux, sur le sérieux des lecteurs?
    9. Furet-Ozouf, ibid., p. 895.
    10. G. Lefebvre, *La Révolution française*, PUF: Paris, 1930-89, p. 501: Bonarparte circa 1798: Lorsque le bonheur du peuple français sera assis sur les mei-lleures lois organiques, l'Europe entière deviendra libre.
    11. P. Gaxotte, ibid., p. 329.
    12. Ibid., p. 340.
    13. J. Orieux, ibid., p. 255.
    14. Solovieff, ibid., p. 171, letter to P.-S. Du Pont de Nemours, May 2, 1800.
    15. Diesbach, *Necker*, ibid., p. 449.
    16. Jasinski, IV, II, p. 348, letter to Joseph Bonaparte, January 17, 1801: Je ne sais plus si vous êtes pour moi, ce Joseph si bon et si aimable, dont la conversation a été les plus douces heures de ma vie.
    17. Ibid., p. 369, letter to P.-S. Du Pont de Nemours, April 20, 1801: Bonaparte a senti avec raison qu'un gouvernement non fondé sur les institutions devait l'être au moins sur les hommes . . . Personne ne regarde ceci comme stable, parce que la France est en rente viagère sur la tête de Bonaparte . . . cette idée ne lui déplait pas . . . mais il ne voudrait pas se rendre moins nécessaire. . . .

18. Staël *Circonstances*, ibid., pp. 120-21: . . . je n'ai de ma vie fait du mal . . . jamais, par moralité peut-être, par fierté sûrement, laissé un ressentiment s'approcher de moi. . . . J'ai employé tout ce que la nature m'avait donné . . . pour être utile aux êtres malheureux.

19. Staël, *De la literature*, Droz, ibid., II, p. 326: Le guerrier sans lumières . . . n'enchaîne point votre imagination; il reste toujours en vous des sentiments qu'il n'a pas captivés, et des idées qui le jugent.

20. Comte d'Haussonville, ibid., p. 100.

21. Solovieff, ibid., p. 206, letter to Villers, August 1, 1802: . . . cette puissance, n'est-ce pas l'âme?

22. M. Levaillant, *Une amitié amoureuse—Madame de Staël et Madam Récamier*, Hachette: Paris, 1956, p. 19: Elle portait un petit chapeau orné de fleurs . . . je fus frappée par la beauté de ses yeux et de son regard . . . Je venais de lire ses *Lettres sur Jean-Jacques Rousseau*, je m'étais passionnée pour cette lecture. J'exprimai ce que j'éprouvais plus par mes regards que par mes paroles; elle m'intimidait et m'attirait à la fois. On sentait tout de suite en elle une personne parfaitement naturelle dans une nature supérieure.

23. Jasinski, ibid., p. 403, letter to Juliette Récamier, September 9, 1801: Comment gouvernez-vous l'empire de la beauté? On vous l'accorde avec plaisir, parce que vous êtes éminemment bonne, et qu'il semble naturel qu'une âme si douce ait un charmant visage pour l'exprimer.

24. Chateaubriand, ibid., II, p. 168: cela formait une réunion qu'il est impossible de peindre sans avoir eu le bonheur d'en être témoin soi-même.

25. Furet-Ozouf, ibid., p. 221.

26. d'Haussonville, ibid., p. 171: Necker to Staël, November 1, 1801.

27. Ibid., p. 165: Sans toi, mon être intérieur se désorganise.

28. Staël *De la literature*, ibid., II, I, ch. XX, pp. 285-86: . . . le talent, c'est la faculté d'appeler à soi . . . les ressources, tous les effets des mouvements naturels; c'est cette mobilité d'âme qui nous fait recevoir de l'imagination l'émotion. . . .

29. Diesbach, *Necker*, ibid., p. 458, and d'Haussonville, ibid., p. 336: . . . Lève la tête dans l'adversité et ne permets pas qu'aucun puissant de la terre te tienne sous ses pieds! (1802).

CHAPTER 10: SAILING, FULL SAILS

1. Solovieff, ibid., p. 176, letter to Madame Pastoret, June 9, 1800: Je fais un roman, je cherche des sujets de tragédie . . . je me prépare une carrière littéraire à l'inverse de ce qu'on fait ordinairement. . . . je viens aux ouvrages d'imagination. Nous verrons après ce que je deviendrai.

2. L, ibid., I, *Delphine* I, letter III, pp. 233, 235, Delphine to Matilde, 1790: . . . je n'ai qu'un désir, c'est d'être aimée des personnes avec qui je vis . . .

laissez chacun chercher au fond de son coeur le soutien qui convient le mieux à son caractère et à sa conscience.

3. Ibid., letter VI, p. 243, Delphine to Louise d'Albémar, April 19, 1790: Je restai à causer . . . avec plusieurs hommes dont la conversation . . . inspire le plus vif intérêt à tous les esprits capables de réflexion et d'enthousiasme . . . c'est peut-être blesser un peu les convenances . . . mais quand . . . les dames . . . sont établies au jeu. . . .

4. Ibid., letter XII, p. 262, Delphine to Louise, May 8, 1790: Jamais on n'a réussi dans un style si simple tant de charmes différents: de la noblesse et de la bonté . . . cette élévation de sentiments, la première des qualités. . . .

5. Ibid., letter XV, p. 272, Delphine to Louise, May 22, 1790: Je dirigeai notre conversation sur ces pensées vers lesquelles la mélancolie nous ramène invinciblement: l'incertitude de la destinée . . . la fatigue de la vie, tout ce vague. . . .

6. Ibid., II, letter VIII, p. 375, Delphine to Louise: Je fus saisie . . . de cette pitié . . . que les fictions n'excitent jamais . . . sans un retour sur nous-mêmes; et je contemplai cette image du malheur comme si . . . menacée au milieu de la mer, j'avais vu de loin, sur les flots, les débris d'un naufrage.

7. Ibid., III, letter XIV, p. 515, Delphine to Léonce: L'enthousiasme que l'amour nous inspire est comme un nouveau principe de vie. Quelques-uns l'ont reçu . . . Les pensées élevées sont aussi nécessaires à l'amour qu'à la vertu.

8. Ibid., I, letter XXIII, Delphine to Louise, June 5, 1790: . . . Ah! Journée trop heureuse, la première et la dernière peut-être de cette vie d'enchantement que la merveilleuse puissance d'un sentiment m'a fait connaître . . . !

9. Ibid., letter XXIV, pp. 294-95, Léonce to Barton, June 6, 1790: Elle a dans le regard quelquechose de sensible et de tremblant, qui semble invoquer un secours . . . et son âme n'est pas faite pour résister seule aux orages du sort. . . .

10. Ibid., III, letter VII, p. 493, Léonce to Delphine: . . . L'univers et les siècles se fatiguent à parler d'amour; mais une fois, dans . . . des milliers de chances, deux êtres se répondent par toutes les facultés de leur esprit et de leur âme. . . .

11. Ibid., letter XXXII, p. 550, Léonce to Delphine, April 20, 1791: Vous aimez la liberté comme la poésie . . . comme tout de qui ennoblit et exalte l'humanité; et les idées que l'on croit devoir être étrangères aux femmes se concilient . . . avec votre aimable nature . . . Cependant . . . quand on vous cite pour aimer la révolution: . . . une femme ne saurait avoir trop d'aristocratie dans ses opinions. . . .

12. Ibid., letter XXXIII, p. 551, Delphine to Léonce, April 24 1791: . . . si j'étais un homme, il me serait aussi impossible de ne pas aimer la liberté . . . que de fermer mon coeur à la générosité . . . à tous les sentiments . . . vrais et . . . purs.

13. Ibid., IV, letter XXXII, p. 671: to the poem by George Lyttleton (1709-73) Léonce adds: Voilà, Delphine, voilà ce que vous êtes; jamais aucune femme avant vous n'a mérité ce portrait!

14. Ibid., V, pp. 691-92, fragments II & III, December 1791: . . . ces tableaux de bonheur . . . m'ont-ils fait illusion . . . ? Non, la souffrance restait au fond . . . sa cruelle serre ne lâchait pas prise . . . j'ai perdu trop tôt le bonheur!

15. Ibid., II, letter XLV, p. 447, Delphine to Louise, November 29, 1790: . . . que le coeur humain est inattendu dans ses développements! Les moralistes méditent sans cesse sur les passions et les caractères . . . contre lesquels ni l'âme ni l'esprit n'ont été mis en garde.

16. Ibid., VI, letter XII, p. 807, Lebensai to Léonce, August 13, 1791: considérez la terre des sommets . . . ne sentez-vous pas que toutes les . . . peines de la société restent au niveau du brouillard des villes . . . ? Les rapports continuels avec les hommes troublent les lumières, étouffent les principes de . . . l'élévation. . . .

17. Ibid., I, p. 240, Delphine to Louise concerning Sophie: . . . il existe une manière de prendre tous les caractères du monde, et les femmes doivent la trouver, si elles veulent vivre en paix sur cette terre. . . .

18. Ibid., II, letter II, p. 347, Delphine to Louise, July 26, 1790: . . . le sort d'une femme est fini quand elle n'a pas épousé celui qu'elle aime . . . on dégrade son carac- tère . . . [cela] ne fait qu'agiter les jours de jeunesse, et dépouiller les dernières années de ces souvenirs . . . l'unique gloire de la vieillesse. . . .

19. Ibid., V, pp. 693-94, fragment V: Arrivée sur la hauteur du Jura, . . . m'avançant à travers un bois de sapins sur le bord d'un précipice, un sentiment . . . sombre s'emparait de moi: . . . penchée . . . ne m'appuyant . . . que sur une branche . . . Des paysans passèrent. Ils me virent vêtue de blanc au milieu de ces arbres noirs, mes cheveux détachés . . . que le vent agitait . . . je les entendis vanter ma beauté . . . Faut-il avouer ma faiblesse? . . . Je plaignis ma jeunesse, et m'éloignant . . . je continuai ma route.

20. Ibid., I, letter III, p. 233.

21. Ibid., I, p. 235.

22. Ibid., I, letter VI, p. 237.

23. Ibid., IV, letter XXX, p. 671.

24. Solovieff, ibid., p. 181, letter to Mme de Pastoret, September10, 1800: Il me faut des années pour refouler tout à fait mon coeur. Je continue mon roman et il est devenu l'histoire de la destinée des femmes présentées sous diverses rapports.

25. L, *Delphine*, ibid., IV, XIV, pp. 728-29: Dans les questions politiques qui divisent maintenant la France, où est la vérité, me direz-vous?

26. Solovieff, ibid., letter to P.-L.Roederer, November 22, 1796, p. 148: En vérité je me crois sûre que l'auteur et moi nous sommes deux; femme jeune et sensible. . . .

27. L, *Delphine*, ibid., fragment III, p. 691: Je suis bien faible; je me fais pitié; tant d'hommes, tant de femmes même, marchent d'un pas assuré dans la route qui leur est tracée, et savent se contenter des jours réguliers et monotones . . . et moi je les traîne . . . épuisant mon esprit . . . comme si j'étais coupable. . . .

28. L, ibid., II, XXVII , p. 418: Sous la prescription de l'opinion, une femme s'affaiblit, mais un homme se relève. . . .

29. Balayé *Ecrire, lutter, vivre*, ibid., p. 76.

30. L, ibid., III, letter XXXIII Delphine to Léonce, p. 551: Ce ne sont pas seulement les lumières de la philosophie qui font adopter les idées comme celle

de la liberté, de la générosité, tous les sentiments de l'amitié . . . il s'y mêle un enthousiasme généreux, qui s'empare de vous comme toutes les passions nobles et fières, et vous domine impérieusement.

CHAPTER 11: THE TEST OF SORROW

1. H. Peyre, *Qu'est-ce que le romantisme?* PUF: Paris, 1971, p. 9.
2. A. Szabo, *Aspects et fonctions du temps dans Delphine*, Annales Benjamin Constant 8-9, Lausanne-Paris, 1988, pp. 195-209.
3. L I, *Quelques réflexions sur le but moral de Delphine*, p. 876: Les femmes règnent en souveraines dans les commencements de l'amour. . . .
4. Jasinski, ibid., IV, II, p. 581, Rosalie de Constant *Cahier vert:* . . . jamais depuis Clarisse je n'avais éprouvé cette illusion complète. . . .
5. Diesbach, *Necker*, ibid., p. 440.
6. Romains, ibid., p. 180, Napoléon, May 4, 1802 : Premier consul, je gouverne; mais ce n'est pas comme militaire, c'est comme magistrat civil. Dans le système féodal, comme dans l'Orient, c'est le plus fort qui commande, . . . [et] qui gouverne.
7. R. Mortier, *Madame de Staël ou la fidélité*, in Cahiers Staëliens new series 28, 1979, pp. 33-40.
8. Solovieff, ibid., p. 214, Chateaubriand to Germaine de Staël January 8, 1803: Avec des ciseaux je ferai une *Delphine* pour moi. . . . Je n'aime point Léonce. . . . Ce qui me charme surtout, c'est que le malheur y est supérieusement exprimé et même si bien que je tremble pour vous. . . .
9. Furet-Ozouf, ibid., p. 221, Napoléon, May 1802: Nous sommes trente millions d'hommes réunis par les Lumières, la propriété et le commerce. Trois ou quatre cent militaires ne sont rien auprès de cette masse.
10. Ibid., p. 224.
11. Solovieff, ibid., pp. 269-70, letter to Necker, April 7, 1804: Il est positif que la mort du duc d'Enghien a produit ici le plus grand effet mais il n'en résultera . . . qu'une pudeur qui empêchera une alliance. . . .
12. Jasinski, ibid., IV, II, letter to C. de Villers, July 20, 1803: Que les hommes sont rares! Et qu'il n'est pas étonnant que le despotisme s'établisse au milieu de tant de gens si bien faits pour servir!
13. Solovieff, ibid., pp. 283-84, letter to C. Hochet, September 17, 1804: . . . je ne crois point à Bonaparte d'animosité contre moi, simplement il trouve que j'ai trop d'existence parmi les étrangers et que sans m'avoir fait faire quelque chose qui me diminue, il ne veut pas de moi debout. . . .
14. G. Poulet, *Madame de Staël et l'Europe*, Klinksieck: Paris, 1970, p. 213.
15. K. Kloocke, *Benjamin Constant Une biographie intellectuelle*, Droz: Genève-Paris, 1984, p. 327.
16. d'Haussonville, ibid., p. 359.

17. d'Haussonville, *Madame de Staël et l'Allemagne*, Calmann-Lévy: Paris, 1928, p. 62, letter Germaine to Necker, December 15, 1803: . . . absence de peine, mais point de plaisir; le plaisir, c'est l'amour, Paris ou la puissance; il faut une de ces trois choses pour combler le coeur, l'esprit et l'activité, tout le reste est métaphysique en jouissance mais réel en douleur si cela manque.
18. Lacretelle, ibid., p. 163.
19. d'Haussonville, ibid., p. 85.
20. N. Boyle, *Goethe:the Poet and the Age*, Clarendon Press: Oxford, 1991-2000, p. 85.
21. Jasinski, ibid., V, I, pp. 340-41, letter to C. Hochet, May 9, 1804: Que me fait l'univers dont je ne peux plus lui parler?
22. Furet-Ozouf, ibid., p. 309.
23. Cahiers Staëliens, 28 Paris, 1980, *Le Journal de Mlle Necker*, p. 59: Qu'il est beau de faire sentir par quelles pensées l'homme d'Etat peut se détacher des . . . intérêts.
24. L, ibid., III, p. 546, *Du caractère de M. Necker et de sa vie privée:* . . . toutes ces vues bienfaisantes réalisées pour la première fois, pénétraient d'admiration et de reconnaissance la classe éclairée et la classe souffrante. . . .
25. Ibid., pp. 549-50: . . . combien alors il était serein! . . . Il attendait les événements avec une sécurité . . . dans toutes les crises où il n'était exposé ni aux peines de coeur ni aux scrupules de la conscience.
26. Jasinski, ibid., IV, II, p. 622, letter to C. Hochet, May 10, 1803: Je suis . . . plus calme, depuis que la nature, redevenue belle, est une sorte de musique continuelle qui rend à l'âme toute son harmonie . . . s'il n'y avait plus de musique, plus de verdure, plus de lune avec le printemps, on ne comprendrait pas d'où naissent . . . ces sentiments si peu analogues avec ceux des courtesans de Saint-Cloud. . . .
27. Comtesse Jean de Pange, *Auguste-Guillaume Schlegel et Madame de Staël*, Albert Paris, 1938, p. 117.
28. Ibid., p. 154: . . . il attribue à moi ce qui est l'effet du pays où nous vivons, car il ne peut douter que je l'aime à jamais comme mon frère. . . .
29. Jasinski, ibid., V, II, p. 501n2.
30. Solovieff, ibid., p. 306, letter to J.-B. Suard, April 9, 1805: C'est peut-être . . . le malheur qui donne à la pensée une cruelle activité. J'ai plus senti la nature ici que je ne l'avais sentie partout ailleurs. . . . J'écrirai une sorte de roman qui serve de cadre au voyage d'Italie. . . .
31. Jasinski, ibid., V, II, p. 517, letter to Vincenzo Monti, March 16, 1805: J'ai senti . . . cet enthousiasme qui tient à l'air, aux parfums, aux merveilles de la nature . . . une nation si favorisée par le ciel et si dégradée par son gouvernement . . . pour qui la vie physique est si belle et la vie morale si bornée . . . n'aime rien que le super-ficiel: . . . elle a besoin de voir plutôt que de sentir et de penser.
32. Sorel, p. 110: Schiller.

CHAPTER 12: THE TEST OF SUCCESS

1. Madame de Staël, *Corinne ou l'Italie*, Gallimard: Paris, 1985, II, ch. III, stanza 20, p. 63: Connaissez-vous cette terre où les orangers fleurissent, que les rayons des cieux fécondent avec amour? Avez-vous entendu les sons mélodieux qui célèbrent la douceur des nuits? Avez-vous respiré ces parfums, luxe de l'air déjà si pur et si doux? Répondez, étrangers, la nature est-elle chez vous belle et bienfaisante?
2. Ibid., XV, ch. II, pp. 398-99: Il existait . . . entre Oswald et Corinne, une sympathie singulière et toute puissante . . . dans le fond de leur âme . . . il y avait des mystères semblables, des émotions puisées à la même source. . . .
3. Ibid., VII, ch. III, pp.192-93: Lord Nelvil, de quelque avantage qu'il fut doué, ne croyait pas l'égaler . . . [cela] lui inspirait des craintes sur la durée de leur affection.
4. Ibid., XIII, ch.V, p. 355: Cette belle Corinne dont les traits animés et le regard plein de vie étaient destinés . . . [au] bonheur, cette fille du soleil, atteinte par des peines secrètes, ressemblait à ces fleurs encore fraîches . . . qu'un point noir . . . menace. . . .
5. Ibid., IX, ch. III, p. 253: . . . il faut, dans le bonheur comme dans le malheur, être en paix avec soi-même.
6. Jasinski, ibid., V, II, pp. 598-99, 613: letters to V. Monti: . . . son beau ciel est dans vos regards, et son climat dans votre âme . . . Ménagerez-vous mon caractère, vous qui êtes l'Italie pour moi?
7. Balayé, *Ecrire, Lutter, Vivre*, ibid., p. 95.
8. L, ibid., II, *De la literature*, II, ch. IV, p. 365: N'est-elle pas une femme extraordinaire? Tout est dit alors; on l'abandonne à ses propres forces, on la laisse se débattre avec la douleur . . . elle promène sa singulière existence . . . entre toutes les classes . . . objet de la curiosité, peut-être de l'envie, et ne méritant . . . que de la pitié.
9. *Corinne*, ibid., XIV, ch. III, p. 377: L'exil est . . . un supplice beaucoup plus cruel que la mort. . . .
10. Solovieff, ibid., pp. 337-38: . . . celui qui dispose de tout se réserve peut-être la décision immédiate de ce grand débat entre le pouvoir et la vertu. . . .
11. *Corinne*, ibid., XVI, ch. I, pp. 431-32: . . . il faut de l'harmonie dans les sentiments et de l'opposition dans les caractères. . . .
12. Ibid., XV, ch. II, p. 399: . . . [une] ressemblance secrète supposait une même nature. . . .
13. Ibid., X, ch.VI, p. 281: . . . les contrastes ne lui permettaient pas de se connaître . . .
14. Solovieff, ibid., pp.340 & 342.
15. Constant de Rebecque, *Correspondance de Benjamin Constant et d'Anna Lindsay*, Plon: Paris, 1933, p. 237: . . . ma vie n'est au fond nulle part qu'en moi-même. Je la laisse prendre, j'en livre les dehors à qui veut s'en

emparer. J'ai tord, car cela m'enlève du temps et des forces . . . l'intérieur est environné d'une barrière que les autres ne franchissent pas.

16. P. Dominique, *Les Polémistes français depuis 1789*, La Colombe: Paris, 1962, pp. 88-90: Chateaubriand circa 1807: Chaque nation a ses vices . . . Le meurtre du duc d'Enghien . . . la guerre d'Espagne et la captivité du pape, décèlent dans Bonaparte une nature étrangère à la France. . . . Bonaparte est un faux homme. . . .

17. Solovieff, ibid., p. 343: . . . j'espère laisser . . . de dignes descendants de mon père. . . .

18. Balayé, *Les Carnets de voyage de Madame de Staël*, Droz: Genève, 1971, p. 32, Frankfort, November 15, 1803: . . . cette idée que les Allemands ont du bon sens et les Français de l'esprit se modifie de mille manières . . . le véritable esprit n'est que la raison appliquée à des objets nouveaux . . . la masse des deux nations sera toujours en opposition; au sommet tout se réunit, parce que le don si rare de la supériorité établit entre . . . tous . . . un langage commun.

19. Charles-Joseph Prince de Ligne, *Mémoires, Lettres et Pensées*, Bourin: Paris, 1989, Cahier XLV, p. 446: Il est sorcier cet homme que les uns croient un Dieu et les autres un Diable, mais jamais un homme. . . . Que peut-il gagner? Qu'il fasse . . . tous les sacrifices possibles pour la paix! C'est en perdant qu'il peut encore acquérir la réputation d'un grand homme qu'il a défaite pour n'être qu'un grand capitaine et le tourment du monde.

20. J. P. Eckermann, *Conversations with Goethe* (1831), tr. G. O'Brien, Ungar: New York, 1964, p. 76.

21. M. Ullrichova, *Madame de Staël et Frédéric Gentz* in *Madame de Staël et l'Europe*, Klincksieck: Paris, 1970, pp. 86-87, Gentz letter to A. H. Müller, May 29, 1808: . . . je la trouvai très à l'aise et très claire, ne s'écartant pas de son sujet, bien ordonnée, cohérente et carrément grande, engageante à la conversation comme encore aucune femme dans le monde . . . Nulle part au monde je n'ai trouvé une telle universalité et profondeur d'âme. . . .

22. Solovieff, ibid., Voght letter to Germaine de Staël, February 1809, p. 379: Vous gagnez de ces batailles qui décident du sort d'une nation.

23. Solovieff, ibid., letter to Prince de Ligne, July 8, 1808, p. 365.

24. *Corinne*, ibid., XIV, ch. I, p. 366: Faut-il imiter les abeilles, don't les essaims se succèdent sans progrès et sans diversité?

CHAPTER 13: THE PATH TO GLORY

1. Solovieff, ibid., p. 434, letter to Thomas Jefferson, November 10, 1812 . . . Vous avez vu les premiers jours de la révolution en France et je me rappelle que chez mon père vous disiez aux hommes exagérés que leurs principes démagogiques amèneraient le despotisme en France. Votre prédiction s'est accomplie. . . .

2. Staël, *De l'Allemagne* Garnier-Flammarion: Paris, 1968, I, II, ch. I, p. 163: Le contraste se fait voir entre les esprits développés dans la solitude et ceux formés par la société. Les impressions du dehors et le recueillement de l'âme, la connaissance des hommes et l'étude des idées abstraites, l'action et la théorie donnent des résultats opposés. La littérature, les arts, la philosopohie, la religion des deux peuples attestent cette différence. . . .
3. Ibid., II, IV, ch. I, p. 244: Luther est . . . celui dont le caractère était le plus allemand, sa fermeté avait quelque chose de rude; sa conviction . . . le courage de l'esprit . . . ce qu'il avait de passionné ne le détournait point des études abstraites. . . .
4. Ibid., I, II, ch. I, p. 341: Goethe . . . ressemble plutôt à la nature . . . et l'on peut aimer mieux son climat du Midi que son climat du Nord, sans méconnaître en lui les talents qui s'accordent avec ces diverses régions de l'âme.
5. Ibid., I, II, ch. I, p. 306: . . . que de génie et . . . que de naturel ne faut-il pas pour s'identifier avec tout ce qu'il y a de beau et de vrai dans tous les pays . . . !
6. E. Vigée-Lebrun, *Souvenirs* (1869), Ed. des femmes: Paris, 1984, pp. 181-85: . . . sa physionomie animée et pleine de génie me donna l'idée de la représenter en Corinne, assise, la lyre en main, sur un rocher . . . Elle n'était pas jolie, mais l'animation de son visage pouvait lui tenir lieu de beauté.
7. *De l'Allemagne*, ibid., II, III, ch. I, p. 128: Kant voulut rétablir . . . l'activité spontanée dans l'âme, la conscience dans la morale. . . .
8. Ibid., II, II, ch. XXVII, p. 34: Le charme de la musique, de la peinture, de la sculpture, de la poésie, et par-dessus tout du langage de l'âme, voilà [pour le déclamateur] ses moyens pour développer dans celui qui l'écoute la puissance des passions. . . .
9. Ibid., II, IV, ch. I, p. 312: Croient-ils connaître la terre? . . . Leur coeur bat-il pour l'écho des montagnes? . . . Comprennent-ils la diversité des pays, l'accent et le caractère des idiomes . . . les chants populaires et les danses leur découvrentils les moeurs et le génie d'une contrée? . . . La nature peut-elle être sentie par des hommes sans enthousiasme?
10. Chateaubriand, ibid., II, XXIX, ch. XI, p. 186: Mille détails de l'oppression de Bonaparte se sont perdus dans la tyrannie générale . . . on demeurait dans la haine du despote.
11. J. de Broglie, *Madame de Staël et sa cour au château de Chaumont*, Plon: Paris, 1936, p. 87, A. de Chamisso: C'est un personnage de tragédie qui doit ou recevoir des couronnes ou en distribuer . . . à ce prix elle peut aimer et vivre . . . elle dépérit dans le bannissement. . . .
12. *De l'Allemagne*, ibid., I, I, ch. XIII, p. 115: . . . l'exil condamne à survivre; les adieux, les séparations, tout est comme à l'instant de la mort. . . .
13. V. Folkenflik, *An Extraordinary Woman—Selected Writings of Germaine de Staël*, Columbia University Press: New York, 1987, p. 356: Staël *Réflexions sur le suicide* (1812):

... Il y a un avenir dans toute occupation, et c'est d'un avenir dont on a sans cesse besoin. Les facultés nous dévorent ... et le travail exerce et dirige ces facultés; enfin, quand on a de l'imagination ... on peut trouver des plaisirs ... dans l'étude des chefs-d'oeuvre de l'esprit humain. ...

14. F. Lotterie, *Conversation sur l'éducation*, Cahiers Staëliens, ibid., 52-2001, pp. 39-51.

15. Romains, ibid., p. 97, Napoléon letter to Joseph Bonaparte, June 24, 1795: ... Nous avons vécu tant d'années ensemble ... nos coeurs se sont confondus et tu sais ... combien le mien est entièrement à toi. Je sens en retraçant ces lignes une émotion dont j'ai eu peu d'exemple dans ma vie.

16. Ibid., pp. 199-202, Napoléon letter to Joseph Bonaparte, March 29, 1808: Je crains que vous ne me trompiez sur la situation de l'Espagne, et que vous ne vous trompiez vous-même ... il y a de l'énergie chez les Espagnols. Vous avez affaire à un peuple neuf ... que n'ont point usé les passions politiques. Je songerai à vos intérêts, n'y songez pas vous-même.

17. J. Orieux, ibid., p. 327.

18. Staël, *Dix Années d'Exil*, Fayard: Paris, 1996, I, p. 45: L'empereur ... m'a persécutée avec un soin minutieux ... une rudesse inflexible, et mes rapports avec lui me l'ont fait connaître longtemps avant que l'Europe eût compris le mot de cette énigme et lorsqu'elle se laissait dévorer par le sphinx ... elle n'avait pas su le deviner.

19. Ibid., pp. 85-86: Le fantôme de l'ennui m'a poursuivie toute ma vie. ... Bonaparte connaissait bien en moi [cette terreur] ... il sait le mauvais côté de chacun. ...

20. Ibid., p. 90: ... le général apprenait de Talleyrand les noms, les usages aristocratiques ... pour donner ... un air d'ancienneté à sa dynastie.

21. Ibid., p. 99: ... Bonaparte étourdissait les anciens cabinets de l'Europe par tant de menaces et de promesses ... qu'ils croyaient gagner en donnant et se réjouissaient du mot de paix comme si ce mot avait conservé le même sens que jadis.

22. Ibid., p. 108: Il fit mettre dans les journaux ... un raisonnement bizarre contre l'opposition ... qu'Angleterre ... le roi y est l'ennemi du peuple; mais dans un pays où le pouvoir exécutif est ... nommé par le peuple, c'est s'opposer à la nation que de combattre son représentant.

23. Ibid., pp. 115-16: Dans un hotel des monnaies, à Pétersbourg, je fus frappée de la violence des machines qu'une seule volonté fait mouvoir ... Bonaparte fait périr des milliers ... et ses agents ... sont aussi insensibles que ce bois et ce fer ... L'impulsion invisible vient d'une volonté ... diabolique ... qui transforme la vie morale en un instrument servile. ...

24. Ibid., II, p. 290: ... il faut encore apprendre à ces présomptueux qui croient trouver la profondeur de la pensée dans les vices de l'âme que, s'il y a ... de l'esprit dans l'immoralité, il y a du génie dans la vertu.

25. Ibid., I, p. 117: L'on ne doit combattre cet homme avec aucune de ses armes. Il doit succomber seulement parce que l'homme a une conscience et l'univers un Dieu.
26. B. Pares, *A History of Russia*, Knopf: New York, 1956, p. 301.
27. *Dix Années d'Exil*, ibid., II, p. 291:... il m'exprima ses regrets de n'être pas un grand général; je répondis qu'un souverain était plus rare et que soutenir l'esprit public par son exemple, c'etait gagner la plus grande des batailles. L'empereur me parla de sa nation avec enthousiasme et de ce dont elle était capable. Il m'indiqua le désir d'améliorer l'état des paysans. Votre caractère, lui dis-je, est une constitution pour votre empire et votre conscience en est la garantie. Quand cela serait vrai, me répondit-il, un homme n'est jamais qu'un accident heureux.
28. Solovieff, ibid., pp. 436-37: Thomas Jefferson, reply to Germaine's letter, May 28, 1813.

CHAPTER 14. THE PRICE OF GLORY

1. Dorothea Schlegel, *Briefen*, ed. E. Wenecke: Weimar, 1914, p. 430.
2. Solovieff, ibid., p. 439, Count Ribbing to Germaine, December 11, 1812:... vous avez tout subjugué, et vos succès retentissent jusqu'ici, tant le charme de votre présence est irrésistible. Ce n'était pas à moi d'en douter.
3. *Madame de Staël Ten Years of Exile*, tr. Doris Beik, Saturday Review Press: New York, 1972, p. 227n, letter to Ribbing, October 20, 1812.
4. *Dix Années*, ibid., p. 308:... je me confirmai dans la résolution de faire rentrer mes fils dans la patrie de leur père en les attachant au service de Suède. ...
5. Gaxotte, ibid., p. 360:... il n'est aucun de vous qui ne veuille retourner en France par un autre chemin que celui de l'honneur.
6. Solovieff, ibid., p. 429: Auguste de Staël to Germaine June 11, 1812:... tu auras de l'émotion, ce dont il faut se garantir... il ne faut plus que regarder devant soi... Adieu, cher ange... nous sommes dans un de ces moments où il faut étouffer son âme comme une chose... nuisible... j'espère que... tu vois qu'il n'est pas possible d'aimer plus que je ne t'aime....
7. Solovieff, ibid., p. 445, letter to Constant, May 20, 1813: J'ai toujours des lettres de vous auprès de moi... je voudrais en recevoir de nouveau. Mon père, vous et Mathieu demeurez dans une partie de mon coeur qui est fermé à jamais... c'est votre admirable esprit qui me fait encore illusion.
8. Comtesse Jean de Pange, *Auguste-Guillaume Schlegel et Madame de Staël*, ibid., p. 432, letter to Schlegel, July 2, 1813: je ne puis me passer de votre entretien: il me semble que je n'ai plus d'idées depuis que nous sommes séparés... N'oubliez pas que nous sommes votre famille.
9. *De l'Allemagne*, ibid., II, III, ch. XIX, p. 218: Rien n'est plus opposé à

la vocation naturelle des femmes que ce qui leur donnerait des rapports de rivalité avec les hommes, et la gloire elle-même ne saurait être pour une femme qu'un deuil éclatant du bonheur.

10. Cahiers Staëliens, *Madame de Staël et la Suède*, 180-1 39 1989-90, pp. 55-72, letter to Carl G. von Brinkman, May 3, 1813–via Norman King, P. Tisseau, baroness von Knorring (*Souvenirs*): . . . Les premiers jours de ma jeunesse ont été tempestueux et méritent souvent le blâme, mais . . . je ne crois pas qu'on puisse être un *homme* sans le culte de la liberté, et la pensée en moi est *home*. . . . Si j'espère de la gloire, c'est par le développement . . . des vertus qui naissent de la liberté et des vices qui naissent du despotisme. . . .

11. Lacretelle, ibid., p. 276.

12. Solovieff, ibid., pp. 453-54, from Schlegel, August 3, 1813: . . . il avait une con-fiance illimitée dans ses forces et son agilité . . . une belle prodigalité de sa vie.

13. Ibid., p. 466.

14. Ibid., p. 472, letter to Constant, January 23, 1814: On ne doit pas dire du mal des Français lorsque les Russes sont à Langres. Que Dieu me banisse plutôt que de m'y faire rentrer par des étrangers!

15. Coppet Colloquium, *Madame de Staël et l'Europe*, 1970, p. 310, letter to Constant of March 22, 1814, quoted by Solovieff: Croyez-vous donc que l'on ne puisse pas se montrer dans une assemblée de princes! Quarante batailles sont aussi une noblesse. Je hais l'homme, mais je blame les événements qui me forcent à lui souhaiter du succès.

16. Adolphe Thiers, *Histoire du Consulat et de l'Empire*, Paulin-Lheureux: Paris, 1860, XVIII, ch. LIV, p. 73.

17. Victor de Pang, *Le plus beau de toutes les fêtes*, Klincksieck: Paris, 1980, p. 59, letter to Rocca, July 1813: Me voici dans la plus belle habitation du monde. . . . c'est là qu'est l'Angleterre telle que je l'aime et l'admire . . . Un parc de deux mille hectares, l'hospitalité la plus noble, la maison la plus belle, des prières en commun le matin et après-dîner.

18. Victor de Pange, ibid., p. 41.

19. P. Quennell, *Byron—a Self-Portrait Letters & Memoirs*, Oxford, 1990, p. 227.

20. Staël, *Considérations sur la Révolution française*, Tallandier: Paris, 1983, ed. J. Godechot, VI, ch. VII, pp. 569-70: Les partisans des principes de la révolution ont soutenu une tyrannie viagère, pour prévenir . . . le retour de despotismes durables. Mais ils n'ont pas vu qu'un genre de pouvoir absolu fraie le chemin à tous les autres, et qu'en redonnant . . . les moeurs de la servitude, Bonaparte a détruit l'énergie de l'esprit public.

21. Solovieff, ibid., p. 515, letter to Louise, countess of Albany, December 20, 1815: J'ai dit, quand à Paris la nouvelle de cet affreux débarquement de Bonaparte m'est arrivé: "S'il triomphe, c'en est fait de la liberté; s'il est battu, de toute indépendance." N'avais-je pas raison?

22. Chateaubriand, ibid., I, XVI, ch. XI, p. 571: Napoléon devint suspect; il fit peur; on perdit confiance en lui . . . ses grandes idées restèrent les mêmes, mais ses bonnes inclinations s'altérèrent et ne soutinrent plus ses . . . qualités.
23. Solov, ibid., p. 183n:Il ne s'agit pas de ce que je veux, mais de ce que je pense.
24. Romains, ibid., I, pp. 79-80: the Lyon *Discours.*
25. Solovieff, ibid., p. 225, letter to Bonaparte, September 26, 1803: Pourquoi renverseriez-vous la destinée d'une femme qui n'a de sa vie fait de mal à personne? . . .

CHAPTER 15: THE TESTAMENT

1. Staël, *Considérations*, ibid., VI, ch. XII, p. 606: C'est une chose remarquable . . . qu'à une certaine profondeur de pensée . . . il n'y a pas un ennemi de la liberté . . . d'un bout du monde à l'autre, les amis de la liberté communiquent par les lumières . . . S'agit-il de l'abolition de la traite des nègres, de la liberté de la presse, de la tolérance religieuse, Jefferson pense comme La Fayette, La Fayette comme Wilberforce; et ceux qui ne sont plus comptent aussi dans la sainte ligue.
2. Solovieff, ibid., p. 516, letter to Jefferson, January 6, 1816: Je n'ai pu me résoudre à retourner en France tant que les étrangers en sont les maîtres . . . Je vais marier ma fille avec le duc de Broglie. C'est un pair de France d'autrefois . . . petit-fils du maréchal et ami de M. de La Fayette, et cela dit tout. Notre famille est encore une petite isle intellectuelle où Franklin, Washington et Jefferson sont révérés comme dans leur patrie. . . .
3. Solovieff, ibid., p. 524: Jefferson to Germaine, September 6, 1816.
4. L, III, *De l'esprit des traductions*, pp. 604-605: Traduire un poète, ce n'est pas prendre un compas, et copier les dimensions de l'édifice; c'est animer du même souffle de vie un instrument différent. . . . A. W. Schlegel a fait une traduction de Shakespeare qui, réunissant l'exactitude à l'inspiration, est tout à fait nationale en Allemagne.
5. Solovieff, ibid., p. 527: Germaine de Staël's testament, October 12, 1816: Je recommande mon âme à Dieu, qui m'a comblée de biens dans ce monde. . . . Je n'ai qu'un conseil à donner à mes enfants, c'est d'avoir présents à l'esprit la conduite, les vertus et les talents de mon père, et de tâcher de l'imiter suivant leur caractère et leurs forces. . . . Je me suis mariée avec M. Albert Jean de Rocca . . . un fils, Louis Alphonse, doit entrer en possession de ses droits. . . .
6. Ibid., p. 529: letter to Wellington Dec.1 1816: J'avais raison quand j'osais vous écrire que votre présence ferait du bien à Paris. Il est malheureux de dépendre des étrangers; mais le génie est cosmopolite et je crois que bien qu'anglais vous seriez généreux envers la France. . . .
7. Ibid., pp. 531-32: letter to Jefferson, February 12, 1817: . . . notre pauvre France est si loin de tout ce que vous répandez de lumières . . . Serons-

nous libres une fois dans ce pays-ci?... Il y a pourtant au fond de cette grande masse... une idée confuse de liberté... Je vais publier un ouvrage... vous y verrez votre nom....

8. Staël, *Considérations*, I, ch. VI, p. 96: La misère accroît l'ignorance... et quand on se demande pourquoi le peuple français a été si cruel..on ne peut en trouver la cause que dans l'absence du bonheur, qui conduit à celle de la moralité.

9. Ibid., I, ch. I, p. 65: Dans la période des affranchissements partiels, les bourgeois des villes ont réclamé quelques droits; car, dès que les hommes se réunissent ils y gagnent au moins autant en sagesse qu'en force.

10. Ibid., I, ch. II, p. 76: Le roi, qui a pensé que les propriétés de ses sujets lui appartenaient, et qui s'est permis tous les genres d'actes arbitraires... ne respectait que lui-même, et n'a jamais pu concevoir ce que c'était qu'une nation.

11. Ibid., I, ch. XXII, p. 162: Comment les esprits de cette trempe veulent-ils prononcer sur les affaires d'un grand peuple? Vit-on jamais des hommes qui ne voulaient pas du raisonnement, s'entendre si mal à s'assurer de la force?

12. Ibid., II, ch. VIII, p. 201: Il y a dans une nation une certaine masse de sentiments qu'il faut ménager comme une force physique. La République a son enthousiasme que Montesquieu appelle son principe; la monarchie a le sien; le despotisme même; mais une constitution qui fait entrer l'humiliation de l'un ou l'autre doit être renversée par l'un ou par l'autre.

13. Ibid., II, cg. XXIII, p. 248:... songez à ce que doivent être des hommes qui, n'ayant jamais exercé aucun droit politique, se trouvent tout à coup en possession d'une jouissance funeste à tous... ils seront longtemps avant de savoir qu'une injustice soufferte par un citoyen... retombe sur la tête de tous.

14. Ibid., III, ch. III, p. 263: On ne peut s'empêcher d'éprouver un sentiment de douleur, lorsqu'on retrace les époques de la révolution où une constitution libre aurait pu être établie....

15. Ibid., III, ch. VI, p. 273:... leurs jurements entremêlés de cris, leurs gestes menaçants, leurs instruments meurtriers, offraient un spectacle épouvantable, et qui pouvait altérer à jamais le respect que la race humaine doit inspirer.

16. Ibid., III, ch. XVI, p. 303: Il semble qu'on descende comme le Dante de cercle en cercle, toujours plus bas dans les enfers. A l'acharnement contre les nobles et les prêtres on voit succéder l'irritation contre les propriétaires... les talents... tout ce qui pouvait rester de grand et généreux....

17. Ibid., III, chs. XXVI and XXVII, pp. 338-39, 344:... la crainte qu'il inspirait était causée par le singulier effet de sa personne.... Un tel être n'ayant point de pareil, ne pouvait ni ressentir, ni faire éprouver de la sympathie... Je sentais une épée froide et tranchante... il méprisait la nation dont il voulait les suffrages. Il ne saurait être naturel que dans le commandement.

18. Ibid., VI, ch. XII, p. 606: Sans doute il faut des lumières pour s'élever audessus des préjugés; mais c'est dans l'âme aussi que les principes de la liberté sont fondés... ils viennent de la nature, ils ennoblissent le caractère. Tout un

ordre de vertus, aussi bien que d'idées, semble former cette chaîne d'or décrite par Homère, qui, rattachant l'homme au ciel, l'affranchit des fers de la tyrannie.

19. Ibid., IV, ch. II, pp. 360-61: ... ne serait-ce pas une leçon pour l'espèce humaine si ces directeurs se relevaient de leur poussière, et demandaient compte à Napoléon de la barrière du Rhin et des Alpes ... de trois millions de Français qui ont péri de Cadix jusqu'à Moscou ... Une nation ne peut faire de pis que de se remettre entre les mains d'un homme ... si elle s'était constituée en respectant les leçons de dix ans ... elle serait encore la lumière du monde.

20. Ibid., I, ch. II, p. 80: Il faut examiner quelle est maintenant la nature des sentiments en harmonie avec le coeur: car le feu sacré n'est et ne sera jamais éteint; mais c'est au grand jour de la vérité seulement qu'il peut reparaître.

21. Ibid., I, ch. III, p. 83: ... toutes les paroles et toutes les actions, les vertus et les passions, les sentiments, les vanités, l'esprit public et la mode, tendaient également au même but.

22. Staël, *Considérations*, ibid., pp. 7, 26.

23. Ibid., ch. I, p. 63: La révolution est une des grandes époques de l'ordre social. Ceux qui la considèrent comme un événement accidentel n'ont porté leur regard ni dans le passé, ni dans l'avenir ... ils ont attribué à ceux du moment ce que les siècles avaient préparé.

24. Ibid., p. 41.

25. Balayé, *Lumières et Liberté*, ibid., p. 236.

26. Furet-Ozouf, ibid., p. 1059.

27. Staël, *Considérations*, ibid., I, ch.VI, p. 96: ... quand on se demande pourquoi le peuple français a été si cruel dans la révolution, on ne peut en trouver de cause que dans l'absence du bonheur, qui conduit à l'absence de moralité.

28. Ibid., IV, ch. XVIII, pp. 422-23: ... l'art de tromper les hommes ... [une] politique [qui] doit tomber à mesure que les lumières s'étendront. ...

29. Ibid., III, ch. XIX, p. 314: ... une religion arrangée à sa manière.

30. Ibid., IV, ch. XVIII, p. 421: ... il y avait dans sa tête une incohérence, trait distinctif de tous ceux qui ne classent pas leurs pensées sous la loi du devoir.

31. Ibid., VIU, ch. XII, pp. 600-601: La liberté a trois sortes d'adversaires en France: les nobles qui ... croient que leurs intérêts ... et ceux du pouvoir ne font qu'un; ceux que la Révolution a dégoûtés des idées qu'elle a profanées; ... tous ceux sans conscience politique.

32. Ibid., p. 602: Quand depuis tant de siècles toutes les âmes généreuses ont aimé la liberté; quand les grandes actions ont été inspirées par elle ... et un ouvrage politique d'une réputation durable a été animé par ce sentiment ... à quoi donc les jeunes gens penseront-ils ... au moins ils seraient des hommes s'ils s'occupaient de leur pays, s'ils se croyaient citoyens, si leur vie était utile de quelque manière.

33. Ibid., I, ch. II, p. 75: Le despotisme du cardinal Richelieu détruisit en entier l'originalité du caractère français, sa loyauté, sa candeur, son indépendance.

34. Ibid., VI, ch. III, p. 606: . . . cette énergie d'indépendance qui sait résister tout. . . .
35. Comtesse Jean de Pange, *Auguste-Guillaume Schlegel et Madame de Staël*, ibid., p. 278: Schlegel: J'ai un vrai culte pour la beauté de votre âme. . . .
36. Ibid., p. 522: Albertine duchesse de Broglie: . . . J'ai perdu à la fois l'objet de mon culte et de ma passion, de mon respect et de ma confiance, celle dont la voix n'a jamais cessé de faire battre mon coeur.

CONCLUSION

1. George Eliot, *Essays*, Routledge & Kegan Paul: London, 1968, p. 55.
2. L, I, ibid. Preface of 1814 to *Lettres sur les écrits et le caractère de Jean-Jacques Rousseau*, p. 2: . . . la culture des lettres m'a valu plus de jouissances que de chagrins . . . il y a dans le développement et le perfectionnement de son esprit . . . un espoir toujours renaissant, que ne saurait offrir le cours ordinaire de la vie.
3. Solovieff, ibid., p. 132: Necker letter to Germaine May 15 1795: Calme ton ambition jusqu'à ce que tu sois dans un pays où tu pourras dire et écrire ce que tu voudras. . . .
4. Ibid., p. 175: Samuel de Constant to Germaine, June 1800: Vous donnez du sentiment et des grâces à l'érudition et vous étendez les bornes de l'esprit. . . .
5. Comte d'Haussonville, *Madame de Staël et Monsieur Necker*, ibid., p. 171: Pauvre petite, te voilà dans la vaste mer et mes regards t'y suivent, car, avec l'esprit des siècles, tu es toute enfant par le caractère. . . .
6. Solovieff, ibid., p. 224n: Necker letter to Germaine, September 20, 1803: . . . il est bien décidé que tu es la personne la plus aimable et la plus spirituelle du monde connu. Ne pouvons-nous rien faire de cela pour ton bonheur?
7. L, II, *De l'influence des passions*, pp. 47-48: . . . la femme qui, en atteignant à une véritable supériorité, pourrait se croire au-dessus de la haine . . . cette femme n'aurait jamais le calme et la force de tête qui caractérisent . . . les hommes les plus célèbres . . . son âme serait trop fortement agitée . . . les talents, unis à une imagination passionnée, éclairent sur les résultats généraux et trompent sur les relations personnelles.
8. Jasinski, ibid., VI, p. 589: letter to Julie de Krüdener February 5, 1809: Je voudrais avoir la force de vous imiter . . . je vois le pour et le contre de tout, et mon désir seul est entier et sans mélange . . . Je vous ai vue plus confiante que moi, et le mauvais côté des hommes et des choses vous frappait moins. Il m'en est resté . . . cette douloureuse disposition dans les plus hautes pensées.
9. L, II, *De la literature*, Preface, pp. 145-47: D'où vient que ce système de la perfectibilité . . . déchaine maintenant toutes les passions politiques? Quel rapport peut-il avoir avec elles?
10. Ibid., *De l'influence des passions*, p. 35: L'ambition dénature le coeur: quand on a tout jugé par rapport à soi, comment se transporter dans un autre?

11. Ibid., *De la literature*, ch. XVI, p. 291: Montesquieu semble donner la vie aux idées, et rappelle à chaque ligne la nature morale . . . au milieu des abstractions.
12. Cahiers Staëliens, 28, 1980, *Journal*, p. 77: L'on respire en ce lieu l'indépendance; toutes les idées ambitieuses paraissent si petites au pied de ses monts qui touchent aux cieux. . . .
13. L, II, *De la literature*, p. 160: . . . l'art d'écrire serait aussi une arme, la parole serait aussi une action, si l'énergie de l'âme s'y peignait tout entière, si les sentiments s'élevaient à la hauteur des idées, et si la tyrannie se voyait ainsi attaquée par . . . l'indignation généreuse et la raison inflexible. . . .

EPILOGUE

1. Victor de Pange, *Le plus beau de toutes les fêtes*, ibid., p. 210: Auguste de Staël to the duchess of Devonshire, September 30, 1817: Le temps ne change rien à ce grand vide que rien ne comblera pour nous: mais il adoucit ces premières impressions dont la force humaine ne supporterait pas la durée.
2. Staël, *Considérations*, ibid., Introduction, p. 41.
3. Benjamin Constant, *De la religion*, Bibliothèque romande Lausanne, 1971, p. 48: Tout ce qui au moral excite l'attendrissement et l'enthousiasme . . . la partie la plus noble de son être.
4. Benjamin Constant, *Oeuvres*, Pléiade-Gallimard: Paris, 1957, III, *Mélanges de littérature et de politique* pp. 826-27 & 840-41: . . . Les deux qualités dominantes de Madame de Staël étaient l'affection et la pitié. Elle avait . . . une grande passion pour la gloire . . . comme toutes les âmes élevées, un grand amour pour la liberté . . . mais [tout cédait] lorsque la moindre circonstance les mettait en opposition avec le bonheur de ceux qu'elle aimait . . . [On est] frappé de cette variété de talent, . . . cette universalité de vues, qui transforme en écrivain politique du premier ordre l'observateur ingénieux des faiblesses de notre nature, le peintre fidèle des souffrances.
5. Cahiers Staëliens, 53, 2002, ibid., p. 157: Auguste de Staël à Germaine September 1811: Je trouve du bonheur à jouer . . . le rôle de chef de famille . . . un protecteur protégé.
6. Comtesse Jean de Pange, *Lettres de femmes du 19ième siècle*, ibid., p. 29.
7. Solovieff, ibid., p. 415: letter to Goethe, March 15, 1811: . . . un homme que j'apprends chaque jour à aimer plus. . . .
8. Chateaubriand, ibid., XXIX, ch. 9, p. 183: Il n'y a rien dans les ouvrages imprimés de Madame de Staël qui approche de ce naturel, de cette éloquence, où l'imagination prête son expression aux sentiments.
9. Ibid., ch. XXII, p. 214: Bonjour, my dear Francis. Je souffre, mais cela ne m'empêche pas de vous aimer.

10. Solovieff, ibid., p. 531: Alexander I to Germaine February 25, 1817: . . . j'aime à penser que si tout en France n'est pas encore au niveau de vos désirs, que s'il existe des obstacles à l'affranchissement de la Restauration, ceux-ci seront levés à une époque prochaine et déterminée: les intentions deviendront alors plus pures. . . .
11. Solovieff, ibid., p. 381: Julie de Krüdener à Germaine March 16 1809: J'ai trouvé quelquefois cet esprit de secte, cette disposition à enchaîner l'esprit humain à des méthodes, à des formes qui choquent . . . tous ceux qui ont dans l'âme quelque chose de vaste.
12. F. Wagener, *Madame Récamier*, J. C. Lattès, Paris, 1968, p. 203: letter Germaine to Juliette from Chaumont 1810: . . . ce séjour va finir. Je ne conçois ni la campagne ni la vie intérieure sans vous . . . Vous étiez le centre doux et tranquille de notre intérieur ici, et rien ne tiendra plus ensemble.
13. Balayé, *Ecrire lutter, vivre*, ibid., p. 295: from Germaine's *Réflexions sur la paix* (1795): Il faut marcher avec son siècle, et ne pass'épuiser dans une lutte rétrograde contre l'irrésistible progrès des lumières. . . .

> Sa nature, à la fois ardente et triste, accessible aux plus nobles passions humaines et toujours prête à s'y livrer, mais entretenant aussi le sentiment du néant de la vie et tourmentée du problème de la destinée . . . Elle était aussi prompte à pardonner qu'à s'offenser. Sa nature généreuse faisait volontiers le premier pas. . . .
>
> Comte O. d'Haussonville, *Madame de Staël et Monsieur Necker*, ibid., p. 343.

SELECT BIBLIOGRAPHY

WORKS OF GERMAINE DE STAËL PUBLISHED SINCE 1820

Oeuvres complètes de Madame la baronne de Staël-Holstein I-XVII. Paris Strasbourg London: Treuttel & Würtz, 1820-1821.
Years of Exile. New York: Collins.
De l'Allemagne. Paris: Villers, C.de.
Oeuvres complètes. Genève: Slatkine, 1836.
Delphine. Philadelphia: Cary & Hart, 1836.
Dix Années: St.Pétersbourg. ed. Fargues, P. F. Paris: Musée littéraire et historique, 1841.
Oeuvres complètes. Paris: Firmin Didot, Treuttel & Würtz, 1844-1861.
Corinne or Italy. tr. Hill, I., Landon, L. E. New York: Derby & Jackson, 1857.
Oeuvres de Madame de Staël-Holstein I-III. Paris: Lefèvre, 1858.
De l'Allemagne. Paris: Didot, 1859.
De l'Allemagne. Paris: Vrin & Garnier, 1874.
Considérations sur la Révolution française. ed. Jullian, E. C. Paris: Hachette, 1896.
Excerpts from *De l'Influence des passions, De la littérature, Delphine, Corinne, De l'Allemagne, Dix Années, Considérations.* ed. Warner-Peale-Hill. New York: Library of the World's Best Literature, 1897.
Considérations sur la Révolution française. ed. Barkhausen, H. Paris: Imprimerie Nationale, 1900.
Fragments d'écrits politiques 1799 inédits. ed. Herriot, E. Paris: Plon, 1904.
Dix Années d'Exil. ed. Gautier, P. Paris: Plon-Nourrit, 1904.
Des circonstances actuelles qui peuvent terminer la Révolution. Paris: Viénot Fischbacher, 1906.

Journal de Jeunesse. ed. Comtesse Jean de Pange. Paris: Occident et Cahiers Staëliens, Attinger, 1930-1932. Also ed. Starobinski, J. Paris: Cahiers staëliens, 1980.
Schazmann, P.-E. *Bibliographie des oeuvres de Madame de Staël.* Paris Neuchâtel: Attinger, 1938.
L'Oeuvre imprimée de Germaine de Staël 1786-1821. ed. Longchamp, F. C. Genève: Cailler, 1949.
De l'Allemagne. ed. Comtesse de Pange & Balayé, S. Paris: Hachette, 1958-1960.
De la littérature I-II. ed. Tieghem, P., Minard. Genève: Droz, 1959. Also ed. Goldzink, J., Gengembre, G. Paris: Flammarion, 1959-1991.
De l'Allemagne. ed. Balayé, S. Paris: Garnier-Flammarion, 1966-1991.
Dix Années d'Exil. re-ed. of the 1904 Gautier by Balayé, S. Paris: Bibliothèque 10/18, 1966.
Carnets de voyage de Madame de Staël. ed. Comtesse de Pange & Balayé, S. Genève: Droz, 1967-1971.
De l'Allemagne. I-II ed. Balayé, S. Paris: Garnier-Flammarion, 1968-1971.
Ten Years of Exile. tr. Beik, D., Gay, P. New York: Saturday Review Press, 1972.
De la littérature. tr. Petroni. Bologna: Patròn, 1974.
Solovieff, G. *Choix de textes de Madame de Staël.* Paris: Klinksieck, 1975.
Corinne ou l'Italie. tr. Kappler Winkler, von Arno & Tachenbuch, D. München: Verlag, 1979.
Corinne ou l'Italie. ed. Hermann, C. Paris: Edition de Femmes, 1979.
Essai sur les fictions, De l'influence des passions. ed. Tournier, M. Paris: Ramsay, 1979.
Des circonstances actuelles qui peuvent terminer la Révolution. ed. Omacini, L. Genève: Droz, 1979.
Mon Journal. ed. Starobinski, J. Paris: Cahiers staëliens 28, 1980.
L'Influenza delle passioni sulla felicita. tr. Cusumano, P., & Perizzi, M. Roma: Melograno, 1981.
Delphine. ed. Omacini, L., & Balayé, S. Paris: Ed. de Femmes, 1981 and Genève: Droz, 1990.
Considérations sur la Révolution française. ed. Godechot, J. Paris: Tallandier, 1983.
Réflexions sur le suicide. ed. Mansau, A. Paris: l'Opale, 1985.
Über Deutschland. ed. Buchholz. F. Frankfurt am Main: Catel & Hitzig, 1985.
Corinne ou l'Italie. ed. Balayé, S. Paris: Gallimard, 1985.
Corinne or Italy. tr. Goldberger, A. New Brunswick, New Jersey: Rutgers University Press, 1987.
An Extraordinary Woman—Selected Writings of Germaine de Staël. ed. Folkenflik, V. New York: Columbia University Press, 1987.
Préface: Prince de Ligne—Lettres et Pensées. Paris: Bourin, 1989.
De la littérature. tr. Milchina, V.A. Moscow: Art, 1989.

SELECT BIBLIOGRAPHY 283

Réflexions sur le procès de la reine. Schirmer Manesse, R. Zurich: Verlag, 1989.
Fragments politiques. ed. Omacini, L. Paris: Cahiers staëliens 42, 1989.
Le portrait de Mélanie. ed. Amend, A.& King, N. Paris: Cahiers Staëliens 42, 1990-1991.
De la littérature. ed. Gengembre, G. & Goldzink, J. Paris: Flammarion, 1991.
Over Duitsland 1803-1808. ed. Uitgeverij. Amsterdam-Antwerpen: Contact, 1993.
Escritos politicos. tr. Portluondo, A. & Mejia, L. S. Madrid: Centro de estudios constitucionales, 1993.
Essai sur les fictions. tr. Yamaguchi, Toshiaki. Kanto: Journal of Arts and Science Guankin University, 1994.
Réflexions sur le procès de la reine par une femme. Cottret, M. Montpellier 4: Presses du Languedoc, 1994.
Perchelet, J. P. *Bibliographie staëlienne.* Paris: Cahiers staëliens 52, 1994-2001.
Delphine tr. Goldberger, Avriel H. De Kalb, Illinois: Northern Illinois University Press, 1995.
Réflexions sur le procès de la reine par une femme. ed. Thomas, Chantal. Paris: Mercure de France, 1996.
Dix Années d'Exil. ed. Balayé, S.& Bonifacio, M.V. Paris: Fayard, 1996.
Mon Journal. Paris: La Nouvelle Revue française 531, 1997.
Oeuvres de Jeunesse. ed. Balayé, S. & Isbell, J. Paris: Desjonquères, 1997.
Corinne ou l'Italie. tr. Natsuo, Sato. Tokyo: Kokushokankokai, 1997.
De la littérature. ed. Blaecke. Paris: Garnier, 1998.
La Folle de la forêt de Sénart, La Folle du Pont Neuf, L'imbécile d'Allemagne. ed. Amend-Söchting, A. Paris: Cahiers staëliens 52 1998-2001.
Corinne ou l'Italie. tr. Raphael, S. Oxford: Oxford University Press, 1999.
Les inconvénients de la vie de Paris (1778). ed. Amend-Söchting, A. Paris: Cahiers staëliens 50, 1999.
Delphine I-II. ed. Didier, B. Paris: Flammarion, 2000.
Oeuvres complètes de Madame de Staël en série, Oeuvres littéraires, Delphine, Corinne. ed. Omacini, L. & Balayé, S. Paris: Champion, H., 2000-2001.
Ten Years of Exile. tr. Goldberger, A. De Kalb, Illinois: Northern Illinois University Press, 2000.
De l'Influence des passions and *Réflexions sur le suicide.* ed. Thomas, C. Paris: Payot-Rivages, 2000.
Du talent d'être aimable en conversation and *De l'éducation de l'âme par la vie.* ed. Balayé, & Lotterie, S. F. Paris: Cahiers staëliens 52 Champion, 2001.

CORRESPONDENCE OF GERMAINE DE STAËL

In addition to the letters collected and presented by Béatrice Jasinski and those offered by Georges Solovieff, the Revue du temps présent (Paris), Comtesse de Pange, M. Ullrichova, P. Zaborov, K. Kloocke, Nicolas-Lelièvre and N. King, bibliographical notices of which are given herewith, the following are Germaine de Staël's correspondents. Names are in alphabetical order. I hope that omissions will be forgiven.

Jasinski, Béatrice. *Madame de Staël, Correspondance Générale:*
  I, I-II *Lettres de Jeunesse.* Paris: Pauvert, 1962.
  II, I *Lettres inédites à Louis de Narbonne.* Paris: Pauvert, 1960.
  II *Lettres diverses.* Paris: Pauvert, 1965.
  III, I *Lettres de Mézery et de Coppet.* Paris: Pauvert, 1968.
  II *Lettres d'une nouvelle républicaine.* Paris: Pauvert, 1972.
  IV,I *Du Directoire au Consulat —*
  II *Lettres d'une républicaine sous le Consulat.* Paris: Pauvert, 1978.
  V,I *France et Allemagne.* Paris: Hachette, 1982.
  II *Le Léman et l'Italie.* Paris: Hachette, 1985.
  VI *De Corinne vers l'Allemagne.* Paris: Klincksieck, 1993.

King, N. *Correspondances suédoises.* Paris: Cahiers staëliens 39, 1987-1988.
Kloocke, K. *Lettres inédites de Madame de Staël.* Paris: Cahiers staëliens 13, 1977.
Nicolas-Lelièvre, C. *A des amis polonais.* Paris: Museum Mickiewiza Cahiers staëliens 20, 1978-1991.
Pange, Comtesse Jean de. *Lettres de femmes.* Monaco: Rocher, 1947.
Solovieff, G. *Madame de Staël et ses amis, ses correspondants —choix de lettres 1778-1817.* Paris: Klincksieck, 1970-1975. Also tr. Jameson, K. Cempee, 2000.
Ullrichova, M. *Lettres de Madame de Staël conservées en Bohême.* Prague: Académie des Sciences Tchécoslovaques, 1960.
Zaborov, P. *Madame de Staël et ses correspondants russes.* Paris: Cahiers staëliens 13, 1971.

Countess of Albany. ed. B.d'Aurevilley. Paris: Lévy, 1863.
Lettres au comte de Balk. Paris: Cahiers staëliens 2, 1964.
P. de Barante. ed. baronne de Barante. Clermond-Ferraud, 1929.
C. de la Bédoyère (1805-1806). Paris: Semaine littéraire, 1925.
C. von Berg. ed. Götze, A. Arch für das Studium der neveren Sprachen und Literaturen Bd 202, 1965.

SELECT BIBLIOGRAPHY 285

J. Bernadotte. ed. Desfailles, P. Paris: Institut Napoléon, 1955.
Joseph Bonaparte. Paris: Revue des deux mondes, 1936-1937.
C. V. de Bonstetten & F. Brun. Genève: Bibliothèque Universelle, 1831.
Byron (1816). King, N. Annales Benjamin Constant 7, 1987.
A. von Chamisso. Cahiers d'études germaniques 28, 1995.
B. Constant, C. de Villers. Kloocke, K, Lang, P. Frankfurt am Main, 1993.
B. Constant, C. de Villers. ed. Isler, M. Hambourg, 1879.
B. Constant (1803-1816). ed. baronne E.de Nolde. Paris: 1928. Also *(1795-1812).* ed. Kra, P.-L. & Rudler, G. Paris: Droz, 1937.
B. Constant. ed. Nolde, E.de. tr. Harwood, C. New York-London: Putnam, 1907.
E. Dumont. ed. Martin, J. Lausanne: Concorde, 1927.
F. von Gentz. ed. King, N. Paris: Cahiers staëliens 40, 1989-1990.
Baron de Gérando. Paris-Metz: Renouard & Blanc, 1868.
Pasteur Gerlach. ed. Hermann, C. Paris: Cahiers staëliens 40,1989.
J. Goethe. Goethe-Jahrbuch, 1884-1887. (current ed. E. Grumach).
Gustave III of Sweden. Paris: Revue des deux mondes, 1856.
E.Hervey duchess of Devonshire (1804-1817) in *Le plus beau de toutes les fêtes.* V. de Pange. Paris: Klincksieck, 1980.
C. Hochet. ed. Mistler, J. Neuchâtel, 1949.
A. de Lameth (1796) Révolution. Paris: Documents historiques V, 1878.
M. Leoni. ed. Balayé, S. Paris: Cahiers staëliens 14, 1971.
C.-J. prince de Ligne. Bulletin de l'Académie royale de langue et de littérature française de Belgique T.xliv 3-4, 1966.
J. Mackintosh. ed. King, N. Paris: Cahiers staëliens 10, 1970.
H. Meister. Usteri, P.-Ritter,E. Paris: Hachette, 1903-1904 and 1963.
V. Monti. ed. Vigo, F. Livorno, 1877.
J. de Müller. ed. Baldensperger, F. Genève: Bibliothèque Universelle & Suisse,1912.
Louis de Narbonne, Adolphe de Ribbing, Benjamin Constant. ed. Beneziglio, J.-L. Paris: Tchou, 1970.
Louis de Narbonne. ed. Solovieff, G. & comtesse de Pange. Paris: Gallimard, 1960.
J. Necker. ed. comte d'Haussonville. Paris: Calmann-Lévy, 1925-1928.
Du Pont de Nemours. Marshall, J.F. Madison, Wisconsin, 1968.
Odier & d'Argenson. ed. d'Argenson, Candaux, J. D. & King, N. Paris: Cahiers Staëliens 38, 1987.
O'Donnell (1805-1817). ed. Mistler. J. Paris: Calmann-Lévy, 1926.
C. Pougens. Paris: Cahiers staëliens 42, 1989-1991.
Juste Constant de Rebecque. ed. Rudler. G. Paris: Droz, 1937.
Madame Récamier. ed. Loménie, E. Beau de. Paris: Domat, 1952.
Ribbing et *Narbonne.* ed. Balayé. S. Figaro littéraire, 14 mars 1959.
A. Ribbing. ed. Balayé, S. & comtesse Jean de Pange. Paris: Gallimard, 1960.
J. Rocca. Genève: Revue de Genève Chapuisat, 1919-1929.

N. von Rosenstein. ed. King, N. Paris: Cahiers staëliens 42, 1990-1991.
Savoye-Rollin. ed. King, N. Paris: Cahiers staëliens 21, 1976.
A. G. Schlegel. ed. comtesse J. de Pange. Paris: Editions Albert, 1938. Also tr. Goverts. Hamburg, 1940.
S. de Sismondi. ed. King, N. & Candaux, J.D. Paris: Cahiers Staëliens 31-32, 1982.
Don Pedro de Souza. ed. d'Andlau, B. Paris: Gallimard, 1979.
Don Pedro de Souza. ed. d'Andlau, B. Paris: Cahiers staëliens 29,1981.
M. de Staël. ed. comtesse de Marois. Paris: Revue des deux mondes, 1932-1939.
J.-B. Suard (1786-1817). Luppé, R. de. Genève: Droz, 1969.
F. Talma. ed. la Batut, G. de. Paris: Montaigne, 1918-1928.
Baron Voght. ed. Kluth, O. Genève: Extrait de Genève, 1958.
A. duke of Wellington. ed. Pange, V.de. Paris: Gallimard, 1961.

The Enlightenment

Bell, Madison Smart. *Lavoisier in the Year One—The Birth of a New Science in an Age of Revolution.* New York London: W. W. Norton, 2005.
Beurekassa, G. *Montesquieu et la Révolution française* and Soumoy-Thibert, G. *Les idées de Madame Necker.* Paris: Société française d'étude du dix-huitième siècle Presses Universitaires de France, 1989.

Cassirer, Ernst. *Kant's Life and Thought.* tr. Haden, J. New Haven & London: Yale University Press, 1981.
———. *The Philosophy of the Enlightenment.* tr. Koelln, F. C. A. & Pettegrove, J. Princeton, New Jersey: Princeton University Press, 1932-1979.
———. *The Question of Jean-Jacques Rousseau.* tr. Gay, P. Indiana University Press, 1954.
———. *Rousseau Kant Goethe.* tr. Gutmann, J. Princeton: Randall, 1945.
Cranston, M. *Jean-Jacques Rousseau* I-III. Chicago: University of Chicago Press, 1982.

Diderot, Denis. *Oeuvres Philosophiques.* Paris: Garnier, 1964.

Fabre, J. *Lumières et romantisme.* Paris: Klincksieck, 1963.
Forestier, L. *Panorama du dix-huitième siècle des Lumières.* Paris: Seghers, 1961.
Furbank, P. N. *Diderot—a Critical Biography.* New York: Knopf, 1992.

Harvey, P. ed. *Oxford Companion to English Literature.* Oxford: Oxford-Clarendon Press, 1932-1958.
Himmelfarb, G. *The Roads to Modernity.* New York: Knopf, 2004.
Hyland, P., O. Gomez, F. Greensides, eds. *The Enlightenment.* London New York: Routledge, 2003.

Kant, Immanuel. *Critique of Practical Reason* (1788). tr. Beck, L. W. New York: Bobbs-Merrill, 1956.
_____. *Observations on the Feeling of the Beautiful and the Sublime*(1764). tr. Goldthwait, J. T., Los Angeles, London: University of California, Berkeley, 1960.
_____. *Religion Within the Limits of Reason Alone* (1792). tr. Greene, T. M. & Hudson, H. H. New York San Francisco London: Harper 1960.

Lanson, G. *Histoire de la littérature française.* Paris: Hachette, 1894-1951.

Montesquieu, Louis de Secondat, Charles. *Oeuvres complètes.* Ed. Caillois, R. Paris: Pleïade I-II Gallimard, 1949-1970.

Pearson, R. *Voltaire Almighty.* New York London: Bloomsbury, 2005.
Porter, R. *The Creation of the Modern World.* New York London: W. W. Norton, 2000.
_____. *Flesh in the Age of Reason.* New York London: W. W. Norton, 2003.

Roche, D. *La France des lumières.* tr. Goldhammer, A. London: Harvard University Press, 1993-1998.
Rousseau, Jean-Jacques. *Du Contrat Social.* ed. Ehrard, J. Paris: Garnier, 1975.
_____. *Emile ou de l'éducation.* ed. Richard, F.& P. Paris: Garnier, 1961.

Trouille, M.S. *Sexual Politics in the Enlightenment.* Albany: SUNY, 1997.
Trousson, R. *Diderot jour après jour.* Paris: Champion, 2006.

Voltaire. *Essai sur les moeurs et l'esprit des nations.* Paris: Editions Sociales, 1962.
_____. *Oeuvres philosophiques.* ed. Vernière, P. Paris: Garnier, 1964.

The French Revolution

Andress, D. *The Terror: The Merciless War for Freedom in Revolutionary France.* New York: Farrar, Strauss & Giroux, 2006.

Badinter, E. & R. *Condorcet (1743-1794) Un intellectuel en politique.* Paris: Fayard, 1988.
Bertaud, J.-P., J. L. Leflon, G. Lefranc, A. Melchior-Bonnet, P. Mermet. *La Révolution française.* Paris: Larousse, 1976.
Bouloiseau, M. *Robespierre.* Paris: Presses Universitaires de France, 1971.
Bourson, P.-A. *Robespierre ou le délire décapité.* Paris: Buchet-Chastel, 1993.

Castelot, A. *Marie Antoinette.* Perrin, 1962.

SELECT BIBLIOGRAPHY

Castries, d. de. *La Fayette pionnier de la liberté*. Paris: Hachette, 1974.
Carlyle, T. *The French Revolution*. New York: Modern Library, 1857.
Chaunu, P. *Le grand déclassement*. Paris: Laffont, 1989.
Cléry, J. B. & A. Firmont. *A Journal of the Terror*. London: The Folio Society, 1955.
Cobb, R. & C. Jones. *Voices of the French Revolution*. Topsfield Mass, 1988.

Dominique, P. *Les polémistes français depuis 1789*. Paris: La Colombe, 1962.
Duby, G. & Mandrou, R. *Histoire de la civilisation française du dix-septième au vingtième siècle*. Paris: Armand Colin, 1958.

Fraisse, G. *Muse de la raison: la démocratie exclusive et la différence des sexes*. Aix-en-Provence: Alinea, 1989.
Fraser, A. *Marie Antoinette The Journey*. London: Phoenix-Orion Books, 2001.
Fumaroli, M. *Quand l'Europe parlait français* Paris: Fallois, 2001.
Furet, F. & M. Ozouf. *Dictionnaire critique de la Révolution française*. Paris: Flammarion, 1988.

Gaxotte, P. *Histoire des Français*. Paris: Flammarion, 1951.

Kennedy, E. *A Cultural History of the French Revolution*. New Haven London: Yale University Press, 1989.
Kermina, F. *Madame Roland ou la passion révolutionnaire*. Paris: Perrin, 1976.

Lanson, G. *Histoire de la littérature française*. Paris: Hachette, 1894-1951.
Lefèbre, G. *La Révolution française*. Paris: Presses Universitaires de France, 1930. Tr. Palmer, B. R. *The Coming of the French Revolution*. Princeton, 1989.
Lever, E. *Louis XVI*. Paris: Fayard, 1985.

Macaulay, B. *The French Revolution*. New York: Encyclopaedia Britannica 21-22, 1911.
Massin, J. *Almanach de la Révolution française*. Paris: Club français du livre, 1963.
May, G. *Elisabeth Vigée Le Brun*. New Haven London: Yale Univ. Press, 2005.
Méthivier, H. *L'Ancien Régime*. Paris: Presses Universitaires de France, 1968.
Mignet, A. *Histoire de la Révolution française*. Paris: Didot-Perrin, 1824.

Necker, Jacques. *De la Révolution* I-II. Paris: Maret, 1797.

Paine, Thomas. *Common Sense*. Mineola, New York: Dover, 1997.

Sauvigny, G. de Berthier de. *Histoire de France*. Paris: Flammarion, 1977.

Schama, S. *Citizens: a Chronicle of the French Revolution.* New York: Knopf, 1989.
Seignobos, C. *Histoire sincère de la nation française.* Paris: Presses universitaires de France, 1969.
Sorel, A. *L'Europe et la Révolution française.* Paris: Plon, 1908.
Tocqueville, A. de. *L'Ancien Régime et la Révolution.* Paris: Gallimard, 1856.
Tudesq, A. J. & J. Rudel. *1789-1848.* Paris: Bordas, 1968.

Vigée-Lebrun, E. *Souvenirs.* Paris: Edition des femmes, 1984.

Napoleon

Bergeron, L. *L'Episode napoléonien (1799-1815).* Paris: Seuil, 1972.
Boime, A. *Art in the Age of Bonapartism (1800-1815).* Chicago London: University of Chicago Press, 1990.
Bourlis, K. ed. *The Age of Napoléon.* New York: Metropolitan Museum of Art & Abrams, 1989.

Castelot, A. *Le fils de l'empereur.* Paris: Presses Pocket, 1962.
Chandler, D. *Napoléon.* New York: Saturday Review Press, 1973.
Chardigny, L. *L'Homme Napoléon.* Paris: Perrin, 1987-1999.
Chateaubriand, F.-R. *Mémoires d'Outre-tombe I-II .* Paris: Pléiade Gallimard, 1946.

Englund, S. *Napoléon A Political Life.* Cambridge: Harvard, 2004.

Jefferson, Thomas. *Life and Selected Writings.* ed. Koch, A. & Peden, W. New York: Random House, 1972-1993.

Lefebvre, G. *Napoléon.* Paris: Presses universitaires de France, 1969.
Ludwig, E. *Napoléon.* tr. Paul, E.-C. New York: Garden City, 1924-1928. tr. Stern, A. Paris: Bibliothèque Historique, Payot, 1928-1929.

Manceron, C. *L'Epopée de Napoléon en mille images.* Paris: Cercle Européen du livre, Laffont, 1964.

Orieux, J. *Talleyrand.* Paris: Flammarion, 1970. tr. Wolf, P. New York: Knopf, 1974.

Pares, B. *A History of Russia.* New York: Knopf, 1956.

Romains, J. *Napoléon par lui-même.* Paris: Perrin, 1963.

Sainte-Beuve, C. A. *Chateaubriand et son groupe littéraire sous l'Empire*. Paris: Calmann Lévy, 1877.
Savant, J. *Tel fut le roi de Rome*. Paris: Fasquelle, 1954.
Schnapper, A. *David*. Paris: Connaissance des Arts, 1989-1990.
Stendhal. *Vie de Napoléon*. Paris: Payot, 1897-1969.
Thiers, A. *Histoire du consulat et de l'empire* I-XX. Paris: Paulin Lheureux, 1845-1862.
Tulard, J. *Napoléon ou le Mythe du Sauveur*. Paris: Fayard, 1977-1987.

Observations from Germaine De Staël's Contemporaries

Note concerning articles published in the Cahiers staëliens: as could be seen in earlier sections of the bibliography, the Cahiers offer a substantial mirroring of Germaine de Staël's era. For nearly eighty years, they have brought together scholars from every part of the world. Beginning in 1930, the Cahiers suffered interruption during World War II, then resumed in 1962 under the care of the Société des études staëliennes which is still active in both Geneva and Paris. Early on, they were published in Paris by Touzot, and in Geneva by Slatkine. Currently they are published in Paris by Honoré Champion. As they are numerous, I have selected articles with strong biographical and critical import, hoping to be forgiven for omissions.

Barante, Prosper de. *Souvenirs*. Paris: Calmann-Lévy, 1890-1897.
Brinkman, Carl Gustaf von. *Lettre sur l'auteur de Corinne* Cahiers staëliens 39 ed. Balayé, S. Paris: Touzot, 987-1990.
Broglie, Albertine de. *Extraits d'un journal d'enfance*. ed. comtesse de Pange. Paris: Revue d'histoire littéraire de la France, 1966.
―――. *Oeuvres diverses de M. le baron Auguste de Staël*. Paris: Treuttel & Würtz, 1829.
Broglie, L.-Victor d. de. *Souvenirs*. Paris: Calmann-Lévy, 1886.
Brun, Friederike. *Quelques interprétations théâtrales de la baronne de Staël-Holstein*. tr. Böschenstein, B.& Michaud, S. F. Cahiers staëliens, 1978.
Byron. *Some Recollections of my Acquaintance with Madame de Staël*. London: Murray's, 1887.

Chateaubriand, François René. *Mémoires d'Outre-tombe I-II*. ed. Moulinier,G. & Levaillant, M. Paris: Pléiade Gallimard, 1946.
Constant, Benjamin. *Adolphe*. ed. Bauër, G. Paris: Imprimerie Nationale 1953.
―――. *Cécile*. Paris: Gallimard, 1951.

_____. *Journal intime, Lettres à sa famille et ses amis.* Melegari, D. & Ollendorf, P. Paris: Stock, 1895-1931.
_____. *Le Cahier rouge.* Paris: Calmann-Lévy, 1907.
_____. *Lettres à Madame Récamier.* Paris: Dentu-Klincksieck, 1864.
_____. *Oeuvres.* Paris: Pléiade Gallimard, 1957.

Goethe, Johann von. *Mémoires.* Paris: Charpentier, 1855.

Jefferson, Thomas. *Life and Selected Writings.* ed. Koch, A. & Peden, W. New York: Random House, 1944-1993.

Ligne, Charles-Joseph pr. de. *Mémoires, Lettres et Pensées.* Paris: Bourin, 1989.

Montmorency, Mathieu de. *Réflexions sur Madame de Staël.* ed. comtesse d'Andlau Cahiers staëliens, 1972.

Rebecque, Constant de. *Correspondance de Benjamin Constant et d'Anna Lindsay.* Paris: Plon, 1933.

Saussure, Albertine Necker de. *Notice sur le caractère et les écrits de Madame de Staël.* Paris: Treuttel & Würtz, 1820-1821, Didot, 1844-1861.
_____. *Réponse à la question en quoi consiste la différence entre le sublime et le beau.* Genève: Annales Benjamin Constant 21 Droz, 1998.
Schlegel, August Wilhelm. *Une étude critique de Corinne ou l'Italie.* tr. Blaesche, A. & Arnaud, J. Cahiers staëliens, 1976.
Schlegel, Dorothea. *Briefen.* ed. Wenecke, E. Weimar, 1914.
Simonde de Sismondi, J-Ch. *Epistolario I-IV.* ed. Pellegrini, C. King, N. Luppé, R. de. Firenze: La Nuova Italia, 1933-1975.

Vigée-Lebrun, Elisabeth. *Memoirs.* tr. Strachey, Lionel. Doubleday & Page, 1903 and G. Braziller, 1989.

Modern Biographical and Critical Studies

Amend-Sôchting, A. *L'Epitre au malheur ou Adèle et Edouard, une méditation de Madame de Staël sur la Terreur.* Paris: Cahiers Rouché-André Chénier 5, 1995.
Amend, A. Lebey, F. Pouzoulet, F. Lotterie, H. Robert. *Carte blanche aux jeunes chercheurs.* Cahiers staëliens 49, 1997-1998.
Amend, A. Principato, A. Sermain, J. P. Brousteau, A. Vanoflen, J. P. Perchellet, J. P. Gengembre, F. Lotterie. *Madame de Staël Sagesse et folie.* Cahiers staëliens 52, 2001.
Anders, K. *Zulma oder die Liebe als Illusion.* Bonn: Romantischer Verlag, 1995.

SELECT BIBLIOGRAPHY

Andlau, B. d'. *La jeunesse de Madame de Staël 1766-1786.* Genève Paris: Droz, 1960-1970.

Bader, W. *El pensiamento politico de Madame de Staël.* Madrid: Sociedad Espanola De literature general y comparada, 1980.

Balayé, S. *Ame et unité du Groupe de Coppet.* Colloque de Coppet, 1998. Paris: Presses Universitaires d'Aix-en-Provence, 2000.

_____. *A propos du Préromantisme—Continuité ou Rupture chez Madame de Staël.* Paris: Klincksieck, 1972.

_____. *Corinne et la ville italienne ou, l'espace extérieur et l'impasse intérieure.* Genève: Slatkine, 1984.

_____. *Delphine et la presse sous le consulat.* Paris: Romantisme 51, 1986.

_____. *Ecrire, lutter, vivre.* Genève: Droz, 1994.

_____. *Madame de Staël et la presse révolutionnaire.* Cahiers staëliens 53, 2002.

_____. *Madame de Staël—Lumières et liberté.* Paris: Klincksieck, 1979.

Bédé, J. A. *Madame de Staël et les mots.* In *Madame de Staël et l'Europe.* Paris: Klincksieck, 1970.

Bernier, O. *The Eighteenth Century Woman.* Garden City, New York: Doubleday, 1981.

Lady Blennerhassett. *Madame de Staël et son temps.* Tr. Dietrich, A. Westhausser, L. Paris: 1887-1890.

Bosse, M. "*Ce hazard qui m'entraîna dans la carrière littéraire.*" Paris: Cahiers staëliens 42, 1990-1991.

_____. *Zulma ou l'esthétique de la Révolution à la lumière de l'Essai sur les fictions.* Colloque de Coppet 4. Paris: Touzot, 1988.

Bowman, F. P. *La Polémique sur les Considérations sur la Révolution.* Colloque de Coppet 4. Lausanne: Institut Benjamin Constant, 1988.

_____. *La Révélation selon Benjamin Constant.* Europe, mars 1968.

Boyle, N. *Goethe: the Poet and the Age.* Oxford: Clarendon Press, 1991-2000.

Broglie, G. de. *Madame de Genlis.* Paris: Perrin, 1985.

Carlyle, T. *The Life of Friedrich Schiller.* London: Chapman & Hall, 1904.

Castries, d. de. *Madame Récamier.* Paris: Hachette, 1971.

Chaffanson, A. *Madame de Staël et sa descendance.* Paris: Palais Royal, 1969.

Colson, L.-C. *Etude de la société dans Corinne ou l'Italie de Madame de Staël.* Case Western Reserve University, 1970.

Craveri, B. *The Age of Conversation.* tr. Waugh, T. New York: New York Review of Books, 2005.

Delon, M. *Le défi de Coppet.* Université de Lausanne, 1997.

_____. *Le Groupe de Coppet.* Lausanne: Payot, 1996.

Diesbach, G. de. *Madame de Staël.* Paris: Perrin, 1983.

_____. *Necker ou la faillite de la vertu.* Paris: Perrin, 1978-1987.
Dubé, P. H. *Bibliographie de la critique sur Madame de Staël 1789-1994.* Genève: Droz, 1998.
Dumont-Wilden, L. *La vie de Benjamin Constant.* Paris: Gallimard, 1930.
Eaubonne, F. d'. *Une femme témoin de son siècle.* Paris: Flammarion, 1966.
Eckermann, J. P. *Conversations with Goethe.* tr. O'Brien, G. New York: Ungar, 1964.
Eliot, George. *Essays.* London: Routledge & Kegan Paul, 1968.

Fabre, J. *Lumières et Romantisme.* Paris: Klincksieck, 1980.
Fabre-Luce, A. *Benjamin Constant.* Paris: Fayard 1933.
Fairweather, M. *Madame de Staël.* Carroll & Graf Constable, 2005.

Gautier, P. *Madame de Staël et Napoléon.* Paris: Plon-Nourrit, 1903.
Garry-Boussel, C. *Statut et fonction du personnage masculin chez Madame de Staël.* Paris: Champion, 2002.
Gengembre, G. *Madame de Staël sous les feux de l'Action française.* Cahiers staëliens 53, 2002.
Gengembre, G. *Delphine, ou la Révolution française: un roman du divorce.* Cahiers staëliens 56, 2005.
Goldberger, A. *Corinne refuses Oswald.* French-American Review VI, 1982.
Gouhier, H. *Benjamin Constant devant la religion.* Paris: Desclée de Brouwer, 1967.
Guillemin, H. *Madame de Staël Benjamin Constant et Napoléon.* Paris: Plon, 1959-1987.
Gutwirth, Madelyn. *Forging a Vocation: Germaine de Staël on Fiction, Power and Passion.* Bulletin for research in the humanities, 1983-1986.
_____. *From J.-J. Rousseau to Germaine de Staël.* Essays in Nineteenth Century European Women Writers, Greenwood Press, 1987.
_____. *Madame de Staël, Novelist—Emergence of the Artist as Woman.* Champaign, Illinois: University of Illinois Press, 1978.
_____. *Madame de Staël Rousseau and the Woman Question.* Modern Language's Association Review, 1970.
_____. *Nature, cruauté, et femmes immolées: les réflexions sur le procès de la reine.* Colloque de Coppet 4. Paris: Touzot, 1988.
Gutwirth, M., S. Goldberger, S. Balayé, M. Hogsett, M. Delon, B. Naginski, K. Zmurlo, E. Sourian, F. P. Bowman. (Colloquium) *Crossing the Borders.* Rutgers University Press, 1991.
Gwynne, G. E. *Madame de Staël et la Révolution française.* Paris: Nizet, 1969.

Haggard, A. *Madame de Staël Her trials and Triumphs.* London: Hutchinson, 1922.

Harris, R. W. *Romanticism and the Social Order 1780-1830.* London: Blandford, 1969.
Harten, E. & H.-C. *Femmes, culture et Révolution.* tr. Chabot, B. Mannoni, E. Paris: Edition des Femmes, 1988.
Haussonville, comte d'. *Auguste de Staël et ses parents.* Cahiers staëliens 53, 2002.
_____. *Coppet. Deux siècles d'histoire littéraire et familiale.* Association des bibliothécaires français 173, 1996.
_____. *Madame de Staël et l'Allemagne.* Calmann-Lévy, 1928.
_____. *Madame de Staël et M. Necker.* Paris: Calmann-Lévy, 1925.
_____. *Necker, Femmes d'autrefois, Hommes d'aujourd'hui.* Paris: Revue des deux mondes, 1913-1914.
Herold, J. C. *Germaine de Staël Mistress to an Age.* tr. Maurois, M. Paris: Plon, 1958-1962.
Hogsett, C. *The Literary Existence of Germaine de Staël.* Carbondale-Edwardsville, Illinois: South Illinois University Press, 1987.

Isbell, J. C. *The Birth of Romanticism–Truth and Propaganda in Germaine de Staël's De l'Allemagne.* Groupe de Coppet. L'Europe. Paris: Touzot, 1994.
Jasinski, B. *L'Engagement de Benjamin Constant, amour et politique 1794-1796.* Paris: Minard, 1971.
_____. *Le Groupe de Coppet 1799-1816.* Colloque de Coppet. Genève: Slatkine, 1974. Paris: Champion, 1977.
_____. *Madame de Staël et l'Angleterre de 1813 à 1814 et les Considérations sur la Révolution française.* Revue d'histoire littéraire de la France, 1966.
Jaume, L. *Coppet. Creuset de l'esprit liberal.* Colloque de Coppet May 1998. Paris: Presses Universitaires d'Aix-en-Provence, 2000.
Johnson-Cousin, D. *Mélodrame et roman noir dans le théâtre révolutionnaire inédit de Madame de Staël.* Toulouse: Presses universitaires du Mirail, 2000.
Jones, R. A. *Madame de Staël and England.* London: London University, 1928.

Kerchove, A. *Benjamin Constant ou le libertin sentimental.* Paris: Albin Michel, 1950.
King, N. *Sismondi Madame de Staël et Delphine—débuts d'une intimité.* Cahiers staëliens 26-27, 1979.
Kloocke, K. *Benjamin Constant–une biographie intellectuelle.* Genève-Paris: Droz, 1984.
Kohler, P. *Madame de Staël au château de Coppet.* Lausanne: Spes, 1929.
_____. *Madame de Staël et la Suisse.* Lausanne-Paris: Droz, 1916. Paris: Attinger, 1930.

Lacretelle, P. de. *Madame de Staël et les hommes.* Paris: Grasset, 1939.

SELECT BIBLIOGRAPHY 295

Lang, A. *Une vie d'Orages—Germaine de Staël.* Paris: Calmann-Lévy, 1958.
Larg, D. Glass. *Madame de Staël—La vie dans l'oeuvre.* Paris: Champion & Vrin, 1924-1928.
Levaillant, M. *Une amitié amoureuse–Madame de Staël et Madame Récamier.* Paris: Hachette, 1956.
Luppé, R. de. *Idées littéraires de Madame de Staël et l'héritage des lumières.* Paris: Vrin, 1969.

Macaulay, B. *William Pitt.* New York: Encyclopaedia Britannica vol.21-22, 1911.
Man, P. de. *Madame de Staël et Jean-Jacques Rousseau.* Paris: Preuves 90, 1966.
Mansel, P. *Charles-Joseph de Ligne Le charmeur de l'Europe.* Paris: Stock, 1992.
Marois, comtesse d'Haussonville,le. *Madame de Staël, Madame Récamier, et Auguste de Staël—A l'ombre de deux femmes.* Revue des deux mondes 12, 1959.
Mortier, R. *Corinne.* Paris: Dix-huitième siècle 12, 1980.
_____. *Madame de Staël et l'héritage des Lumières.* Colloque de Coppet I.Genève: Droz, 1969.
_____. *Madame de Staël ou la fidélité.* Cahiers staëliens 28, 1979.

Omacini, L. *Benjamin Constant correcteur de Madame de Staël.* Cahiers staëliens 25, 1979.
_____. *Delphine et la tradition du roman épistolaire.* Cahiers staëliens 56, 2005.

Pailleron, M. L. *Madame de Staël—les Romantiques.* Paris: Hachette, 1931.
Pange, Comtesse Jean de. *Germaine de Staël.* Paris: Gallimard, 1962.
_____. *Le dernier amour de Madame de Staël.* Genève, La Palatine, 1944.
_____. *Monsieur de Staël.* Paris: Portiques, 1931.
Pange, Victor de. *Le plus beau de toutes les fêtes.* Paris: Klincksieck, 1980.
Perchellet, J.-P. *La fonction Romanesque des épisodes théâtraux dans Corinne.* Cahiers staëliens 52, 2001.
Peyre, H. *Qu'est-ce que le Romantisme?* Paris: Presses Universitaires de France, 1971.
Poulet, G. *Benjamin Constant par lui-même.* Paris: Seuil, 1968.
_____. *La pensée critique de Madame de Staël.* Paris: Preuves & Corti, 1966-1971.
Poulet, G. Bédé, G. A. King, N. Ullrichova, M. Solovieff, G. Bowman, F. P. Mortier, R. *Madame de Staël et l'Europe.* Paris: Klincksieck, 1966-1971.
Postgate, H. *Madame de Staël.* Boston: Twayne, 1969.

Rosset, F. *De Ferney à Coppet.* Center for Seventeenth and Eighteenth Century Studies UCLA, 1997 and Geneva: Slatkine, 1998.

Smurlo, K. M. *Le feu et le discours féminin: la danse de l'héroïne staëlienne.* Nineteenth Century French Studies, 1986-1987.
Solovieff, G. *Madame de Staël et August Wilhelm Schlegel—natures complémentaires et/ou antinomiques?* Cahiers staëliens 37, 1985-1986.
Sorel, A. *Madame de Staël.* Collection des grands écrivains français. Paris: Hachette, 1893-1907.
Starobinski, J. *Suicide et mélancolie chez Madame de Staël.* Paris: Preuves, 1966.
Stevens, A. *Madame de Staël—A Study of her Life and Times.* New York: Harper, 1881.
Szabo, A. *As pects et fonctions du temps dans Delphine.* Paris-Lausanne: Annales Benjamin Constant 8-9, 1988.

Walser-Wilhelm, D.& P. *A la charnière du temps: Charles-Victor de Bonstetten et Madame de Staël, Madame de Staël et Friederike Brun.* tr. A. Kolde. Geneva: Slatkine, 2005.
Wagener, F. *Madame Récamier 1777-1849.* Paris: J.-C.Lattès, 1968.

INDEX

Les Actes des Apôtres, 68
Aeschylus, 120, 136
Albany, Louise of, 131
Alembert, Jean Le Rond d', 18, 20, 50
Alexander I of Russia, 10, 184, 188, 197, 201, 233-34
Alfieri, 131, 136
Alighieri, Dante 119, 161, 212
L'Année littéraire, 21
L'Ami des patriotes, 69
L'Ami du peuple, 65, 67-68
L'Ami du roi, 68
Athenaüm, 118
Augustus of Prussia, 173
Aurelius, Marcus, 121

Bacon, Francis, 121
Bailly, Jean, 38, 76, 84
Balk, Piotr F. de, 181
Ballanche, Pierre, 135
Barante, Prosper de, 168, 172, 182, 201
Barras, Paul de, 80, 86, 96, 109-13, 126-27
Beaumarchais, Pierre Caron de, 26, 49
Bentham, Jeremy, 136

Bernadotte, Jean Baptiste, 10, 135, 194-95, 197, 201
Bernardin de Saint-Pierre, Henri, 26, 50, 109, 133
Berthier, Louis de, 113, 134, 199-200
Biblioteca italiana, 207
Biographie universelle, 182
Biran, Maine de, 182
Blake, William, 88
Blücher, Gebhard pr., 203
Bonald, Louis de, 97, 135
Bonaparte, Jérôme, 153, 197
Bonaparte, Joseph, 131, 153, 155-56, 197, 200, 203
Bonaparte, Joséphine (Beauharnais), 95-96, 109, 201
Bonaparte, Lucien, 153, 162
Bonaparte, Napoléon (see Napoléon I)
Bonstetten, Charles-Victor, 82, 133, 160, 232
Bourrienne, Louis de, 156
Brienne, Etienne Loménie de, 35-36, 54
Brinkman, Carl von, 171, 196-97
Brissot, Jacques, 35, 69, 84
Broglie, Victor de, 205-208

INDEX

Brougham, Henry, 208
Brun, Friederika, 133, 173
Buffon, Georges de, 20, 25, 68
Burke, Edmund, 88
Burney, Fanny, 81
Byron, George Gordon L., 10, 182, 198, 202, 206-208

Cabanis, G., 47, 135
Calderon, 161
Calonne, Charles de, 25, 34, 54
Cambacérès, J.-J. de, 86, 129, 131, 156
Capelle, Benoît, 181
Carnot, Lazare, 202
Chamisso, Adalbert, 181
Charles-August of Saxony-Weimar, 158
Charles X of France (comte d'Artois), 33, 35, 61
Charrière, Isabelle de, 50, 98
Chateaubriand, François René de, 10, 88, 128, 133, 135-36, 153-55, 173, 180-82, 197, 202, 206, 208, 217, 233
Chénier, André de, 47, 79, 121
Chénier, M. J., 88, 96, 98
La Chronique scandaleuse, 68
Le Citoyen français, 132
Clef du Cabinet des Souverains, 132
Colbert, Jean-Baptiste, 27
Condillac, Etienne de, 19
Condorcet, M. Jean m. de, 37, 47-49, 72, 76-77, 83-84, 96, 107, 121, 129
Constant, Benjamin, 10, 48, 66, 82, 85-86, 88-89, 91, 93, 97-99, 104, 110-12, 125-29, 132, 134-35, 152, 154, 157-62, 168-69, 171-73, 182, 194, 196-99, 201-202, 205, 208, 222, 229-31
Constant, Rosalie de, 152
Constant de Rebecque, Samuel, 223
Correspondance littéraire, philosophique et critique, 51, 82, 97
Courrier de l'Europe, 35, 39

Danton, Georges, 66, 74-75, 78-79, 108
Darnley, John, 200
Daunou, Pierre, 132-33, 136
David, Louis, 153
Davy, Humphrey, 208
Desmoulins, Camille, 69
Diderot, Denis, 17-23, 25, 33, 59, 82, 99, 123
Dryden, John, 19
Dumouriez, Charles F., 78

Edgeworth, Maria, 172
The Edinburgh Review, 198
Encyclopédie—Dictionnaire raisonné des sciences, des arts et des métiers, 18, 21-23, 33, 50
Enghien, Louis de Bourbon-Condé, d. d', 155, 206
Euripides, 136

Fauriel, Claude, 134
Fénelon, François de, 117
Ferdinand VII of Spain, 197
Fichte, J. G., 88
Fielding, Henry, 118
Flahaut, Adèle de (Madame Talleyrand), 131
Fontanes, Louis de, 156
Fontenelle, Bernard de, 21
Foster, Elizabeth (d.of Devonshire), 201
Fouché, Joseph, 127, 131, 134, 153, 185, 199, 202-203, 206
Fox, Charles, 81, 85
Francis II of Austria, 185
Franklin, Benjamin, 207
Frederick Wilhelm II of Prussia, 75

Garrick, David, 20
Gazette française, 85
Gazette littéraire de l'Europe, 68
Genlis, Félicité de, 88, 127-28, 134, 152, 160, 172, 206
Gentz, Frederick von, 175

INDEX 299

Geoffrin, Marie-Thérèse, 18
Gérando, Joseph de, 132-34, 136, 160, 173, 222
Gibbon, Edward, 88
Glück, Christoph von, 20
Godwin, William, 88, 136
Goethe, Johann von, 20, 82, 97, 104, 119, 121, 123, 135, 158-59, 161, 167, 169, 172, 174-75, 178-79, 182, 185, 206, 222
Gray, Thomas, 19
Grey, Charles, 200
Grey, Jane, 55-56
Grimm, Melchior von, 21-22, 51, 82, 97
Guibert, Jacques de, 47, 70
Guizot, François, 231
Gustave III of Sweden, 49-50, 69, 76, 87, 91

Hegel, G. W. F., 183
Helvétius, Claude, 18
Mme Helvétius, 18
Herder, J. G., 88, 118, 135
Hervey, Elizabeth, 10
Hochet, Claude, 159, 173
Holbach, Paul Henri d', 18, 22, 59, 82
Mme d'Holbach, 18
Homer, 120, 212
Horace, 120
Humboldt, W., 129, 135, 162, 206
Hume, David, 22, 33, 88

Les Indépendants, 69
Isabey, Jean-Baptiste, 114

Jacobi, Friedrich, 179
Jaucourt, François de, 76
Jefferson, Thomas, 10, 20, 36, 39, 47-48, 67, 79, 131, 171, 177, 189, 205, 207, 209, 222, 237
Jordan, Camille, 130, 156, 173, 181, 222
Journal de la cour et de la ville, 68
Journal des Débats, 69, 151, 202
Journal des Hommes libres, 125, 127
Journal littéraire de Lausanne, 86
Journal de Paris, 39, 85
Journal politique national, 68-69

Kant, Immanuel, 23, 49, 88, 133, 135-36, 157, 167, 179, 243
Kléber, Jean-Baptiste, 110
Kleist, H. von, 183
Klopstock, Friedrich, 156, 178
Krüdener, Julie de, 133, 136, 160, 175, 201, 234

Laclos, Choderlos de, 65
La Fayette, M. Joseph m. de, 20, 36, 38, 40, 47-48, 63, 65-67, 69, 71-72, 75-76, 99, 129, 201
La Fontaine, Jean de, 123
La Harpe, Jean F. de, 86, 118, 124
Lamartine, Alphonse de, 231
Lameth, Alexandre de, 81, 93
La Mettrie, Julien de, 58
Lannes, Jean, 155, 185
Lansdowne, Henry m. of, 200
La Lanterne magique nationale, 68
Laplace, P., 98
Launay, Bernard Jordan m. de, 31
Lavater, Johann, 222
Lavoisier, Antoine de, 49, 79, 108
Lebrun, Charles, 129, 131, 134
Leibniz, Gottfried W., 179
Leopold II of Austria, 74-75
Lessing, Gotthold, 19, 178
Ligne, Charles de, 174
Locke, John, 19, 21, 88, 179
Louis XIV of France, 27
Louis XV of France, 26, 31, 33, 71
Louis XVI of France, 26, 32-36, 38, 40, 48, 61-63, 67, 74-77, 84, 129
Louis XVIII of France (comte de Provence), 33, 199-200, 206, 208, 217
Lyttleton, George, 141

300 INDEX

Machiavelli, N., 121
Macpherson, James, 20, 59, 123
Maistre, J. de, 97, 182
Malesherbes, Chrétien de, 34, 84, 210
Marat, Jean-Paul, 65, 68, 77-78, 108
Marie-Antoinette of France, 32-34, 67, 76, 78-79, 84
Marie-Louise of Austria, 185
Marie Thérèse of Austria, 78
Marmontel, Jean-François, 20, 124, 141
Maurepas, Jean-Frédéric de, 33
Meilhan, Sénac de, 108
Meister, Henri, 10, 51, 82, 97, 114
Mercier, L.-S., 108
Mercure de France, 69, 128, 151-52, 173
Metastasio, 167
Metternich, Clemens von, 174-75, 185, 206
Milton, John, 19
Mirabeau, Honoré Riqueti de, 36, 61-62, 66, 68, 73
Monge, Gaspard, 113
Le Moniteur, 169
Montaigne, Michel de, 121
Montesquieu, Charles de Secondat de, 13, 19-20, 22-23, 26, 33, 50, 120, 127, 131, 157
Monti, Vincenzo, 162-63, 168, 172, 183, 207
Montmorency, M. de, 48, 81, 90, 160, 180, 183, 201, 208, 231-33
Müller, Jean de, 182
Murat, Joachim, 156, 197
Murray, John, 198

Napoléon I, 10, 13-14, 59, 80, 95-96, 103, 107-10, 112-14, 125-32, 134-35, 151-56, 170-71, 174-75, 180, 183-86, 194-95, 199-200, 202-203
Napoléon II, 198-99
Narbonne-Lara, Louis de, 10, 48, 69, 71-72, 75-77, 80-82, 86-88, 91, 153, 185, 197
Necker, Jacques, 14, 24-27, 32, 34-35, 37-40, 54, 61-62, 67-68, 70-71, 77, 80-81, 112, 126-27, 132, 134, 153, 159-60
Necker, Suzanne (Curchod), 14, 17-20, 22-24, 47, 71, 80, 128
Ney, Michel d'Elchingey, 188, 200, 206
Nicolle, 180, 182
Nouvelles politiques et étrangères, 86
Novalis, F., 135

L'Orateur du peuple, 68
O'Donnell, Maurice, 162-63, 174, 181
Orléans, Philippe d' (Philippe Egalité), 35, 64-65, 75, 79
Ouvrard, G., 185, 202
Ovid, 94, 120

Paine, Thomas, 47-48, 50, 88
Pange, François de, 82, 84, 95, 104, 222
Pastoret, Adelaide de, 146
Petrarch, 167
Philippart, J., 201
Pitt, William the Younger, 44, 81-83, 109
Pliny, 121
Plutarch, 167
Pope, Alexander, 19
Prud'hon, P., 183
Le Publiciste, 152, 160

Racine, Jean, 19, 94, 123
Radcliffe, Ann, 172
Rameau, Jean-Philippe, 22
Randall, Frances, 182, 217, 231
Récamier, Juliette, 10, 95, 133-34, 136, 160, 172-73, 180, 183, 234-35

INDEX 301

Restif de la Bretonne, N., 50
Ribbing, L.-Adolf, 10, 82, 87-92, 97, 223, 232
Richardson, Samuel, 19, 54, 118, 123
Richelieu, Armand Du Plessis cardinal de, 35
Richelieu, Armand d. de, 206, 207, 210, 213
Richter, Jean Paul, 88, 118, 133, 158
Rilliet-Huber, Catherine, 20, 183
Robespierre, Maximilien de, 37, 75, 78-80, 108-109, 121
Rocca, Alphonse de, 209
Rocca, John, 182-83, 187, 196, 201, 208-209, 230
Roederer, P., 85-86, 96, 125, 136, 146
Roland, Jean Marie, 74, 79
Roland, Manon, 79, 84
Rousseau, Jean-Jacques, 12-13, 22-23, 25, 33, 37, 49-50, 57-60, 70, 92, 107, 120, 123, 126, 133, 174, 204, 213, 219, 242
Rovigo, A. de, (Savary), 180-81

Sade, Donatien de, 49
Sabran, Elzéar de, 173, 183
Saint-Just, Louis de, 79, 108-109
Saint-Lambert, J. F. de, 19
Saint-Simon, C. de, 183
Sand, George, 169
Saussure, Albertine (Necker) de, 9, 112, 125, 160, 207, 232
Schelling, F. W., 88, 135, 136
Schiller, Friedrich, 10, 88, 135, 158, 160, 163, 178
Schlegel, A. Wilhelm, 10, 118, 135, 161-62, 175, 180-83, 198, 207, 231-32
Schlegel, Dorothea, 193
Schlegel, Friedrich, 118, 135
Scott, Walter, 198
Senancour, E. de, 160
Seneca, 120

Shakespeare, William, 19, 81, 120
Sieyès, Emmanuel, 32, 37, 48-49, 66, 86, 95-96, 110, 126, 129
Sismondi, Simonde de, 10, 133, 135-36, 160-61, 174-75, 182, 208
Smith, Adam, 47-48
Souza, Pedro de, 10, 162-63
Spectateur du Nord, 98, 135
Spenser, Edmund, 117
Staël, Albert de, 76, 195, 198, 200-201
Staël, Albertine de Staël (de Broglie), 9, 99, 174, 195, 205, 207-208, 217, 231
Staël, Auguste de, 9, 71, 159, 180, 195, 198, 230-31
Staël-Holstein, Eric de, 45-46, 71, 99, 125-26, 128, 134-35, 153
Staël-Holstein, Germaine (Necker) de:
  appearance: 46, 49, 114
  attitude toward Mirabeau: 64-72
    toward Robespierre: 79, 83, 212, 215, 222
    toward Napoléon: 132, 134, 155-56, 186, 199, 202-204, 212, 215-16, 222, 225
  character: 17-18, 26-27, 43, 46, 49, 77, 91, 112
  on happiness: 93, 196-97
  love for France: 64, 69, 72, 81, 83, 84, 87, 89, 93-94, 100, 107, 187, 196, 198-99, 202, 208-10, 216-17, 222, 226
  love for her children: see Auguste, Albert, and Albertine de Staël
  philosophical affinities: 196-97, 219, 221, 223-24
  relationship with Jacques Necker: 26-27, 40, 49-50, 63, 69, 81, 112, 136, 159, 187, 213, 223
  relationship with Suzanne Necker: 17-21, 71, 76, 81, 128

Germaine's salons: 47-48, 86, 99-100, 125-26, 129, 134-35, 198, 201
venerations:
  Shakespeare: 121, 123
  Racine: 20, 106, 121, 123, 157, 194
  Voltaire: 120, 123, 181
  Montesquieu: 19, 39, 58, 93, 106, 120, 123
works in their order of composition:
  Journal de jeunesse: — 1785: 27, 43-44, 50, 54, 92, 224
  Zulma: 1785: 88, 91-92
  Mirza, Adelaïde et Théodore, Pauline: 1786: 70, 91
  Sophie ou les sentiments secrets: 1786-1787: 53-54, 56, 91, 224
  Jane Gray: 1787: 55-56, 91
  Lettres sur le caractère et les écrits de Jean-Jacques Rousseau: 1787-1788: 57-60, 70, 91, 115, 126
  Eloge de Guibert: 1790: 91
  La folle de la forêt de Sénart: 1790: 51, 91, 224
  Rosamonde: 1791: 70
  A quels signes peut-on reconnaître l'opinion de la majorité de la nation: 1792: 69, 73, 91
  Réflexions sur le procès de la Reine, par une femme: 1793: 78-79
  Réflexions sur la paix, adressées à M. Pitt et aux Français: 1794: 82-83, 85, 109
  Réflexions sur la paix intérieure: 1795: 83, 104
  Epître au malheur: 1795: 84, 86-87
  Essai sur les fictions: 1795: 12, 115-19, 136, 148
  De l'influence des passions sur le bonheur des individus et des nations: 1796: 78, 88, 90-94, 96-97, 99, 111, 126, 148, 161, 220, 225
  Des circonstances actuelles qui peuvent terminer la Révolution et des principes qui doivent fonder la République en France: 1799: 104-106, 221, 224
  De la littérature considérée dans ses rapports avec les institutions sociales: 1800: 104, 115, 119-28, 132-33, 138, 148, 170
  Delphine: 1802-1803: 11, 90, 113, 125, 134, 136-48, 151-54, 156-57, 160, 168, 170, 183, 216, 220, 225-26
  Réflexions sur le but moral du roman 'Delphine': 1803: 151-52
  Du caractère de M. Necker et de sa vie privée: 1804: 160
  Agar dans le désert: 1806: 136
  Corinne ou l'Italie: 1807:11, 113, 151, 165-76, 196, 220
  Préface pour les lettres et pensées du prince de Ligne: 1809: 174
  La Sunamite, Capitaire Kernadec, Signora Fantastici, Mannequin: 1810: 174, 181
  Sapho: circa 1811: 182
  De l'Allemagne: 1810-1813: 11, 113, 177-80, 186, 198, 201
  Dix Années d'exil: 1810-1813: 113, 183, 185, 187, 194, 229

Réflexions sur le suicide:
  1813: 182
De l'esprit des traductions
  1816: 207
Des considérations sur les principaux événements de la Révolution française:
  1812-1817: 113, 196, 205-206, 208-17, 225-26, 229, 232
on writing: 60, 82, 92, 96-100, 103-104, 113, 115, 124, 132, 144-45, 147, 173, 175, 180, 219, 222-23, 226-27
Stendhal, 119
Sterne, Lawrence, 19, 26
Suard, J. B., 20, 68-69, 86, 97, 152, 158
Swedenborg, Immanuel, 49
Swift, Jonathan, 19

Tacitus, 120
Talleyrand, C.-M. de, 37, 48-49, 64-65, 69, 72, 78, 81, 110-11, 113-14, 127, 129-30, 181, 184, 197, 201, 206
Tallien, J. Lambert, 86
Talma, François J., 181
Tencin, Claudine de, 50
Tieck, L., 135
Tocqueville, A. de, 231
Turgot, Robert de, 24-25, 32-34, 210

Vigée-Lebrun, Elisabeth, 10, 173, 175, 179
Vigny, Alfred de, 231
Villers, Charles de, 10, 98, 136, 157-58, 160, 179, 207
Virgil, 27, 120, 167
Voght, Kaspar de, 175
Volney, C., 108, 119
Voltaire, F. M. (Arouet), 13-14, 20, 22, 26, 34, 48-49, 58, 106, 120, 123, 173, 222

Washington, George, 65, 207
Wellington, A. Wellesley d. of, 10, 201, 203, 206, 208-209, 217
Werner, Zacharias, 181
Wieland, Christoph, 19, 82, 97, 158
Wilberforce, W., 200, 202